Spire Study System
Capture. Crosstrain. Conquer.

ASVAB
Study Guide

Spire Study System & ASVAB Test Prep Guide with
ASVAB Practice Test Review Questions for the
Armed Services Vocational Aptitude Battery

STUDY SYSTEM + TEST PREP GUIDE + PRACTICE TEST QUESTIONS

Thank you for purchasing the ASVAB Study Guide from Spire Study System!

Your opinion matters!

As a dedicated educational publisher, we depend on you, our customer, to provide feedback (email: MyBookFeedback@outlook.com). We want to know what we did well and what areas we could further improve.

Likewise, your comments can help other shoppers make informed decisions about whether our system is right for them. If you are happy with your purchase, please take a few minutes to leave a review on Amazon!

Thank you for trusting Spire Study System for your test prep needs. We are always here for you.

Andrew T. Patton

Andrew T. Patton
Chief Editor
Spire Study System
Email: MyBookFeedback@outlook.com

ISBN: 978-1-950159-07-9

Printed in the United States of America

Table of Contents

INTRODUCTION

OVERVIEW OF THE ASVAB EXAM

The Armed Services Vocational Aptitude Battery (ASVAB) is a comprehensive, multi-part test designed to evaluate the strengths, skills, and potential of individuals interested in pursuing a career in the U.S. military. Since its inception in 1968, the ASVAB has become one of the most widely administered aptitude tests in the world, playing a critical role in military enlistment, career exploration, and job placement within the armed forces. The ASVAB serves as both a military entrance exam and a tool for career guidance.

The ASVAB is primarily used to determine whether a candidate is qualified to enlist in the U.S. military and to assess their aptitude for specific military occupational specialties (MOS). The exam consists of multiple subtests, each focused on a different skill set, such as verbal comprehension, mathematical reasoning, and mechanical knowledge. In total, the ASVAB has nine or ten subtests, depending on whether the computerized version (CAT-ASVAB) or paper-based version is taken. The exam covers a broad range of subjects, allowing the military to assess both general academic abilities and specialized technical skills.

The ASVAB measures an individual's potential in four key areas:

- Verbal Skills: This includes the Word Knowledge (WK) and Paragraph Comprehension (PC) subtests, which evaluate reading comprehension and vocabulary knowledge.

- Math Skills: The Arithmetic Reasoning (AR) and Mathematics Knowledge (MK) subtests assess problem-solving abilities and mathematical proficiency.

- Science and Technical Skills: Subtests such as General Science (GS), Electronics Information (EI), Auto and Shop Information (AS), and Mechanical Comprehension (MC) evaluate a candidate's technical knowledge and understanding of scientific principles.

- Spatial Abilities: The Assembling Objects (AO) subtest measures spatial orientation and the ability to visualize objects and how they fit together.

The ASVAB plays a vital role in military enlistment. Each military branch—Army, Navy, Air Force, Marines, Coast Guard, and Space Force—uses ASVAB scores to determine an applicant's eligibility to enlist and suitability for various military jobs. The scores from the ASVAB are used to calculate the Armed Forces Qualification Test (AFQT) score, which is the most critical score for enlistment purposes. The AFQT score, based on four sections of the ASVAB (Arithmetic Reasoning, Mathematics Knowledge, Paragraph Comprehension, and Word Knowledge), determines whether an individual qualifies to join the military. The higher the AFQT score, the more job options are available to the candidate.

Who Should Take the ASVAB

The ASVAB is primarily intended for individuals who are considering a career in the U.S. military, but its utility extends beyond just military enlistment. Various groups of people could benefit from taking the ASVAB.

Potential Military Recruits

The most obvious group that should take the ASVAB is those who are planning to enlist in the U.S. Armed Forces. Every branch of the military, including the Army, Navy, Air Force, Marine Corps, Coast Guard, and Space Force, requires prospective recruits to take the ASVAB as part of the enlistment process. The ASVAB provides a detailed assessment of a recruit's strengths and weaknesses across a variety of skills and subjects, ensuring they are placed in roles where they will succeed and benefit the military.

The ASVAB serves two critical purposes for potential recruits:

- Eligibility for Military Service: Your ASVAB score helps determine whether you qualify for military enlistment. Each branch of the military has its own minimum score requirements, particularly the Armed Forces Qualification Test (AFQT) score, which is derived from four sections of the ASVAB.

- Job Placement: The ASVAB assesses your aptitude in areas such as mechanics, electronics, and mathematics, helping military branches place you in a role that aligns with your strengths. A higher ASVAB score gives you more options when selecting a military occupational specialty (MOS).

For anyone who has already decided to join the military, the ASVAB is a critical step in the recruitment process, and preparing for it is essential to open up the widest range of career opportunities within the armed forces.

High School Students Exploring Career Options

Another significant group that can benefit from taking the ASVAB is high school students unsure about their future career path and whether they plan to join the military. The ASVAB Career Exploration Program, offered at many high schools, allows students to assess their skills and strengths in various areas such as verbal comprehension, math, science, and technical skills. This program is especially useful for those who are still deciding between military and civilian career paths.

Students who take the ASVAB as part of the Career Exploration Program receive a score report that highlights their skills and how those skills align with different types of careers. This information can help students:

- Identify Strengths: The ASVAB reveals areas where a student excels, guiding them toward careers that match their natural abilities.

- Explore Career Fields: Based on their ASVAB results, students can explore military and civilian careers they may not have considered before.

- Make Informed Decisions: Even if a student does not plan to enlist in the military, the ASVAB can help them make well-informed decisions about post-secondary education or job training programs.

Individuals Considering a Change in Career

Adults considering a career change or re-entering the workforce after a period of absence may also find the ASVAB to be a helpful resource. For those who may not have had the opportunity to take the ASVAB earlier in life, the test provides a structured way to assess their aptitudes and explore new career possibilities.

For example, someone who has worked in a civilian field for years and is now interested in joining the military or exploring technical fields may benefit from taking the ASVAB to gauge their readiness. Additionally, those who have completed higher education or vocational training can use the ASVAB to confirm whether their skills match their career interests, particularly if they are interested in highly technical or specialized military roles.

Individuals Seeking to Retake the ASVAB

For individuals who have already taken the ASVAB but are unsatisfied with their scores, there is the option to retake the test. Some may feel that their initial performance does not reflect their true capabilities due to insufficient preparation or test anxiety. Retaking the ASVAB can allow them to improve their scores, which may open doors to more desirable job placements or even enhance their chances of enlisting in a branch with higher score requirements.

In later sections, we will discuss the specific requirements and conditions for retaking the ASVAB, as well as how scores from multiple attempts are used by the military.

ASVAB vs AFQT

The ASVAB (Armed Services Vocational Aptitude Battery) and the AFQT (Armed Forces Qualification Test) are closely related but serve different purposes in the military recruitment and qualification process. While the ASVAB is a comprehensive test used to measure a broad range of skills and aptitudes, the AFQT is a specific score derived from the ASVAB results that determines whether an individual is eligible to enlist in the U.S. military.

ASVAB

The ASVAB is a multi-part aptitude test that covers a wide range of subjects and skill areas. The U.S. military uses it to assess a candidate's strengths and weaknesses across various domains, including verbal, math, science, technical, and spatial abilities. The ASVAB is designed to help the military place recruits into roles that match their skills, ensuring both the individual and the military benefit from the right job fit.

The ASVAB consists of nine or ten subtests, depending on whether you take the computerized or paper-based version. These subtests include:

1. General Science (GS)

The General Science subtest measures knowledge of physical and biological sciences. It covers topics from a broad range of scientific disciplines, including Biology, Earth Science (geology, meteorology), Physics, and Chemistry.

Candidates are asked questions that test their understanding of basic scientific principles and their ability to apply them to practical situations. This subtest is particularly important for roles in technical and engineering fields where a strong foundation in science is critical.

2. Arithmetic Reasoning (AR)

The Arithmetic Reasoning subtest evaluates the ability to solve arithmetic word problems. These problems often involve real-world scenarios where candidates must apply basic math concepts to solve issues related to time, money, distance, or quantities. The AR subtest assesses logical thinking and problem-solving skills rather than purely mathematical knowledge. A strong performance in this section is important for any role that requires critical thinking and numerical problem-solving, such as technical or engineering positions.

3. Word Knowledge (WK)

The Word Knowledge subtest measures the candidate's ability to understand the meaning of words based on context and synonyms. Questions often involve selecting the closest synonym for a given word or interpreting the meaning of a word in a sentence. A high score in Word Knowledge indicates a strong vocabulary and verbal skills, which are valuable in nearly all military occupations, especially those involving communication, writing, or intelligence gathering.

4. Paragraph Comprehension (PC)

The Paragraph Comprehension subtest evaluates the ability to understand and interpret written material. Candidates read brief passages and answer questions based on the content. This subtest measures how well a candidate can grasp main ideas, draw inferences, and make logical conclusions from the information provided. This skill is essential for roles involving reading and processing written instructions or reports.

5. Mathematics Knowledge (MK)

The Mathematics Knowledge subtest assesses a candidate's understanding of high school-level mathematical concepts. Topics covered include: Algebra, Geometry, Basic number theory.

The questions in this subtest focus on applying mathematical principles to solve equations and problems. This subtest is critical for technical roles that require mathematical precision, such as engineering, electronics, and other technology-based positions.

6. Electronics Information (EI)

The Electronics Information subtest measures knowledge of electrical concepts, including: Circuits, Currents, Batteries, Electrical components like resistors, capacitors, and transistors.

Candidates are asked to demonstrate their understanding of how electrical systems work, often through practical questions related to diagnosing or repairing electrical problems. This subtest is particularly relevant for positions in the military that deal with electrical engineering, communications, and radar technology.

7. Auto and Shop Information (AS)

The Auto and Shop Information subtest assesses knowledge of automotive maintenance, repair, and shop practices. The test covers: Vehicle components and systems, Common automotive tools, Shop safety and techniques.

The questions range from identifying the purpose of various tools to explaining how different mechanical systems in a car work. This subtest is especially important for candidates interested in mechanical and maintenance roles in the military, such as working on vehicles or heavy equipment.

Based on how you take the ASVAB test (computer-based or paper-based), you either take Auto and Shop Information as one subtest, or take them as two separate subtests, which we will discuss shortly.

8. Mechanical Comprehension (MC)

The Mechanical Comprehension subtest evaluates understanding of mechanical and physical principles, including: Levers and pulleys, Gears and wheels, Laws of motion, Properties of fluids.

Candidates must demonstrate how mechanical devices operate and how physical laws influence their functions. This subtest is key for roles involving engineering, mechanics, and other positions that require hands-on technical skills.

9. Assembling Objects (AO)

The Assembling Objects subtest measures spatial reasoning and the ability to visualize how different parts fit together. Candidates are given images of disassembled objects and must determine how the pieces should be arranged. This section is particularly important for jobs that require good spatial awareness and the ability to work with complex machinery or technical diagrams, such as in fields like aviation or construction.

The ASVAB is offered in two formats: the computerized version (CAT-ASVAB) and the paper-and-pencil version (P&P-ASVAB). While both formats test the same content areas, there are some key differences in the way the test is administered and scored.

CAT-ASVAB (Computerized Adaptive Test): The CAT-ASVAB is the most commonly administered version of the test. It is adaptive, meaning that the difficulty of each question adjusts based on how well you answered the previous one. If you answer a question correctly, the next question will be more challenging; if you answer incorrectly, the next question will be easier.

On the CAT-ASVAB, you are allowed to work at your own pace. Once you finish a section, you can immediately move on to the next without having to wait for others. After completing all the sections, you are free to leave the testing room. However, unlike the paper version, once you submit an answer on the CAT-ASVAB, you cannot go back to review or change it.

If you're running low on time, it's better to keep answering thoughtfully rather than making random guesses. Here is why: even though the CAT-ASVAB does not explicitly penalize you for guessing in the traditional sense, the structure of the test inherently discourages random guessing. In the CAT-ASVAB, the difficulty of the next question is based on whether you answer the current question correctly. When you guess randomly and answer incorrectly, the next question the adaptive algorithm selects for you will be easier, which limits your ability to score higher. This process can indirectly lower your score since easier questions contribute less to the overall score than more difficult ones. Thus, while there's no direct deduction for wrong answers, random guessing can negatively affect your performance by leading to easier subsequent questions, which may result in a lower final score.

You might find it reassuring though to know that even though there are time limits imposed on each subtest in the CAT-ASVAB, the vast majority of examinees complete the individual subtests before the time expires. Most candidates complete it in about 1.5 to 2 hours. Your test scores will generally be available immediately after your testing session at the testing site.

P&P-ASVAB (Paper-and-Pencil Test): The P&P-ASVAB is the traditional format and is still offered at some MET sites and high schools. Unlike the CAT-ASVAB, the P&P-ASVAB allows you to review and change your answers within the same subtest, but you cannot return to a previous subtest or move ahead to the next one until instructed. If you run out of time on the P&P-ASVAB, it's beneficial to make random guesses for unanswered questions, as there is no penalty for guessing in the P&P-ASVAB format. The paper-and-pencil version takes about 3 hours to complete.

Another main difference between the CAT-ASVAB (computer-based) and the P&P-ASVAB (paper-based) tests lies in the way Auto Information (AI) and Shop Information (SI) are administered. In the CAT-ASVAB, these are two separate subtests, but in the P&P-ASVAB, they are combined into one subtest. This results in 10 sections for the CAT-ASVAB and 9 for the P&P-ASVAB. Despite this difference, the combined Auto & Shop score (AS) is reported for both formats.

ASVAB Test Lengths and Time Limits

The table below shows the number of questions and time limits in each of CAT-ASVAB's and P&P-ASVAB's subtests.

ASVAB Test Lengths and Time Limits

CAT-ASVAB			P&P-ASVAB		
Test	Number of Questions	Time Limit (minutes)	Test	Number of Questions	Time Limit (minutes)
GS	15	12	GS	25	11
AR	15	55	AR	30	36
WK	15	9	WK	35	11
PC	10	27	PC	15	13
MK	15	31	MK	25	24
EI	15	10	EI	20	9
AI	10	7	AS	25	11
SI	10	6	MC	25	19
MC	15	22	AO	25	15
AO	15	18			
Total	135	197	**Total**	225	149

However, the inclusion of possible tryout questions in CAT-ASVAB makes each subtest's number of questions and time limits uncertain—you may or may not run into the tryout questions in a given subtest. These tryout questions are new items being tested for future use and do not impact your score. They are included to assess how well they function and ensure they meet fairness standards before they are officially scored. Tryout questions also help maintain consistency between the scores of current and future test-takers. Each test-taker may encounter tryout questions in 2 to 4 of the subtests, with up to 15 of these questions randomly scattered throughout. Test candidates won't know which questions are tryouts.

Additional time is provided when tryout questions are part of the subtest. The following table shows the CAT-ASVAB subtests' length and time limits with and without possible tryout questions included.

CAT-ASVAB Test Lengths and Time Limits

Subtest	Number of Scored Questions	Subtest Time Limit **Without** Tryout Questions	Number of Possible Tryout Questions	Subtest Time Limit **With** Tryout Questions
General Science (GS)	15	12	15	25
Arithmetic Reasoning (AR)	15	55	15	113
Word Knowledge (WK)	15	9	15	18
Paragraph Comprehension (PC)	10	27	15	75
Mathematics Knowledge (MK)	15	31	15	65
Electronics Information (EI)	15	10	15	21
Auto Information (AI)	10	7	15	18
Shop Information (SI)	10	6	15	17
Mechanical Comprehension (MC)	15	22	15	42
Assembling Objects (AO)	15	18	15	38

Regardless of whether you take the paper- or computer-based ASVAB, the subject areas covered in the test are the same, and both versions are valid for determining military enlistment eligibility and job placement.

AFQT

The AFQT (Armed Forces Qualification Test) is a subset of the ASVAB that determines whether a candidate is eligible to enlist in the U.S. military. The AFQT score is calculated using the results from four specific sections of the ASVAB:

- Arithmetic Reasoning (AR)
- Mathematics Knowledge (MK)
- Word Knowledge (WK)
- Paragraph Comprehension (PC)

These four sections are considered to be the most critical in assessing a candidate's overall aptitude for military service, as they focus on basic math and verbal skills. The AFQT score is expressed as a percentile, indicating how a candidate performed in comparison to a nationally representative sample of test-takers. For example, an AFQT score of 60 means the candidate scored better than 60% of the reference group.

The AFQT is used by all branches of the military (Army, Navy, Air Force, Marine Corps, Coast Guard, and Space Force) to determine whether a candidate meets the minimum qualifications for enlistment. Each branch has its own minimum AFQT score requirements, which may vary depending on the needs of the service and the desired job roles.

Key Differences Between the ASVAB and AFQT

Purpose: The ASVAB is a comprehensive test that measures skills and aptitudes across various domains. It is used to determine both eligibility for enlistment and qualification for specific military jobs. The AFQT, on the other hand, is a specific score derived from the ASVAB and is solely used to determine whether a candidate qualifies for enlistment in the military.

Subtests Involved: The ASVAB includes nine or ten subtests, depending on the format, covering a wide range of skills and knowledge. The AFQT, however, only uses four subtests from the ASVAB: Arithmetic Reasoning, Mathematics Knowledge, Word Knowledge, and Paragraph Comprehension. These sections focus on verbal and mathematical skills that are deemed essential for military service.

Scoring: ASVAB scores are reported as standard scores for each individual subtest, and composite scores (also known as line scores) are used to determine eligibility for specific military jobs. The AFQT score, however, is expressed as a percentile and only reflects the candidate's performance in the four key areas. This score is primarily used to determine if the individual can enlist in the military, not what job they qualify for.

Use in Job Placement: The ASVAB helps determine which military jobs (or MOS) a candidate is qualified for based on their performance across all subtests. Each military job has specific line score requirements that are calculated from different combinations of ASVAB subtests. The AFQT, in contrast, is only concerned with enlistment eligibility and does not factor into job placement.

How the AFQT and ASVAB Scores Work Together

While the AFQT score is the first hurdle for enlistment, the broader ASVAB scores are used to identify a candidate's aptitude for various military careers. A high AFQT score means a candidate is eligible to enlist, but it does not guarantee qualification for every job. Once a candidate qualifies for enlistment based on their AFQT score, the individual line scores from the other ASVAB subtests come into play. These line scores help determine which specific roles within the military the candidate is best suited for.

ASVAB Registration and Testing: What to Know

Where to Take the ASVAB

The ASVAB is administered at various locations, depending on your reason for taking the test:

Military Entrance Processing Stations (MEPS): MEPS are facilities located throughout the country that handle all aspects of the military enlistment process, including administering the ASVAB. If you are taking the ASVAB as part of your enlistment process, you will most likely take it at a MEPS. The computerized version of the ASVAB (CAT-ASVAB) is generally administered here.

Military Entrance Test (MET) Sites: MET sites are satellite locations that offer the ASVAB in a paper-and-pencil format (P&P-ASVAB). These locations are often found in areas without easy access to a MEPS, such as National Guard armories or federal office buildings. While the paper-and-pencil version is less common today, it is still available at some locations.

High Schools: While the ASVAB is an essential part of the enlistment process, it is also widely administered as part of career exploration programs in high schools across the United States. Many high schools offer the ASVAB as part of the ASVAB Career Exploration Program, which helps students assess their skills and explore both military and civilian career options. High school students interested in taking the ASVAB should speak with their guidance counselor about the test's availability at their school. This version is typically administered in the paper-and-pencil format.

How to Register for the ASVAB

The registration process for the ASVAB depends on where and why you're taking the test:

For Military Enlistment: If you are taking the ASVAB as part of the enlistment process, you must contact your local military recruiter. The recruiter will guide you through the necessary steps, including scheduling your ASVAB at a MEPS or MET site. The recruiter will also help ensure that you meet the basic requirements for enlistment, such as age, citizenship, and health, before scheduling the test.

For High School Students: If your school participates in the ASVAB Career Exploration Program, you can register for the test through your school's guidance counselor or career advisor. There is no cost to take the ASVAB through this program, and students are under no obligation to enlist in the military after taking the test.

Other Test-Takers: If you are not currently enrolled in high school and are taking the ASVAB for career exploration purposes, you may still be able to take the test through a military recruiter. Contact your local recruitment office for guidance on how to proceed.

What to Expect on Test Day

Understanding what to expect on test day can help reduce anxiety and improve your performance. Here are some key things to keep in mind:

Identification: Bring a valid form of photo identification, such as a driver's license, passport, or school ID. You will not be allowed to take the ASVAB without proper identification.

Prohibited Items: Electronic devices, including cell phones, smartwatches, and calculators, are not allowed in the testing area. You will be provided with any materials necessary for completing the test, such as scratch paper and pencils.

Time Management: For the CAT-ASVAB, you will need to pace yourself carefully since you cannot go back to previous questions. For the P&P-ASVAB, you have more flexibility to return to earlier questions, but time management is still crucial since each subtest is timed individually.

Breaks: You will have scheduled breaks during the test. Make sure to take advantage of these breaks to clear your mind and stay focused.

Test Environment: The testing environment will be quiet and closely monitored to ensure that all test-takers follow the rules. If you are taking the test at a MEPS or MET site, expect a more formal atmosphere, while high school testing environments may feel more familiar.

Outcomes and Implications of ASVAB Scores

In this section, we will explore how ASVAB scores are used by the military, the meaning behind the Armed Forces Qualification Test (AFQT) score, and how your individual subtest scores affect your job opportunities.

ASVAB Scores and Military Enlistment Eligibility

The ASVAB serves as the primary tool for assessing whether a candidate is eligible to join the U.S. military. Each branch of the military (Army, Navy, Air Force, Marines, Coast Guard, and Space Force) sets minimum score requirements based on the Armed Forces Qualification Test (AFQT) score, which is derived from four specific sections of the ASVAB: Arithmetic Reasoning (AR), Mathematics Knowledge (MK), Word Knowledge (WK), and Paragraph Comprehension (PC).

The AFQT score is expressed as a percentile, comparing your performance to a nationally representative sample of test-takers. While the military branches establish minimum score requirements, these thresholds can and do change over time. The minimum required scores are influenced by the military's current recruiting needs, which can fluctuate depending on factors like the size of the force, specific role shortages, or broader strategic goals.

Therefore, the required AFQT scores for enlistment are not static and may vary from year to year or even month to month. It's important to regularly check with a recruiter to understand the most up-to-date score requirements for the branch you're interested in. Failing to meet the minimum AFQT score for a branch may result in needing to retake the ASVAB or considering alternative career paths.

Military Job Placement (MOS) and Line Scores

Beyond the AFQT score, ASVAB results are used to calculate what are known as line scores—composite scores that determine which specific military jobs or MOS (Military Occupational Specialties) a candidate qualifies for. Line scores are calculated from various combinations of ASVAB subtests, depending on the job or career field you are interested in.

Each branch of the military has its own system for grouping ASVAB subtest scores to match candidates with job roles. For example, the Army uses line scores such as General Technical (GT), Clerical (CL), Combat (CO), Field Artillery (FA), and more. These line scores are made up of different ASVAB subtests:

- General Technical (GT): Derived from Word Knowledge (WK) and Paragraph Comprehension (PC), this score is used for roles requiring strong verbal and analytical skills.

- Combat (CO): This typically includes subtests like Arithmetic Reasoning (AR), Auto and Shop Information (AS), and Mechanical Comprehension (MC), which indicate suitability for mechanical and combat-related jobs.

The specific line scores you need will vary depending on the job or MOS you want to pursue. High scores in certain subtests can open up more advanced or technical career paths, while lower scores may limit your options to more general roles.

Implications for Career Exploration

For high school students or individuals taking the ASVAB as part of the Career Exploration Program, the test's outcomes can be equally valuable. The ASVAB provides a comprehensive profile of your skills and abilities, helping you explore potential career paths that match your strengths. The ASVAB Career Exploration Program offers a detailed score report that highlights how your performance in specific areas (such as verbal, math, science, and technical skills) aligns with various civilian and military careers.

Even if you do not plan to join the military, your ASVAB scores can serve as a useful career assessment tool, guiding you toward careers that suit your natural abilities. The program encourages individuals to consider how their strengths can be applied in different fields, whether in healthcare, engineering, communications, or technical trades.

Understanding Your ASVAB Score Report

After you complete the ASVAB, you will receive a score report that provides a breakdown of your performance across each of the subtests. This report includes:

- Standard Scores: These scores show how you performed on each subtest relative to a national sample of test-takers. A score of 50 is considered average.

- Composite Scores: Depending on the branch of the military you are interested in, these scores combine the results of various subtests to assess your qualifications for specific job roles.

- AFQT Score: As previously discussed, your AFQT score determines your eligibility for enlistment and is based on four key ASVAB subtests.

If you are taking the ASVAB as part of the Career Exploration Program, your score report will also include resources to help you explore potential career fields based on your strengths. You may be encouraged to look into both military and civilian careers that align with your skill set.

Communicating with Your Recruiter

After receiving your scores, your recruiter will review them with you and explain the types of jobs for which you qualify. It's important to communicate your interests and career goals so your recruiter can help you find roles that align with your strengths and aspirations. If your scores do not qualify you for the role you want, your recruiter can also help you explore ways to improve your scores or consider alternative career paths within the military.

Exploring Civilian Career Paths Using Your Scores

For those taking the ASVAB as part of the Career Exploration Program, your scores can serve as a valuable tool in identifying civilian career paths that align with your abilities and interests. The ASVAB provides insights into your strengths in areas such as verbal, mathematical, technical, and mechanical skills, which can be applied to a wide range of careers outside of the military.

Score Interpretation for Civilian Careers: The ASVAB score report highlights your strengths in various areas and matches them to career fields that are likely to align with your abilities. For example, if you perform well in subtests related to electronics and mechanical comprehension, careers in engineering, automotive technology, or industrial design may be worth exploring. On the other hand, strong scores in verbal and math skills might suggest a natural fit for roles in education, communications, or finance.

Using Career Exploration Tools: The ASVAB Career Exploration Program provides access to career exploration tools, including an interest inventory that can help you better understand how your skills and personal interests align with different career fields. These tools allow you to explore a variety of career options, both military and civilian, and provide detailed information about the qualifications and educational requirements for each.

Using ASVAB Scores for Enlistment and Beyond

If your goal is to join the military, your ASVAB scores are a crucial part of your enlistment process. However, using those scores effectively can extend far beyond initial enlistment. Throughout your military career, your ASVAB scores can impact opportunities for career advancement, specialized training, and eligibility for certain roles.

Advanced Roles and Specialization: High ASVAB scores in certain areas may qualify you for advanced or specialized roles in fields such as intelligence, cybersecurity, aviation, or medical services. These roles often come with additional training and educational opportunities that can enhance your military career and provide valuable experience for civilian careers post-service.

Opportunities for Reclassification: As your military career progresses, you may have the opportunity to reclassify into a different job role based on new interests or changing needs within the service. In many cases, your original ASVAB scores will still be used to determine eligibility for reclassification. If you did not initially qualify for a specialized role, you may also have the chance to retake the ASVAB to improve your line scores (more on this in Section 9).

Educational and Training Benefits: The ASVAB is just the beginning of your career journey. Once you enlist, many military roles come with access to educational benefits, such as the GI Bill, and specialized training programs. Your ASVAB scores can help guide you into roles that will give you access to training in fields like electronics, healthcare, mechanics, or information technology, which can be valuable both during your service and when transitioning to a civilian career.

Long-Term Implications of Your ASVAB Scores

ASVAB scores have long-term implications not only for your initial enlistment but also for your career trajectory within the military. High scores in key areas can lead to more specialized, high-responsibility roles that come with additional benefits, such as leadership opportunities, higher pay, and increased job satisfaction. Your ASVAB scores can also play a role in:

Promotion: Certain military promotions and career advancements are based on your job performance and qualifications, and your ASVAB scores can be a factor in determining your eligibility for more senior positions.

Specialized Schools: Some military careers require attendance at specialized schools or training programs. High ASVAB scores can make you a more competitive candidate for these programs.

In summary, the ASVAB is more than just a test to determine military eligibility—it's a tool that helps you navigate your career both in the military and beyond. In the next section, we will explore the process of retaking the ASVAB and how you can improve your scores to open up more career opportunities.

Retaking the ASVAB

Retaking the ASVAB is a common step for individuals who want to improve their scores, whether to qualify for enlistment, gain access to more specialized military occupations, or increase their chances of securing a role in a specific branch. While preparing for and performing well on the ASVAB the first time is ideal, retaking the test offers candidates another opportunity to better align their scores with their career goals. This section will cover the reasons for retaking the ASVAB, the eligibility requirements, and how to improve your scores for a second attempt.

Reasons for Retaking the ASVAB

There are various reasons why someone might choose to retake the ASVAB. Some of the most common include:

Improving AFQT Scores for Enlistment Eligibility: The AFQT score, which is derived from four ASVAB subtests—Arithmetic Reasoning (AR), Mathematics Knowledge (MK), Word Knowledge (WK), and Paragraph Comprehension (PC)—determines whether a candidate qualifies for military enlistment. If your AFQT score does not meet the minimum requirement for the branch you want to join, retaking the test can give you another chance to meet or exceed that threshold.

Qualifying for More Specialized Jobs (MOS): Even if you meet the enlistment requirements with your AFQT score, your ASVAB line scores may not qualify you for certain specialized military roles or jobs you desire. For example, technical jobs in electronics, mechanics, or aviation may require higher scores in subtests such as Electronics Information (EI) or Mechanical Comprehension (MC). Retaking the ASVAB to improve your line scores can expand your career options.

Branch-Specific Score Requirements: Some military branches have stricter score requirements than others. For instance, the Coast Guard generally requires a higher AFQT score than other branches. If you are set on joining a specific branch, but your initial scores fall short, a second attempt may give you the opportunity to achieve the required score.

Gaining Access to Advanced Training and Education: A high ASVAB score can qualify you for specialized training programs or schools within the military, which can enhance your career prospects both during and after your service. If your initial ASVAB score didn't meet the requirements for these programs, retaking the test could open new doors.

Eligibility for Retaking the ASVAB

While retaking the ASVAB is allowed, specific rules and waiting periods apply to when and how you can retake the test. Understanding these rules is essential before you schedule another attempt.

Initial Waiting Period: If you want to retake the ASVAB after your first attempt, you must wait a minimum of 30 days from your test date. This waiting period gives candidates time to study and prepare for a stronger performance on their next attempt.

Second Retake: If you need to take the ASVAB a third time, you must wait an additional 30 days after your second attempt. This applies whether you are retaking the test to improve scores or due to circumstances beyond your control, such as illness on the test day.

Subsequent Retakes: After your third attempt, the waiting period increases to six months before you are eligible to retake the ASVAB again. This longer waiting period encourages candidates to take sufficient time to prepare before attempting the test again.

Limits on Retakes: While there is no strict limit on how many times you can retake the ASVAB, military recruiters often advise candidates to prepare thoroughly before each attempt. Multiple low scores could indicate to recruiters that you may struggle in certain areas, so retaking the ASVAB too many times without improvement may hurt your prospects.

What Happens After You Retake the ASVAB?

Once you retake the ASVAB, your most recent scores will replace your previous ones. Whether your scores improve or remain the same, the military will use your most recent scores for enlistment and job qualification purposes. If your retake yields higher scores, it could open up new career opportunities within the military or qualify you for more specialized roles.

Discuss Your Scores with Your Recruiter: After receiving your new scores, review them with your military recruiter. They can help you understand how your updated scores affect your enlistment eligibility and job options. Your recruiter can also provide advice on next steps, such as further test preparation or applying for advanced military training programs.

Apply Your Improved Scores: Higher scores can improve your eligibility for certain military benefits, training programs, and career paths. For example, if your new ASVAB scores qualify you for a job that requires technical skills, you may gain access to advanced training that can benefit you both during your military service and after you transition to civilian life.

Retaking the ASVAB can be a valuable option for candidates who want to improve their scores and expand their career opportunities. However, this study guide aims to help you achieve satisfactory scores the first time and won't have to take it again! We will discuss effective test preparation strategies next.

ACE THE ASVAB: STRATEGIES FOR SUCCESS

You know you will have to take the ASVAB. No matter how good a student you have been in the past, those butterflies in your stomach flutter anyway. Luckily, you still have a few weeks or months to prepare. Now what?

Your performance on the test will be largely determined by 1) how well you've studied the relevant materials in the past and 2) how well you familiarize and prepare for the test in the weeks and months prior to the test.

Based on our own test-taking experiences and scientific studies of test preparation, memorization, and cognitive psychology, we summarized the following strategies to facilitate and optimize your test preparation.

Choose the Right Test Preparation Tool

Test preparation tools can include courses, books, tutors, flash cards, and so on. Depending on your individual needs and current readiness, the best tool or combination of tools can be different. You are the most qualified person to assess what's best for yourself. When chosen properly, the right tool(s) can save you considerable time and enhance your test performance.

This book strives to strike the right balance between comprehensiveness and conciseness. We provide sufficient coverage to enable you to pass the test with a comfortable safety margin or earn a high score, but keep things relatively concise to help you get ready for the test as quickly as feasible.

Study the Preparation Materials with Systematic Repetition

We ourselves have been tested countless times in academic and professional settings. Based on those experiences and scientific research, we know that learning is more effective when repeated in spaced-out sessions.

Information repeatedly learned over a spaced-out period allows a learner to better remember and better recall the information being learned. In fact, strategically spaced repetition has been scientifically proven to better encode information into long-term memory.

When applying this learning principle, you will want to be systematic about test preparation: First, start early so that you do not have to cram right before the test. Second, while studying new materials, methodically review the older materials you studied a few days ago, well before your memory begins to fade. Using this strategy, you can go through the exam preparation materials at an aggressive rate and still maintain satisfactory retention because you repeatedly reinforce your fading memories.

Another highly beneficial practice can also be helpful: as you take practice tests, take note of those questions you answered incorrectly, or you answered correctly but want to review again anyway. Then write down the page number and question number for each. In the days and weeks that follow, you can systematically revisit the questions multiple times so that you can commit the current information to memory.

Apply Memorization Techniques

Rule number one for memorization is comprehension. A good understanding will go a long way in ensuring long-term memory and effective recall. However, rote memorization is still invariably needed in almost all studies. In such situations, the application of various memorization techniques can help tremendously with retaining information effectively.

Many books have been written on this subject. But most advice boils down to two techniques: imagination and association. These techniques are beyond the scope of this book, but a quick Google search will generate ample resources. You will be amazed how handy these techniques can be in test preparation and beyond.

Take Practice Tests

Taking practice tests is beneficial on multiple fronts:

- Helps familiarize you with the format, coverage, and difficulty level of the test.

- Helps you apply the knowledge you have learned in a different context, reinforcing memory retention.
- Helps you learn from having to figure out the correct answer since you'll probably run into questions where you don't know the answer, or you answer incorrectly.
- Boosts your confidence and eases your nervousness when taking the actual exam thanks to performing increasingly better on practice exams.
- Consequently, taking practice tests is an integral part of preparing for any test.

Devote Yourself

For tests with set dates that you have no choice over, plan early and leave yourself enough time to prepare.

For those tests that you can choose a test date, you have your choice of two diametrically different approaches to prepare:

- Approach #1. Devote every hour you can to preparing for the exam, and then take it as soon as you feel ready.
- Approach #2. Fall prey to all the distractions in life, and study the materials at your leisure, halfheartedly in a drawn-out process. Procrastinate until you have your back against a wall and must take the test.

The more drawn-out the process, the more time you will have to spend reinforcing fading memories. In the end, you spend more total hours on exam preparation if you adopt the second approach.

Thus, in test preparation, if you would like to reduce the cumulative amount of "pain" you must endure and increase your odds of scoring well, then the best approach is to completely commit yourself to a single-minded, intensive preparation period. You can then take the exam when you feel confident and ready.

ASVAB 60-Day Test Prep Study Plan

The study plan on the following page is designed to help you prepare effectively for the ASVAB exam in 60 days. It is realistic and works for a typical high school student in his/her junior or senior year or someone with equivalent academic preparedness. Here's how you can optimize your study sessions by following the plan:

1. Daily Focus and Goal Setting

Each day of the plan is intentionally focused on one or two core areas. By dedicating specific days to each area, you avoid overloading yourself and maintain a steady, focused progression. Ensure you set realistic goals for each session, such as completing a certain number of pages, a chapter, or finishing a set of practice questions.

2. Efficient Time Management

- Study Blocks: Allocate at least a couple of hours per day to your studies, breaking them into shorter, focused blocks (e.g., 30–45 minutes per block). Use techniques like the Pomodoro method (25 minutes study, 5 minutes break) to stay focused and avoid burnout.

- Prioritize Weak Areas: If you know certain sections are more challenging for you, e.g., math, then plan to spend more time on these areas.

3. Balancing Study and Review

- Initial Study Days: We designed the study plan so that you start with studying new materials, which builds your foundational skills and familiarity with test concepts.

- Review Days: We include dedicated review days dispersed throughout the test preparation. Reviews days are critical for reinforcing knowledge and identifying areas where you may need additional practice. Use these days to go over key concepts, formulas, and incorrect answers from practice tests, etc.

4. Practice Tests and Test Simulation

- Practice Under Real Conditions: On practice test days, take full-length practice tests in one sitting, replicating test-day conditions. This will help you gauge your readiness and stamina for the actual exam.

- Analyze Your Performance: Use the review days following each practice test to analyze your mistakes and review the correct answers. Look for patterns in your errors—whether it's certain types of math problems or recurring grammar mistakes—and focus on improving those areas.

60-Day Study Plan

Day 1	Day 2	Day 3	Day 4	Day 5	Day 6
Introduction	Word Knowledge	Word Knowledge	Paragraph Comprehension	Paragraph Comprehension	Math §1
Day 7	**Day 8**	**Day 9**	**Day 10**	**Day 11**	**Day 12**
Math §1	Math §1	Math §2	Math §2	Math §2	Review Word Knowledge
Day 13	**Day 14**	**Day 15**	**Day 16**	**Day 17**	**Day 18**
Math §3	Math §3	Review Paragraph Comprehension	Math §4	Math §4	Review Math §1-2
Day 19	**Day 20**	**Day 21**	**Day 22**	**Day 23**	**Day 24**
Review Math §3-4	Arithmetic Reasoning	Arithmetic Reasoning	General Science §1	General Science §1	General Science §2
Day 25	**Day 26**	**Day 27**	**Day 28**	**Day 29**	**Day 30**
General Science §2	Review Arithmetic Reasoning	General Science §3	General Science §3	Review General Science §1-3	Electronic Information
Day 31	**Day 32**	**Day 33**	**Day 34**	**Day 35**	**Day 36**
Electronic Information	Electronic Information	Automotive Information	Automotive Information	Automotive Information	Review Electronic Information
Day 37	**Day 38**	**Day 39**	**Day 40**	**Day 41**	**Day 42**
Shop Information	Shop Information	Shop Information	Review Automotive Information	Mechanical Comprehension	Mechanical Comprehension
Day 43	**Day 44**	**Day 45**	**Day 46**	**Day 47**	**Day 48**
Mechanical Comprehension	Review Shop Information	Assembing Objeects	Assembing Objeects	Review Math §1-2	Review Math §3-4
Day 49	**Day 50**	**Day 51**	**Day 52**	**Day 53**	**Day 54**
Review Mechanical Comprehension	Review Arithmetic Reasoning	Review General Science §1-3	Review Electronic Information	Test 1	Review Test 1
Day 55	**Day 56**	**Day 57**	**Day 58**	**Day 59**	**Day 60**
Review Auto and Shop Information	Test 2	Review Test 2	Review Mechanical Comprehension	Test 3	Review Test 3

I'm Ready!

5. Rest and Recharge

Remember to schedule short breaks during your study sessions to maintain focus and retain information more effectively. Even a 5-minute break can help reset your mind. If you make good progress and end up ahead of the study plan, feel free to take a day off from time to time.

6. Building Confidence for Test Day

- Final Reviews: The last couple of weeks are dedicated to reviewing and taking practice tests. These days are designed to boost your confidence by reinforcing what you've learned.

- Positive Mindset: Use these final days to cultivate a positive mindset. Remind yourself of how much progress you've made, and trust in the preparation you've done.

By sticking to this study plan, managing your time effectively, and focusing on both learning and review, you'll be well-prepared to tackle the ASVAB exam with confidence. It is always advisable to start preparing for the test early though. If you have more than 60 days to prepare, the best time to get started is right away!

SUCCESS SKILLS FOR TEST DAY

Time Management

Each ASVAB subtest has strict time limits. Hence, managing your time effectively is essential. Practice pacing yourself by taking timed practice tests. During the test, avoid spending too much time on difficult questions—make your best guess and move on, as you won't have time to dwell on every question.

Staying Calm and Focused

Test anxiety can hinder performance, so practice relaxation techniques like deep breathing or visualization to stay calm during the exam. Maintaining focus for the entire test is crucial, as it's a lengthy process. Breaks are built into the test, so use them to refresh your mind.

Reading and Following Instructions Carefully

Ensure you read and understand all instructions before beginning each subtest. Rushing through instructions or missing key details can lead to avoidable mistakes. Particularly in sections like Paragraph Comprehension, understanding the instructions is crucial to answering correctly.

Answer Every Question

With four possible answers for every question, the ASVAB offers a chance at scoring points even when you're unsure of the correct answer. Educated guessing is a skill you can develop. Look for contextual clues within the question and eliminate the most obviously incorrect answers to improve your odds of guessing correctly. Since there's no penalty for wrong answers on P&P-ASVAB, it's to your advantage to answer every question. With CAT-ASVAB, randomly guessing can result in wrong answers, an easier next question, and potentially drag down your score. So, on the questions you are not sure, you will want to deliberately eliminate a few answers you can determine are wrong first, and then pick the most plausible answer from the remaining ones.

Finally, be mindful that on the computer-based ASVAB, once you move on to the next question, you can't go back, so be confident in your answers before proceeding.

Rest and Hydration

Ensure you get a good night's sleep before the test. Being well-rested helps with concentration and memory. Staying hydrated also supports cognitive function, but avoid excessive caffeine, as it can increase anxiety.

By practicing these strategies and remaining calm, focused, and prepared, you will improve your chances of performing well on the test day.

CONQUER TEST ANXIETY

Dealing with test anxiety is a crucial skill that can significantly impact one's academic and professional life. Test anxiety is a type of performance anxiety that occurs when an individual feels an intense fear or panic before, during, or after an examination. It can manifest through various symptoms, including nervousness, difficulty concentrating, negative thoughts, physical symptoms such as headaches or nausea, and even panic attacks. Fortunately, there are effective strategies to manage and overcome test anxiety, ensuring that it doesn't hinder one's ability to perform to the best of their abilities.

Test anxiety can stem from fear of failure, lack of preparation, previous negative experiences, or high pressure to perform well. Identifying the root cause is essential in developing a targeted approach to manage anxiety.

One of the most effective ways to reduce test anxiety is thorough preparation. Begin studying well in advance of the test date. This allows ample time to understand the material, reducing the likelihood of feeling overwhelmed as the test approaches. Create a study plan that breaks down the material into manageable sections. Use organizers, such as outlines, flashcards, or mind maps, to make the study process more efficient and less daunting.

Simulating test conditions can help alleviate anxiety. Practice with timed quizzes or tests in a quiet environment. This not only helps with time management but also makes the actual test environment feel more familiar.

Mindset and Attitude Adjustments

Transform negative thoughts into positive affirmations. Instead of thinking, "I'm going to fail," tell yourself, "I'm prepared and will do my best." Positive thinking can enhance self-confidence and reduce nervousness. Furthermore, accept that it's okay to be nervous and that feeling anxious doesn't mean you will perform poorly. Recognize that anxiety can sometimes motivate you to prepare better.

Relaxation Techniques

Deep breathing exercises can be effective in managing physical symptoms of anxiety. Techniques such as the 4-7-8 method, where you inhale for four seconds, hold your breath for seven seconds, and exhale for eight seconds, can help calm the nervous system.

The Progressive Muscle Relaxation technique can also help. This involves tensing and then slowly relaxing each muscle group in the body to reduce the physical symptoms of stress and anxiety.

During the Test

If you find yourself becoming anxious, pause for a moment, take a few deep breaths, and refocus on the question in front of you. Avoid dwelling on what you might have gotten wrong or what's coming next.

Test anxiety is a common challenge that many face, but it doesn't have to be a barrier to success. By understanding its causes, implementing effective study and preparation strategies, adopting relaxation techniques, and seeking support when needed, individuals can overcome test anxiety. Remember, the goal is not to eliminate anxiety completely but to manage it effectively so that it doesn't interfere with performance.

CHAPTER 1: WORD KNOWLEDGE

INTRODUCTION

The Word Knowledge (WK) subtest of the ASVAB measures a candidate's ability to understand the meanings of words through definitions and synonyms. This section evaluates vocabulary skills, which are crucial not only for communication but also for succeeding in various military roles that involve reading, writing, intelligence gathering, and following instructions. A solid grasp of vocabulary is key to performing well in other ASVAB subtests as well, such as Paragraph Comprehension (PC).

In the Word Knowledge subtest, you'll encounter questions where you're given a word and asked to select the best synonym or the closest meaning from four answer choices. The test aims to assess your understanding of word meanings based on context and your ability to decipher unfamiliar words.

Example Questions

Question 1: The word <u>diligent</u> most nearly means:

    A) Careless
    B) Hardworking
    C) Lazy
    D) Uncertain

Answer: B) Hardworking

Explanation: "Diligent" describes someone who is hardworking and consistently puts effort into their tasks. By eliminating opposites like "careless" and "lazy," you can narrow down to the correct answer.

Question 2: The weather was <u>harsh</u> during the hike.

A) mild
B) gentle
C) extreme
D) pleasant

Answer: C) extreme
Explanation: "Harsh" means severe or extreme, so the closest synonym is "extreme."

Question 3: The word most opposite in meaning to <u>indifferent</u> is:

A) uninterested
B) passionate
C) neutral
D) careless

Answer: B) passionate
Explanation: "Indifferent" means lacking interest or concern, so the antonym is "passionate," which indicates strong interest or intense emotion.

These examples show how the Word Knowledge subtest focuses on assessing your vocabulary through quick identification of word meanings. The key to success is building a strong vocabulary and developing strategies to approach unfamiliar words. In the next sections, we will cover specific techniques to decipher words and improve your overall performance on this subtest.

BUILDING BLOCKS OF WORDS

Understanding how to break down a word into its parts—prefixes, suffixes, and roots—is an essential skill for improving your vocabulary and performing well on the ASVAB Word Knowledge subtest. Many words in the English language are derived from Greek and Latin, and by learning the meaning of common word parts, you can often infer the meaning of unfamiliar words. This section will explain how to use these components to decode word meanings effectively.

Prefixes and Suffixes

By recognizing common prefixes (beginning parts of words) and suffixes (endings of words), you can often deduce the general meaning of words, even if you've never encountered them before. Both Greek and Latin origins heavily influence English, making these word components valuable tools for decoding language.

Prefixes

Prefixes appear at the start of a word and modify its meaning, often giving clues about direction, negation, or intensity. By learning some common prefixes, you can better guess the meaning of a word.

For example:

- Anti- (against): *Antibiotic* – a substance that works *against* bacteria.

- Pre- (before): *Preview* – a look *before* the main event.

- Re- (again): *Rewrite* – to write *again*.

Below is a table of **common prefixes**:

Prefix	Variations	Meaning	Examples
Anti-	Ant-	Against or opposite	Anti-inflammatory, antagonist
De-		Opposite	Decontaminate, deconstruct
Dis-		Not or opposite	Disagree, discontent, disable
En-	Em-	Cause to	Encourage, empower, embolden
Ex-		Out of, from, former	Export, ex-husband, exclude
In-	Im-, Il-, Ir-	Not	Incapable, impossible, illegitimate, irrational
Inter-		Between or among	Interact, international, interconnect
Mis-		Wrongly	Misunderstand, misplace, misuse
Non-		Not	Noncompliant, nonsense
Over-		Too much	Overcook, overestimate, overload
Post-		After	Postpone, post-war, postscript
Pre-		Before	Predict, pretest, preheat
Pro-		In favor of, forward	Proactive, promote, propel
Re-		Again or back	Rewrite, redo, replay
Semi-		Half, partly	Semicircle, semiannual, semiconscious
Sub-		Under	Submarine, substitute, subway
Super-		Above or over	Superhero, superimpose, supernatural
Trans-		Across or beyond	Transport, transmit, translate
Under-		Too little, below	Underestimate, underpaid, underground
Un-		Not	Unfair, unjust

Suffixes

Suffixes are added to the end of a word and often indicate the word's function in a sentence, such as whether it's a noun, verb, adjective, or adverb. They can also modify the meaning to reflect qualities, actions, or conditions.

For example:

- -able (capable of): *Manageable* – something that is capable of being managed.

- -ful (full of): *Hopeful* – full of hope.

- -ly (in the manner of): *Quickly* – done in a quick manner.

Below is a table of **common suffixes**:

Suffix	Variations	Meaning	Examples
-able	-ible	Capable of being	Readable, edible, manageable
-al		Relating to, characteristic of	Personal, natural, cultural
-ed		Past tense, having been	Walked, jumped, decorated
-en		To make or become	Strengthen, lengthen, darken
-er	-or	One who, more (comparative)	Teacher, actor, greater
-ful		Full of	Hopeful, thankful, beautiful
-ic	-ical	Pertaining to, related to	Artistic, musical, logical
-ing		Present participle, action	Running, cooking, swimming
-ion	-tion, -ation	The action or state of	Celebration, operation, promotion
-ist		A person who practices	Artist, scientist, biologist
-ity	-ty	State or quality	Clarity, responsibility, certainty
-ive	-ative, -itive	Having the nature of	Creative, sensitive, addictive
-ize	-ise	To make or become	Realize, organize, maximize
-less		Without	Hopeless, fearless, meaningless
-ly		In a manner	Quickly, softly, happily
-ment		Action or process	Development, engagement, movement
-ness		State of, quality of	Kindness, darkness, weakness
-ous	-eous, -ious	Full of, having qualities of	Curious, dangerous, mysterious
-ship		Position held, condition	Friendship, leadership, partnership
-sion	-tion	State or result of	Explosion, confusion, transition
-y		Characterized by, full of	Happy, sunny, tricky

By mastering common prefixes and suffixes, you can greatly improve your ability to infer the meaning of unfamiliar words on the ASVAB. Prefixes give you clues about the basic meaning or direction of the word, while suffixes often define the word's part of speech and refine its meaning.

Root Words

A root word is the core part of a word that carries the most essential meaning. Prefixes and suffixes are added to root words to modify their meaning, but the root remains central to understanding the word's fundamental idea. By learning common Greek and Latin roots, you'll be able to break down complex words and infer their meanings, even if you've never seen them before. Below are tables of commonly used Greek and Latin roots, their meanings, and examples.

Common Greek Root Words

Root	Meaning	Examples
Bio	Life	Biology, biography, biosphere
Geo	Earth	Geography, geology, geocentric
Therm	Heat	Thermometer, thermal, thermostat
Phon	Sound	Telephone, phonograph, symphony
Graph	Write or draw	Autograph, graphic, photography
Chron	Time	Chronology, chronic, synchronize
Hydr	Water	Hydration, hydroplane, hydroelectric
Path	Feeling or disease	Empathy, pathology, sympathy
Scope	See, view	Telescope, microscope, periscope
Tele	Distant	Telephone, television, telegraph

Root	Meaning	Examples
Psych	Mind	Psychology, psychiatrist, psyche
Auto	Self	Autonomy, autobiography, automatic
Macro	Large	Macroeconomics, macroscopic
Micro	Small	Microscope, microchip, microorganism
Mono	One	Monologue, monotheism, monopoly
Poly	Many	Polygon, polytheism, polygamy
Anti	Against	Antibiotic, antidote, anticlimax
Astro	Star, outer space	Astronomy, astronaut, asteroid
Photo	Light	Photograph, photosynthesis, photon
Meter	Measure	Thermometer, speedometer, barometer

Common Latin Root Words

Root	Meaning	Examples
Aud	Hear	Audible, audience, auditory
Bene	Good	Benefit, benevolent, benefactor
Cent	One hundred	Century, percent, centennial
Dict	Say, speak	Dictate, dictionary, predict
Form	Shape	Formation, reform, uniform
Ject	Throw	Eject, project, injection
Lum	Light	Illuminate, luminous, luminary
Mal	Bad	Malfunction, malnourished, malice
Mater	Mother	Maternal, maternity, matriarch
Mort	Death	Mortal, mortuary, immortality
Port	Carry	Transport, portable, import
Rupt	Break	Rupture, erupt, disrupt
Script	Write	Manuscript, prescription, inscription
Spect	See, look	Spectator, inspect, perspective
Struct	Build	Construct, structure, infrastructure
Tract	Pull, drag	Tractor, attract, contract
Vid/Vis	See	Video, vision, visible
Voc	Call	Vocal, invoke, advocate
Scrib	Write	Scribble, describe, inscription
Vit/Viv	Life	Vital, survive, revive

Applying Root Words to Decode Meanings

By recognizing these root words, you can better understand unfamiliar terms. For instance, if you encounter the word "auditory", knowing that "aud" means "hear" helps you quickly conclude that this word relates to hearing. Similarly, if you see "benevolent", you can break it down into "bene" (good) and "volent" (wishing), which tells you it means someone who is kind or wishing well.

Here is one more example: "thermometer". The root "therm" relates to heat, and the root "Meter" means "measure" or "measuring device". Hence, it makes sense that "thermometer" means a device that measures heat or temperature.

By learning and applying these common prefixes, suffixes, Greek and Latin root words, you can greatly improve your ability to decode unfamiliar words on the ASVAB Word Knowledge subtest. These roots not only help you determine the meaning of individual words but also strengthen your overall vocabulary, providing an edge in other parts of the ASVAB and beyond.

INFERRING A WORD'S MEANING THROUGH CONTEXT

One of the most effective strategies for deciphering unfamiliar words on the ASVAB Word Knowledge subtest is using context clues. These are hints or information within the sentence or passage that help you infer the meaning of an unknown word. There are several types of context clues that can assist you in determining the meaning without needing to know the exact definition. Let's explore the different kinds of context clues:

1. Definition Context Clues

Sometimes, the author provides a direct definition or explanation of the word right in the sentence or nearby. This is often signaled by phrases like "which means" or "that is."

Example: The artifact, which is an ancient object, was found in the ruins.

Explanation: The sentence directly defines the word "artifact" as an ancient object.

2. Synonym/Restatement Context Clues

In some instances, the unfamiliar word is explained or restated using a synonym, a word with the same or similar meaning, within the sentence.

Example: The student was meticulous, or very careful, in completing her project.

Explanation: The word "meticulous" is restated using its synonym "very careful," helping to clarify its meaning.

3. Antonym/Contrast Context Clues

Words with opposite meanings, known as antonyms, are sometimes used to infer the meaning of an unfamiliar word. Words like "but," "however," and "on the other hand" signal a contrast in meaning.

Example: Unlike her apathetic classmates, Jane was deeply concerned about the environment.

Explanation: By contrasting Jane's behavior with her classmates' indifference, you can infer that "apathetic" means showing little or no interest or concern.

4. Example Context Clues

Sometimes, the word is explained by providing examples. Words like "such as," "including," or "for example" often introduce these context clues.

Example: Large predators, such as lions, wolves, and sharks, are at the top of their respective food chains.

Explanation: By listing examples of "predators" like lions, wolves, and sharks, the sentence helps clarify the meaning of the word.

5. Cause and Effect Context Clues

In this type of clue, you infer the meaning of a word based on the cause or effect presented in the sentence.

Example: The river overflowed due to the torrential downpour, flooding the nearby homes.

Explanation: Since the downpour caused the river to overflow, you can infer that "torrential" means something very heavy or intense.

6. General Inference Context Clues

Sometimes, the meaning of a word can be inferred based on the general mood or atmosphere of the sentence or passage, even if no direct clues are given.

Example: The dark clouds and distant thunder gave the day a foreboding feeling.

Explanation: The overall mood suggests that "foreboding" relates to a sense of fear or something bad about to happen.

Practice Example: The professor's lecture was <u>convoluted</u>, making it difficult for the students to understand.

A) clear
B) complicated
C) engaging
D) simple

Answer: B) complicated
Explanation: The context indicates that the lecture was difficult to understand, which points to the word "convoluted" meaning complicated or intricate.

By using these different types of context clues—definition, synonym, antonym, example, cause and effect, and general inference—you can oftentimes figure out the meaning of unfamiliar words.

INFERRING MEANING BY IDENTIFYING CONNOTATION

Another effective strategy for deciphering unfamiliar words on the ASVAB Word Knowledge subtest is understanding whether the word carries a positive or negative connotation. Connotation refers to the implied or emotional meaning behind a word, beyond its literal definition. Words can evoke feelings or ideas that hint at whether they are used to describe something favorable or unfavorable. This technique can help you quickly eliminate wrong answer choices and guide you toward the correct one, even if you're not entirely familiar with the word itself.

1. Positive Connotation

Words with a positive connotation suggest something good, desirable, or favorable. They often evoke feelings of happiness, approval, or success. Even if you don't know the exact definition of a word, recognizing a positive connotation can help you choose the most appropriate synonym or antonym.

Example Word: Admirable
Connotation: Positive
Meaning: Worthy of admiration or praise.
Associated Words: Respectable, commendable.

If the word carries a positive connotation, you can rule out answer choices that have negative implications.

2. Negative Connotation

Words with a negative connotation convey something undesirable, harmful, or unpleasant. These words typically suggest disapproval, failure, or negativity. Understanding this can help you identify the correct answer by eliminating words with positive meanings.

Example Word: <u>Hostile</u>
Connotation: Negative
Meaning: Unfriendly or antagonistic.
Associated Words: Aggressive, belligerent.

If a word has a negative connotation, you can eliminate answer choices that describe positive or neutral ideas.

3. Neutral Connotation

Some words may have a neutral connotation, meaning they neither evoke strong positive nor negative feelings. These words often describe things factually, without implying approval or disapproval.

Example Word: <u>Academic</u>
Connotation: Neutral
Meaning: Relating to education or scholarly work.
Associated Words: Educational, scholarly.

Understanding connotation can help you interpret the word in its context and lead you to the correct answer.

Practice Example 1: The <u>turbulent</u> weather caused the flight to be delayed.
A) calm
B) stormy
C) glorious
D) pleasant

Answer: B) stormy
Explanation: "caused the flight to be delayed" has a negative connotation. Here, we derived the connotation not from

the word being tested, but from the context of the sentence. It has to be a negative weather pattern that led to a delayed flight. Hence, you would eliminate positive or neutral answer choices like "calm", "glorious", or "pleasant" and lean toward an answer like "stormy".

Practice Example 2: The treaty was seen as a **pivotal** moment in the history of the conflict.

A) minor
B) insignificant
C) crucial
D) irrelevant

Answer: C) crucial
Explanation: The word "pivotal" has a positive and significant connotation, meaning something that is of great importance or critical. Words like "minor" and "insignificant" have opposite, less impactful meanings. The best answer is "crucial," which matches the importance implied by "pivotal."

Use This Strategy on the ASVAB

When approaching a question in the Word Knowledge subtest, look at the context in which the word is used. Ask yourself:

- Does this word suggest something good, bad, or neutral?
- Can I match the connotation to one of the answer choices?
- Can I eliminate choices that clearly do not fit the tone of the word?

This strategy works especially well when you're unsure about the exact meaning of a word but can sense whether it's being used in a positive, negative, or neutral way.

By practicing this approach, you can improve your ability to infer meanings on the ASVAB, even when you're unfamiliar with the specific word.

INFERRING MEANING BY REPLACING WITH ANSWER CHOICES

A powerful strategy to use on the ASVAB Word Knowledge subtest is replacing the unfamiliar word with the answer choices. This method allows you to test each possible answer by fitting it into the sentence where the unfamiliar word appears, helping you determine which option makes the most sense in context. This approach is particularly helpful when you're unsure of a word's meaning but have a sense of the overall meaning of the sentence.

Example

Original Sentence: The scientist's hypothesis was <u>tenuous</u>, lacking sufficient evidence to be convincing.

A) strong
B) flimsy
C) irrefutable
D) elaborate

Step 1: Read the sentence carefully. The context suggests that the scientist's hypothesis is weak or not well-supported.

Step 2: Replace the word "tenuous" with each answer choice.

A) strong

"The scientist's hypothesis was strong, lacking sufficient evidence to be convincing."

(This doesn't make sense because "strong" contradicts the idea of lacking evidence.)

B) flimsy

"The scientist's hypothesis was flimsy, lacking sufficient evidence to be convincing."

(This fits well since "flimsy" implies weak or not convincing, matching the sentence.)

C) irrefutable

"The scientist's hypothesis was irrefutable, lacking sufficient evidence to be convincing."

(This doesn't fit because "irrefutable" means something that cannot be disproven, which doesn't match the idea of lacking evidence.)

D) elaborate

"The scientist's hypothesis was elaborate, lacking sufficient evidence to be convincing."

(While "elaborate" suggests something detailed or complex, it doesn't align with the idea of lacking evidence.)

Step 3: Eliminate options that don't make sense, which include "strong," "irrefutable," and "elaborate."

Step 4: Choose the best-fitting answer. In this case, B) flimsy is the correct choice.

Why This Strategy Works

This method works because it allows you to focus on the overall meaning of the sentence, which often provides enough information to guide you toward the right answer. Even if you don't know the meaning of the unfamiliar word, the context in which it is used and the logical flow of the sentence can help you find the correct answer.

Practice Example: The king's authority was <u>unassailable</u>; no one could question or challenge it.

A) vulnerable
B) invincible
C) questionable
D) uncertain

Answer: B) invincible
Explanation: The sentence indicates that the king's authority was beyond challenge, which aligns with the meaning of "invincible."

The replacement strategy is a simple yet effective tool for figuring out unfamiliar words. By substituting each answer choice into the sentence, you can quickly eliminate a few incorrect options and narrow down to the ones that best fit the context. This method helps you make logical, informed guesses, even when you are unfamiliar with the word itself.

GUESSING A CHOICE THROUGH PARTS OF SPEECH

Understanding a word's part of speech—whether it's a noun, verb, adjective, or adverb—you can often eliminate incorrect answer choices and make a better-informed guess.

The Four Key Parts of Speech

1. Nouns: Words that represent a person, place, thing, or idea.

Example: The house was built last year.
In this sentence, "house" is a noun, as it refers to a place.

2. Verbs: Words that describe an action, occurrence, or state of being.

Example: She runs every morning.
Here, "runs" is the verb, indicating an action.

3. Adjectives: Words that describe or modify nouns.

Example: The bright sun shone all day.
"Bright" is an adjective because it describes the noun "sun."

4. Adverbs: Words that modify verbs, adjectives, or other adverbs, often describing how something is done.

Example: She ran quickly to catch the bus.
"Quickly" is an adverb because it modifies the verb "ran."

Example

Original Sentence: The students were <u>assiduous</u>, always making sure to complete their homework on time.

The word "assiduous" most nearly means:

A) slow
B) careful

C) intelligence
D) lazy

Step 1: Identify the part of speech. The word "assiduous" is used to describe the students, which makes it an adjective.

Step 2: Eliminate options that don't match the part of speech. After "The students were", the sentence needs an adjective. Choice A, B, D are adjectives, but C) intelligence is a noun, which can be eliminated based on part of speech.

Step 3: Replace the word "assiduous" with choice A, B, D to see which fits best.

- "Slow" doesn't fit the context of completing homework on time.
- "Careful" fits, as it suggests paying attention to the task, which matches the idea of doing homework properly.
- "Lazy" contradicts the context of the sentence, which implies hard work and dedication.

Answer: B) careful
Explanation: "Assiduous" is an adjective meaning careful or hardworking, which aligns with the context of students consistently completing their homework on time.

Practice Example: The diplomat's response was <u>circumspect</u>, carefully avoiding any controversial remarks.

A) reckless
B) cautious
C) spontaneous
D) prudence

Answer: B) cautious
Explanation: We can immediately eliminate D) Prudence, which is a noun, not an adjective, and doesn't fit the sentence grammatically. "Circumspect" means being cautious or wary, especially in speech or action. In this context, the word "cautious" matches the diplomat's careful approach to avoiding controversy.

GUESSING A CHOICE THROUGH THE ELIMINATION METHOD

When you are unsure of the correct answer, you can improve your chances of selecting the right one by eliminating obviously incorrect choices. This method is especially useful when the word is completely unfamiliar, as it allows you to rule out options that don't fit, thus increasing your odds of guessing correctly.

Steps to Use the Elimination Method:

1. Read the Sentence Carefully: Start by understanding the context of the sentence. Even if you don't know the meaning of the word, the surrounding words and overall sentence structure can give you clues.

2. Eliminate Clearly Wrong Choices: Begin by eliminating any answer choices that are clearly incorrect based on context or part of speech. For example, if the word you're analyzing is an adjective, eliminate any options that are verbs or nouns.

3. Compare Remaining Choices: Once you've narrowed down the choices, evaluate the remaining options in the sentence to see which one makes the most sense. Consider both meaning and connotation (whether the word has a positive, negative, or neutral tone).

4. Make an Educated Guess: After eliminating the weakest choices, select the answer that best fits the sentence context, even if you are not entirely sure of the word's exact meaning.

Example:

Original Sentence: The witness's <u>reticent</u> nature made it difficult to get detailed information from her.

A) talkative
B) mute
C) silent
D) nervous

Step 1: Read the sentence carefully. The sentence suggests that the witness was not providing detailed information, indicating that "reticent" likely relates to withholding or not speaking much.

Step 2: Eliminate clearly wrong choices. "Talkative" (A) is the opposite of what is described, so it can be eliminated. "Nervous" (D) may seem plausible but doesn't directly fit the context of not providing information.

Step 3: Compare remaining choices. "Silent" (C) fits well, as being quiet could explain why the witness wasn't sharing details. "Mute" (B) has the right connotation, but is generally not used to describe someone's nature or personality.

Step 4: Make an educated guess. The word "silent" (C) makes the most sense given the context of the witness's reluctance to speak.

Answer: C) silent
Explanation: "Reticent" means being reserved or unwilling to share information, which aligns with the idea of someone being quiet or silent during questioning.

When everything else fails, the elimination method is a powerful strategy that allows you to systematically rule out incorrect answers and improve your chances of making an educated guess. Even when faced with unfamiliar words, you can use context and logic to eliminate the least likely options and focus on those that fit best. In the next section, we'll discuss how to build your vocabulary over time to improve overall performance on the test.

INCREASE YOUR VOCABULARY IN A HURRY

Let's face the truth, a large vocabulary takes years to build. If you have only 2 to 3 months before your ASVAB test, you're running out of time to increase your vocabulary the organic way: reading widely. Don't despair though, you can still adopt efficient and focused strategies to maximize your vocabulary growth in a short period of time. Here are some realistic steps you can take:

1. Invest in a SAT or ASVAB Vocabulary Book

SAT or ASVAB vocabulary books are excellent tools for learning test-relevant words in a structured way. These books provide lists of high-frequency words, definitions, and examples to help you understand their usage. Aim to study around 20-30 words a day. Dedicate about 30-45 minutes each day to reviewing and memorizing new words. Focus on learning their meanings, usage in sentences, and common synonyms/antonyms.

2. Use Flashcards/Apps for Active Recall

Flashcards/Apps are helpful for quick vocabulary building. The easiest is to use apps like Quizlet or Anki that already have word sets for ASVAB and SAT prep. Focus on active recall by testing yourself daily. Start with 10-15 cards, and gradually increase the number as you master words. Use spaced repetition, a technique where you review words at increasing intervals, to reinforce your memory. This is crucial for retaining new vocabulary in a short timeframe.

3. Focus on Word Roots, Prefixes, and Suffixes

Learning Greek and Latin root words, along with prefixes and suffixes, helps you infer the meaning of unfamiliar words. This strategy allows you to break down words and grasp their meanings more quickly. Study 5-10 roots or affixes each day and practice applying them to unfamiliar words.

WORD KNOWLEDGE PRACTICE SET

Time: 9 minutes for 15 questions

Each question below includes an underlined word. You may be asked to determine which one of the four answer choices most closely matches the meaning of the underlined word, or which choice has the opposite meaning. If the word is used within a sentence, your task is to select the option that most accurately reflects its meaning in the context of that sentence. This practice subtest reflects the number of questions and time limits you'll encounter on the CAT-ASVAB Word Knowledge subtest without any tryout questions.

1. The word abhor most nearly means:

A) love
B) tolerate
C) detest
D) ignore

2. The word abridge most nearly means:

A) extend
B) shorten
C) complicate
D) dismiss

3. The word most opposite in meaning to cognizant is:

A) aware
B) unaware
C) mindful
D) conscious

4. The student's response was concise, giving only the necessary information.

A) long-winded
B) vague
C) brief
D) confusing

5. The artist's work was praised for its novel approach to traditional techniques.

A) outdated
B) original
C) copied
D) repetitive

6. The word fortuitous most nearly means:

A) unlucky
B) random
C) accidental
D) lucky

7. The word malleable most nearly means:

A) rigid
B) flexible
C) breakable
D) unchanging

8. The word frugal most nearly means:

A) wasteful
B) generous
C) economical
D) lavish

9. The professor's disdain for lazy students was obvious.

A) respect
B) contempt
C) affection
D) compassion

10. The committee will convene next week to discuss the proposal.

A) dismiss
B) meet
C) argue
D) ignore

11. The politician's brazen actions left the public shocked.

A) timid
B) bold
C) cautious
D) uncertain

12. The weather forecast indicated a precarious situation with the incoming storm.

A) safe
B) dangerous
C) boring
D) mild

13. The word obstinate most nearly means:

A) stubborn
B) agreeable
C) indifferent
D) flexible

14. The word infallible most nearly means:

A) imperfect
B) foolproof
C) weak
D) flawed

15. The word animosity most nearly means:

A) hatred
B) love
C) indifference
D) Support

Answers and Explanations

1. C) detest. "Abhor" refers to an intense hatred or disgust. Words like "love" and "tolerate" are opposites, making "detest" the best match.

2. B) shorten. "Abridge" means to reduce or shorten something. The opposite would be to extend, making "shorten" the correct answer.

3. B) unaware. "Cognizant" means being aware or knowledgeable, so the antonym is "unaware."

4. C) brief. "Concise" means giving a lot of information in a brief and clear manner, making "brief" the closest synonym.

5. B) original. "Novel" in this context means new and original, making "original" the best synonym.

6. D) lucky. "Fortuitous" refers to something happening by chance in a positive way, making "lucky" the best match.

7. B) flexible. "Malleable" describes something that can be shaped or changed easily, such as a flexible material or a person's opinions.

8. C) economical. "Frugal" refers to being careful with money and resources, making "economical" the closest synonym.

9. B) contempt. "Disdain" means a feeling of contempt or scorn, especially towards something regarded as unworthy.

10. B) meet. "Convene" means to come together for a meeting or gathering.

11. B) bold. "Brazen" refers to bold or shameless actions, especially in a negative sense.

12. B) dangerous. "Precarious" means unstable or dangerous, so the closest synonym is "dangerous."

13. A) stubborn. "Obstinate" means being stubborn or unyielding, unwilling to change one's opinion.

14. B) foolproof. "Infallible" means incapable of making mistakes or being wrong, making "foolproof" the best fit.

15. A) hatred. "Animosity" describes strong hostility or dislike.

CHAPTER 2: PARAGRAPH COMPREHENSION

INTRODUCTION

The Paragraph Comprehension subtest of the ASVAB assesses your ability to read, interpret, and extract information from written passages. This subtest evaluates how well you can understand, synthesize, and infer information from a variety of texts—a vital skill in both military and civilian careers.

In this subtest, you'll encounter four main types of questions that are designed to measure your reading comprehension skills. Each question type requires a different approach, and understanding how to tackle them effectively will help you maximize your score. The question types are as follows.

Main Idea Questions: These questions ask you to identify the primary point or central theme of a passage. You'll need to focus on what the author is trying to communicate overall, rather than on specific details.

Detail Questions: Detail questions require you to focus on specific facts or statements found within the text. These questions will test your ability to locate and recall particular pieces of information, often presented in a straightforward manner.

Inference Questions: Inference questions require you to deduce conclusions that are not explicitly stated but are implied by the text. You'll need to analyze the passage and draw logical conclusions based on the information provided.

Vocabulary in Context: These questions ask you to determine the meaning of a word based on how it is used within the passage. You'll need to analyze the surrounding words and sentences to figure out the most appropriate definition.

We now discuss these question types in greater detail.

QUESTIONS REGARDING MAIN IDEAS AND THEMES

The ability to determine central ideas and themes in a passage is pivotal for a test taker preparing for the ASVAB. This skill assesses your capacity to grasp the essence of what you read, identifying the main point or message the author intends to communicate and the underlying concepts or insights that recur throughout the text.

Understanding the central idea and themes is crucial because it forms the backbone of comprehension. It's about seeing beyond the words to grasp the 'why' and 'what' of the text. This ability is foundational, enhancing your reading comprehension and preparing you for academic success.

Strategies for Success:

- **Preview and Predict:** Start by examining titles, headings, and introductory sentences to determine the passage's main focus.

- **Note Repetitions:** Pay attention to ideas, phrases, or motifs repeated throughout the text; these often indicate key themes.

- **Summarize:** Try to encapsulate the passage's main point in a single sentence. This exercise forces you to distill the essence of what you've read.

- **Ask Questions:** While reading, continually ask yourself, "What's the main point here?" and "What themes are emerging?"

- **Context Clues:** Use context clues around unfamiliar words or concepts to understand their importance to the central idea or themes.

Application in Test Preparation:

To prepare for this question type, engage with a wide range of reading materials. After reading a piece, practice writing a brief summary of the central idea and list out potential themes. Discuss these with peers or mentors to explore different perspectives and interpretations. Utilize practice tests to familiarize yourself with how the ASVAB frames these questions, and review explanations for both correct and incorrect answers to deepen your understanding.

Common Pitfalls and How to Avoid Them:

- **Getting Lost in Details:** Don't let minor details distract you from the overall message. Always tie specifics back to the main idea or themes.

- **Overgeneralization:** Avoid too broad interpretations. Ensure your understanding of the central idea or themes is specific and supported by the text.

- **Misinterpreting the Text:** This can happen if you rush or skim too quickly. Take your time to fully engage with the passage, rereading complex or dense parts.

Example Passage 1

The development within the young of the attitudes and dispositions necessary to the continuous and progressive life of a society cannot take place by direct conveyance of beliefs, emotions, and knowledge. It takes place through the intermediary of the environment. The social environment consists of all the activities of fellow beings that are bound up in the carrying on of the activities of any one of its members. It is truly educative in its effect in the degree in which an individual shares or participates in some conjoint activity. By doing his share in the associated activity, the individual appropriates the purpose which actuates it, becomes familiar with its methods and subject matters, acquires needed skill, and is saturated with its emotional spirit.

Question: Which of the following statements best reflects the main idea of the passage?

A) The environment's role in education is mainly to ensure physical survival.
B) Young people acquire societal attitudes and skills by engaging in shared social activities.
C) Education primarily occurs through the direct transmission of knowledge and values.
D) The best way to develop societal attitudes in the young is through individual reflection.

Answer: B) Young people acquire societal attitudes and skills by engaging in shared social activities.

Explanation: The passage discusses how young individuals develop essential attitudes and dispositions for societal life through participation in social activities rather than direct transmission of beliefs or solitary study. It emphasizes that education is fostered within the social environment through shared experiences and activities. Option B accurately captures the essence of this idea. In contrast, options A, C, and D present inaccurate interpretations of the passage, suggesting either a physical, direct, or solitary approach to education, which the passage does not support.

Example Passage 2

In this Autobiography I shall keep in mind the fact that I am speaking from the grave. I am literally speaking from the grave, because I shall be dead when the book issues from the press. I speak from the grave rather than with my living tongue, for a good reason: I can speak thence freely. When a man is writing a book dealing with the privacies of his life—a book which is to be read while he is still alive—he shrinks from speaking his whole frank mind; all his attempts to do it fail, he recognizes that he is trying to do a thing which is wholly impossible to a human being. The frankest and freest and privatest product of the human mind and heart is a love letter; the writer gets his limitless freedom of statement and expression from his sense that no stranger is going to see what he is writing.

Question: The author's main purpose of this passage is to

A) Emphasize the limitations that living authors face when writing autobiographies.
B) Argue the superiority of love letters as forms of expression.
C) Illustrate the challenges of writing about one's private life for public consumption.
D) Explain the author's decision to write as if speaking from the grave in his autobiography.

Answer: D) Explain the author's decision to write as if speaking from the grave in his autobiography.

Explanation: The passage primarily focuses on the author's rationale for adopting a unique narrative perspective in his autobiography — that of speaking from the grave. This approach is chosen to achieve a level of frankness and freedom not possible when one is constrained by the considerations and repercussions of speaking as a living person. While the passage touches upon the nature of writing about private matters and compares it to the freedom found in love letters, these points serve to support the main argument rather than constitute the central idea themselves. Thus, the correct answer is D, as it directly addresses the author's intention to use posthumous narration as a means to express himself without reservation.

QUESTIONS REGARDING DETAILS

Detail-oriented questions on the ASVAB evaluate your ability to identify and understand specific information within the text. These questions test your ability to pick out facts, examples, and other particulars that support the main idea or themes of the passage.

Being adept at locating details is essential for thorough comprehension. It enables you to gather evidence, understand the structure of arguments, and appreciate the nuances of the narrative or exposition. This skill is crucial for academic research, critical analysis, and practical decision-making.

Strategies for Success:

- **Active Reading and Mental Notes:** As you read, note where the key facts, names, dates, and specific information are mentioned. In a computer-based test, you won't be able to underline the text, but mental notes will still help you quickly locate details when answering questions.

- **Practice Skimming:** Improve your skimming skills to quickly locate information within the text without having to read everything thoroughly a second time.

- **Understand Question Types:** Familiarize yourself with how detail questions are phrased. Knowing if a question asks for a fact, an example, or an explanation can guide you on what to look for.

- **Context Is Key:** Always consider the detail within the passage's context to ensure correct interpretation.

Application in Test Preparation:

Engage with texts across a variety of subjects and formats. After reading, challenge yourself to recall specific details without looking back at the text. Use practice tests to hone your ability to find and interpret details.

Common Pitfalls and How to Avoid Them:

- **Overlooking Details:** Important details can be easily missed if you read too quickly. Slow down and ensure you're fully processing the information.

- **Confusing Similar Details:** Pay attention to the nuances that differentiate similar pieces of information within the text to avoid mixing them up.

- **Relying Too Much on Memory:** Don't assume you remember all the details correctly. Double-check the passage to confirm your answers.

Example Passage 1

The *Endurance* steamed along the front of this ice-flow for about seventeen miles. The glacier showed huge crevasses and high pressure ridges, and appeared to run back to ice-covered slopes or hills 1000 or 2,000 ft. high. Some bays in its front were filled with smooth ice, dotted with seals and penguins. At 4 a.m. on the 16th we reached the edge of another huge glacial overflow from the icesheet. The ice appeared to be coming over low hills and was heavily broken. The cliff-face was 250 to 350 ft. high, and the ice surface two miles inland was probably 2,000 ft. high.

Question: According to the passage, which of the following is not true?

A) The *Endurance* traveled along the front of the ice-flow for approximately seventeen miles.
B) The glacier was devoid of any crevasses and pressure ridges.
C) Seals and penguins were spotted on some smooth ice areas in front of the glacier.
D) The ice surface two miles inland from the cliff-face was estimated to be around 2,000 ft. high.

Answer: B) The glacier was devoid of any crevasses and pressure ridges.

Explanation: The passage describes the *Endurance*'s journey along the front of an ice-flow, detailing the presence of "huge crevasses and high-pressure ridges" in the glacier. This directly contradicts option B, which falsely claims that the glacier was devoid of crevasses and pressure ridges. Options A, C, and D are all supported by the passage: A) states the distance the *Endurance* traveled along the ice-flow, C) mentions the wildlife observed on the smooth ice, and D) provides an estimation of the ice surface's height two miles inland. Therefore, B is the correct answer as it is the only statement not corroborated by the passage, making it untrue according to the provided text.

Example Passage 2

The dock was still for a moment. Then a barrel toppled from a pile of barrels, and a figure moved like a bird's shadow across the opening between mounds of cargo set about the pier. At the same time two men approached down a narrow street filled with the day's last light. The bigger one threw a great shadow that aped his gesticulating arms behind him on the greenish faces of the buildings. Bare feet like halved hams, shins bound with thongs and pelts, he waved one hand in explanation, while he rubbed the back of the other on his short, mahogany beard.

Question: According to the passage, which is the most accurate description of the bigger man?

A) He was quietly observing from the shadows, unnoticed.
B) He carried a barrel on his shoulder as he walked.
C) He was barefoot, with his shins wrapped, and had a short mahogany beard.
D) He was wearing heavy boots and a long coat as he gestured animatedly.

Answer: C) He was barefoot, with his shins wrapped, and had a short mahogany beard.

Explanation: The passage vividly describes the bigger man's appearance and actions as he walks down a narrow street. It specifically mentions that his "bare feet like halved hams, shins bound with thongs and pelts," indicating that he is barefoot and has his shins wrapped. Additionally, it describes him as having a "short, mahogany beard," which he rubs with the back of his hand. These details collectively match option C, making it the most accurate description of the bigger man according to the passage. Options A, B, and D do not accurately reflect the details provided; A suggests he was hiding, B incorrectly mentions him carrying a barrel, and D describes attire not mentioned in the passage. Therefore, C is the correct answer.

UNDERSTANDING RELATIONSHIPS AND MAKING INFERENCES

This type of question evaluates your ability to understand the relationships between various elements within the text and to make logical inferences based on the provided information. It requires a deeper level of comprehension, moving beyond the literal content to grasp the implied meanings and connections.

The skill of making inferences and understanding relationships is crucial for real-world problem-solving and critical thinking. It allows you to read between the lines, draw conclusions from subtle cues, and connect the dots in complex situations. This skill is invaluable in academics, professional settings, and everyday life, where not everything is stated explicitly.

Strategies for Success:

- **Look for Clues:** Pay attention to the text's tone, word choice, and any hints the author might give to imply relationships or to set the groundwork for inferences.

- **Connect Ideas:** Identify how different parts of the passage relate to each other through cause and effect, contrast, or similarities.

- **Read Actively:** Ask questions as you read. Consider what is stated and what can be reasonably assumed. Question why the author included certain details and what they signify.

- **Use Background Knowledge:** Apply your own knowledge and experiences to understand unstated aspects of the passage. This can help fill in gaps and make informed inferences.

- **Practice Predicting:** Try to anticipate the author's direction or the conclusion of arguments or narratives. Such attempts prepare you to make inferences and understand relationships.

Application in Test Preparation:

Engage with a wide variety of reading materials, including those that are complex or outside your comfort zone. After reading, practice articulating the relationships you've identified and the inferences you've made. Discussing texts with others can also reveal different perspectives and deepen your understanding. Utilize practice tests to familiarize yourself with these questions' format and refine your analytical skills.

Common Pitfalls and How to Avoid Them:

- **Overreaching:** Be cautious not to extend your inferences beyond what is reasonably supported by the text. Your conclusions should always be grounded in the passage.

- **Ignoring the Context:** Every inference or relationship identified should be contextual. Avoid making assumptions based on external knowledge not supported by the passage.

- **Overlooking Subtlety:** The most crucial connections or implications are often subtle. Ensure you don't gloss over these finer points in your reading.

Example Passage 1

Once upon a time Jeremiah the prophet had asked for only one thing, that he might get away from that strange cityful of perverse men to whom it was his hard lot to be the mouthpiece of a God they were forgetting. He was tired of them. "O that I had in the wilderness a lodging place of wayfaring men that I might leave my people and go from them." Well, time passed on. The people got no wiser, and Jeremiah's burden certainly got no lighter. But the very chance he prayed for came. He had a clear and honorable opportunity to go to the lodge in the wilderness, or anywhere else he liked, away from the men who had disowned his teaching. His work was done apparently, and he had failed. Yet with the door standing invitingly open, see what Jeremiah did! He "went and dwelt among the people that were left in the land." He had his chance and he did not take it!

Question: Which of the following does this passage imply about Jeremiah?

A) Jeremiah eventually abandoned his people due to their persistent disregard for his teachings.
B) Despite his frustrations and the opportunity to leave, Jeremiah chose to stay with his people.
C) Jeremiah found solace and success in solitude, away from the city and its perverse inhabitants.
D) The people eventually embraced Jeremiah's teachings, leading to a harmonious relationship.

Answer: B) Despite his frustrations and the opportunity to leave, Jeremiah chose to stay with his people.

Explanation: The passage describes Jeremiah's deep-seated desire to escape from a difficult situation where he felt his message was not being received by a people increasingly disconnected from their faith. Despite his frustrations and the clear opportunity to leave for a quieter life in the wilderness—an opportunity he had explicitly wished for—Jeremiah decides against taking this path. When presented with a real chance to abandon the very people who had disregarded his teachings, he instead chooses to remain among them. This decision underlines a sense of duty or commitment to these people despite the personal toll it had taken on him. The passage does not suggest that he abandoned his people (A), found success in solitude (C), or that his teachings were embraced, leading to harmony (D). Instead, it clearly illustrates Jeremiah's dedication to his role and people by staying with them against his earlier desires to leave, making option B the correct and most accurate interpretation.

Example Passage 2:

In the old days Hortons Bay was a lumbering town. No one who lived in it was out of sound of the big saws in the mill by the lake. Then one year there were no more logs to make lumber. The lumber schooners came into the bay and were loaded with the cut of the mill that stood stacked in the yard. All the piles of lumber were carried away. The big mill building had all its machinery that was removable taken out and hoisted on board one of the schooners by the men who had worked in the mill. The schooner moved out of the bay toward the open lake carrying the two great saws, the traveling carriage that hurled the logs against the revolving, circular saws and all the rollers, wheels, belts and iron piled on a hull-deep load of lumber. Its open hold covered with canvas and lashed tight, the sails of the schooner filled and it moved out into the open lake, carrying with it everything that had made the mill a mill and Hortons Bay, a town.

Question: What is the likely fate of the town of Hortons Bay?

A) It will experience a revival as a tourist destination.
B) It will become a thriving fishing community.
C) It will grow into a major industrial city.
D) It will likely decline or become abandoned.

Answer: D) It will likely decline or become abandoned.

Explanation: The passage vividly depicts Hortons Bay's transition from a bustling lumbering town to a place stripped of its defining industry. With the removal of the mill's machinery, including the saws and other equipment vital for its lumber operations, and the transportation of these resources out of town, the narrative strongly implies that Hortons Bay's economic foundation has been dismantled. The specific mention that "everything that had made the mill a mill and Hortons Bay, a town" was carried away leaves little room for interpreting a future for Hortons Bay that involves economic prosperity or community sustainability in its current form. Options A, B, and C suggest potential futures that are not supported by the passage's depiction of the town's deindustrialization and the essential elements of its identity and economy being physically removed. Therefore, the most logical conclusion is option D.

VOCABULARY IN CONTEXT QUESTIONS

Vocabulary in Context questions require you to determine the meaning of a word based on how it is used within a passage. These questions test not just your knowledge of word definitions, but also your ability to infer meaning from context. The key to answering these questions is to analyze the surrounding words, phrases, and overall tone of the passage to deduce what the unfamiliar word likely means in that specific setting.

In many cases, the word's definition may vary from its usual meaning, so understanding the context is crucial. Let's explore strategies for tackling these questions and provide examples.

How to Approach Vocabulary in Context Questions:

- Read the Entire Passage: Don't just focus on the word itself. Read the sentence and the surrounding sentences to gather clues about how the word is used.

- Look for Contextual Clues: These could be definitions, synonyms, antonyms, or descriptive phrases within the passage that help define the word.

- Test Each Answer Choice: Substitute each answer choice into the sentence to see which one fits best with the meaning of the sentence.

- Eliminate Incorrect Choices: Discard any answers that don't fit logically in the context of the passage.

Example Passage 1

The towering castle ruins, weathered by centuries of storms and sun, stood majestically at the edge of the cliff, as if meant to glorify the power of time itself. Wildflowers grew in every crack of the stone walls, softening the structure's once formidable appearance. Below, the waves crashed relentlessly, echoing the relentless passage of time. Travelers who visited the site couldn't help but feel humbled, their voices hushed by the ancient beauty that seemed to radiate from every stone.

Question 1: In this passage, *glorify* most nearly means

A) Exaggerate
B) Celebrate
C) Ignore
D) Ruin

Answer: B) Celebrate

Explanation: *glorify* in this context suggests the castle's ruins highlight or honor the enduring passage of time, making *celebrate* the correct answer. The other options do not fit the tone or meaning.

Example Passage 2

The country near the mouth of the river is wretched in the extreme: on the south side a long line of perpendicular cliffs commences, which exposes a section of the geological nature of the country. The strata are of sandstone, and one layer was remarkable from being composed of a firmly cemented conglomerate of pumice pebbles, which must have travelled more than four hundred miles, from the Andes. The surface is everywhere covered up by a thick bed of gravel, which extends far and wide over the open plain. Water is extremely scarce, and, where found, is almost invariably brackish. The vegetation is scanty; and although there are bushes of many kinds, all are armed with formidable thorns, which seem to warn the stranger not to enter on these inhospitable regions.

Question 1: In this passage, *brackish* mostly nearly means

A) Boiling
B) Fresh
C) Salty
D) Clear

Answer: C) Salty

Explanation: *Brackish* refers to water that has more salinity than freshwater but not as much as seawater, making *salty* the correct meaning. From the context, one can also rule out A, B, or D, even if one is not familiar with the word *brackish*.

Question 2: A word that could be properly substituted for *inhospitable* most nearly means?

A) Welcoming
B) Unfriendly
C) Populated
D) Sheltered

Answer: B) Unfriendly

Explanation: *Inhospitable* refers to an environment that is harsh and difficult to live in, thus *unfriendly* is the term that most closely matches the meaning in this context.

PARAGRAPH COMPREHENSION PRACTICE SET

Time: 27 minutes for 10 questions

This section presents reading paragraphs followed by questions or incomplete statements. Your task is to read the paragraph and choose the option that best completes the statement or answers the question. This practice subtest simulates the number of questions and time constraints you'll face on the CAT-ASVAB Paragraph Comprehension subtest, without any tryout questions.

The military force of the U.S.T. *Buford* is in command of a Colonel of the United States Army, tall and severe-looking, about fifty. In his charge are a number of officers and a very considerable body of soldiers, most of them of the regular army. Direct supervision over the deportees is given to the representative of the Federal Government, Mr. Berkshire, who is here with a number of Secret Service men. The Captain of the Buford takes his orders from the Colonel, who is the supreme authority on board.

1. Which of the following conclusions about the command structure on board of *Buford* can most reasonably be drawn from the passage?

A) The Colonel and Mr. Berkshire share equal authority on the Buford.
B) The Secret Service men are in charge of the military operations.
C) The Colonel is the supreme authority on board the Buford.
D) Mr. Berkshire commands the military personnel and the Captain.

The word "idealism" is used by different philosophers in somewhat different senses. We shall understand by it the doctrine that whatever exists, or at any rate whatever can be known to exist, must be in some sense mental. This doctrine, which is very widely held among philosophers, has several forms, and is advocated on several different grounds. The doctrine is so widely held, and so interesting in itself, that even the briefest survey of philosophy must give some account of it.

2. What's the author's attitude about the "doctrine" in this passage?

A) Dismissive
B) Critical
C) Neutral
D) Supportive

In 1857, Russell, Majors & Waddell were sending supply trains to Salt Lake for General Johnston's army, offering high wages. A respected wagon master, Lewis Simpson, invited the author to join as an "extra hand." The author found the offer appealing due to the good pay and light responsibilities, which involved covering for sick drivers while also riding his own mule and taking on minor supervisory duties.

3. What can be inferred from this passage about the author's likely next course of action?

A) The author will decline the offer due to the risks involved.
B) The author will accept the offer because of the high wages and responsibilities.
C) The author will negotiate for a higher salary.
D) The author will recommend someone else for the position.

At first glance, the horizontal strata of valleys suggest they were carved by water, but this would require the removal of massive amounts of rock. The author questions this explanation and rejects the idea of subsidence. The shape of the valleys and peaks leads to the conclusion that water action is insufficient to explain these formations. Some locals even compare the valleys to a rugged seacoast due to their structure.

4. According to the passage, how does the author view the role of water action in shaping the observed geography?

A) As the predominant force.
B) As negligible or non-contributory.
C) As causing subsidence in the valleys.
D) As influencing the drainage from the summit.

When the party came out of the Yellowstone, Adams went on alone to Seattle and Vancouver to inspect the last American railway systems yet untried. They, too, offered little new learning, and no sooner had he finished this debauch of Northwestern geography than with desperate thirst for exhausting the American field, he set out for Mexico and the Gulf, making a sweep of the Caribbean and clearing up, in these six or eight months, at least twenty thousand miles of American land and water.

5. The primary purpose of the passage is to

A) critique the American railway systems.
B) illustrate the extent of Adams' travels across America.
C) compare different geographic regions of America.
D) highlight the inadequacies of American geography.

Descartes determined that he would believe nothing which he did not see quite clearly and distinctly to be true. Whatever he could bring himself to doubt, he would doubt, until he saw reason for not doubting it. By applying this method he gradually became convinced that the only existence of which he could be quite certain was his own. He imagined a deceitful demon, who presented unreal things to his senses in a perpetual phantasmagoria; it might be very improbable that such a demon existed, but still it was possible, and therefore doubt concerning things perceived by the senses was possible.

6. Which of the following best describes what "phantasmagoria" means in the passage?

A) A systematic method of doubt
B) A state of clear and distinct truth
C) A deceptive, shifting sequence of illusions
D) A demon's improbable existence

Shirley was, I believe, sincerely glad of being relieved from so burdensome a charge as the conduct of an army must be to a man unacquainted with military business. I was at the entertainment given by the city of New York to Lord Loudoun, on his taking upon him the command. Shirley, though thereby superseded, was present also. There was a great company of officers, citizens, and strangers, and, some chairs having been borrowed in the neighborhood, there was one among them very low, which fell to the lot of Mr. Shirley. Perceiving it as I sat by him, I said, "They have given you, sir, too low a seat." "No matter," says he, "Mr. Franklin, I find a low seat the easiest."

7. The passage's author conveys Shirley's attitude by

A) highlighting his relief at no longer being in command.
B) describing his discomfort at the social event.
C) illustrating his humility in accepting a lower seat.
D) emphasizing his displeasure with Lord Loudoun.

The mansion stood isolated atop the hill, its walls painted in vibrant, mismatched colors that clashed with the surrounding landscape. A peculiar tower spiraled toward the sky in an uneven fashion. The grounds were overgrown with wild plants, yet within the disarray, there was a sense of peculiar order. Visitors were both drawn to and bewildered by its strangeness, as if the house itself reflected the personality of its mysterious and eccentric owner.

8. In this passage, *eccentric* most nearly means

A) Ordinary
B) Unusual
C) Dull
D) Stylish

I became certain that truth, sincerity, and integrity were vital to living a fulfilling life. Rather than following religious commands, my past experiences had taught me that actions were inherently good or bad based on their outcomes. These values guided me, and with some luck, I avoided significant immoral behavior during my youth, even when away from my father's guidance.

9. What convinced the author to value truth, sincerity, and integrity?

A) Reflection on life experiences.
B) Religious teachings.
C) His father's influence.
D) Observing the consequences of his actions.

Historians sometimes face great difficulty maintaining a clear narrative due to fragmented and unreliable historical records. In such cases, they must compare and conjecture from available fragments to construct a plausible account of events. For example, when studying the fall of the Roman Empire, historians might have to infer details about military campaigns from incomplete letters or inscriptions, piecing together how leaders responded to barbarian invasions.

10. What method would the author likely agree with?
A) Ignoring unreliable fragments
B) Recreating details from available records for continuity
C) Relying on archaeology
D) Collecting and comparing fragments

Answers and Explanations

1. C) The Colonel is the supreme authority on board the Buford.

Explanation: The passage explicitly states that "The Captain of the Buford takes his orders from the Colonel, who is the supreme authority on board," indicating that the Colonel holds the highest command over all operations and personnel on the Buford.

2. C) Neutral

Explanation: The author describes the doctrine of idealism as "widely held" and "interesting," and mentions the need to discuss it in a survey of philosophy, suggesting a neutral, objective attitude toward the subject.

3. B) The author will accept the offer because of the high wages and responsibilities.

Explanation: The passage mentions the high wages and the appealing nature of the "extra hand" position as significant inducements for the author, suggesting he is likely to accept the offer.

4. B) As negligible or non-contributory.

Explanation: The author dismisses the idea that water action shaped the valleys, stating that its influence is insignificant given the scale of the formations. The author argues that the structure of the valleys cannot be explained by erosion processes.

5. B) illustrate the extent of Adams' travels across America.

Explanation: The passage details Adams' extensive travels from the Yellowstone to Seattle, Vancouver, and then on to Mexico and the Caribbean, emphasizing the broad scope of his geographic exploration within America.

6. C) A deceptive, shifting sequence of illusions

Explanation: In the passage, "phantasmagoria" refers to the array of unreal things that Descartes imagined a deceitful demon presented to his senses, indicating a misleading or illusory spectacle.

7. C) illustrating his humility in accepting a lower seat.

Explanation: Shirley's response to the low seat, "No matter, Mr. Franklin, I find a low seat the easiest," suggests humility and acceptance, which the author conveys through this anecdote from the social event.

8. B) Unusual

Explanation: "Eccentric" refers to something unconventional or strange, making "unusual" the correct choice in this context. The other options do not fit the description of the house.

9. A) Reflection on life experiences.

Explanation: The author emphasizes that personal experiences led him to value these principles, rather than religion or external influences.

10. B) Recreating details from available records for continuity

Explanation: The author suggests that, in the absence of reliable historical records, historians should use conjecture to fill in gaps while ensuring that these guesses are plausible. Instead of ignoring fragments or solely relying on facts, the author supports recreating plausible details to maintain a continuous narrative, thus making B the correct choice. This method helps form a coherent story without sacrificing historical integrity entirely.

CHAPTER 3: MATHEMATICS KNOWLEDGE

INTRODUCTION

The ASVAB Mathematics Knowledge (MK) subtest assesses your understanding of high school-level mathematics concepts. This subtest focuses on algebra, geometry, and basic mathematical principles, including number theory, equations, and mathematical operations. You'll need to apply these concepts to solve straightforward problems without the aid of a calculator.

What to Expect

The MK subtest assesses both your computational abilities and your capacity to think critically about mathematical relationships. Key topics covered include the following.

Algebraic Concepts: This includes solving linear and quadratic equations, working with inequalities, and simplifying polynomials. You'll encounter problems that require basic algebraic manipulation, such as solving for unknown variables or interpreting algebraic expressions. You may also need to understand functions and their properties.

Geometry: Expect questions on calculating the area, perimeter, volume, and surface area of various geometric shapes. You will also need to apply the Pythagorean theorem, identify properties of angles and triangles, and solve problems involving the relationships between angles in polygons.

Number Theory and Arithmetic Operations: This includes a range of topics such as working with fractions, decimals, percentages, ratios, and proportions. Understanding prime numbers, factors, multiples, and the basic properties of integers is essential. You'll also be expected to perform basic operations like addition, subtraction, multiplication, and division accurately and efficiently.

Mathematical Properties and Rules: Understanding mathematical properties such as the distributive property, associative and commutative properties, and rules for working with exponents and square roots will be important for certain questions.

Data Analysis and Probability: Though not the primary focus, you may encounter basic questions on interpreting data from graphs or charts, calculating averages, and understanding probability.

You can find the time limit and number of questions for the paper- and computer-based test in the "ASVAB Test Lengths and Time Limits" section of this book's Introduction chapter.

Types of Questions

Questions on this subtest are generally straightforward, requiring the direct application of mathematical formulas and principles. You won't need to solve complex word problems (these are on the Arithmetic Reasoning subtest), but you'll be tested on your ability to work with numbers and equations directly. The questions often resemble typical problems you'd find in high school math exams, where you solve for unknowns or work through geometric problems step by step.

For example:

Algebraic question: Solve for x in the equation: $2x + 3 = 11$.

Geometry question: Calculate the volume of a cylinder with a given radius and height.

Arithmetic question: Simplify a fraction or convert a decimal to a percentage.

Arithmetic Reasoning vs Mathematics Knowledge Subtests

While both subtests assess your mathematical ability, their focus differs.

Arithmetic Reasoning: This subtest evaluates your ability to solve word problems that require mathematical reasoning and practical application, often focusing on real-world scenarios.

Mathematics Knowledge: In contrast, this subtest focuses on abstract, theoretical math concepts and the ability to solve equations and work through mathematical principles directly.

Now, let's start to get you well-prepared by reviewing some basic math concepts first!

§1. Mathematics Fundamentals

Whole Number Operations

Whole numbers are non-negative integers that include zero and all positive integers. They form the basic building blocks of arithmetic and are essential for mathematical operations. Whole numbers don't include fractions or decimals, making them suitable for simple arithmetic tasks. Examples of whole numbers include 0, 1, 2, 3, 56, 327, etc. They can be used in various contexts, such as counting objects, keeping track of scores, or measuring discrete quantities. For instance, if you have five apples, three friends, and two books, each of these counts can be expressed as whole numbers, making it easier to perform addition, subtraction, and other arithmetic operations.

Order of Operations (PEMDAS)

Order of Operations, commonly remembered by the acronym PEMDAS, dictates the order in which mathematical operations should be performed to ensure consistency and accuracy. PEMDAS stands for:

- Parentheses: Operations inside parentheses are performed first.
- Exponents: After parentheses, handle powers and roots.
- Multiplication and Division: Next, solve any multiplication or division from left to right.
- Addition and Subtraction: Finally, perform addition and subtraction from left to right.

Examples:

1. $3 + 2 \times 4$: According to PEMDAS, multiplication is done before addition. So, $2 \times 4 = 8$. Then, apply the addition: $3 + 8 = 11$.

2. $(2 + 3)^2$: Operations inside the parentheses come first. So, $2 + 3 = 5$. Then, apply the exponent: $5^2 = 25$.

3. $8 \div 2 \times 3$: Multiplication and division are handled from left to right. So, $8 \div 2 = 4$, and then $4 \times 3 = 12$.

Estimation

Estimation in mathematics is a method of roughly calculating an answer or checking the accuracy of a solution. It provides a way to arrive at a reasonable approximation quickly and efficiently.

Example 1: A tablet costs 244.99, but there is a 20% discount. Approximately how much does it cost now?

Solution: In this problem, the word "approximately" indicates that estimation is needed. The amount can be rounded to 250 or 240 for simplicity. However, rounding to 250 is straightforward, especially for percentage calculations.

Now, 20% of $250 is $50, allowing us to estimate the new cost: $250 - $50 = $200. This estimate is fairly close to the actual cost of $195.99, showing that rounding and approximate calculations can lead to reasonable results.

Example 2: Estimate a sensible answer to 54,893 x 29.

Solution: To approach this problem efficiently, we round 54,893 to the nearest ten thousand: 50,000. Similarly, 29 rounds to 30. The rounded values allow for quicker calculations: 50,000 x 30 = 1,500,000.

Rounding

Rounding to the Nearest Integer

Focus on the digit immediately following the decimal point:

If this digit is between 0 and 4, drop the decimal part, leaving the integer part as it is.

If this digit is between 5 and 9, drop the decimal part and add 1 to the integer.

Example 1: round 12.7 to the nearest integer

Solution: The digit immediately after the decimal point is 7, so the decimal part is dropped, and 1 is added to the integer part, making the number 13.

Rounding to the Nearest Ten

Focus on the ones digit:

If the digit is between 0 and 4, change it to 0, keeping the other digits the same.

If the digit is between 5 and 9, change it to 0 and add 1 to the tens digit.

Example 2: round 347 to the nearest ten

Solution: The ones digit is 7, so it changes to 0, and 1 is added to the tens digit, making the number 350.

Rounding to the Nearest Hundred

Focus on the tens digit:

If the digit is between 0 and 4, change it and the ones digit to 0.

If the digit is between 5 and 9, change it and the ones digit to 0 and add 1 to the hundreds digit.

Example 3: round 2836 to the nearest hundred

Solution: The tens digit is 3, which changes to 0, along with the ones digit, making the number 2800.

You must get the idea now! If you are asked to round to the nearest thousand, million, billion, trillion, and so on, just follow similar procedures as the above.

Inequalities

Inequalities provide a way to compare two values or expressions that are not necessarily equal. Common symbols used to express inequalities include:

$<$ (less than): Indicates that the value on the left is smaller than the value on the right.

$>$ (greater than): Indicates that the value on the left is larger than the value on the right.

$\leq$ (less than or equal to): Indicates that the value on the left is smaller than or equal to the value on the right.

$\geq$ (greater than or equal to): Indicates that the value on the left is larger than or equal to the value on the right.

Below is a summary of inequalities symbols, their meanings, and how they appear on the number line.

Symbol	Meaning	On the Number Line
$<$	Less than	Open circle
$>$	Greater than	Open circle
$\leq$	Less than or equal to	Closed circle
$\geq$	Greater than or equal to	Closed circle

Example 1: Comparing Numbers Directly

Solution: Compare 45 and 38:

Since $45 > 38$, we write the inequality as: $45 > 38$.

Example 2: Inequality Expressions

For more complex scenarios, the ASVAB test may require evaluating and simplifying expressions. Consider the expressions $2x + 10$ and $4x - 8$. Question: when the first expression is larger than the second? To find out, we write an inequality:

$$2x + 10 > 4x - 8.$$

Rearranging by subtracting 2x and adding 8 from both sides:

$$10 + 8 > 4x - 2x$$

$$18 > 2x.$$

Dividing both sides by 2:

$$9 > x.$$

This example shows how inequalities can help find ranges of values for variables.

Example 3: Inequalities in Real-Life Context

In practical applications, inequalities may compare numerical data. For example, a store offers a discount on products that cost at least $50. A customer has a coupon for 15% off any qualifying item. Question: should the customer qualify to use the coupon, how much will he/she save at a minimum?

We write an inequality to show how much the customer would save: $Savings \geq 0.15 * 50$.

This inequality shows that the customer would save at least $7.50 with the coupon.

This is illustrated on the following number line.

Below are more examples of inequalities illustrated on a number line.

Example 4: $-5 < X \leq 12$

Example 5: $X \leq -1 \ or \ X > 3$

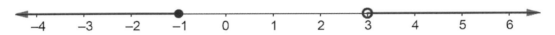

FRACTION OPERATIONS

In this section, we will review arithmetic operations with fractions, including addition, subtraction, multiplication, and division of fractions and mixed numbers, estimation and rounding.

Basic Fraction Concepts

Fraction: A way to represent parts of a whole, a fraction consists of a numerator and a denominator separated by a fraction bar. For example: In the fraction $\frac{3}{4}$, 3 parts of a whole that is divided into 4 equal parts are considered. The top part of a fraction is the **numerator**, indicating how many parts of the whole are being considered. The bottom part of a fraction is the **denominator**, indicating into how many parts the whole is divided. In the above example, 3 is the numerator, and 4 is the denominator. The numbers 3 and 4 are also called the **terms** of the fraction. The term on top of the fraction bar is the numerator, and the term on the bottom is the denominator.

Proper Fractions: Fractions where the numerator is less than the denominator. For example: $\frac{3}{5}$ is a proper fraction because the numerator, 3, is less than the denominator, 5.

Improper Fractions: Fractions where the numerator is greater than or equal to the denominator. For example: $\frac{7}{5}$ is a proper fraction because the numerator, 7, is bigger than the denominator, 5.

Reciprocals: Two numbers whose product is 1. Essentially, you flip the numerator and the denominator. For example: $\frac{7}{11}$ is the reciprocal $\frac{11}{7}$.

Zero as Numerator: Indicates that the fraction represents zero, as nothing is taken from the whole. For example: $\frac{0}{9} = 0$.

Zero as Denominator: This is undefined in mathematics because you cannot divide by zero.

Mixed Number: A whole number combined with a proper fraction. A mixed number is a way to express a number that includes both a whole part and a fraction part. It combines a whole number (like 1, 2, 3, and so on) with a proper fraction (where the top number, or numerator, is smaller than the bottom number, or denominator), e.g., $2\frac{1}{2}$.

Converting an Improper Fraction to a Mixed Number

Converting an improper fraction to a mixed number involves turning a fraction where the numerator (top number) is larger than the denominator (bottom number) into a number that shows how many whole parts there are, along with a proper fraction. Let's go through how to do this with an example.

Example: Convert $\frac{22}{7}$ to a Mixed Number.

Solution: This can be achieved by the following steps.

1. Divide the Numerator by the Denominator: Divide 22 by 7. When you divide 22 by 7, the quotient (the whole number part of the division) is 3, because 7 goes into 22 three times completely.

2. Calculate the Remainder: To find out how much is left over, multiply the whole number part (3) by the denominator (7), which equals 21. Subtract this product from the original numerator: $22 - 21 = 1$.

3. The Whole Number: The quotient from your division (3) is the whole number part of the mixed number.

4. The Fraction Part: The remainder (1) is the new numerator, while the denominator remains the same (7), so the fraction part is $\frac{1}{7}$.

5. Write the Mixed Number: Combine the whole number and the fraction part to form the mixed number, which is $3\frac{1}{7}$.

This conversion demonstrates how an improper fraction can be expressed more intuitively as a mixed number, making it easier to visualize and understand.

Converting a Mixed Number to an Improper Fraction

Converting a mixed number to an improper fraction involves combining the whole number and the fractional parts into a single fraction, where the numerator is larger than the denominator.

Example: Convert $3\frac{2}{5}$ to an improper fraction.

Solution: This can be achieved by the following steps.

1. Multiply the Whole Number by the Denominator: Multiply the whole number part of the mixed number (3) by the denominator of the fraction part (5). This calculation represents the total number of fifths in the three whole parts: $3 \times 5 = 15$

2. Add the Numerator of the Fraction Part: Add the numerator of the fraction part (2) to the result from the first step. This step accounts for all the parts: $15 + 2 = 17$

3. Write the Improper Fraction: The sum from the second step (17) becomes the new numerator, and the original denominator (5) stays the same. So, the improper fraction is: $\frac{17}{5}$.

This improper fraction, $\frac{17}{5}$, represents the total number of fifths in $3\frac{2}{5}$. This method ensures that all parts of the mixed number are accounted for, translating it back into a single fraction format. This can be particularly useful in calculations involving multiple fractions or when needing a consistent format for mathematical operations.

Equivalent Fractions

Equivalent fractions are fractions that, although they have different numerators and denominators, actually represent the same value or portion of a whole. This concept is crucial for simplifying fractions, comparing them, and performing operations like addition and subtraction when the fractions involved have different denominators.

How to Find Equivalent Fractions: To find equivalent fractions, you multiply or divide the numerator and the denominator of a fraction by the same non-zero number. Here are the steps for each method.

Multiplication method

1. Choose a number (other than zero) to multiply both the numerator and the denominator.

2. This number is known as the 'scale factor'.

Example: Find two equivalent fractions for $\frac{1}{4}$.

Solution 1: Multiply both the numerator and the denominator by 2:

$$\frac{1 \times 2}{4 \times 2} = \frac{2}{8}$$

Solution 2: Multiply both the numerator and the denominator by 3:

$$\frac{1 \times 3}{4 \times 3} = \frac{3}{12}$$

Division method

If both the numerator and the denominator can be evenly divided by the same number (this number is known as the 'common divisor'), you can simplify the fraction by dividing the numerator and denominator with the common divisor.

Example: Find an equivalent fractions for $\frac{6}{9}$.

Solution: Since both 6 and 9 are divisible by 3, divide both by 3:

$$\frac{6 \div 3}{9 \div 3} = \frac{2}{3}$$

These examples illustrate how you can either increase or decrease the terms of a fraction while keeping its value unchanged.

The Fundamental Property of Fractions

The Fundamental Property of Fractions, also known as the Multiplicative Property of Equality, states that multiplying the numerator and the denominator of a fraction by the same non-zero number does not change the value of the fraction.

$$\text{If a, b, and c are numbers, and } b \neq 0 \text{ and } c \neq 0, \text{ then: } \frac{a}{b} = \frac{a \cdot c}{b \cdot c}$$

Both the multiplication method and the division method of finding equivalent fractions utilize the Fundamental Property of Fractions.

Greatest Common Divisor (GCD)

The Greatest Common Divisor (GCD), also known as the Greatest Common Factor (GCF), is the largest number that can evenly divide both the numerator and the denominator of a fraction without leaving a remainder. Finding the GCD is crucial for simplifying fractions to their lowest terms.

Steps to Find the GCD:

1. List the Factors of Each Number: Begin by listing all the factors (numbers that divide without leaving a remainder) for both the numerator and the denominator.

2. Identify the Common Factors: Compare the lists of factors for both the numerator and the denominator and identify the numbers that appear in both lists.

3. Select the Largest Common Factor: The largest number in the list of common factors is the GCD.

Example: Find the GCD of 18 and 24.

Solution:

- Factors of 18: 1, 2, 3, 6, 9, 18

- Factors of 24: 1, 2, 3, 4, 6, 8, 12, 24

Common Factors are: 1, 2, 3, 6

Greatest Common Factor is: 6

Thus, the GCD of 18 and 24 is 6.

Cancellation and Lowest Terms

Cancellation and simplifying fractions to their lowest terms are are used to simplify calculations and make fractions easier to understand and compare.

Cancellation involves dividing both the numerator and the denominator of a fraction by the same non-zero number. This process reduces the fraction to a simpler form, often making it easier to work with in calculations. A fraction is in its **lowest terms** (or simplest form) when the numerator and the denominator have no common factors other than 1. This means the fraction cannot be simplified any further.

Steps for Simplifying Fractions:

1. **Identify a Common Factor**: Find a number that divides evenly into both the numerator and the denominator.

2. **Divide Both Terms**: Divide the numerator and the denominator by this common factor.

3. **Repeat if Necessary**: Continue this process with the new fraction until no further common factors can be found.

Example 1: Simplifying $\frac{18}{24}$.

Solution: First, identify the **greatest common divisor (GCD)** for 18 and 24, which is 6.

Then, divide both the numerator and the denominator by 6:

$$\frac{18 \div 6}{24 \div 6} = \frac{3}{4}$$

Now, $\frac{3}{4}$ is in its lowest terms because the only common factor between 3 and 4 is 1.

Example 2: Simplifying $\frac{40}{60}$.

Solution: The GCD for 40 and 60 is 20. Divide both the numerator and the denominator by 20:

$$\frac{40 \div 20}{60 \div 20} = \frac{2}{3}$$

$\frac{2}{3}$ is in its lowest terms, as 2 and 3 are coprime (they have no common factors other than 1).

These examples show how cancellation reduces fractions to their simplest form, facilitating easier manipulation and comparison of fractional values.

Multiplication of Fractions

Multiplying fractions is straightforward once you understand the basic rule: multiply the numerators together to get the new numerator, and multiply the denominators together to get the new denominator.

Steps for Multiplying Fractions:

1. Multiply the Numerators: Take the numerator of each fraction and multiply them together.

2. Multiply the Denominators: Take the denominator of each fraction and multiply them together.

3. Simplify the Resulting Fraction: If possible, simplify the new fraction by dividing both the numerator and the denominator by their greatest common divisor (GCD).

Example 1: Multiply $\frac{1}{4}$ and $\frac{3}{5}$.

Solution: $\frac{1}{4} \times \frac{3}{5} = \frac{1 \times 3}{4 \times 5} = \frac{3}{20}$

Example 2: Multiply $\frac{7}{8}$ and $\frac{12}{15}$

Solution: $\frac{7}{8} \times \frac{12}{15} = \frac{7 \times 12}{8 \times 15} = \frac{84}{120}$

Simplify $\frac{84}{120}$ by finding the GCD of 84 and 120, which is 12. Divide both the numerator and the denominator by 12:

$$\frac{84 \div 12}{120 \div 12} = \frac{7}{10}$$

This example shows how multiplication of fractions can also involve simplification to reduce the fraction to its lowest terms.

Pre-cancelling when Multiplying Fractions

Pre-cancelling (also known as cross-cancelling) when multiplying fractions is a technique that simplifies the multiplication process by reducing the fractions before actually performing the multiplication. This method involves cancelling common factors between the numerators and denominators of the fractions involved in the multiplication. It makes calculations easier and helps to avoid dealing with unnecessarily large numbers.

Steps for Pre-cancelling:

1. **Identify Common Factors**: Look for any common factors that the numerator of one fraction has with the denominator of the other fraction.

2. **Cancel the Common Factors**: Divide the common factors out before multiplying.

3. **Multiply the Remaining Numbers**: Multiply the simplified numerators and denominators to get the final answer.

Example: Multiply $\frac{14}{45}$ by $\frac{27}{28}$

Solution: Here's how you can pre-cancel. From the first fraction $\frac{14}{45}$, and the second fraction $\frac{27}{28}$:

- Notice that 14 in the numerator of the first fraction and 28 in the denominator of the second fraction share a common factor of 14.

- Notice that 27 in the numerator of the second fraction and 45 in the denominator of the first fraction share a common factor of 9.

Pre-cancel the common factors:

$\frac{14}{28}$ reduces to $\frac{1}{2}$ (14 divided by 14 is 1, 28 divided by 14 is 2).

$\frac{27}{45}$ reduces to $\frac{3}{5}$ (27 divided by 9 is 3, 45 divided by 9 is 5).

Now multiply the simplified fractions:

$$\frac{1}{2} \times \frac{3}{5} = \frac{1 \times 3}{2 \times 5} = \frac{3}{10}$$

The entire process of solving this problem can be written this way:

$$\frac{14}{45} \times \frac{27}{28} = \frac{14}{28} \times \frac{27}{45} = \frac{1}{2} \times \frac{9 \times 3}{9 \times 5} = \frac{1}{2} \times \frac{3}{5} = \frac{1 \times 3}{2 \times 5} = \frac{3}{10}$$

This example shows how pre-cancelling simplifies the process of multiplying fractions, making the multiplication straightforward and reducing the numbers involved.

Division of Fractions

Division of fractions involves reversing the process of multiplication by using the reciprocal of the divisor. The **reciprocal** of a fraction is obtained by swapping its numerator and denominator. This method, often summarized by the phrase "invert and multiply," simplifies the process of dividing fractions.

Steps for Dividing Fractions:

1. **Find the Reciprocal**: Take the reciprocal of the fraction that you are dividing by (the divisor).

2. **Multiply the Fractions**: Multiply the first fraction (the dividend) by the reciprocal of the second fraction.

Example 1: Divide $\frac{3}{7}$ by $\frac{6}{5}$

Solution: $\frac{3}{7} \div \frac{6}{5} = \frac{3}{7} \times \frac{5}{6} = \frac{3 \times 5}{7 \times 6} = \frac{15}{42}$

As illustrated, the division of fractions is handled through the "invert and multiply" technique, transforming a division problem into a multiplication problem that is often simpler to solve.

Dividing fractions where one or both numbers are mixed fractions involves converting those mixed fractions to improper fractions first, and then following the "invert and multiply" method. Let's go through this with a detailed example.

Example 2: Divide $2\frac{1}{3}$ by $1\frac{1}{2}$

Solution: Convert Mixed Fractions to Improper Fractions first:

$$2\frac{1}{3} = \frac{2 \times 3 + 1}{3} = \frac{6 + 1}{3} = \frac{7}{3}$$

$$1\frac{1}{2} = \frac{1 \times 2 + 1}{2} = \frac{2 + 1}{2} = \frac{3}{2}$$

Invert the Divisor ($1\frac{1}{2}$) and Multiply:

$$\frac{7}{3} \div \frac{3}{2} = \frac{7}{3} \times \frac{2}{3} = \frac{7 \times 2}{3 \times 3} = \frac{14}{9}$$

Here the entire process:

$$2\frac{1}{3} \div 1\frac{1}{2} = \frac{7}{3} \div \frac{3}{2} = \frac{7}{3} \times \frac{2}{3} = \frac{7 \times 2}{3 \times 3} = \frac{14}{9}$$

Adding and Subtracting Fractions

The process of adding and subtracting fractions varies slightly depending on whether the fractions have the same denominator or different denominators.

Adding and Subtracting Fractions with the Same Denominator

When fractions have the same denominator (the bottom number of the fraction), the process is straightforward:

1. **Keep the Denominator**: The denominator remains the same.

2. **Add/Subtract the Numerators**: Simply add or subtract the numerators (the top numbers of the fractions) as indicated.

Example 1: Add $\frac{3}{7}$ and $\frac{2}{7}$

Solution: $\frac{3}{7} + \frac{2}{7} = \frac{3+2}{7} = \frac{5}{7}$

Example 2: Subtracting $\frac{5}{7}$ from $\frac{6}{7}$

Solution: $\frac{6}{7} - \frac{5}{7} = \frac{6-5}{7} = \frac{1}{7}$

Adding and Subtracting Fractions with Different Denominators

When fractions have different denominators, you must first find a common denominator before you can add or subtract them. This often involves finding the **Least Common Denominator** (LCD), which is the smallest number that both denominators can divide into without a remainder.

1. **Find the Least Common Denominator (LCD):** Determine the smallest common multiple of the denominators.

2. **Adjust the Fractions**: Convert each fraction to an equivalent fraction with the LCD as the new denominator.

3. **Add/Subtract the Adjusted Numerators**: With the same denominators, add or subtract the numerators.

Example 1: adding $\frac{1}{4}$ and $\frac{1}{6}$

Solution: Observe that the LCD of 4 and 6 is 12. Convert $\frac{1}{4}$ to $\frac{3}{12}$ and convert $\frac{1}{6}$ to $\frac{2}{12}$

Now, add the adjusted fractions:

$$\frac{1}{4} + \frac{1}{6} = \frac{3}{12} + \frac{2}{12} = \frac{3+2}{12} = \frac{5}{12}$$

Combined operations with fractions and mixed numbers

Combined operations with fractions and mixed numbers involve performing multiple arithmetic operations—such as addition, subtraction, multiplication, and division—on numbers in fractional and mixed number forms.

Steps for Combined Operations:

1. Convert Mixed Numbers: If the problem involves mixed numbers, convert them to improper fractions first. This simplifies the process of combining them with other fractions.

2. Find a Common Denominator: For addition and subtraction, ensure all fractions involved have a common denominator. This may involve converting each fraction to an equivalent form.

3. Perform Operations: Apply the relevant arithmetic operations. If the operation is addition or subtraction, combine the numerators as appropriate. For multiplication or division, follow the standard rules for fractions.

4. Simplify: Always simplify the resulting fraction to its lowest terms. This may involve finding the greatest common divisor (GCD) and reducing the fraction.

Example: Calculate $1\frac{2}{3} - \frac{3}{4} \times \frac{5}{6} + \frac{1}{2}$

Solution: Step 1: Convert Mixed Numbers

Convert $1\frac{2}{3}$ to an improper fraction:

$$1\frac{2}{3} = \frac{1 \cdot 3 + 2}{3} = \frac{5}{3}$$

Step 2: Perform Multiplication First by following PEMDAS rules.

Calculate $\frac{3}{4} \times \frac{5}{6}$:

$$\frac{3}{4} \times \frac{5}{6} = \frac{3 \cdot 5}{4 \cdot 6} = \frac{15}{24} = \frac{5}{8}$$

Step 3: Perform Subtraction

Subtract $\frac{5}{8}$ from $\frac{5}{3}$ (first find a common denominator, which is 24):

$$\frac{5}{3} = \frac{40}{24}, \quad \frac{5}{8} = \frac{15}{24}$$

$$\frac{40}{24} - \frac{15}{24} = \frac{25}{24}$$

Step 4: Add $\frac{1}{2}$ (convert $\frac{1}{2}$ to $\frac{12}{24}$):

$$\frac{25}{24} + \frac{12}{24} = \frac{37}{24}$$

Step 5: Simplify or Convert to Mixed Number

The result $\frac{37}{24}$ can be expressed as a mixed number:

$$\frac{37}{24} = 1\frac{13}{24}$$

Summary: When performing combined operations with fractions and mixed numbers, the key is to handle one operation at a time, simplify at each step, and always keep track of the order of operations to ensure accuracy.

DECIMAL OPERATIONS

Decimals are a way of expressing numbers that are not whole, using a base of ten. Here's an introduction to some fundamental concepts of decimals:

Decimal Point: The decimal point separates the whole number part from the fractional part of a number. It is denoted by a dot (.)

Writing Whole Numbers as Decimals: Any whole number can be written as a decimal by adding a decimal point and zeros. For example, the whole number 25 can be written as a decimal: 25=25.0. This shows that 25 is equivalent to 25 plus zero tenths.

Powers of Ten: Decimals are based on powers of ten. Each place to the right of the decimal point represents a negative power of ten. The first place to the right of the decimal point is the tenths place (10^{-1}), the next is the hundredths place (10^{-2}), and so on. Conversely, places to the left of the decimal point represent positive powers of ten, like tens (10^1), hundreds (10^2), etc.

Leading Zeros: In decimal fractions that fall strictly between -1 and 1, the leading zero digits between the decimal point and the first non-zero digit are essential for conveying the magnitude of a number and must not be omitted. For instance, for decimal 0.000357, the three zeros between decimal point and number 3 cannot be omitted.

The zero that appears immediately to the left of the decimal point, such as the 0 in 0.468, is sometimes dropped, although the decimal point must remain. Most of the time though, the zero to the left of the decimal point is not omitted. Keeping the zero to the left of the decimal point enhances clarity.

Trailing Zeros: Zeros after the last non-zero digit in a decimal number can affect the precision in a scientific or mathematical context but do not change the value of the number. For example: Compare 0.2500 and 0.25. The first number, 0.2500, suggests a precision measurement to the ten-thousandths place. This indicates a higher precision than 0.25, which suggests a precision measurement to the hundredths place. However, the two numbers are equal in value.

Decimal Place Values

Each position or place in a decimal number has a value based on powers of ten.

- Tenths (10^{-1}): This is the first place to the right of the decimal point. Each unit in this place is one-tenth of a whole.
- Hundredths (10^{-2}): The second place to the right of the decimal point, where each unit is one-hundredth of a whole.
- Thousandths (10^{-3}): The third place to the right of the decimal point, where each unit is one-thousandth of a whole.
- And so on, with ten-thousandths, hundred-thousandths, etc.

Example: Consider the decimal number 45.6789. Here's how each digit fits into the place value system:

- 4 is in the tens place (10^1),
- 5 is in the units or ones place (10^0),
- 6 is in the tenths place (10^{-1}),
- 7 is in the hundredths place (10^{-2}),
- 8 is in the thousandths place (10^{-3}),
- 9 is in the ten-thousandths place (10^{-4}).

Each position affects the value of the number. For instance, the 6 in 45.6789 contributes 6 tenths to the value, or 0.6. The 7 contributes 7 hundredths, or 0.07, and so on.

Multiplying and Dividing Decimals by Powers of 10

When you multiply a decimal by a power of 10, shift the decimal point to the right by as many places as there are zeros in the power of 10.

Example: Multiply 4.567 by 100 (which is 10^2): 4.567×100=456.7

The decimal point moves two places to the right.

When you divide by a power of 10, shift the decimal point to the left by as many places as there are zeros in the power of 10.

Example: Divide 3.25 by 1000 (which is 10^3): 3.25÷1000=0.00325

The decimal point moves three places to the left.

If the number of zeros exceeds the number of digits before the decimal in the original number, you may need to add leading zeros. For example, multiplying 0.123 by 10^5 results in 12300, and dividing 0.00456 by 10^2 results in 0.0000456.

Rounding of Decimal Numbers

Rounding decimal numbers is used to make them easier to work with, particularly when precision is less critical. Rounding involves increasing or decreasing a number to a certain place value.

Steps for Rounding Decimals:

1. Identify the Place Value to round to: Determine the decimal place to which you want to round. This could be to the nearest tenth, hundredth, thousandth, etc.

2. Look at the Digit Immediately to the Right: This is the deciding digit.

3. If the deciding digit is 5 or higher, round up by adding one to the digit in the place you are rounding to and dropping all digits to the right.

4. If the deciding digit is less than 5, round down by keeping the digit in the place you are rounding to the same and dropping all digits to the right.

Example: Round 14.5379 to the nearest tenth, hundredth, and thousandth:

To the Nearest Tenth: The digit in the tenths place is 5. Look at the next digit (3). Since it's less than 5, the 5 stays the same. Hence, 14.5379≈14.5.

To the Nearest Hundredth: The digit in the hundredths place is 3. Look at the next digit (7). Since it's 5 or higher, round up the 3 to a 4. Hence, 14.5379≈14.54.

To the Nearest Thousandth: The digit in the thousandths place is 7. Look at the next digit (9). Since it's 5 or higher, round up the 7 to an 8. Hence, 14.5379≈14.538.

Adding and Subtracting Decimals

The key to successfully performing adding and subtracting decimals is ensuring the decimal points of all numbers involved are lined up correctly. Here's how to add and subtract decimals:

Steps for Adding Decimals

1. Align the Decimal Points: Write the numbers so that the decimal points are vertically aligned.

2. Fill in Missing Places: If the numbers have different numbers of digits after the decimal point, add zeros to the ends of the shorter decimals to make them equal in length.

3. Add as Whole Numbers: Ignore the decimal point and add the numbers as if they were whole numbers.

4. Place the Decimal Point: In the sum, place the decimal point directly below the other decimal points.

Example: Add 2.75 and 3.006

Solution: Write the numbers with aligned decimal points:

$$
\begin{array}{r}
2.75 \\
+ \quad 3.006 \\
\hline
5.756
\end{array}
$$

Steps for Subtracting Decimals

1. Align the Decimal Points: As with addition, ensure the decimal points are vertically aligned.

2. Fill in Missing Places: Pad the number with fewer decimal places with zeros.

3. Subtract as Whole Numbers: Ignore the decimal point temporarily and subtract as if they were whole numbers.

4. Place the Decimal Point: Ensure the decimal point in the result lines up with the decimal points above.

Example: Subtract 7.82 from 10.5:

Solution: Write the numbers with aligned decimal points and pad with zeros if necessary:

$$
\begin{array}{r}
10.50 \\
- \quad 7.82 \\
\hline
2.68
\end{array}
$$

Key Points in this example are:

Alignment: When aligning decimals, it is crucial to be accurate with the placement of decimal points to ensure correct calculations.

Zero Padding: Adding zeros to the ends of shorter decimals does not change their value but helps make the addition and subtraction operations straightforward.

Carry/Borrow: In subtraction, remember to borrow as you would with whole numbers when subtracting one digit from another that is smaller. Similarly, remember to carry over in addition when sums of digits exceed 9.

Multiplying and Dividing Decimals

When multiplying decimals, it's crucial to handle the decimal points correctly to ensure the product has the correct number of decimal places.

Steps for Multiplying Decimals:

1. **Ignore the Decimal Points**: Multiply the numbers as if they were whole numbers.

2. **Count Decimal Places**: Add up the total number of decimal places in both factors.

3. **Place the Decimal Point**: In the product, position the decimal point so that it has the combined number of decimal places from the factors.

Example: Multiply 3.2 by 2.5

Solution: Multiply as whole numbers: 32×25=800

Count decimal places: 1+1=2

Position the decimal point: 3.2×2.5=8.00 or simply 8.

Steps for Dividing Decimals:

1. Make the Divisor a Whole Number: Shift the decimal point in the divisor right until it is a whole number, doing the same shift to the dividend.

2. Divide as Whole Numbers: Perform the division as you would with whole numbers.

3. Place the Decimal Point: Insert the decimal point in the quotient based on the initial shifts made.

Example: Divide 6.75 by 1.5

Solution: Steps for Dividing Decimals:

1. Make the Divisor a Whole Number: We'll adjust the divisor 1.5 to make it a whole number by shifting the decimal point to the right, so 1.5 becomes 15.

2. Adjust the Dividend Accordingly: Shift the decimal point in the dividend the same number of places as the divisor to maintain the balance. So, 6.75 becomes 67.5.

3. Divide as Whole Numbers: Perform the division on the adjusted numbers.

4. Position the Decimal Point: After the division, ensure the decimal point in the quotient is correctly placed based on the shifts made.

5. Now, perform the division:

$$\frac{67.5}{15} = 4.5$$

PERCENTAGE

Percents are a way to express a number as a fraction of 100. The word "percent" comes from the Latin phrase "per centum," which means "by the hundred." This makes percents very useful for describing proportions and comparisons.

For example, imagine you have a jar of 100 marbles, and 25 of them are red. You could say that 25% of the marbles are red. This percentage tells us how many marbles out of every 100 are red, making it easy to understand proportions even if the total number of marbles were to change.

Here's a simple mathematical example involving percents: Suppose you scored 45 out of 50 questions correct on a test. To find out the percentage of questions you got right, you divide the number of questions you answered correctly by the total number of questions, and then multiply by 100 to convert it to a percentage. The equation looks like this:

$$\text{Percentage} = \left(\frac{\text{Correct answers}}{\text{Total questions}}\right) \times 100$$

Plugging in the numbers:

$$\text{Percentage} = \left(\frac{45}{50}\right) \times 100$$

This calculation shows you got 90% of the questions correct.

Any problem involving percents can be expressed in the form "A is P percent of B." In this statement, one of the values A, B, or P is typically unknown. To handle such problems mathematically, we translate the statement into an equation:

$$A = \left(\frac{P}{100}\right) \times B$$

If we divide both sides of this equation by B, we derive the formula for P, the percentage:

$$\frac{A}{B} = \frac{P}{100}$$

This equation shows that the percentage P can be calculated by dividing A by B and then multiplying the result by 100. Let's explore this concept through three practical examples:

Example 1: Finding the Unknown Percent

Suppose you have savings of $500 and you learn that it is a part of your annual savings goal. If your total savings goal is $2000, what percent of your goal have you already saved?

Using the formula: $P = \left(\frac{A}{B}\right) \times 100$ to calculate the percent:

$$P = \left(\frac{500}{2000}\right) \times 100 = 25\%$$

So, you have saved 25% of your annual savings goal.

Example 2: Finding the Total (B)

Imagine you scored 92% on a test, and this percentage represents getting 46 questions correct. How many questions were on the test?

Rearrange the formula to solve for B: $B = \frac{A}{(P/100)}$, plug in the values:

$$B = \frac{46}{92\%} = \frac{46}{0.92} = 50$$

There were about 50 questions on the test.

Example 3: Finding the Part (A)

You want to buy a laptop that is on sale for 30% off its original price of $800. How much discount are you getting?

Apply the formula: $A = \left(\frac{P}{100}\right) \times B$

Calculate the discount: $A = 30\% \times 800 = 240$

You get a $240 discount on the laptop.

These examples demonstrate how versatile the percent formula is for solving various real-world problems involving percentages.

Percentage Increase and Decrease

Percentage increase and decrease are important concepts used to describe how much something grows or reduces in proportion over time.

Percentage increase is used to measure how much a quantity has grown relative to its original amount. It's calculated by finding the difference between the new value and the original value, dividing that difference by the original value, and then multiplying the result by 100 to convert it to a percentage. Here's the formula for calculating percentage increase:

$$\text{Percentage Increase} = \left(\frac{\text{New Value} - \text{Original Value}}{\text{Original Value}}\right) \times 100$$

Example: Suppose last year a store sold 150 units of a product, and this year the store sold 180 units. The percentage increase in sales is calculated as follows:

$$\text{Percentage Increase} = \left(\frac{180 - 150}{150}\right) \times 100 = 20\%$$

This means that sales increased by 20% from last year.

Percentage decrease is used to measure how much a quantity has reduced relative to its original amount. The formula is similar to that of percentage increase, but it starts with the original value being higher than the new value. Here's how to calculate percentage decrease:

$$\text{Percentage Decrease} = \left(\frac{\text{Original Value} - \text{New Value}}{\text{Original Value}}\right) \times 100$$

Example: If a car's value decreases from $20,000 to $15,000 over a year, the percentage decrease is:

$$\text{Percentage Decrease} = \left(\frac{20000 - 15000}{20000}\right) \times 100 = 25\%$$

This calculation shows that the car's value has decreased by 25%.

These calculations help us understand changes in terms of percentages, which are easier to compare than just absolute numbers. Percentage increases and decreases offer a clear and standardized method of measurement.

Convert between Percentages, Fractions, and Decimals

Converting between percentages, fractions, and decimals allows you to interpret and compare different forms of numerical expressions.

1. From Percentages to Fractions and Decimals

Converting Percentages to Fractions

To convert a percentage to a fraction, you simply place the percentage number over 100 and then simplify the fraction if possible.

Example: Convert 75% to a fraction.

Solution: First, write the percentage as a fraction: $\frac{75}{100}$. Then, simplify the fraction by dividing the numerator and the denominator by their greatest common divisor, which is 25 in this case:

$$\frac{75 \div 25}{100 \div 25} = \frac{3}{4}$$

Converting Percentages to Decimals

To convert a percentage to a decimal, divide the percentage by 100 or simply move the decimal point two places to the left.

Example: Convert 75% to a decimal.

Solution: Divide 75 by 100: $75 \div 100 = 0.75$

2. From Fractions and Decimals to Percentages

Converting Fractions to Percentages

To convert a fraction to a percentage, divide the numerator by the denominator to get a decimal, and then multiply by 100 to get the percentage.

Example: Convert 3/4 to a percentage.

Solution: First, divide the numerator by the denominator: $3 \div 4 = 0.75$

Then, multiply by 100 to convert to a percentage: $0.75 \times 100 = 75\%$

Converting Decimals to Percentages

To convert a decimal to a percentage, multiply the decimal by 100.

Example: Convert 0.75 to a percentage.

Solution: Multiply by 0.75 by 100: $0.75 \times 100 = 75\%$

3. Convert between Decimals and Fractions

Converting Decimals to Percentages

To convert a decimal to a percentage, multiply the decimal by 100. This shift of the decimal point two places to the right transforms the decimal into a percentage, as it essentially converts the decimal into a fraction with a denominator of 100.

Example: Convert 0.85 to a percentage.

Solution: Multiply the decimal by 100 to get the percentage: $0.85 \times 100 = 85\%$

This means 0.85 is equivalent to 85%.

Converting Decimals to Fractions

To convert a decimal to a fraction, the steps are as follows:

1. Write down the decimal divided by 1 (e.g., 0.85/1).

2. Multiply both the numerator (the top number) and the denominator (the bottom number) by 10 for every number after the decimal point. This step is necessary to eliminate the decimal point.

3. Simplify the resulting fraction by dividing both the numerator and the denominator by their greatest common divisor.

Example: Convert 0.85 to a fraction.

Solution: Express the decimal as a fraction: $\frac{0.85}{1}$. Since there are two digits after the decimal, multiply both the numerator and the denominator by 100 (10 raised to the power of 2):

$$\frac{0.85 \times 100}{1 \times 100} = \frac{85}{100}$$

Simplify the fraction:

$$\frac{85 \div 5}{100 \div 5} = \frac{17}{20}$$

Thus, the decimal 0.85 is equivalent to the fraction $\frac{17}{20}$.

NUMBER COMPARISONS AND EQUIVALENTS

One type of ASVAB test question is comparing values between fractions, decimals, and percentages.

Comparing Decimals

The key to comparing decimal values is understanding the place value of each digit. The digits to the left of the decimal point represent whole numbers, while the digits to the right represent fractions of a whole (tenths, hundredths, etc.).

Steps for Comparing Decimals:

1. Align Decimal Points: Make sure both numbers are written with their decimal points in the same position. If one number has fewer decimal places than the other, add zeros to make the numbers have the same number of decimal places.

2. Compare Whole Numbers: Look at the digits to the left of the decimal point. The number with the larger whole number is greater.

3. Compare Decimal Places: If the whole numbers are the same, compare each decimal place from left to right. The number with the larger digit in the first differing decimal place is greater.

Example: Find the largest among the following decimal numbers: 0.756, 0.765, 0.76, and 0.75.

Solution: Align the decimal points and pad with zeros if necessary to ensure that all have the same number of decimal places:

- 0.756
- 0.765
- 0.760 (added a zero)
- 0.750 (added a zero)

Compare from left to right: The whole number part is the same for all numbers: 0. The tenths place (first digit after the decimal point) is also the same: 7. The hundredths place is where differences appear:

- 0.756 has a 5
- 0.765 has a 6
- 0.760 has a 6
- 0.750 has a 5

The thousandths place further distinguishes the numbers with 0.765 having the largest value (5 compared to 0).

Hence, the answer is that 0.765 is the largest number among the group of numbers given.

Comparing Fractions

Comparing fractions with the same denominator is straightforward, so let's go directly to comparing Fractions with the different denominators. There are two methods: 1.) Cross Multiplication method, and 2.) Common Denominator Method.

Example 1: Compare $\frac{7}{9}$ and $\frac{8}{11}$ using Cross Multiplication Method.

Solution: Observe that $7 \times 11 = 77$, $8 \times 9 = 72$. Since $77 > 72$, we conclude that:

$$\frac{7}{9} > \frac{8}{11}$$

Example 2: Compare $\frac{7}{9}$ and $\frac{8}{11}$ using Common Denominator Method.

Solution: Convert $\frac{7}{9}$ and $\frac{8}{11}$ to fractions with a common denominator: the LCD of 9 and 11 is 99. So, convert $\frac{7}{9}$ to $\frac{77}{99}$ (by multiplying both numerator and denominator by 11). Convert $\frac{8}{11}$ to $\frac{72}{99}$ (by multiplying both numerator and denominator by 9).

Since $\frac{77}{99} > \frac{72}{99}$, we conclude that $\frac{7}{9} > \frac{8}{11}$.

Comparing Decimals, Fractions, and Percents

Some ASVAB questions ask you to compare a mixture of Decimals, Fractions, and Percents. The two primary strategies are converting each value to a decimal or a fraction, depending on which method is easier. Let's explore both methods.

Convert All to Decimals

This method involves converting every value into a decimal, which allows for a direct comparison between the numbers.

Steps:

- Fractions to Decimals: Divide the numerator by the denominator.

- Percentages to Decimals: Divide the percentage by 100.

Example: Compare these values: $\frac{3}{4}$, 0.65, and 80%.

Solution: Convert the fraction to a decimal: $\frac{3}{4}$=0.75.

Convert the percentage to a decimal: 80%=0.80

Now, compare all values as decimals: 0.75, 0.65, 0.80.

Conclusion: The correct order from smallest to largest is 0.65, 0.75, and 0.80. Hence, the original values can be order from smallest to largest as 0.65, $\frac{3}{4}$, 80%.

Convert All to Fractions

This method involves converting all values to fractions before making comparisons. This method is preferable if converting all values to decimals is cumbersome. Consider the following example.

Example: Rank the value of $\frac{5}{11}$, $\frac{7}{13}$, and 45%, from smallest to largest.

Solution: It is obvious converting $\frac{5}{11}$ and $\frac{7}{13}$ into decimals is not the easiest task if you are doing long division manually. At the same time, it is obvious 45% can readily be converted into a fraction. Based on these observations, we can determine that the best step forward is probably to compare the three values as fractions using the cross-multiplication method.

1. Convert 45% to a fraction: $45\% = \frac{45}{100} = \frac{9}{20}$. So, the three values to compare become: $\frac{5}{11}$, $\frac{7}{13}$, and $\frac{9}{20}$.

2. Compare $\frac{5}{11}$ and $\frac{7}{13}$. Cross-multiply to find: $5 \times 13 = 65$, $7 \times 11 = 77$.

   Since $65 < 77$, we know $\frac{5}{11} < \frac{7}{13}$.

3. Compare $\frac{7}{13}$ and $\frac{9}{20}$. Cross-multiply to find: $7 \times 20 = 140$, $9 \times 13 = 117$.

   Since $140 > 117$, $\frac{7}{13} > \frac{9}{20}$.

4. Now that we know $\frac{7}{13}$ is the largest value, we still need to compare $\frac{5}{11}$ and $\frac{9}{20}$. Cross-multiply to find: $7 \times 20 = 140$, $9 \times 13 = 117$. Since $140 > 117$, $\frac{7}{13} > \frac{9}{20}$.

5. Hence, we conclude that: $\frac{9}{20} < \frac{5}{11} < \frac{7}{13}$.

An astute test-take may also be able to determine $\frac{7}{13}$ to be bigger than $\frac{5}{11}$ and 45% by noticing that $\frac{7}{13}$ is larger than 0.5, while the other two items are smaller than 0.5. This will help save two cross-multiplication comparisons.

In conclusion, when faced with ASVAB comparisons questions between decimals, fractions, and percents, it is advisable to first assess quickly which method above is easier and then solve the problem accordingly.

PRE-ALGEBRA CONCEPTS

ASVAB evaluates your ability to interpret numerical data and apply mathematical concepts in real-world situations. You'll handle rates, ratios, proportions, unit conversions, and so on, all crucial for practical problem-solving in daily life and non-STEM academic fields.

We will also cover the following Pre-Algebra concepts in this section: rational numbers, exponents, radicals, fractional exponents, and scientific notation.

Real Numbers

Real numbers form the comprehensive set of numbers used in mathematics, including rational and irrational ones. They represent all points on the number line and include various number types, from the simplest counting numbers to complex fractional and irrational forms.

Types of Real Numbers:

Natural Numbers: These are also known as counting numbers, which are the numbers used for counting objects. They start from 1 and continue infinitely: 1, 2, 3, 4, 5,...

Integers: This set includes all natural numbers, their negatives, and zero. Unlike natural numbers, integers cover both positive and negative values: ...,−3, −2, −1, 0, 1, 2, 3,...

Rational Numbers: Any number that can be expressed as a ratio (or fraction) of two integers is a rational number. This set includes all integers and fractions where the denominator is not zero. Examples include: 34, -2, $-\frac{5}{7}$, 0.75, $\frac{49}{57}$ ...

Irrational Numbers: These are numbers that cannot be expressed as simple fractions. They have non-terminating, non-repeating decimal representations. Famous examples include:

- $\sqrt{2}$ (the square root of 2)

- π (the ratio of a circle's circumference to its diameter)

To recap, real numbers encompass all rational and irrational numbers. This vast collection allows for accurate representation and measurement of distances, quantities, and other numerical concepts.

Absolute Value

The absolute value of a number is its distance from zero on the number line, regardless of direction. It is always a non-negative value. The notation for absolute value is two vertical bars surrounding the number, like this: $|x|$.

Examples:

- $|5| = 5$ because 5 is 5 units away from zero.

- $|-8| = 8$ because -8 is 8 units away from zero.

- $|0| = 0$ because 0 is exactly at zero.

Absolute value is handled similarly to parentheses in the order of operations (PEMDAS):

- P: Parentheses (including absolute value bars)

- E: Exponents (including roots)

- MD: Multiplication and Division (left to right)

- AS: Addition and Subtraction (left to right)

This means that any operation inside the absolute value bars should be evaluated first, and the result's absolute value is taken afterward.

Examples:

- Simple Absolute Value: $|-4| = 4$

- Absolute Value with Expressions: $|5 - 8| = |-3| = 3$

- Combining Absolute Value with Other Operations:

$$3 \times |4 - 6| + 2 = 3 \times |-2| + 2 = 3 \times 2 + 2 = 6 + 2 = 8$$

- Absolute Value with Nested Operations: $|(2^3 - 10)| = |8 - 10| = |-2| = 2$

In all these cases, operations inside the absolute value bars are completed first, followed by taking the absolute value itself and then any other arithmetic operations outside the bars.

Rates

In arithmetic, a rate is a specific kind of ratio that compares two quantities with different units. It is a measure of one quantity relative to another, allowing us to understand how one variable changes with respect to another. Rates are commonly used to describe things like speed, price per unit, or productivity, etc.

Examples of Rates:

1. **Speed (Distance/Time):**

    - Speed is often expressed as a rate, such as miles per hour (mph) or kilometers per hour (km/h).

    Example: If a car travels 120 miles in 2 hours, its speed is: $\frac{120\ miles}{2\ hours} = 60\ mph$

2. **Price (Cost/Unit):**

    - Prices are rates that indicate how much something costs per unit.

    Example: If a 10-pound bag of apples costs $20, the cost per pound is:

$$\frac{20\ dollars}{10\ pounds} = 2\ dollars\ per\ pound$$

3. **Productivity (Output/Time):**

    - Productivity rates describe the output or result produced within a given period.

Example: If a worker assembles 300 items in 8 hours, the productivity rate is:

$$\frac{300 \ items}{8 \ hours} = 37.5 \ items \ per \ hour$$

Unit Conversion

When you know the rate between two units, you can easily convert from one to the other. This is particularly useful when dealing with measurements like speed, currency, and volume.

Example: Suppose you have a speed of 60 miles per hour (mph) and want to convert it to kilometers per hour (km/h). The conversion rate is: 1 mile=1.60934 kilometers.

To convert 60 mph to km/h, multiply by the conversion factor:

$$60 \ mph \times 1.60934 \ km/mile = 96.56 \ km/h$$

Therefore, 60 mph is equivalent to approximately 96.56 km/h.

Unit Rate

A unit rate is a rate where the denominator is reduced to 1. For example, if the speed of a vehicle is 60 mph, the rate is a unit rate—"miles per one hour," or simply "miles per hour". This contrasts with "miles per every two hours", or "miles per every 10 minutes", which are also rates, but not unit rates.

Ratios and Proportional Relationships

A **ratio** is a comparison of two or more numbers, often representing how many times one quantity is contained within another. Ratios can be written in different ways, including:

- Fraction Form: $\frac{a}{b}$

- Colon Form: a:b

- Word Form: "a to b"

Example: 3/5 or 3:5 or "3 to 5" are all ratios expressed differently but are equal in value.

In practice, you might encounter questions involving simplifying ratios, finding equivalent ratios, or comparing different ratios.

A **proportional relationship** occurs when two quantities always have the same ratio or are directly proportional. In other words, as one quantity increases or decreases, the other changes at a consistent rate.

These relationships can often be expressed as: $y = kx$, where y and x are the variables in the relationship, k is the constant of proportionality.

Example: If a recipe calls for 3 cups of flour to make 24 cookies, you can determine the cups of flour needed for 48 cookies through a proportion:

$$\frac{3}{24} = \frac{x}{48}$$

Cross-multiplying gives:

$$x = \frac{3 \times 48}{24} = 6$$

This shows that 6 cups of flour are needed to make 48 cookies.

You may get asked these types of questions on the test:

- **Proportional Reasoning**: Questions may ask you to determine the missing value in a proportion or identify if two sets of values are proportional.

- **Rates and Unit Rates**: These could involve calculating unit prices, speeds, or other rates.

- **Scale Factors**: You might need to work with maps, diagrams, or blueprints involving scaling.

Exponents

Exponents represent repeated multiplication of a base number. Understanding different types of exponents and their applications is fundamental in algebra and scientific calculations. Here's an overview of various exponent concepts.

Positive Whole-Number Exponents

A positive whole-number exponent represents how many times a base number is multiplied by itself. It's a form of repeated multiplication that simplifies large calculations.

General Form: If a is the base and n is the exponent (a positive whole number), then:

$$a^n = a \times a \times a \times \ldots (n \text{ times})$$

Examples:

- $2^3 = 2 \times 2 \times 2 = 8$

- $5^4 = 5 \times 5 \times 5 \times 5 = 625$

- $10^2 = 10 \times 10 = 100$

Properties of Positive Whole-Number Exponents:

1. **Multiplying with the Same Base:** When multiplying two expressions with the same base, add their exponents: $a^m \times a^n = a^{m+n}$

   Example: $2^3 \times 2^2 = 2^{3+2} = 2^5 = 32$

2. **Dividing with the Same Base:** When dividing two expressions with the same base, subtract their exponents: $a^m \div a^n = a^{m-n}$

   Example: $7^5 \div 7^2 = 7^{5-2} = 7^3 = 343$

3. **Power of a Power:** When raising an expression with an exponent to another power, multiply the exponents: $(a^m)^n = a^{m \times n}$

   Example: $(3^2)^3 = 3^{2 \times 3} = 3^6 = 729$

Zero Exponents

Any nonzero base raised to the power of zero equals 1. This rule simplifies calculations involving expressions with zero exponents.

General Rule: $a^0 = 1$, where $a \neq 0$

Example: $(-5)^0 = 1$

This rule applies because, by definition, an expression like $a^n \div a^n$ equals 1.

Meanwhile, $a^n \div a^n = a^{(n-n)} = a^0$. Hence, $a^0 = 1$.

Negative Exponents

A negative exponent represents the reciprocal of a base raised to the corresponding positive exponent. This concept flips the base to its reciprocal and changes the sign of the exponent to positive. Sounds confusing? The example below will clarify it.

General Rule: For any nonzero number a and positive integer n:

$$a^{-n} = \frac{1}{a^n}$$

Examples:

- $4^{-2} = \frac{1}{4^2} = \frac{1}{16}$

- $10^{-3} = \frac{1}{10^3} = \frac{1}{1000} = 0.001$

- $(2x)^{-3} = \frac{1}{(2x)^3} = \frac{1}{8x^3}$

Properties of Negative Exponents:

1. **Multiplying with the Same Base:** When multiplying two expressions with the same base, add the exponents even if one or both are negative: $a^m \times a^{-n} = a^{m-n}$

   Example: $5^3 \times 5^{-2} = 5^{3-2} = 5^1 = 5$

2. **Dividing with the Same Base:** When dividing two expressions with the same base, subtract the exponents: $\frac{a^m}{a^{-n}} = a^{m+n}$

   Example: $\frac{2^4}{2^{-2}} = 2^{4+2} = 2^6 = 64$

3. **Power of a Power:** When raising a base with a negative exponent to another power, multiply the exponents: $(a^{-m})^n = a^{-m \times n}$

   Example: $(3^{-2})^4 = 3^{-8} = \frac{1}{3^8}$

Negative exponents allow for easy representation of reciprocals and small values. They are commonly used in scientific notation and simplify algebraic expressions involving division and reciprocal relationships.

Radicals

Radicals represent roots of numbers and provide a way to express roots in a simplified form. The most common type is the square root, but radicals can represent other roots like cube roots, fourth roots, etc.

Examples:

- **Square Root ($\sqrt{x}$):** The square root of a number x is a value y such that $y^2 = x$. Example: $\sqrt{16} = 4$ because $4^2 = 16$.

- **Cube Root ($\sqrt[3]{x}$):** The cube root of a number x is a value y such that $y^3 = x$.

   Example: $\sqrt[3]{27} = 3$ because $3^3 = 27$.

- **General Roots:** Other roots follow the same pattern, $\sqrt[n]{x}$ represents a radical where n is called the **root** of the radical.

   Example: $\sqrt[4]{81} = 3$

Properties of Radicals:

1. **Product Rule:** The product of two radicals can be combined into a single radical: $\sqrt[n]{a} \times \sqrt[n]{b} = \sqrt[n]{a \times b}$

   Example: $\sqrt{4} \times \sqrt{9} = \sqrt{36} = 6$

2. **Quotient Rule:** The quotient of two radicals can also be combined: $\sqrt[n]{\frac{a}{b}} = \frac{\sqrt[n]{a}}{\sqrt[n]{b}}$.

   Example: $\frac{\sqrt{25}}{\sqrt{4}} = \sqrt{\frac{25}{4}} = \frac{5}{2}$

Fractional Exponents

Fractional exponents are another way to represent roots or radicals. Instead of using the radical symbol, a root is expressed as an exponent in fractional form. This notation provides a concise way to represent both roots and powers.

General Form:

If a is the base and $\frac{m}{n}$ is the fractional exponent: $a^{\frac{m}{n}} = \sqrt[n]{a^m}$

where: n is the root (index), m is the power to which the base is raised before taking the root.

Examples:

- **Square Root** (Fractional Exponent as $\frac{1}{2}$): The square root of a number a is expressed using a fractional exponent as: $a^{\frac{1}{2}} = \sqrt{a}$.

  Example: $25^{\frac{1}{2}} = \sqrt{25} = 5$

- **Cube Root** (Fractional Exponent as $\frac{1}{3}$): The cube root of a number a is expressed using a fractional exponent as: $a^{\frac{1}{3}} = \sqrt[3]{a}$

  Example: $27^{\frac{1}{3}} = \sqrt[3]{27} = 3$.

- **Combining Roots and Powers:** A fractional exponent like $\frac{3}{4}$ indicates that the base should first be raised to the power of 3, and then the fourth root is taken: $a^{\frac{3}{4}} = \sqrt[4]{a^3}$.

  Example: $16^{\frac{3}{4}} = \sqrt[4]{16^3} = \sqrt[4]{4096} = 8$

Powers of 10

Powers of 10 refer to multiplying the base 10 by itself a certain number of times. They are especially important because our number system is based on powers of 10. This notation helps represent very large or very small numbers conveniently.

General Form:

If n is a positive integer, a power of 10 is expressed as: $10^n = 10 \times 10 \times 10 \times \dots$ (n times)

Examples: Positive Powers of 10

- $10^1 = 10$
- $10^3 = 10 \times 10 \times 10 = 1000$
- $10^6 = 1,000,000$ (one million)

A positive power of 10 shows how many zeros follow the number 1 in the standard form we write numbers, e.g., 1000, 1,000,000.

Examples: Negative Powers of 10

- $10^{-1} = \frac{1}{10} = 0.1$
- $10^{-2} = \frac{1}{10^2} = \frac{1}{100} = 0.01$
- $10^{-6} = 0.000001$ (one millionth)

A negative power of 10 shows how many decimal places the 1 is shifted to the left of the decimal point.

Scientific Notation

Powers of 10 are used extensively in scientific notation, a method to express very large or very small numbers. Scientific notation combines a coefficient and a power of 10: $a \times 10^n$, where a is a number between 1 and 10, n is an integer representing the power of 10.

Examples:

- The mass of Earth is approximately 5.97×10^{24} kilograms, a very large number.
- The mass of a hydrogen atom is about 1.67×10^{-27} kilograms, a very small number.

Calculations involving scientific notation follow the same rules as ordinary exponents. Here's a guide to handling scientific notation in various arithmetic operations:

Multiplication: To multiply numbers in scientific notation, multiply the coefficients and add the exponents of the powers of 10.

Example: $(2.5 \times 10^3) \times (4 \times 10^2)$

Solution:

1. Multiply the coefficients: $2.5 \times 4 = 10$
2. Add the exponents: $10^3 \times 10^2 = 10^{3+2} = 10^5$
3. Combine the results: $10 \times 10^5 = 1.0 \times 10^6$

Division: To divide numbers in scientific notation, divide the coefficients and subtract the exponents of the powers of 10.

Example: $\frac{4.8 \times 10^5}{2 \times 10^3}$

Solution:

1. Divide the coefficients: $\frac{4.8}{2} = 2.4$

2. Subtract the exponents: $10^5 \div 10^3 = 10^{5-3} = 10^2$

3. Combine the results: 2.4×10^2

Addition and Subtraction: When adding or subtracting numbers in scientific notation, make sure the exponents are the same before combining the coefficients.

Example: $(3.5 \times 10^4) + (2.3 \times 10^3)$

Solution:

1. Adjust the second term so the exponents match: $2.3 \times 10^3 = 0.23 \times 10^4$

2. Add the coefficients: $3.5 + 0.23 = 3.73$

3. Combine with the power of 10: 3.73×10^4

Summary of the Exponent Operation Rules

Now that we have spent so much time on exponents, let's summarize all the fundamental rules of exponent operations in one table.

Rule	Example
$x^n x^m = x^{n+m}$	$7^3 \cdot 7^2 = 7^5$
$\dfrac{x^n}{x^m} = x^{n-m}$	$\dfrac{5^5}{5^3} = 5^{5-3} = 5^2 = 25$
$x^0 = 1 \ provided \ x \neq 0$	$39^0 = 1$
$(x \cdot y)^n = x^n \cdot y^n$	$(3 \cdot 4)^2 = 3^2 \cdot 4^2 = 9 \cdot 16 = 144$
$\left(\dfrac{x}{y}\right)^n = \dfrac{x^n}{y^n}$	$\left(\dfrac{1}{3}\right)^2 = \dfrac{1^2}{3^2} = \dfrac{1}{9}$
$(x^n)^m = x^{n \cdot m}$	$(2^3)^4 = 2^{3 \cdot 4} = 2^{12}$
$x^{-n} = \dfrac{1}{x^n} \ provided \ X \neq 0$	$10^{-3} = \dfrac{1}{10^3}$

§2. ALGEBRAIC REASONING

Algebra is a branch of mathematics that focuses on the manipulation of symbols and variables to represent and solve equations and expressions. It extends the basic principles of arithmetic by using letters (variables) to stand in for numbers. This allows for the generalization of mathematical concepts and relationships. Key concepts of Algebra include the following.

Variables: Symbols (typically letters) that represent unknown or general values. Examples include x and y.

Coefficients: Numerical values that multiply the variables. For instance, in the expression $3x$, 3 is the coefficient, meaning the variable x is multiplied by 3.

Terms: A term is a single mathematical expression involving a number (coefficient), a variable, or both, separated by addition or subtraction. Examples of terms include: $4x, -5y, 7$.

Expressions: Combinations of terms involving variables, numbers, and arithmetic operations (addition, subtraction, multiplication, and division). Example: $3x + 2y - 5$. This expression includes three terms: $3x, 2y, -5$. Notice that a minus sign is always included with the term that it immediately precedes. In this case, the third term is -5. To make it easier, the forgoing expression can be alternatively written as: $3x + 2y + (-5)$.

Equations: Statements that two expressions are equal, often containing one or more unknowns (variables). Example: $2x + 3 = 7$.

Inequalities: Statements that compare two expressions using inequality symbols such as greater than ($>$), less than ($<$), greater than or equal to ($\geq$), or less than or equal to ($\leq$). Example: $4x - 1 < 9$

Functions: Relationships between two sets of variables, usually expressed as a rule or equation. Example: $f(x) = x^2 - 4$.

EVALUATING ALGEBRAIC EXPRESSIONS

Evaluating algebraic expressions means finding the value of an expression by substituting specific values for the variables involved and then performing the necessary calculations.

Steps for Evaluating Algebraic Expressions:

1. **Identify the Expression:** The expression is a combination of variables, coefficients, constants, and arithmetic operators like addition, subtraction, multiplication, and division.

2. **Substitute Values:** Replace the variables with specific numerical values provided in the problem.

3. **Perform the Calculations:** Follow the order of operations (PEMDAS): Parentheses, Exponents, Multiplication and Division (from left to right), Addition and Subtraction (from left to right).

Example: Given $x = 2$ and $y = 4$, evaluating $3x + 5y - 7$.

Solution: Substitute the values of x and y into the above expression:

$$3x + 5y - 7 = 3 \cdot 2 + 5 \cdot 4 - 7 = 6 + 20 - 7 = 19$$

OPERATIONS OF ALGEBRAIC EXPRESSIONS

In algebra, **like terms** are terms that contain the same variables raised to the same power. The coefficients (numbers in front of variables) can be different. For instance, in the expression:

$3x^2 + 4x - 5 + 7x^2 - 2x + 8$, like terms are as follows:

- $3x^2$ and $7x^2$ are like terms because both contain the variable x raised to the power of 2.

- $4x$ and $-2x$ are like terms because both contain the variable x raised to the power of 1.

- -5 and 8 are like terms because they are constants (terms without variables).

Addition and Subtraction

To add or subtract algebraic expressions, combine like terms.

Example: Simplify $3x^2 + 4x - 5 + 7x^2 - 2x + 8$

Solution:

1. Combine like terms involving x^2: $3x^2 + 7x^2 = 10x^2$
2. Combine like terms involving x: $4x - 2x = 2x$
3. Combine the constants: $-5 + 8 = 3$
4. Final Result: $10x^2 + 2x + 3$

Multiplication

To multiply algebraic expressions, apply the distributive property and combine like terms.

Example: Multiply the following: (x+3)(x−2)

Solution:

1. Distribute x over x−2: $x \cdot (x - 2) = x^2 - 2x$
2. Distribute 3 over $x - 2$: $3 \cdot (x - 2) = 3x - 6$
3. Add the results: $x^2 - 2x + 3x - 6 = x^2 + x - 6$

The above process is also called the **FOIL** method of multiplying two binomials. The acronym "FOIL" stands for: First, Outer, Inner, Last.

First: Multiply the first terms of each binomial.

Outer: Multiply the outer terms of each binomial.

Inner: Multiply the inner terms of each binomial.

Last: Multiply the last terms of each binomial.

In some cases, an algebraic expression is complicated by parentheses, and simplifying it requires removing the parentheses. To achieve this, distribute the term that directly precedes the parentheses by multiplying it with each term inside. Let's tackle an example where a polynomial is multiplied by a binomial:

Example: Multiply the following: $(2x^2 - 3x + 4)(3x + 5)$

Solution: Distribute each term in the polynomial $(2x^2 - 3x + 4)$ over the terms in the binomial $(3x + 5)$.

1. **First Term:** Distribute $2x^2$

    $2x^2 \cdot 3x + 2x^2 \cdot 5 = 6x^3 + 10x^2$

2. **Second Term:** Distribute $-3x$

    $-3x \cdot 3x + (-3x) \cdot 5 = -9x^2 - 15x$

3. **Third Term:** Distribute 4

    $4 \cdot 3x + 4 \cdot 5 = 12x + 20$

4. **Combine the Results:**

    $6x^3 + 10x^2 - 9x^2 - 15x + 12x + 20$

5. **Simplify by Combining Like Terms:**

    $6x^3 + (10x^2 - 9x^2) + (-15x + 12x) + 20 = 6x^3 + x^2 - 3x + 20$

Division

For division, expressions are often divided through factorization or by reducing fractions.

Example: Divide the following: $\frac{2x^2-8}{2x}$

Solution:

1. Factor out 2 from the numerator: $2x^2 - 8 = 2(x^2 - 4)$

2. Recognize that $x^2 - 4$ is a difference of squares: $x^2 - 4 = (x + 2)(x - 2)$

3. Substitute back to rewrite the original expression: $\frac{2(x+2)(x-2)}{2x}$

4. Cancel out the common factor of 2 and reduce: $\frac{(x+2)(x-2)}{x}$

GCF Factoring

The greatest common factor (GCF) of a set of terms is the largest expression that divides each term evenly. Factoring out the GCF is the most basic type of polynomial factoring and simplifies expressions by grouping common factors.

Steps to Factor Out the GCF:

1. **Identify the GCF**: Determine the largest factor shared by all terms in the polynomial.

2. **Factor Out the GCF**: Divide each term by the GCF, leaving a simpler polynomial inside parentheses.

3. **Rewrite**: Multiply the GCF by the simplified polynomial inside the parentheses.

Example 1: Factor out the GCF from: $12x^3 - 18x^2 + 24x$

Solution:

1. Identify the GCF: The GCF of 12, 18, and 24 is 6. The common variable is x, and the smallest power among all terms is x. Thus, the GCF is $6x$.

2. Factor Out the GCF: Divide each term by $6x$:
   $$12x^3 \div 6x = 2x^2, \quad 18x^2 \div 6x = 3x, \quad 24x \div 6x = 4$$

3. Rewrite the Expression: $12x^3 - 18x^2 + 24x = 6x(2x^2 - 3x + 4)$

Example 2: GCF Factoring to Simplify Division: $\frac{15\ ^3+20x^2}{5x}$

Solution:

1. Factor Out the GCF (Numerator): The GCF of the numerator, $15x^3 + 20x^2$, is $5x^2$. Thus, factor it out: $15x^3 + 20x^2 = 5x^2(3x + 4)$

2. Rewrite the Expression: $\frac{15x^3+20x^2}{5x} = \frac{5x^2(3x+4)}{5x}$

3. Simplify the Division: Cancel out the common factor of 5x: $\frac{5x^2}{5x} = x$,

   leaving: $x(3x + 4) = 3x^2 + 4x$.

   Hence, $\frac{15x^3+20x^2}{5x} = \frac{5x^2(3x+4)}{5x} = x(3x + 4) = 3x^2 + 4x$.

FACTORING

Factoring is a fundamental algebraic process used to simplify expressions, solve equations, and understand polynomial functions. Factoring involves breaking down a complex expression into simpler, multiplied components known as factors. These factors, when multiplied together, reconstruct the original expression. Factoring can simplify calculations and reveal useful properties and relationships within algebraic expressions.

Greatest Common Factor (GCF) and Factoring by Grouping

Mastering the techniques of finding the greatest common factor (GCF) and factoring by grouping are essential for simplifying and solving algebraic expressions. This section will guide you through both processes, helping you break down more complex polynomial expressions.

Finding the Greatest Common Factor (GCF)

The GCF of two or more expressions is the largest expression that divides each of the original expressions without leaving a remainder. Finding the GCF is often the first step in factoring polynomials effectively.

Steps to Find the GCF:

1. **List Factors**: List all factors (or use prime factorization) of each term in the expression.

2. **Identify Common Factors**: Identify the largest factor that is common to all terms.

Example: Finding the GCF of $12x^2$ and $18x$

Solution:

1. Prime Factorization:

$$12x^2 = 2 \times 2 \times 3 \times x \times x$$

$$18x = 2 \times 3 \times 3 \times x$$

2. Common Factors: The common prime factors are 2, 3, and x.

3. Greatest Common Factor: The GCF is $6x$ (since $2 \times 3 \times x = 6x$).

Factoring by Grouping

Factoring by grouping involves rearranging and grouping terms in a polynomial to simplify factoring, especially useful for polynomials with four or more terms.

Steps to Factor by Grouping:

1. **Group the Terms**: Arrange the polynomial into groups that have a common factor.

2. **Factor Out the GCF from Each Group**: Apply the GCF method within each group.

3. **Factor Out the Common Binomial Factor**: Look for and factor out the common binomial factor from the grouped terms.

Example: Factoring $x^3 + 3x^2 + 2x + 6$ by Grouping

Solution:

1. Group the Terms: $x^3 + 3x^2$ and $2x + 6$

2. Factor Out the GCF from Each Group:

   - From $x^3 + 3x^2$, factor out x^2, resulting in $x^2(x + 3)$

   - From $2x + 6$, factor out 2, resulting in $2(x + 3)$

3. Factor Out the Common Binomial Factor: The common factor is $x + 3$, hence:

$$x^3 + 3x^2 + 2x + 6 = x^2(x + 3) + 2(x + 3)$$
$$= (x^2 + 2)(x + 3)$$

By understanding and applying these methods, you can efficiently simplify and solve a variety of polynomial expressions.

Factoring Quadratics $x^2 + bx + c$

Quadratic expressions in the standard form $x^2 + bx + c$ are a common sight in algebra. These are polynomials where the highest exponent is 2, and they do not have a coefficient in front of x^2. The goal of factoring such quadratics is to express them as the product of two binomials. This section will guide you through the process of factoring these types of quadratics using a straightforward method that involves finding two numbers.

The key to factoring a quadratic expression of the form $x^2 + bx + c$ is to find two numbers that multiply to c (the constant term) and add up to b (the coefficient of x). These numbers will be used to create the binomials.

Steps to Factor $x^2 + bx + c$:

1. **Identify the Numbers**: Find two numbers that multiply to give the constant term c, and at the same time, add up to the coefficient b.

2. **Write the Binomials**: Use these numbers to write two binomials. The binomials will have the form $(x + m)(x + n)$, where m and n are the numbers identified in the first step.

Example: Factor $x^2 + 5x + 6$

1. Identify the Numbers: We need two numbers that multiply to 6 (the constant term) and add to 5 (the coefficient of x). After checking possible pairs, we find that 2 and 3 fit the requirements because $2 \times 3 = 6$ and $2 + 3 = 5$.

2. Write the Binomials: Using the numbers 2 and 3, we can write the quadratic as $(x + 2)(x + 3)$.

Check the Factorization: To verify, expand $(x + 2)(x + 3)$ using the distributive property (also known as the FOIL method for binomials):

$$(x + 2)(x + 3) = x^2 + 3x + 2x + 6 = x^2 + 5x + 6$$

The expansion matches the original expression, confirming our factorization is correct.

Factoring Quadratics $ax^2 + bx + c$

Factoring quadratic expressions where the leading coefficient (a) is not 1, such as in the general form $ax^2 + bx + c$, can be more challenging than factoring when $a = 1$. This section will introduce a method known as the "ac method" or "splitting the middle term," which is effective for tackling these more complex quadratics.

The ac method involves manipulating the middle term of the quadratic by finding two numbers that multiply to ac (the product of the coefficients of x^2 and the constant term) and add up to b (the coefficient of x). These numbers are then used to split the middle term, allowing the expression to be factored by grouping.

Steps to Factor $ax^2 + bx + c$:

1. **Multiply and Find**: Calculate ac and find two numbers that multiply to ac and add up to b.

2. **Split the Middle Term**: Use these numbers to split the middle term into two terms.

$$ax^2 + bx + c = ax^2 + nx + mx + c$$

3. **Group and Factor**: Group the terms in pairs and factor out the greatest common factor from each group: $(ax^2 + nx) + (mx + c)$

4. **Factor Out the Common Binomial Factor**: Extract the common binomial factor from the grouped terms to complete the factorization.

Example: Factor $6x^2 + 11x + 4$

Solution:

1. Multiply and Find: Calculate $ac = 6 \times 4 = 24$.

2. Find two numbers that multiply to 24 and add to 11. These numbers are 8 and 3.

3. Split the Middle Term: Rewrite the middle term using 8 and 3: $6x^2 + 8x + 3x + 4$.

4. Group and Factor: Group the terms: $(6x^2 + 8x) + (3x + 4)$.

5. Factor out the GCF from each group: $2x(3x + 4) + 1(3x + 4)$.

6. Factor Out the Common Binomial Factor: The common factor is $(3x + 4)$, so the expression factors as $(2x + 1)(3x + 4)$.

$$6x^2 + 11x + 4 = 2x(3x + 4) + 1(3x + 4)$$
$$= (2x + 1)(3x + 4)$$

By following these steps, you can successfully factor quadratic expressions with a leading coefficient greater than one.

Factoring Perfect Square Trinomials

Perfect square trinomials are a special form of quadratic expressions that result from squaring a binomial. These trinomials are always in the form of $ax^2 + 2abx + b^2$ or $ax^2 - 2abx + b^2$ where the square of the first term and the square of the last term are perfect squares, and the middle term is twice the product of the square roots of these squares. Factoring perfect square trinomials is straightforward once you recognize the pattern.

Steps to Factor $ax^2 + 2abx + b^2$ or $ax^2 - 2abx + b^2$

To factor a perfect square trinomial, you need to identify whether it can be written as the square of a binomial. Here are the steps to follow:

1. **Identify the Squares:** Ensure that the first and last terms are perfect squares.

2. **Check the Middle Term:** Verify that the middle term is twice the product of the roots of the first and last terms.

3. **Write the Binomial:** Express the trinomial as the square of a binomial.

Example: Factor $x^2 + 6x + 9$

Solution:

1. Identify the Squares: The first term x^2 is the square of x, and the last term 9 is the square of 3.

2. Check the Middle Term: The middle term $6x$ should be twice the product of x and 3, which it is: $2 \cdot 3 \cdot x = 6x$.

3. Write the Binomial: Since all conditions are satisfied, the trinomial can be written as the square of a binomial: $(x + 3)^2$.

$$x^2 + 6x + 9 = (x + 3)^2$$

Factoring Differences of Squares $a^2 - b^2$

The difference of squares is a common algebraic pattern that is simple to factor once recognized. This pattern applies to expressions where two terms are squared and subtracted from each other, taking the general form $a^2 - b^2$. Factoring differences of squares relies on a fundamental algebraic identity, making it a quick and effective process.

Steps to Factor $a^2 - b^2$

To factor a difference of squares, you utilize the identity $a^2 - b^2 = (a - b)(a + b)$. Here are the steps to factor such expressions:

1. **Identify the Squares**: Ensure both terms are perfect squares.

2. **Apply the Difference of Squares Formula**: Write the expression as the product of two binomials, one representing the sum of the square roots and the other the difference of the square roots.

Example: Factor $x^2 - 16$

Solution:

1. Identify the Squares: The first term, x^2, is the square of x, and the last term, 16, is the square of 4.

2. Apply the Difference of Squares Formula: Since x^2 and 16 are perfect squares, apply the formula $a^2 - b^2 = (a - b)(a + b)$ with $a = x$ and $b = 4$.

$$x^2 - 16 = (x - 4)(x + 4)$$

This straightforward factorization shows how the difference of squares identity simplifies the process, quickly breaking down the expression into a product of binomials.

Factoring the Sum or Difference of Cubes

Factoring the sum or difference of cubes involves breaking down expressions that are either the sum or the subtraction of two cubed terms. These expressions take the forms $a^3 + b^3$ and $a^3 - b^3$, respectively. The factoring of these forms is based on specific algebraic identities, which allow for simplification into products of binomials and trinomials.

Factoring $a^3 + b^3$ and $a^3 - b^3$

To factor the sum or difference of cubes, you use the following identities:

- For the sum of cubes: $a^3 + b^3 = (a + b)(a^2 - ab + b^2)$

- For the difference of cubes: $a^3 - b^3 = (a - b)(a^2 + ab + b^2)$

The mnemonic "SOAP" is a helpful way to remember the signs used in the formulas for factoring the sum or difference of cubes. There are a total of three plus or minus signs to the right of the equal sign in the above two formulas. Here's how each letter in the mnemonic corresponds to these three plus or minus signs in the formulas:

1. **S - Same**: This stands for the first sign in the binomial part of the factorization formula, which is the same as the sign in the original cubic expression. For instance:

   - In $a^3 + b^3$, the sign between a and b in the binomial $(a + b)$ is positive.

   - In $a^3 - b^3$, the sign between a and b in the binomial $(a - b)$ is negative.

2. **O - Opposite**: This represents the first sign in the trinomial part of the factorization formula, which is the opposite of the sign in the binomial. For example:

   - In $a^3 + b^3 = (a + b)(a^2 - ab + b^2)$, the sign after a^2 is negative, which is the opposite of the positive sign in $(a + b)$.

   - In $a^3 - b^3 = (a - b)(a^2 + ab + b^2)$, the sign after a^2 is positive, opposite the negative sign in $(a - b)$.

3. **AP - Always Positive**: This refers to the last sign in the trinomial part of the factorization formula, which is always positive, regardless of whether the expression is a sum or a difference of cubes. This means:

   - Both $a^2 - ab + b^2$ in the sum of cubes and $a^2 + ab + b^2$ in the difference of cubes end with a positive term $(+b^2)$.

Example: Factor $x^3 - 27$

Solution:

1. Identify the Cubes: The term x^3 is the cube of x, and 27 is the cube of 3.

2. Apply the Difference of Cubes Formula: Since the expression involves subtraction, use the difference of cubes formula: $a^3 - b^3 = (a - b)(a^2 + ab + b^2)$ with $a = x$ and $b = 3$.

$$x^3 - 27 = (x - 3)(x^2 + 3x + 9)$$

General Strategy of Factoring Polynomials

Factoring polynomials efficiently requires a systematic approach, ensuring each polynomial is broken down into its simplest form. Below is a structured method to guide you through the factoring process:

Step 1—Identify the Greatest Common Factor (GCF): Check if there is a GCF in all terms of the polynomial. If one exists, factor it out first. This simplifies the polynomial, reducing the complexity of further factoring steps.

Step 2—Analyze the Structure of the Polynomial: Determine the type of polynomial and apply the appropriate factoring technique:

Binomial Factors:

Sum of Squares: Note that sums of squares generally do not factor over the real numbers.

Sum of Cubes: Apply the sum of cubes formula: $a^3 + b^3 = (a + b)(a^2 - ab + b^2)$

Difference of Squares: Factor as the product of conjugates using $a^2 - b^2 = (a - b)(a + b)$

Difference of Cubes: Use the difference of cubes formula: $a^3 - b^3 = (a - b)(a^2 + ab + b^2)$

<u>Trinomial Factors:</u>

Simple Form ($x^2 + bx + c$): Undo the FOIL process by finding two numbers that multiply to c and add to b.

Complex Form ($ax^2 + bx + c$): Check if a and c are perfect squares and fit the trinomial square pattern where the first term, ax^2, and the last term, c, must both be perfect squares, and the middle term, bx, must be twice the product of the square roots of ax^2 and c.

Otherwise, use trial and error or the "ac" method, finding two numbers that multiply to ac and add to b, then group and factor.

<u>Polynomials with More than Three Terms:</u>

Grouping Method: Group terms to create factorable chunks, typically aiming for common factors or binomial factors within the groups.

Step 3—Verification: Check if the polynomial is factored completely. Ensure that no further factorization is possible. Multiply the factors to verify that they combine to form the original polynomial.

The following table summarizes the factoring methods we have covered, and the general strategy of factoring polynomials.

Table: General Strategy of Factoring Polynomials

Category	Type	Formula/Method
GCF		Always check for and factor out the GCF first.
Binomial	Difference of Squares	$a^2 - b^2 = (a - b)(a + b)$
	Sum of Squares	Sums of squares do not factor (over real numbers)
	Sum of Cubes	$a^3 + b^3 = (a + b)(a^2 - ab + b^2)$
	Difference of Cubes	$a^3 - b^3 = (a - b)(a^2 + ab + b^2)$
Trinomial	Simple: $x^2 + bx + c$	Look for two numbers that multiply to c and add to b
	Complex: $ax^2 + bx + c$	Use the 'ac' method
More than 3 terms	Grouping	Group terms to factor by common factors

FUNCTIONS

A function is a relation that uniquely associates each element of a given set, called the domain, with an element in another set, known as the range. In simpler terms, a function takes an input, applies a specific rule to it, and then produces <u>exactly one output</u>. Below are a couple of examples:

- Numerical Example: Consider the function $f(x) = x + 3$. If the input x is 2, then the output $f(2)$ is $2 + 3 = 5$.

- Real-life Example: Consider the relationship between the distance traveled and the amount of fuel used by a vehicle. This function, often referred to as the fuel efficiency function, calculates the fuel consumption based on the distance traveled.

Function Notation

Function notation is a concise way to represent functions. The notation $f(x)$ denotes a function named f evaluated at an input x. Here, f represents the function itself, and x is the variable or input to the function. The expression $f(x)$ represents the output of the function.

Example: In the function $f(x) = x^2 - 4x + 4$,

- $f(0) = 0^2 - 4 \times 0 + 4 = 4$

- $f(2) = 2^2 - 4 \times 2 + 4 = 0$

Different Representations of Functions

Functions can be represented in various forms, each providing different insights:

1. **Verbal Descriptions**: Describing the relationship in words, such as "add three to any number."

2. **Equations**: A mathematical statement like $f(x) = 2x + 1$ that defines the output for each input.

3. **Tables**: Listing input values alongside their corresponding output values.

4. **Graphs**: Visual representations, where the input values are plotted on the x-axis, and the output values are plotted on the y-axis.

Evaluating Linear and Quadratic Functions

Linear Functions

Linear functions are functions of the form $f(x) = mx + b$, where m is the slope and b is the y-intercept. Evaluating a linear function means substituting a value for x and calculating the corresponding y value.

Example: For the function $f(x) = 3x + 2$, find $f(4)$.

To find f(4), substitute x=4: $f(4) = 3(4) + 2 = 14$

Quadratic Functions

Quadratic functions are expressed as $f(x) = ax^2 + bx + c$, with a, b, and c being constants. Evaluating a quadratic function involves substituting the x value into the equation and calculating the result.

Example: For $f(x) = x2 - 5x + 6$, find $f(3)$.

To evaluate $f(3)$, substitute $x = 3$: $f(3) = 3^2 - 5 \cdot 3 + 6 = 0$

RADICAL FUNCTIONS

Radical functions are functions that involve a variable within a radical symbol, most commonly a square root. These functions are characterized by the presence of roots, such as square roots, cube roots, or higher-order roots. The general form of a radical function is: $f(x) = \sqrt[n]{x}$, where n is the degree of the root.

Domain of Radical Functions

The domain of a radical function includes all the values of x for which the expression under the radical is defined. This depends on the type of radical:

1. **Square Root Functions**: For a function of the form $f(x) = x$ or $f(x) = \sqrt{g(x)}$ the expression under the square root must be non-negative. Therefore, the domain is found by solving: $g(x) \geq 0$. For example, for $f(x) = \sqrt{x - 2}$, the domain is determined by $x - 2 \geq 0$, so $x \geq 2$.

2. **Higher-Order Root Functions**: For functions involving even roots (such as fourth roots), the domain also requires the expression under the radical to be non-negative. For odd roots (such as cube roots), the expression under the radical can be any real number, so the domain is all real numbers.

Range of Radical Functions

The range of a radical function depends on the values that the function can output:

1. **Square Root Functions**: Since the square root function $\sqrt{x}$ produces non-negative values, the range of $f(x) = \sqrt{x}$ is $y \geq 0$. For $f(x) = \sqrt{g(x)}$, the range is determined by evaluating the function over its domain.

2. **Higher-Order Root Functions**: The range of functions involving even roots is also non-negative. For odd roots, the range is all real numbers because these functions can produce both positive and negative values.

Examples

1. Square Root Function: $f(x) = \sqrt{x-1}$

    - Domain: $x - 1 \geq 0 \Rightarrow x \geq 1$

    - Range: $y \geq 0$

2. Cube Root Function: $f(x) = \sqrt[3]{x+2}$

    - Domain: All real numbers (since cube roots are defined for all real numbers)

    - Range: All real numbers

Determining the domain and range helps in graphing the function accurately and understanding its behavior within the specified intervals.

Simplifying Radical Expressions

Simplifying radical expressions involves rewriting them in their simplest form. This process includes reducing the radicand (the expression under the radical) and rationalizing the denominator if necessary.

Steps to Simplify Radical Expressions

1. **Factor the Radicand**: Break down the expression inside the radical into its prime factors or simpler expressions.

    - For example, $\sqrt{50}$ can be factored as $\sqrt{25 \cdot 2}$

2. **Simplify the Radical**: Apply the property $\sqrt{a \cdot b} = \sqrt{a} \cdot \sqrt{b}$ to separate the factors.

    - Simplify each part: $\sqrt{25 \cdot 2} = \sqrt{25} \cdot \sqrt{2} = 5\sqrt{2}$.

3. **Combine Like Terms**: If you have multiple radical terms, combine like terms by ensuring they have the same radicand.

    - For example, $3\sqrt{2} + 5\sqrt{2} = 8\sqrt{2}$

4. **Rationalize the Denominator**: If a radical expression is in the denominator, multiply the numerator and the denominator by a term that will eliminate the radical in the denominator.

    - For example, to simplify $\frac{1}{\sqrt{3}}$ multiply by $\frac{\sqrt{3}}{\sqrt{3}}$ to get $\frac{\sqrt{3}}{3}$.

Examples:

1. Simplifying a Single Radical: Simplify $\sqrt{72}$

    - Factor 72 : $72 = 36 \times 2$

    - Simplify: $\sqrt{72} = \sqrt{36 \times 2} = \sqrt{36} \cdot \sqrt{2} = 6\sqrt{2}$.

2. Combining Like Radicals: Simplify $2\sqrt{3} + 4\sqrt{3}$

    - Combine like terms: $2\sqrt{3} + 4\sqrt{3} = (2+4)\sqrt{3} = 6\sqrt{3}$.

3. Rationalizing the Denominator: Simplify $\frac{5}{\sqrt{7}}$

    - Multiply by $\frac{\sqrt{7}}{\sqrt{7}}$: $\frac{5}{\sqrt{7}} \cdot \frac{\sqrt{7}}{\sqrt{7}} = \frac{5\sqrt{7}}{7}$.

4. Simplifying a Radical with a Variable: Simplify $\sqrt{18x^3}$

    - Factor: $18x^3 = 9 \times 2 \times x^2 \times x$

    - Simplify: $\sqrt{18x^3} = \sqrt{9 \times 2 \times x^2 \times x} = \sqrt{9} \cdot \sqrt{2} \cdot \sqrt{x^2} \cdot \sqrt{x} = 3x\sqrt{2x}$

Tips for Simplifying Radical Expressions

- **Perfect Squares**: Look for perfect squares within the radicand to simplify.

- **Prime Factorization**: Use prime factorization to break down complex radicands.

- **Rationalization**: Always rationalize the denominator if a radical is present.

Graphing Radical Functions

Below are the two most common radical functions along with their corresponding graphs. Although there are countless variations of radical functions, understanding the principles of function transformations allows us to determine their approximate shapes and locations based on these two graphs below. Radical functions with even roots all resemble a transformed (translated, dilated, or flipped) graph of $f(x) = \sqrt{x}$, while those with odd roots resemble a transformed graph of $y = \sqrt[3]{x}$.

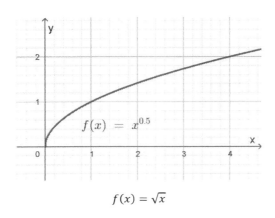

$$f(x) = \sqrt{x}$$

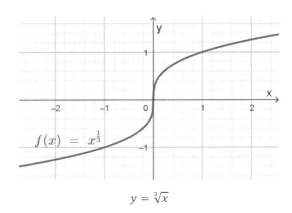

$$y = \sqrt[3]{x}$$

LINEAR EQUATIONS

A one-variable linear equation is an equation with a single unknown variable, typically denoted by x, and it forms a straight line when graphed on the coordinate plane. The standard form of a one-variable linear equation is: $ax + b = 0$ where: a and b are constants (with $a \neq 0$), and x is the unknown variable.

Solve One-Variable Linear Equations

To solve a linear equation means finding the value of the unknown variable that makes the equation true.

Steps to Solve:

1. **Isolate the Variable**: Rearrange the equation to express the unknown variable (x) on one side of the equation.

2. **Simplify**: Combine like terms or reduce fractions as needed.

3. **Solve for the Variable**: Perform arithmetic operations to obtain the value of the unknown variable.

Example 1—Simple Equation: Solve the equation: $2x + 5 = 13$

Solution:

1. Isolate $2x$: Subtract 5 from both sides.

$$2x + 5 - 5 = 13 - 5$$
$$2x = 8$$

2. Solve for x: Divide both sides by 2.

$$x = \frac{8}{2} = 4$$

Example 2—Fractional Coefficients: Solve the equation: $\frac{3x}{5} - 2 = 1$

Solution:

1. Isolate the Fractional Term: Add 2 to both sides.

$$\frac{3x}{5} - 2 + 2 = 1 + 2$$
$$\frac{3x}{5} = 3$$

2. Solve for x: Multiply both sides by 5 to clear the fraction.

$$3x = 3 \cdot 5$$
$$3x = 15$$

3. Divide both sides by 3.

$$x = \frac{15}{3} = 5$$

Example 3— Cross-Multiplication: Solve the equation: $\frac{2x-1}{3} = \frac{x+4}{5}$

Solution:

1. **Cross-Multiply**: Multiply the numerator on one side by the denominator on the other, and vice versa:

$$5 \cdot (2x - 1) = 3 \cdot (x + 4)$$

2. **Simplify Both Sides**: Perform the multiplication:

$$10x - 5 = 3x + 12$$

3. **Isolate the Variable**: To solve for x, get all the x-terms on one side of the equation by subtracting $3x$ from both sides:

$$10x - 3x - 5 = 12$$
$$7x - 5 = 12$$

4. **Solve for x**: Add 5 to both sides to isolate $7x$, and then divide by 7:

$$7x - 5 + 5 = 12 + 5$$
$$7x = 17$$
$$x = \frac{17}{7}$$

Example 4— Multiplying LCD: Solve the equation: $\frac{x}{4} + \frac{3}{2} = \frac{x-1}{3}$

Solution:

1. **Identify the LCD:** The denominators in the equation are 4, 2, and 3. The least common denominator (LCD) for these is 12.

2. **Multiply Each Term by the LCD:** Multiply both sides of the equation by 12 to clear the fractions.

$$12 \cdot \left(\frac{x}{4} + \frac{3}{2}\right) = 12 \cdot \frac{x-1}{3}$$
$$12 \cdot \frac{x}{4} + 12 \cdot \frac{3}{2} = 4(x - 1)$$
$$3x + 18 = 4x - 4$$

3. **Solve for x:**

$$3x - 4x = -18 - 4$$
$$-x = -22$$
$$x = 22$$

Solving Equations in Terms of Other Variables

Sometimes, an equation involves multiple variables, and the goal is to solve for one variable in terms of the others. This allows us to express that variable as a function of the remaining variables. The steps to solve equations in terms of other variables are not any different from what we have already discussed above.

Example: Solve for x in terms of y in the equation: $2x + 3y = 12$

Solution:

$$2x = 12 - 3y$$
$$x = \frac{12 - 3y}{2}$$

Solving Inequalities

Linear inequalities are similar to linear equations, but instead of using an equal sign (=), they involve inequality signs like <, >, ≤, or ≥. The goal is to find the range of values that satisfy the given inequality.

Interval notation is a method used to represent the set of all solutions to an inequality. It describes the range of numbers that satisfy a condition or a series of conditions. The notation uses parentheses () and square brackets [] to show whether endpoints are included or excluded from the interval.

- **Parentheses ()**: Used to exclude endpoints. For instance, (a, b) means all values between a and b, but not including a or b.

- **Square Brackets []**: Used to include endpoints. For example, $[a, b]$ includes both a and b in the range.

- **Infinity** (∞) and **Negative Infinity** ($-\infty$): Represent unbounded intervals. Infinity symbols are always used with parentheses because infinity itself isn't a specific number that can be included.

Examples: Inequality solution and corresponding interval:

- $x > 3$ is equivalent to $(3, \infty)$

- $2 \leq x < 7$ is equivalent to $[2,7)$

- $x \leq -5$ is equivalent to $(-\infty, -5]$

Using interval notation provides a concise and standardized way to describe ranges of values that satisfy various conditions in inequalities.

Basic Steps for Solving Linear Inequalities

1. **Isolate the Variable**: Rearrange the inequality to isolate the unknown variable on one side, while keeping the other terms on the opposite side. This often involves addition, subtraction, multiplication, or division.

2. **Simplify if Needed**: Combine like terms or reduce fractions.

3. **Consider the Direction of the Inequality**: If you multiply or divide both sides of the inequality by a negative number, remember to reverse the direction of the inequality sign.

4. **Write the Solution**: Express the solution in interval notation or using inequality symbols.

Example 1—Simple Inequality: Solve the inequality: $3x - 7 < 5$

Solution:

$$3x - 7 + 7 < 5 + 7$$
$$3x < 12$$
$$x < \frac{12}{3} = 4$$
$$x < 4$$

The solution is all values of x less than 4. Interval Notation: $(-\infty, 4)$.

Here is how the solution looks like on a number line:

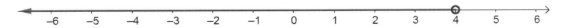

Example 2—Reversing the Inequality: Solve the inequality: $-2x + 8 \geq 4$

Solution:

$$-2x + 8 - 8 \geq 4 - 8$$
$$-2x \geq -4$$

Divide both sides by -2 to solve for x. Remember to reverse the direction of inequality because we are dividing both sides with a negative number.

$$x \leq \frac{-4}{-2} = 2$$
$$x \leq 2$$

The solution is all values of x less than or equal to 2. Interval Notation: $(-\infty, 2]$.

Here is how the solution looks like on a number line:

Solving Systems of Equations

A system of two equations consists of two equations with two variables, typically represented as x and y. The goal is to find a solution that satisfies both equations simultaneously.

Methods for Solving Systems of Equations

1. Substitution Method: This method involves solving one equation for one variable and substituting that expression into the other equation to find the second variable.

Example: Solve the following system:

$$x + 2y = 8 \quad (1)$$
$$3x - y = 1 \quad (2)$$

Solution:

1. Solve equation (1) for x:

$$x = 8 - 2y$$

2. Substitute $x = 8 - 2y$ into equation (2):

$$3(8 - 2y) - y = 1$$
$$24 - 6y - y = 1$$
$$24 - 7y = 1$$
$$-7y = -23$$
$$y = \frac{-23}{-7} = \frac{23}{7}$$

3. Substitute back to find x:

$$x = 8 - 2 \cdot \frac{23}{7}$$
$$x = 8 - \frac{46}{7} = \frac{56}{7} - \frac{46}{7} = \frac{10}{7}$$

So, the solution is: $\left(\frac{10}{7}, \frac{23}{7}\right)$.

2. Elimination Method: This method involves adding or subtracting the equations after multiplying one or both by suitable factors to cancel out one of the variables.

Example: Solve the following system:

$$2x + 3y = 11 \quad (1)$$
$$4x - y = 5 \quad (2)$$

Solution:

1. Multiply equation (2) by 3 to match the coefficients of y in equation (1):

$$3(4x - y) = 3(5)$$
$$12x - 3y = 15$$

2. Add equations (1) and the transformed (2) to eliminate y:

$$(2x + 3y) + (12x - 3y) = 11 + 15$$
$$14x = 26$$
$$x = \frac{26}{14} = \frac{13}{7}$$

3. Substitute $x = \frac{13}{7}$ into equation (1) to find y:

$$2 \cdot \frac{13}{7} + 3y = 11$$
$$\frac{26}{7} + 3y = 11$$
$$3y = 11 - \frac{26}{7} = \frac{77}{7} - \frac{26}{7} = \frac{51}{7}$$
$$y = \frac{\frac{51}{7}}{3} = \frac{51}{21} = \frac{17}{7}$$

So, the solution is: $\left(\frac{13}{7}, \frac{17}{7}\right)$.

QUADRATIC EQUATIONS

Quadratic equations are characterized by their standard form $ax^2 + bx + c = 0$, where a, b, and c are coefficients and $a \neq 0$. These equations often appear in various scientific, engineering, and mathematical contexts, representing parabolic shapes when graphed. This section introduces methods to solve quadratic equations, including factoring, using the quadratic formula, and completing the square.

Method 1: Factoring

Factoring involves expressing the quadratic equation in a product form $(px + q)(rx + s) = 0$, where p, q, r, and s are numbers that satisfy the equation. This method works best when the quadratic can be easily decomposed into factors.

Steps:

1. **Write the equation in standard form**: Ensure the equation is in the form $ax^2 + bx + c = 0$.

2. **Factor the quadratic**: Look for two numbers that multiply to ac (the product of the coefficient of x^2 and the constant term) and add up to b (the coefficient of x). Break down the middle term using the identified pairs and factor by grouping.

3. **Set each factor to zero**: Solve $px + q = 0$ and $rx + s = 0$ for x.

Example: Solve $x^2 - 5x + 6 = 0$ by factoring.

Solution:

1. Factor pairs of 6 that add up to -5 are -2 and -3.

2. Factor the quadratic: $(x - 2)(x - 3) = 0$.

3. Set each factor to zero: $x - 2 = 0$ or $x - 3 = 0$, so $x = 2$ or $x = 3$.

Method 2: Quadratic Formula

The quadratic formula is a universal method that can solve any quadratic equation, regardless of its coefficients. The formula is derived from the process of completing the square.

Formula:

$$x = \frac{-b \pm \sqrt{b^2 - 4ac}}{2a}$$

Steps:

1. **Identify coefficients a, b, and c.**

2. **Substitute into the quadratic formula**: Plug the values of a, b, and c into the formula.

3. **Calculate the discriminant**: $b2 - 4ac$. The nature of the roots depends on the discriminant (real and distinct, real and equal, or complex).

4. **Solve for x**: Compute the values using plus and minus versions of the formula.

Example: Solve $2x^2 - 4x - 6 = 0$ using the quadratic formula.

Solution:

1. Substitute $a = 2, b = -4, c = -6$ into the formula.

2. Compute the discriminant: $(-4)^2 - 4 \times 2 \times (-6) = 16 + 48 = 64$.

3. Solve for x: $x = \frac{-(-4) \pm \sqrt{64}}{2 \times 2} = \frac{4 \pm 8}{4}$. So, $x = 3$ or $x = -1$.

Method 3: Completing the Square

Completing the square involves rewriting the quadratic equation in a way that it forms a perfect square trinomial $(dx + e)^2 + f = 0$, which can then be solved by taking square roots.

Solution:

1. **Isolate the quadratic and linear terms**: Move the constant term to the other side of the equation.

2. **Divide through by** a if $a \neq 1$.

3. **Complete the square**: Add and subtract the square of half the coefficient of x inside the equation.

4. **Factor and solve for** x.

Example: Solve $x^2 - 6x + 5 = 0$ by completing the square.

Solution:

1. Move the constant term: $x^2 - 6x = -5$.

2. Half the coefficient of x is -3, square it to get 9, add and subtract 9: $x^2 - 6x + 9 = 4$.

3. Factor and solve: $(x - 3)^2 = 4$, so $x - 3 = \pm 2$, thus $x = 5$ or $x = 1$.

Which Method to Choose

Choosing the right method to solve a quadratic equation—whether to factor, complete the square, or use the quadratic formula—depends largely on the equation's complexity and the specific coefficients involved.

Factoring is the fastest and most straightforward for equations with simple, small integer coefficients and obvious roots. However, not all quadratics neatly factor, especially those with large or complex coefficients. In these cases, completing the square can be useful for deriving the vertex form and understanding the equation's geometric properties, although it can be algebraically demanding.

The quadratic formula is the most universally applicable method, capable of solving any quadratic equation, but it can be computationally intensive.

Simplifying complex quadratic equations is always a good idea before attempting to solve it. Steps such as factoring out the greatest common divisor, rationalizing fractions, or methodically testing factor combinations can make solving the equation easier regardless of the chosen method.

SETTING UP ALGEBRA WORD PROBLEMS

ASVAB algebra word problems require translating real-world situations into mathematical expressions and equations. Understanding how to identify key information and represent it mathematically is crucial to solving them effectively.

Steps to Set Up and Solve Algebra Word Problems

1. Read and Understand the Problem: Identify the important information given in the problem and determine the unknowns to be found.

2. Assign Variables to the Unknowns: Choose symbols, typically letters like x, y, etc., to represent unknown quantities.

3. Write an Equation or System of Equations: Translate the relationships and conditions described in the word problem into mathematical expressions or equations. Ensure that each equation accurately represents the conditions in the problem.

4. Solve the Equation(s): Use algebraic methods like substitution or elimination (for systems) to find the value(s) of the unknown variable(s).

5. Interpret and Verify: Interpret the solution back into the context of the problem to ensure it makes sense. Verify by substituting back into the original equations if necessary.

Translating English Sentences into Math Equations

Different phrases and words can hint at mathematical operations. Here are some common phrases and their mathematical equivalents:

- Addition: "Sum of," "more than," "increased by," "plus."

  Example: "Five more than x" translates to $x + 5$.

- Subtraction: "Difference," "less than," "decreased by," "minus."

  Example: "Ten less than x" translates to $x - 10$.

- Multiplication: "Product of," "times," "of."

  Example: "Twice x" translates to $2x$.

- Division: "Quotient of," "divided by," "per."

  Example: "Half of x" translates to $\frac{x}{2}$.

- Equals: "Is," "are," "will be," "gives."

  Example: "The result is ten" translates to $= 10$.

Example 1— Setting Up a Proportion Problem: A juice recipe requires 4 oranges to make 500 ml of juice. If you need to make 750 ml of juice, how many oranges do you need?

Solution: Assign Variables: Let x represent the number of oranges needed to make 750 ml of juice.

1. Write the Proportion: Set up a ratio comparing oranges to juice in the original recipe: $\frac{4}{500}$

2. Set up a similar ratio for the desired quantity: $\frac{x}{750}$

3. Create an Equation: Establish the proportion by setting the two ratios equal:

$$\frac{4}{500} = \frac{x}{750}$$
$$4 \cdot 750 = 500 \cdot x$$
$$3000 = 500x$$
$$x = \frac{3000}{500} = 6$$

4. Interpret the Solution: You will need 6 oranges to make 750 ml of juice.

Example 2— Setting Up an Equation with One Unknown: In five years, John will be twice as old as he was three years ago. How old is John now?

Solution: Assign Variables: Let x represent John's current age.

1. Write an Equation: In five years, John's age will be $x + 5$. Three years ago, John's age was $x - 3$.

2. The problem says that in five years, John will be twice as old as he was three years ago. Therefore, the equation becomes:

$$x + 5 = 2(x - 3)$$
$$x + 5 = 2x - 6$$
$$5 = 2x - x - 6$$
$$5 = x - 6$$
$$x = 5 + 6 = 11$$

3. Interpret the Solution: John is currently 11 years old.

Example 3— Setting Up Systems of Equations: Sarah is twice as old as Jane. Five years ago, Sarah was three times as old as Jane was. How old are Sarah and Jane now?

Solution: Assign Variables: Let x represent Sarah's current age. Let y represent Jane's current age.

1. Write Equations: From "Sarah is twice as old as Jane," the equation becomes: $x = 2y$.

    From "Five years ago, Sarah was three times as old as Jane," the equation becomes:

$$x - 5 = 3(y - 5)$$

2. Solve the System: Substitute $x = 2y$ into the second equation:

$$2y - 5 = 3(y - 5)$$
$$2y - 5 = 3y - 15$$
$$2y - 3y = -15 + 5$$
$$-y = -10$$
$$y = 10$$

3. Find x by substituting back into the equation $x = 2y$:

$$x = 2 \cdot 10 = 20$$

4. Interpret the Solution: Sarah is 20 years old, and Jane is 10 years old.

5. Verify: Five years ago, Sarah was $20 - 5 = 15$ and Jane was $10 - 5 = 5$. Thus, Sarah was three times as old as Jane five years ago, confirming the solution is correct.

LINEAR APPLICATIONS AND GRAPHS

Linear equations can be used to model relationships between two variables in many real-life situations. When graphed, these relationships form straight lines, and their general form is:
$y = mx + c$, where y is the dependent variable, x is the independent variable, m is the slope (rate of change), and c is the y-intercept (the value of y when $x = 0$).

Here, it's crucial to distinguish between the input variable (often represented as x) and the output variable (often represented as y). Here's a clear understanding of each:

Input Variable (x): The input variable is the independent variable in a function or equation. It represents the values you can freely choose or manipulate. For instance, in a business context, x might represent the number of products manufactured. In science, x could represent time.

In a function $y = f(x)$, x is the value provided to the function.

Output Variable (y): The output variable is the dependent variable in a function or equation. Its value depends on the input variable and the relationship defined by the function or equation. For instance, in business, y might represent the total revenue earned. In science, y could represent the distance traveled after a certain period.

In the function $y = f(x)$, y is the value calculated after plugging in the input x.

Example—Travel Distance and Speed: Suppose you're driving a car at a constant speed of 60 mph (miles per hour). The distance (y) traveled depends on the amount of time (x) spent driving. The relationship between distance and time can be expressed using the equation: $y = 60x$.

- **Input (x):** This represents the amount of time (in hours) spent driving.

- **Output (y):** This represents the total distance traveled in miles.

For example: If you drive for 4 hours ($x = 4$), the distance traveled (y) is: $y = 60 \cdot 4 = 240$.

So, the output variable y (distance traveled) is 240 miles after driving for 4 hours at a speed of 60 mph. This example illustrates how the input (x representing time) directly influences the output (y representing distance traveled) based on a linear relationship.

Such a linear relationship between speed and travel distance can also be illustrated in a graph, as shown here.

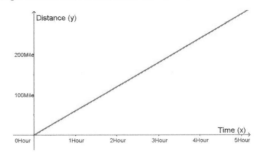

Linear Functions: Slope-Intercept Form ($y = mx + c$)

In linear equation $y = mx + c$, y is the output or dependent variable, x is the input or independent variable, m is the slope, which represents the rate of change, and c is the y-intercept, the value of y when $x = 0$. Let's examine the concept of slope and intercept further.

Slope (m): The slope is the ratio of the vertical change (rise) to the horizontal change (run) between two points on a line. A positive slope means the line is increasing, while a negative slope means the line is decreasing. If the slope is zero, the line is horizontal (constant function).

Intercept (c): The y-intercept is the point where the line crosses the y-axis, representing the value of y when $x = 0$.

Example—Continuing the Travel Example with an Intercept: In the previous travel example, we assumed that the starting point is zero miles (no intercept). However, let's consider that the car has already traveled 30 miles before starting to drive at a constant speed. The equation now changes to: $y = 60x + 30$, where $m = 60mph$ is the speed (slope), $c = 30$ miles is the initial distance already traveled (intercept).

In this case, if you drive for 4 hours ($x = 4$), the total distance traveled (y) is:

$$y = 60 \cdot 4 + 30 = 240 + 30 = 270$$

So, after driving for 4 hours, the total distance covered is 270 miles, including the 30 miles already covered. The relationship between time and distance can also been expressed graphically as follows.

Compare the two figures and one will notice the second one has an intercept while the first one does not.

Graphing Linear Functions

Graphing linear functions involves plotting the relationship between an independent variable (x) and a dependent variable (y) on a two-dimensional plane.

Steps to Graph a Linear Equation

1. Identify the Slope and Intercept: The equation $y = mx + c$ provides the slope (m) and the y-intercept (c). The slope (m) measures the steepness of the line. The intercept (c) indicates the point where the line crosses the y-axis.

2. Plot the Y-Intercept: Mark the point on the y-axis where the line will pass. This is given by the y-intercept (c).

3. Use the Slope to Plot Another Point: The slope m is often written as a fraction $\Delta y / \Delta x$ (change in y over change in x). From the y-intercept, use the slope to find a second point on the graph: Move vertically by Δy (up if positive, down if negative). Move horizontally by Δx (right if positive, left if negative).

4. Draw the Line: Once you have two points, draw a straight line through them to complete the graph.

Example: Graphing the Equation $y = 2x + 3$

1. Identify Slope and Intercept: The slope (m) is 2, which means a vertical change of +2 for every horizontal change of +1. The y-intercept (c) is 3, meaning the line crosses the y-axis at $y = 3$.

2. Plot the Y-Intercept: Mark the point (0,3) on the y-axis.

3. Use the Slope to Find Another Point: Start at (0,3). Move up by 2 units (due to the slope's numerator) and right by 1 unit (due to the slope's denominator), reaching the point (1,5).

4. Draw the Line: Draw a line passing through the points (0,3) and (1,5).

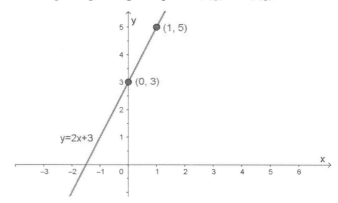

Note that the y-intercept marks the starting point of the line on the y-axis, and the slope controls the line's angle. Since the line will have a positive slope (2), it slants upward from left to right.

Writing Equations in Point-Slope Form

The point-slope form is particularly useful when you have a known point on the line and the slope. The equation in point-slope form is given by: $y - y_1 = m(x - x_1)$, where m is the slope of the line, (x_1, y_1) is a known point on the line.

Steps to Write an Equation in Point-Slope Form

1. Identify the Slope (m) and a Point (x_1, y_1): The slope indicates the rate of change or steepness of the line. A known point on the line helps anchor the line's position.

2. Substitute the Values into the Point-Slope Formula: Plug in the known slope (m) and the coordinates of the known point (x_1, y_1) into the formula.

3. Simplify or Leave in Point-Slope Form: You can either keep the equation in point-slope form or rearrange it to another form like slope-intercept ($y = mx + c$).

Example: Write the equation of a line with a slope of 3 passing through the point $(2, -1)$.

Solution: Identify the Slope (m) and Point (x_1, y_1): $m = 3$, $(x_1, y_1) = (2, -1)$. Substitute into the Formula:

$$y - (-1) = 3(x - 2)$$
$$y + 1 = 3(x - 2)$$

This is the equation of the line in point-slope form. If you prefer, you can convert this to slope-intercept form by expanding and simplifying.

Writing Equations from Two Known Points

When given two points, you can find the equation of the line that passes through them using the slope formula and the point-slope form. Here's a step-by-step process:

Steps to Write a Linear Equation from Two Known Points

1. Find the Slope (m): Use the slope formula to calculate the slope between the two points: $m = \frac{y_2 - y_1}{x_2 - x_1}$. This formula calculates the rate of change between the two given points, (x_1, y_1) and (x_2, y_2).

2. Substitute the Slope and One Point into Point-Slope Form: $y - y_1 = m(x - x_1)$

3. Simplify or Convert to Slope-Intercept Form: You can keep the equation in point-slope form or convert it to slope-intercept form $(y = mx + c)$ by expanding and simplifying.

Example: Find the equation of the line that passes through the points $(1,2)$ and $(3,-4)$.

Solution:

1. Calculate the Slope: $m = \frac{-4-2}{3-1} = \frac{-6}{2} = -3$

2. Substitute into Point-Slope Form: Use the point-slope form formula
   $y - y_1 = m(x - x_1)$ with $m = -3$ and the point $(1,2)$: $y - 2 = -3(x - 1)$

3. Simplify: Expand and simplify to convert to slope-intercept form:

$$y - 2 = -3x + 3$$
$$y = -3x + 5$$

This equation in slope-intercept form $(y = -3x + 5)$ is the equation of the line that passes through the points $(1,2)$ and $(3,-4)$.

Parallel and Perpendicular Lines

In a two-dimensional coordinate system, lines can be parallel or perpendicular to each other based on the relationship of their slopes.

Parallel Lines

Parallel lines have the same slope but different y-intercepts. If two lines have the same slope (m), they are parallel and never intersect.

Example: Suppose the equation of an existing line is: $y = 4x + 2$. Any line parallel to this one will have the same slope, $m = 4$, but a different y-intercept (c).

Examples of a parallel lines include: $y = 4x - 3$, $y = 4x + 18$, $y = 4x - \frac{11}{17}$

Perpendicular Lines

Perpendicular lines intersect at right angles (90°). If the slope of one line is m, then the slope of any line perpendicular to it is the negative reciprocal, $-\frac{1}{m}$.

Example 1: Suppose the equation of an existing line is: $y = \frac{3}{4}x + 5$. The slope of this line is $m = \frac{3}{4}$. The slope of any line perpendicular to it will be the negative reciprocal: $m_\perp = -\frac{4}{3}$.

An example of a perpendicular line equation (using slope $m_\perp$ and an arbitrary y-intercept):

$$y = -\frac{4}{3}x + 1$$

By analyzing or adjusting the slopes of linear equations, you can quickly determine if lines are parallel or perpendicular to each other.

Example 2: Find a line that is perpendicular to the equation $y = 2x + 3$ and passes through the point $(1, 5)$.

Solution:

1. Identify the Slope of the Given Line: The given line is: $y = 2x + 3$. The slope (m) is 2.

2. Find the Perpendicular Slope: The slope of a line perpendicular to this one is the negative reciprocal. If the original slope is m=2, the perpendicular slope $(m_\perp)$ is:
$$m_\perp = -0.5$$

3. Use the Point-Slope Formula: We'll use the point-slope formula to find the equation of the perpendicular line: $y - y_1 = m(x - x_1)$. Here, $(x_1, y_1) = (1,5)$ and $m = -0.5$.

    Substitute into the Point-Slope Formula: $y - 5 = -0.5(x - 1)$

4. Simplify the Equation:

$$y - 5 = -0.5x + 0.5$$
$$y = -0.5x + 5.5$$

Hence, the equation of the line perpendicular to the equation $y = 2x + 3$ and passes through the point $(1, 5)$ is: $y = -0.5x + 5.5$.

§3. Geometric and Spatial Reasoning

In the ASVAB Mathematics Test, you won't need to tackle geometric proofs, and the exam only covers a well-defined list of practical geometry topics, which we will cover below.

Perimeter, Circumference, Area, and Volume

The perimeter and circumference formula of common geometric shapes is summarized in the following table. The ASVAB test will usually give you the needed formula except the simplest.

Shape	Formula	Description
Rectangle	Perimeter of a rectangle $P = 2(l + w)$	l and w are length and width
Square	Perimeter of a square $P = 4s$	s is the length of one side
Triangle	Perimeter of a triangle $P = a + b + c$	a, b, c are the length of the three sides
Circle	Circumference of a circle $C = 2\pi r$ (or $C = \pi d$)	r is the radius, d is the diameter

Area

Here's a table summarizing the formulas for calculating the area of common geometric shapes.

Shape	Formula	Description
Triangle	$A = \dfrac{1}{2} bh$	b is the base, h is the height
Square	$A = s^2$	s is the length of one side
Rectangle	$A = lw$	l and w are the length and width
Parallelogram	$A = bh$	b is the base, h is the height
Trapezoid	$A = \dfrac{1}{2}(a + b)h$	a and b are the bases, h is the height
Circle	$A = \pi r^2$	r is the radius

Volume

Here's a table summarizing the formulas for calculating the volume of common geometric shapes.

Shape	Formula	Description
Rectangular Prism	$V = lwh$	$l, w,$ and h are the length, width, and height of the prism
Right Cylinder	$V = \pi r^2 h$	r is the radius of the base, h is the height of the cylinder
Sphere	$V = \dfrac{4}{3}\pi r^3$	r is the radius of the sphere

PYTHAGOREAN THEOREM

The Pythagorean Theorem is a fundamental principle in geometry that relates the lengths of the sides of a right triangle.

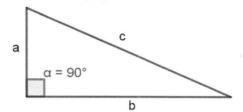

According to the theorem, the square of the length of the hypotenuse (the side opposite the right angle) is equal to the sum of the squares of the lengths of the other two sides. This relationship is usually expressed with the formula:

$$c^2 = a^2 + b^2$$

Here, c represents the length of the hypotenuse, and a and b represent the lengths of the other two sides. The Pythagorean Theorem is frequently used in trigonometry to solve problems involving right triangles. Let's go through a couple of examples where we apply the Pythagorean Theorem.

Example 1—Finding the Hypotenuse: Suppose you have a right triangle with legs of lengths 3 cm and 4 cm. You want to find the length of the hypotenuse.

According to the Pythagorean Theorem: $c^2 = a^2 + b^2$

Plugging in the values:

$$c^2 = 3^2 + 4^2$$
$$c^2 = 9 + 16$$
$$c^2 = 25$$
$$c = \sqrt{25}$$
$$c = 5\ cm$$

So, the hypotenuse is 5 cm long.

Example 2—Finding a Leg of the Triangle: Imagine you know the hypotenuse of a right triangle is 10 cm and one of the legs is 8 cm. You need to find the length of the other leg.

Using the Pythagorean Theorem: $c^2 = a^2 + b^2$

Let b be the unknown side, and rearrange the equation: $b^2 = c^2 - a^2$

Substitute the known values:

$$b^2 = 10^2 - 8^2$$
$$b^2 = 100 - 64$$
$$b^2 = 36$$
$$b = 6\ \text{cm}$$

The unknown leg measures 6 cm.

DISTANCE FORMULA

The distance formula is used to calculate the distance between two points in a coordinate system. It is derived from the Pythagorean Theorem, which we just discussed. The formula provides the distance between two points (x_1, y_1) and (x_2, y_2) in a 2-dimensional Cartesian plane. The distance d between two points (x_1, y_1) and (x_2, y_2) is given by:

$$d = \sqrt{(x_2 - x_1)^2 + (y_2 - y_1)^2}$$

The expression $(x_2 - x_1)^2 + (y_2 - y_1)^2$ calculates the sum of the squares of the differences in the x and y coordinates. This is analogous to finding the square of the lengths of the two legs in a right triangle, where the line segment between the two points forms the hypotenuse.

Example: Calculating Distance Between Two Points

Let's calculate the distance between two points, $A(1,2)$ and $B(4,6)$.

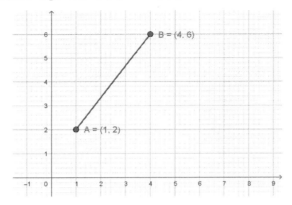

Using the distance formula:

$$d = \sqrt{(x_2 - x_1)^2 + (y_2 - y_1)^2}$$

Plugging in the coordinates:

$$d = \sqrt{(4-1)^2 + (6-2)^2}$$
$$d = \sqrt{3^2 + 4^2}$$
$$d = \sqrt{9 + 16}$$
$$d = \sqrt{25}$$
$$d = 5 \text{ units}$$

Thus, the distance between points A and B is 5 units.

INTERSECTING LINE THEOREMS

Intersecting lines create a variety of angles and geometric relationships that are governed by several theorems. Here's an overview:

Vertical Angles Theorem

If two lines intersect, then the vertical angles are congruent.

Example:

Given lines AB and CD intersecting at point E:

$$\angle AEC = \angle BED$$

$$\angle AED = \angle BEC$$

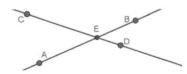

Linear Pair Theorem

If two angles form a linear pair, then they are supplementary (their measures add up to 180°).

Example:

Given lines AB and CD intersecting at point E:

$$\angle AEC + \angle CEB = 180°$$

$$\angle AED + \angle DEB = 180°$$

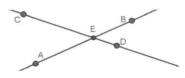

Corresponding Angles Postulate (with Parallel Lines)

If a transversal intersects two parallel lines, then each pair of corresponding angles is congruent.

Example:

Given parallel lines AB and CD intersected by transversal EF :

$$\angle AEF \cong \angle CDF$$

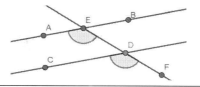

Alternate Interior Angles Theorem (with Parallel Lines)

If a transversal intersects two parallel lines, then each pair of alternate interior angles is congruent.

Example:

Given parallel lines AB and CD intersected by transversal EF :

$$\angle BED \cong \angle CDE$$

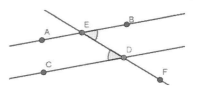

Same-Side Interior Angles Theorem (with Parallel Lines)

If a transversal intersects two parallel lines, then each pair of same-side interior angles is supplementary.

Example:

Given parallel lines AB and CD intersected by transversal EF :

$$\angle AEF + \angle CDE = 180°$$

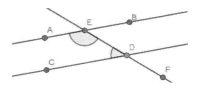

Alternate Exterior Angles Theorem (with Parallel Lines)

If a transversal intersects two parallel lines, then each pair of alternate exterior angles is congruent.

Example:

Given parallel lines AB and CD intersected by transversal EF :

$$\angle ABE \cong \angle DCF$$

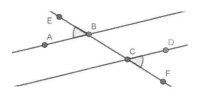

Now, let's put to these theorems to use in the following example.

Example: Given MN and ST are parallel lines, and $\angle a = 30°$, find all the rest of the angles.

Solution:

Step 1: Identify the Vertical Angles

The vertical angle opposite $\angle a$ is $\angle c$ Hence, $\angle c = \angle a = 30°$.

Step 2: Identify the Linear Pairs

Angles a and d form a linear pair, so they add up to 180°.

$$\angle d = 180° - \angle a = 180 - 30° = 150°$$

Since b and d are vertical angles: $\angle b = \angle d = 150°$

Step 3: Identify the Corresponding Angles

Since MN and ST are parallel, $\angle a$ corresponds to $\angle h$. Hence, $\angle h = \angle a = 30°$.

Similarly, $\angle d$ corresponds to $\angle g$. Hence, $\angle g = \angle d = 150°$.

$\angle e$ corresponds to $\angle b$ Hence, $\angle e = \angle b = 150°$.

$\angle f$ corresponds to $\angle c$ Hence, $\angle f = \angle c = 30°$.

Example: Given angle $\angle a = 36°$, find $\angle \theta$

Solution:

From the diagram:

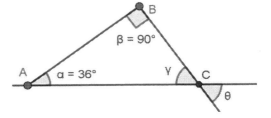

1. Identify Angles in Triangle $\triangle ABC$: $\alpha = 36°, \beta = 90°$.

2. Triangle Sum Theorem: The sum of the angles in a triangle is $180°$.

$$\alpha + \beta + \gamma = 180°$$
$$36° + 90° + \gamma = 180°$$
$$\gamma = 180° - 36° - 90°$$
$$\gamma = 54°$$

3. Find $\angle \theta$: since $\angle \theta$ and $\angle \gamma$ are vertical angles. $\angle \theta = \angle \gamma = 54°$.

TRIANGLE CONGRUENCY THEOREMS

Triangle congruency describes a condition where two triangles are exactly identical in shape and size. Two triangles are congruent if all their corresponding sides are equal in length and all their corresponding angles are equal in measure. When two triangles are congruent, they can be perfectly overlaid on each other, with every corresponding side and angle matching precisely.

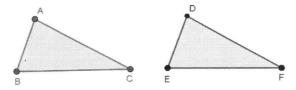

If two triangles $\triangle ABC$ and $\triangle DEF$ are congruent, this relationship is denoted as:
$\triangle ABC \cong \triangle DEF$. This means that $AB = DE$, $BC = EF$, $CA = FD$ and $\angle A = \angle D, \angle B = \angle E, \angle C = \angle F$.

SSS (Side-Side-Side) Congruency

Two triangles are congruent if all three sides of one triangle are equal to all three sides of another triangle. This is known as the SSS congruency criterion.

If $AB = DE$, $BC = EF$, $CA = FD$, then $\triangle ABC \cong \triangle DEF$.

SAS (Side-Angle-Side) Congruency

Two triangles are congruent if two sides and the included angle of one triangle are equal to two sides and the included angle of another triangle. This is known as the SAS congruency criterion.

If $AB = DE$, $AC = DF$, $\angle A = \angle D$, then $\triangle ABC \cong \triangle DEF$.

ASA (Angle-Side-Angle) Congruency

Two triangles are congruent if two angles and the included side of one triangle are equal to two angles and the included side of another triangle. This is known as the ASA congruency criterion.

If $\angle A = \angle D$, $\angle B = \angle E$, $AB = DE$, then $\triangle ABC \cong \triangle DEF$.

AAS (Angle-Angle-Side) Congruency

Two triangles are congruent if two angles and a non-included side of one triangle are equal to two angles and the corresponding non-included side of another triangle. This is known as the AAS congruency criterion.

If $\angle A = \angle D$, $\angle B = \angle E$, $BC = EF$, then $\triangle ABC \cong \triangle DEF$.

HL (Hypotenuse-Leg) Congruency (Right Triangles Only)

Two right triangles are congruent if the hypotenuse and one leg of one triangle are equal to the hypotenuse and one leg of another triangle. This is known as the HL congruency criterion.

If $AC = DF$, $BC = EF$, and $\angle C = \angle F = 90°$, then $\triangle ABC \cong \triangle DEF$.

SSA (Side-Side-Angle) ≠ Congruency

There is one side and angle combination that does not prove triangle congruency: SSA. The SSA (Side-Side-Angle) condition fails to prove that a pair of triangles are congruent due to the possibility of multiple non-congruent triangles satisfying this condition. To understand why, let's look at the following scenario:

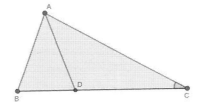

Consider triangles $\triangle ABC$ and $\triangle ACD$ as shown in the figure. Clearly, triangles $\triangle ABC$ and $\triangle ACD$ are not congruent. In fact, $\triangle ABC$ includes all of $\triangle ACD$ and then some. However, the two triangles share the same angle $\angle C$ and the same side AC. Also, they have one side where the length is equal: $AB = AD$.

The key here is the two sides that $\triangle ABC$ and $\triangle BCD$ have the same length ($AB = AD$, $AC = AC$) don't inscribe their shared angle, $\angle C$, leading to a SSA situation. If the two congruent sides inscribe the angle of equal value, leading to a SAS situation, then the two triangles will be congruent without any ambiguity.

AAA (Angle-Angle-Angle) ≠ Congruency

This should be self-evident. Two triangles with all three angles being equal can differ greatly in size. So, AAA does not necessarily guarantee two triangles are congruent.

Here is a tip on how to remember these theorems and exceptions: ALL combinations of three elements of A and S, be it AAS, ASA, SSA, SSS, will prove congruency, except AAA, and SSA. It is easy to remember AAA does not prove congruency—again, it is self-evident.

As for remembering SSA, the author has always remembered it as ASS instead. Should you associate it with anything other than a donkey though, it is on you, not me. The author's innocence is proven by a poem he wrote for this situation:

> Two asses live on a farm,
>
> Both tan and both tame.
>
> One is healthy and one is lame,
>
> Two asses are NOT always the same!

TRIANGLE SIMILARITY THEOREMS

Triangle similarity describes a condition where two triangles have the same shape but not necessarily the same size. Two triangles are similar if their corresponding angles are equal, and their corresponding sides are proportional. This means that one triangle can be obtained from the other by scaling (enlarging or reducing), possibly followed by a translation, rotation, or reflection.

If two triangles $\triangle ABC$ and $\triangle DEF$ are similar, this relationship is denoted as: $\triangle ABC \sim \triangle DEF$, which means that $\angle A = \angle D$, $\angle B = \angle E$, $\angle C = \angle F$ and $\frac{AB}{DE} = \frac{BC}{EF} = \frac{CA}{FD}$.

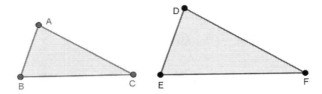

AA (Angle-Angle) Similarity

Two triangles are similar if two angles of one triangle are congruent to two angles of the other triangle. This is known as the AA similarity criterion. When two triangles are similar, their corresponding sides are proportional, and their corresponding angles are equal.

If $\angle A = \angle D$ and $\angle B = \angle E$, then $\triangle ABC \sim \triangle DEF$.

SSS (Side-Side-Side) Similarity

Two triangles are similar if the corresponding sides of one triangle are proportional to the corresponding sides of the other triangle. This is known as the SSS similarity criterion.

If $\frac{AB}{DE} = \frac{BC}{EF} = \frac{CA}{FD}$, then $\triangle ABC \sim \triangle DEF$.

SAS (Side-Angle-Side) Similarity

Two triangles are similar if one angle of one triangle is congruent to one angle of the other triangle, and the lengths of the sides inscribing these angles are proportional. This is known as the SAS similarity criterion.

If $\frac{AB}{DE} = \frac{AC}{DF}$ and $\angle A = \angle D$, then $\triangle ABC \sim \triangle DEF$.

TRIANGLE CONGRUENCY AND SIMILARITY QUESTIONS

On the ASVAB Test, some questions may ask you to prove that a pair of triangles are congruent. These questions typically require you to be familiar with the four congruency theorems and apply them to the question to establish triangle congruency.

Example 1: For triangle ABC and triangle DEF, if $\angle A$ is congruent to $\angle D$, which of the following must be true in order to prove that triangles ABC and DEF are congruent?

A. $\angle B = \angle E$ and $AC = DF$

B. $BC = EF$ and $DF = AC$

C. $AB = DE$ and $BC = EF$

D. $\angle C = \angle F$ and $\angle B = \angle E$

Answer: A

Explanation: Triangles are congruent if they meet the SSS, SAS, AAS, or ASA criterion. Here, choice A will satisfy AAS, so it is correct. Choice B and C constitute SSA situation, choice D constitutes AAA situation. Hence, B, C, and D are not correct answers.

Other ASVAB questions give you some choices and may ask you to identify a pair of similar triangles. This type of question often involves some calculation, such as creating and solving a proportion, before you can decide.

Example 2: Triangle ABC and triangle DEF are shown below. If $\angle A$ is congruent to $\angle D$ and $AC = 4, DE = 3, DF = 6$, which of the following must be true for triangles ABC and DEF to be similar?

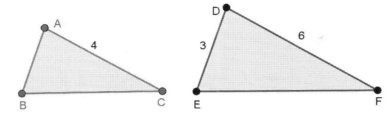

A. $AB = 1.5$

B. $AB = 2$

C. $AB = 2.5$

D. $AB = 3$

Answer: B

Explanation: Two triangles are similar if one angle of one triangle is congruent to one angle of the other triangle, and the lengths of the sides inscribing these angles are proportional. This is known as the SAS similarity criterion. So, to have $\triangle ABC \sim \triangle DEF$, it must be true that: $\frac{AB}{DE} = \frac{AC}{DF}$ and $\angle A = \angle D$. Thus, $\frac{AB}{3} = \frac{4}{6} \Rightarrow AB = \frac{3 \times 4}{6} = 2$.

Hence, B is the right choice.

§4. PROBABILISTIC AND STATISTICAL REASONING

Probability is a measure of how likely an event is to occur. It's a value between 0 and 1, where 0 means the event will not happen, and 1 means it will definitely happen. For example, if you toss a coin, the probability of it landing on heads is 0.5, meaning there's a 50% chance of it happening.

Key Probability Terms

- **Experiment:** A procedure that results in one or more outcomes. Tossing a coin is an example of an experiment.

- **Outcome:** A possible result of an experiment. For example, "heads" is an outcome of tossing a coin.

- **Sample Space:** The set of all possible outcomes. For example, for a coin toss, the sample space is {Heads,Tails}.

- **Event:** A subset of the sample space, representing one or more outcomes that we're interested in. If we're only interested in getting "heads," that outcome is an event.

CALCULATING PROBABILITY

Simple Probability: Simple probability refers to the likelihood of a single event occurring.

Formula: The probability of an event E is:

$$P(E) = \frac{Number\ of\ favorable\ outcomes}{Total\ number\ of\ possible\ outcomes}$$

Example: If you roll a six-sided die, the probability of rolling a 4 is:

$$P(Rolling\ a\ 4) = \frac{1}{6}$$

Compound Probability: Compound probability involves finding the likelihood of two or more events occurring together. For independent events (events that don't affect each other), multiply their probabilities to get Compound Probability.

Example: If you roll a die and flip a coin, the probability of rolling a 3 <u>and</u> flipping heads is:

$$P(Rolling\ a\ 3) \cdot P(Flipping\ Heads) = \frac{1}{6} \cdot \frac{1}{2} = \frac{1}{12}$$

Conditional Probability: Conditional probability is the likelihood of an event occurring given that another event has already happened.

Example: If 80% of students in a class pass math and 60% of those who pass also pass science, the probability of a student passing science given that they passed math is:

$$P(\ Pass\ Science\ |\ Pass\ Math\ ) = \frac{0.6}{0.8} = 0.75$$

Table-Based Probability Questions

On ASVAB, probability questions are sometimes based on facts presented in a table. So, let's use the following example to review the three types of probabilities.

Example: Let's consider a table summarizing the distribution of animals in a nature reserve based on two traits: whether they are mammals or reptiles and whether they are nocturnal or diurnal.

Table of Animal Distribution

	Nocturnal	Diurnal	**Total**
Mammal	15	30	45
Reptile	10	25	35
Total	**25**	**55**	**80**

Simple Probability: Find the probability that a randomly chosen animal is nocturnal.

From the table, 25 animals are nocturnal out of a total of 80.

$$P(Nocturnal) = \frac{25}{80} = 0.3125$$

Compound Probability: Find the probability that a randomly chosen animal is both a mammal and nocturnal.

From the table, 15 animals are both mammals and nocturnal.

$$P(Mammal\ and\ Nocturnal) = \frac{15}{80} = 0.1875$$

Conditional Probability: Find the probability that an animal is a reptile given that it is diurnal.

From the table, 25 out of the 55 diurnal animals are reptiles.

$$P(Reptile \mid Diurnal) = \frac{25}{55} \approx 0.455$$

DESCRIPTIVE STATISTICS

Descriptive statistics involve methods for summarizing and organizing data, providing simple insights into the patterns and characteristics of a dataset. Instead of analyzing every individual data point, descriptive statistics condense information into meaningful measures to help understand trends, variability, and distribution.

Measures of Central Tendency

Mean, median, and mode are measures of central tendency, used to describe the central point or typical value within a dataset. Each measure provides different insights into the nature of the data.

Mean (Average): The mean is the sum of all data values divided by the total number of values. It is influenced by every value in the dataset.

$$\text{mean} = \frac{x_1 + x_2 + \cdots + x_n}{n}$$

where:

- $x_1, x_2, \ldots, x_n$ are the data values,

- n is the number of data points.

Example: Given the dataset {3,5,7,8,10}, what is the mean?

Solution: mean $= \frac{3+5+7+8+10}{5} = \frac{33}{5} = 6.6$

Median: The median is the middle value when all data values are arranged in ascending or descending order. If the number of data points is even, the median is the average of the two middle values.

Example: Given the dataset {3,5,7,8,10}, the median value is 7 because it is the third value in a dataset with five numbers.

If the dataset were {3,5,7,8}, the median would be: $\frac{5+7}{2} = \frac{12}{2} = 6$.

Mode: The mode is the most frequently occurring value(s) in a dataset. There can be one mode (unimodal), more than one mode (bimodal or multimodal), or no mode if no value repeats.

Example: Given the dataset {3,5,5,8,10}, the mode is 5 because it occurs most frequently (twice). If the dataset were {3,3,5,5,8,10}, the mode would be both 3 and 5, making the dataset bimodal.

Measures of Dispersion (Spread)

The range of data helps describe the spread of values within a dataset. Here are some basic concepts:

Maximum (Max): The maximum is the largest value in a dataset.

Example: In the dataset {2,4,6,8,10}, the maximum value is: Max = 10.

Minimum (Min): The minimum is the smallest value in a dataset.

Example: In the dataset {2,4,6,8,10}, the minimum value is: Min = 2.

Range: The range is the difference between the maximum and minimum values in a dataset.

Range = Max − Min

Example: In the dataset {2,4,6,8,10}: Range = 10 − 2 = 8

Quantile: A quantile divides the data into intervals containing an equal number of data points.

Common quantiles include:

- Quartile: Divides data into four equal parts.
- Percentile: Divides data into 100 equal parts.

Example: Given the dataset {3,5,7,9,11,13,15}, let's find the first quartile (Q_1) and the third quartile (Q_3).

Solution: The following table illustrates how we analyze the data.

3	5	7	9	11	13	15
Minimum	First Quartile		Median		Third Quartile	Maximum

←———————— Lower half ————————→ ←———— Upper half ————————→

Hence, $Q_1 = 5$, $Q_3 = 13$.

In this example, the first quartile (Q_1) marks the value below which 25% of the data falls, and the third quartile (Q_3) marks the value below which 75% of the data falls. Together, these measures provide insight into the data's spread and distribution, helping identify potential outliers and the overall range of values.

Visual Representations

Graphical displays offer a visual way to analyze and interpret data. They reveal trends, patterns, and outliers that might not be evident through raw numbers alone. Here are three common types of data visualization tools appearing on ASVAB: histograms, box plots, and scatterplots.

Histogram

A histogram is a bar graph that displays the distribution of a dataset. The data is grouped into intervals (bins), and each bar represents the frequency (or count) of values within that interval.

Interpretation:

- **Height of Bars:** Indicates how many data points fall within each interval.
- **Shape:** The shape of the histogram provides insight into the data distribution (e.g., skewed, symmetric).
- **Outliers:** Bars that are separate from the main distribution can indicate outliers.

Example: A histogram depicting the scores of students on a test might show that most scores fall between 70 and 95, with an outlier below 50.

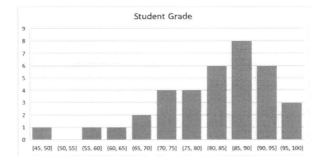

Box Plot (Box-and-Whisker Plot)

Definition: A box plot shows the data distribution by dividing it into quartiles and highlighting the median. It also displays potential outliers using whiskers.

Interpretation:

- **Box:** Represents the interquartile range (IQR) between the first quartile (Q_1) and third quartile (Q_3), which contains the middle 50% of the data.
- **Median Line:** Divides the box into two halves, showing the median of the data.
- **Whiskers:** In the usual convention, they extend from the box to the minimum and maximum values within a specified range.

Example: A box plot showing employee salaries might reveal that the median salary is near $82,000, while outliers earning above $100,000 form a distinct tail.

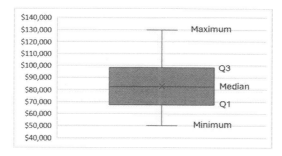

Scatter Plot

Definition: A scatter plot displays data points on a Cartesian plane to illustrate the relationship between two variables.

Interpretation:

- **Trend:** Points that form an upward or downward pattern indicate positive or negative correlations, respectively.
- **Clusters:** Groups of points in different areas may suggest different categories or clusters of data.
- **Outliers:** Points that lie far from the main cluster may represent outliers.

Example: A scatter plot comparing advertising expenditure and sales revenue might reveal that higher ad spending correlates with higher revenue.

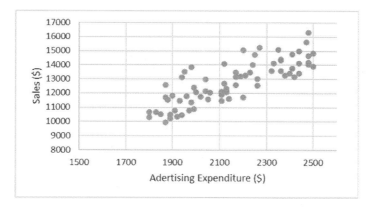

MATHEMATICS KNOWLEDGE PRACTICE SET 1

Time: 31 minutes for 15 questions

Select the correct answer from the choices given. This practice subtest reflects the number of questions and time limits you'll encounter on the CAT-ASVAB Mathematics Knowledge subtest without any tryout questions.

1: $(3 + 5)^2 - 12/3 =$

A) 58
B) 62
C) 60
D) 64

2: What is the difference between 45.678 and 19.234, to the nearest integer?

A) 24
B) 26
C) 27
D) 28

3: 72 is 30% of what number?

A) 210
B) 230
C) 240
D) 220

4: Sara paid $45 for a jacket that was originally priced at $60. By what percent was the jacket discounted?

A) 15%
B) 20%
C) 25%
D) 30%

5: $0.85, \frac{2}{3}$, and 80%.

Which of the following correctly orders these numbers from least to greatest?

A) $\frac{2}{3}, 0.85, 80\%$
B) $80\%, \frac{2}{3}, 0.85$
C) $0.85, 80\%, \frac{2}{3}$
D) $\frac{2}{3}, 80\%, 0.85$

6. Which of the following points (x, y) lies on the graph of $7x + 3y = 26$?

A) (1,3)
B) (2,5)
C) (4,3)
D) (2,4)

7. A cyclist traveled a distance of 45 kilometers in 3 hours. On average, how much distance did the cyclist cover each hour?

A) 12 km
B) 15 km
C) 18 km
D) 20 km

8. A circle has a diameter of 12 meters. What is the area, in square meters, of this circle? (The area of a circle with a radius of r , is equal to πr^2.)

A) 36π
B) 38π
C) 24π
D) 48π

9. The cost of renting a bicycle is $10 per hour. In addition, a flat helmet rental fee of $5 is charged. Which of the following represents the total cost, in dollars, of the bicycle and helmet rental for h hours?

A) $10h + 5$
B) $10h + 15$
C) $15h$
D) $10h - 5$

10. What is the value of $1.5 + 4 \times 3.2 - 10$?

A) 4.8
B) 5.3
C) 4.3
D) 6.3

11. The box plot below summarizes the calories of food a group of lab mice consume per day. What could be the range of these mice's calorie intake per day?

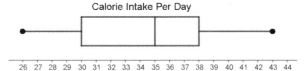

Calorie Intake Per Day

26 27 28 29 30 31 32 33 34 35 36 37 38 39 40 41 42 43 44

A) 14
B) 15
C) 16
D) 17

12. There are 24 books on a shelf. 8 of the books are fiction, and the rest are non-fiction. What is the ratio of fiction books to non-fiction books on the shelf?

A) 1 to 2
B) 1 to 3
C) 1 to 1
D) 2 to 3

13. Which equation represents the line shown?

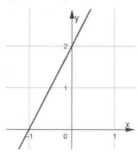

A) $y = -x + 2$
B) $y = x - 1$
C) $y = 2x + 2$
D) $y = 2x - 1$

14. Which of the following is equivalent to $\left(\frac{3}{4}\right)^{-2}$?

A) $\frac{9}{16}$
B) $-\frac{9}{16}$
C) $\frac{16}{9}$
D) $-\frac{16}{9}$

15. $1.25 \div 10^{-3} =$

A) 12.5
B) 125
C) 1250
D) 12500

Practice Set 1 Answers and Explanations

1. C) 60. Explanation: $(3+5)^2 - \frac{12}{3} = 64 - 4 = 60$

2. B) 26. Explanation: $45.678 - 19.234 \approx 26.444 \approx 26$

3. C) 240. Explanation: We know $0.30 \times N = 72$. Hence, $N = \frac{72}{0.30} = 240$.

4. C) 25%. Explanation: $\frac{60-45}{60} \times 100 = \frac{15}{60} \times 100 = 25\%$

5. D) $\frac{2}{3}$, 80%, 0.85. Explanation: Convert Each to Decimals: $\frac{2}{3} \approx 0.6667$, $80\% = 0.80$. Order the Decimals from Least to Greatest: 0.6667, 0.80, 0.85.

6. D) (2,4). Explanation: When faced with such problems, try each pair of solutions in the equation to see if it is true. Here, $7 \times 2 + 3 \times 4 = 14 + 12 = 26$. So D is correct.

7. B) 15 km. Explanation: Total distance = 45 km, Total time = 3 hours. 45/3 = 15.

8. A) 36π. Diameter = 12 meters, thus, Radius = $\frac{\text{Diameter}}{2} = \frac{12}{2} = 6$ meters.

Area = $\pi r^2 = \pi(6)^2 = \pi \times 36 = 36\pi$ square meters.

9. A) $10h + 5$

10. C) 4.3. Explanation: $1.5 + 4 \times 3.2 - 10 = 1.5 + 12.8 - 10 = 1.5 + 2.8 = 4.3$

11. D) 17. Explanation: The range is the difference between the maximum and minimum values in a dataset. Range = Max − Min. So, $43 - 26 = 17$.

12. A) 1 to 2. Explanation: Total books = 24, Fiction books = 8, Non-fiction books = $24 - 8 = 16$. Ratio of fiction books to non-fiction books = $\frac{8}{16} = \frac{1}{2}$.

13. C) $y = 2x + 2$. Explanation: From the graph, the line's slope is 2, while it intersects y-axis at (0,2). So, $y = 2x + 2$.

14. C) $\frac{16}{9}$. Explanation: $\left(\frac{3}{4}\right)^{-2} = \left(\frac{4}{3}\right)^2 = \frac{4^2}{3^2} = \frac{16}{9}$.

15. C) 1250. Explanation: $\frac{1.25}{10^{-3}} = 1.25 \times 10^3 = 1.25 \times 1000 = 1250$.

MATHEMATICS KNOWLEDGE PRACTICE SET 2

Time: 31 minutes for 15 questions

Select the correct answer from the choices given. This practice subtest reflects the number of questions and time limits you'll encounter on the CAT-ASVAB Mathematics Knowledge subtest without any tryout questions.

1. Solve the following problem and choose the best $\frac{9.68}{2}$

A) 4.86
B) 4.84
C) 4.82
D) 4.87

2. To the nearest integer, what is the product of 15.7 and 4.8?

A) 74
B) 75
C) 76
D) 77

3. What is the sum of 23.85 and 2.155, to the nearest integer?

A) 26
B) 27
C) 25
D) 24

4. If 35% of a number N is 14, what is the value of N?

A) 35
B) 40
C) 45
D) 50

5. Which of the following has the least value?

A) 40% of 60
B) 60% of 40
C) 40% of 40
D) 60% of 60

6. Which of the following fractions is greater than $\frac{1}{3}$ and less than $\frac{2}{3}$?

A) $\frac{1}{6}$
B) $\frac{2}{5}$
C) $\frac{3}{4}$
D) $\frac{5}{6}$

7. Which of the following is equivalent to $\frac{3}{2} \times \frac{4}{5}$?

A) $\frac{7}{10}$
B) $\frac{6}{10}$
C) $\frac{3}{5}$
D) $\frac{6}{5}$

8. The bar graph represents the number bags of each type of fruit in a grocery store. Which fruit has the most number of bags in the store?

A) Apple
B) Banana
C) Cherry
D) Date

9. At a hardware store, nails cost $0.05 each and screws cost $0.10 each. Jenna spent less than $5.00 on 20 nails and x screws. Which inequality represents this situation?

A) $\left(\frac{0.05+0.10}{2}\right)x < 5.00$
B) $20(0.05) + 0.10x < 5.00$
C) $20(0.10) + 0.05x < 5.00$
D) $20(0.05 + 0.10)x < 5.00$

10. Based on the relationship between elevation and temperature established in the graph, what's the temperature at 5,000 ft?

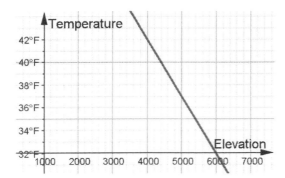

A) 35°
B) 36°
C) 37°
D) 38°

11. A rectangular field has an area of 1500 square feet. If the width of the field is 20 feet less than the length, what is the perimeter, in feet, of the field?

A) 140
B) 150
C) 160
D) 185

12. Which expression is equivalent to $5(d - 2^3) + 2d$?

A) $5d - 20$
B) $7d - 40$
C) $5d - 30$
D) $7d - 30$

13. In a triangle, one angle measures 40°, and another measures 60°. What is the measure of the third angle?

A) 80°
B) 100°
C) 70°
D) 60°

14. A right triangle has an area of 24 square units and one of its legs measures 6 units. What is the perimeter of the triangle?

A) 18 units
B) 24 units
C) 20 units
D) 22 units

15. Simplify the following polynomial expression:

$(3x^2 + 4x - 5) - (2x^2 - 3x + 6)$

A) $x^2 + 7x - 11$
B) $5x^2 + x + 1$
C) $x^2 + 7x - 1$
D) $x^2 + x - 11$

Practice Set 2 Answers and Explanations

1. B) 4.84. Explanation: $\frac{9.68}{2} = 4.84$

2. B) 75. Explanation: $15.7 \times 4.8 = 75.36 \approx 75$

3. A) 26. Explanation: $23.85 + 2.155 = 26.005 \approx 26$

4. B) 40. Explanation: We know $0.35 \times N = 14$. Thus, solving the equation: $N = \frac{14}{0.35} = 40$.

5. C) 40% of 40. Explanation: A. $0.40 \times 60 = 24$. B. $0.60 \times 40 = 24$. C. $0.40 \times 40 = 16$. D. $0.60 \times 60 = 36$.

6. B) $\frac{2}{5}$. Explanation: Convert the Fractions to Decimals: $\frac{1}{3} \approx 0.3333$, $\frac{2}{3} \approx 0.6667$, $\frac{1}{6} \approx 0.1667$, $\frac{2}{5} = 0.4$, $\frac{3}{4} = 0.75$, $\frac{5}{6} \approx 0.8333$. Identify the Fraction Between $\frac{1}{3}$ and $\frac{2}{3}$: $0.3333 < 0.4 < 0.6667$.

7. D) $\frac{6}{5}$. Explanation: $\frac{3}{2} \times \frac{4}{5} = \frac{3 \times 4}{2 \times 5} = \frac{12}{10} = \frac{6}{5}$.

8. B) Banana. Explanation: The bar associated with banana is the tallest.

9. B) $20(0.05) + 0.10x < 5.00$.

10. C) 37°. This can be observed in the graph: when elevation is at 5000, temperature is at 37°.

11. C) 160. Explanation: Let l = length of the field, w = width of the field. We know $w = l - 20$.

   Hence, Area $= l \times w \implies 1500 = l \times (l - 20) \implies 1500 = l^2 - 20l \implies l^2 - 20l - 1500 = 0$.

   Solve the quadratic equation: $l = \frac{-b \pm \sqrt{b^2 - 4ac}}{2a}$, where $a = 1$, $b = -20$, $c = -1500$.

   So, $l = \frac{-(-20) \pm \sqrt{(-2)^2 - 4 \cdot 1 \cdot (-150)}}{2 \cdot 1} = \frac{20 \pm \sqrt{400 + 6000}}{2} = \frac{20 \pm \sqrt{6400}}{2} = \frac{20 \pm 80}{2}$.

   Hence, $l = \frac{20 + 80}{2}$ or $l = \frac{20 - 8}{2}$. Thus, $l = 50$ (since length cannot be negative).

   $w = l - 20 \implies w = 50 - 20 = 30$. Perimeter $= 2(l + w) = 2(50 + 30) = 2 \times 80 = 160$ feet.

12. B) $7d - 40$. Explanation: $5(d - 2^3) + 2d = 5(d - 8) + 2d \implies 5d - 40 + 2d \implies 7d - 40$.

13. A) 80°. Explanation: The sum of the internal angles of a triangle always equals 180°. Given that two of the angles are 40° and 60°, you can find the third angle by subtracting their sum from 180°: 180°−(40°+60°)=180°−100°=80°. Thus, the measure of the third angle is 80°.

14. B) 24 units. Explanation: The area formula for a triangle is: $\frac{1}{2} \times$ base $\times$ height $= 24$.

   Given that one leg (which serves as the base or height) of the right triangle is 6 units, we can find the other leg using this equation. First, solve for the unknown height:

   $\frac{1}{2} \times 6 \times$ height $= 24 \implies 3 \times$ height $= 24 \implies$ height $= \frac{24}{3} = 8$ units

   Now that we know both legs (6 units and 8 units), we can apply the Pythagorean theorem to find the hypotenuse:

   hypotenuse $= \sqrt{6^2 + 8^2} = \sqrt{36 + 64} = \sqrt{100} = 10$ units

   Finally, the perimeter of the triangle is the sum of all three sides: Perimeter $= 6 + 8 + 10 = 24$ units.

15. A) $x^2 + 7x - 11$. Explanation: simplify as follows.

   $$(3x^2 + 4x - 5) - (2x^2 - 3x + 6) = (3x^2 - 2x^2) + \left(4x - (-3x)\right) + (-5 - 6) = x^2 + 7x - 11$$

CHAPTER 4: ARITHMETIC REASONING

INTRODUCTION

The Arithmetic Reasoning subtest of the ASVAB focuses primarily on solving word problems. It measures your ability to understand and apply mathematical concepts to real-world scenarios. Rather than focusing on abstract calculations, this section requires you to interpret and solve problems based on the information provided in a practical context. These word problems often involve basic arithmetic, percentages, ratios, proportions, and occasionally some elementary algebra. These questions test not only a student's math skills but also their ability to comprehend English, requiring careful interpretation of problem descriptions to determine how to approach the solution.

Success in this section depends on your ability to break down the problem, identify the relevant mathematical operations, and apply logical reasoning to arrive at the correct solution. With practice, you'll become more comfortable navigating these types of questions and sharpening your problem-solving skills.

Basic steps when faced with word problems include:

- **Understand the Problem**: Carefully read and comprehend the problem to identify key instructions and requirements.

- **Identify Key Information**: Keep a mental note of relevant data, units, and mathematical operations required.

- **Plan and Solve**: Translate the word problem into mathematical expressions, equations, or series of calculations, then solve step by step.

Below are examples of the type of word problems you may run into in the ASVAB Arithmetic Reasoning subtest.

ARITHMETIC WORD PROBLEMS

Addition/Subtraction Problem

Example 1: After her gym session, Sarah decided to do some shopping. She purchased new workout gear for $35.75 and bought two protein bars from the counter, each costing $1.25. Afterward, she treated herself to a smoothie, which was $6.50. What was the total amount that Sarah spent on these three purchases?

Solution:

Workout Gear: 35.75

Protein Bars: 2×1.25=2.50

Smoothie: 6.50

Total = 35.75 + 2.50 + 6.50 = 44.75.

Sarah spent a total of $44.75 on her shopping trip.

Example 2: Charlotte, a baker, starts Monday with an inventory of 5,275 cookies at her bakery. During the day, she sells 600 cookies to customers and bakes more batches to keep up with the demand. By the end of the day, her bakery's cookie count has reached 5,700. How many cookies did Charlotte's bakery bake on Monday?

Solution: Initial Cookie Count (Monday Morning): 5,275

Cookies Sold During the Day: 600

Final Cookie Count (Monday Evening): 5,700

First, find out how many cookies should have been there if no new batches were baked:

Expected Count = 5275 − 600 = 4675

Now, calculate how many new cookies were baked to reach the final count of 5,700:

Cookies Baked = 5700 − 4675 = 1025

So, Charlotte's bakery baked 1,025 cookies on Monday to replenish the inventory after the sales.

Multiplication/Division Problem

Example 1:   As part of a community outreach project, Carlos plans to distribute a 45-page brochure to each of the 20 organizations in his network. In addition, he wants to keep an extra 5% of the total number of brochures as a backup for any additional requests. How many pages will Carlos need to produce in total?

Solution: Step 1: Calculate the total number of brochures required, including the backup:

$$\text{Total Brochures} = 20 \times 1.05 = 21$$

Step 2: Calculate the total number of pages required: Total Pages=45×21=945.

Carlos will need to produce a total of 945 pages.

Example 2:   A biologist needs to collect 528 leaf samples from various tree species in a forest research project. The project requires the biologist to divide the samples evenly among 24 research sites in the forest. How many leaf samples should be collected at each site?

Solution: Divide the total number of samples by the number of sites: $\text{Samples per Site} = \frac{528}{24} = 22$.

At each research site, one will need to collect 22 leaf samples.

Maximum/Minimum Problem

Example 1: A chemical storage tank can hold a maximum of 4,500 liters of liquid. Jordan needs to fill it with barrels of ethanol, each containing 400 liters. What is the maximum number of whole barrels that Jordan can fill the tank with?

Solution: Divide the tank's capacity by the volume per barrel:

$$\text{Maximum Barrels} = \frac{4500}{400} = 11.25.$$

Since the tank can only hold whole barrels, round down to the nearest whole number: Maximum Barrels=11. Jordan can fill the tank with a maximum of 11 barrels of ethanol.

Example 2:   As part of a new diet, Benjamin plans to drink at least 2,000 milliliters of water each day. He uses a reusable bottle that holds 300 milliliters. How many full bottles does Benjamin need to drink each day to reach his goal?

Solution: Divide the daily water goal by the capacity of the bottle:

$$\text{Bottles Required} = \frac{2000}{300} \approx 6.67.$$

Since Benjamin can only drink whole bottles, round up to the nearest whole number: Bottles Required=7. Benjamin needs to drink at least 7 full bottles of water daily to meet his goal of 2,000 milliliters.

Parts of the Whole Problem

Example 1: In a local astronomy club, members voted on a new logo design. Design A received 36.2% of the votes, Design B garnered 29.4%, and Design C obtained 14.8%. The remaining votes were given to Design D. What percentage of the votes did Design D receive?

Solution: First, calculate the total percentage that Designs A, B, and C collectively obtained: 36.2+29.4+14.8=80.4.

To find the percentage of votes for Design D, subtract the total above from 100%: 100−80.4=19.6. Thus, Design D received 19.6% of the votes.

Example 2: A space research team is studying the different types of stars in a newly discovered star cluster. They determined that $\frac{1}{3}$ of the stars are red dwarfs and $\frac{1}{4}$ are white dwarfs. The remaining stars are either neutron stars or main-sequence stars. What fraction of the stars are neutron stars or main-sequence stars?

Solution: To find the fraction of neutron stars or main-sequence stars, first calculate the total fraction of stars that are either red dwarfs or white dwarfs.

Step 1: Find a common denominator to add the fractions $\frac{1}{3}$ and $\frac{1}{4}$. The least common denominator (LCD) is 12.

Step 2: Add the fractions: $\frac{1}{3} + \frac{1}{4} = \frac{4}{12} + \frac{3}{12} = \frac{7}{12}$. This sum represents the fraction of stars that are either red dwarfs or white dwarfs.

Step 3: Subtract this from 1 to find the fraction of stars that are neutron stars or main-sequence stars.

$$1 - \frac{7}{12} = \frac{12}{12} - \frac{7}{12} = \frac{5}{12}$$

So, $\frac{5}{12}$ of the stars are neutron stars or main-sequence stars.

ALGEBRA WORD PROBLEMS

Algebra Word Problems often require you to set up and solve equations based on real-world scenarios. If you're not already familiar with the process of setting up algebra word problems, please review the "Setting Up Algebra Word Problems" section from the previous chapter before diving into the examples below. Mastering the ability to translate word problems into algebraic expressions is key to solving these types of questions efficiently.

Example 1—Age Problem: Sarah is twice as old as her brother, Tom. In 4 years, the sum of their ages will be 44. How old are Sarah and Tom now?

Solution: Let Tom's current age be x. Since Sarah is twice as old as Tom, her age is $2x$.

In 4 years, Tom's age will be $x + 4$ and Sarah's age will be $2x + 4$. The problem states that the sum of their ages in 4 years will be 44. Therefore, we can set up the following equation: $(x + 4) + (2x + 4) = 44$.

Simplify the equation: $3x + 8 = 44$

Subtract 8 from both sides: $3x = 36$

Now, divide both sides by 3: $x = 12$

So, Tom is 12 years old, and Sarah is: $2x = 2 \times 12 = 24$

Thus, Tom is 12 years old, and Sarah is 24 years old.

Example 2—Distance Problem: A car rental company charges a base fee of $50 plus $0.20 per mile driven. If the total cost to rent a car for a day is $90, how many miles were driven?

Solution: Let the number of miles driven be x.

The total cost is given by the base fee plus the charge per mile, so the equation is: $50 + 0.20x = 90$

Subtract 50 from both sides: $0.20x = 40$

Now, divide both sides by 0.20: $x = \frac{40}{0.20} = 200$

Thus, 200 miles were driven.

GEOMETRY WORD PROBLEMS

Geometry Word Problems in the ASVAB Arithmetic Reasoning subtest test your ability to apply geometric principles to solve real-life problems. You'll encounter problems involving shapes, areas, volumes, perimeters, and other essential geometry concepts. It is crucial to recall formulas related to geometric shapes and be comfortable translating the given information into these formulas.

Example 1—Perimeter of a Rectangle: A rectangular garden has a length that is 5 feet longer than its width. The total perimeter of the garden is 50 feet. What are the dimensions of the garden?

Solution: Let the width of the garden be x The length is 5 feet longer than the width, so the length is $x + 5$.

The formula for the perimeter P of a rectangle is: $P = 2 \times (\text{length} + \text{width})$

Substitute the given values into the formula: $50 = 2 \times ((x + 5) + x)$. Solve the equation:

$$50 = 2 \times (2x + 5)$$
$$25 = 2x + 5$$
$$20 = 2x$$
$$x = 10$$

So, the width of the garden is 10 feet, and the length is: $x + 5 = 10 + 5 = 15$ feet

Thus, the dimensions of the garden are 10 feet by 15 feet.

Example 2—Area of a Triangle:

A triangular plot of land has a base of 12 meters and a height of 8 meters. What is the area of the triangle?

Solution: The formula for the area A of a triangle is: $A = \frac{1}{2} \times$ base $\times$ height

Substitute the given values into the formula: $A = \frac{1}{2} \times 12 \times 8$

Simplify the calculation: $A = \frac{1}{2} \times 96 = 48$ square meters. Thus, the area of the triangle is 48 square meters.

Example 3—Finding Angles within a Triangle: In a particular triangle, one angle is twice the size of the second angle, and the third angle is 20 degrees larger than the second angle. What are the measures of the three angles?

Solution: Let the second angle be x degrees.

The first angle is twice the size of the second angle, so the first angle is $2x$.

The third angle is 20 degrees larger than the second angle, so the third angle is $x + 20$.

We know that the sum of the three angles in a triangle is always 180 degrees, so we can set up the following equation:

$$2x + x + (x + 20) = 180$$
$$4x + 20 = 180$$
$$4x = 160$$
$$x = 40$$

So, the second angle is 40 degrees. Now, find the other two angles: The first angle is $2x = 2 \times 40 = 80$ degrees. The third angle is $x + 20 = 40 + 20 = 60$ degrees. Thus, the three angles of the triangle are 40 degrees, 80 degrees, and 60 degrees.

Arithmetic Reasoning vs Mathematics Knowledge

In this chapter, we explored the various types of word problems you may encounter on the ASVAB Arithmetic Reasoning subtest, including arithmetic, algebra, and geometry problems. Each type of problem requires a different approach, but they all emphasize the ability to apply mathematical concepts to real-world situations. While the Arithmetic Reasoning subtest focuses on word problems and logical reasoning, it's important to recognize the blurred line between this section and the Mathematics Knowledge subtest. Both assess your mathematical ability, but Arithmetic Reasoning emphasizes comprehension and problem-solving in everyday contexts, while the Mathematics Knowledge subtest leans more toward direct calculations and the understanding of formal mathematical principles.

ARITHMETIC REASONING PRACTICE SET

Time: 55 minutes for 15 questions

Select the correct answer from the choices given. This practice subtest reflects the number of questions and time limits you'll encounter on the CAT-ASVAB Arithmetic Reasoning subtest without any tryout questions.

1. A concert organizer charged $12 for each ticket. The organizer collected a total of $288 from ticket sales. How many tickets were sold?

A) 20
B) 22
C) 24
D) 26

2. The wholesale price of a chair is $80. The retail price of the chair is 15% more than the wholesale price. What is the retail price of the chair?

A) $90
B) $92
C) $94
D) $96

3. Lucas bought a 24-pack of water bottles. The pack was $\frac{1}{3}$ full before Lucas decided to refill it with new bottles. Each new bottle cost $0.75. How much did Lucas spend, in dollars, to refill the pack to its full capacity?

A) $12.00
B) $10.50
C) $9.75
D) $11.25

4. Liam bought some apples for $1 each and some pineapples for $4 each. He bought 2 more apples than pineapples and spent a total of $17. How many pineapples did Liam buy?

A) 1
B) 2
C) 3
D) 4

5. At 7 a.m., a hiker at Death Valley National Park was at an elevation of -200 feet relative to sea level. By 3 p.m. on the same day, the hiker reached an elevation of 1300 feet above sea level. What was the change in elevation, in feet, for the hiker from 7 a.m. to 3 p.m.?

A) -100 feet
B) 1200 feet
C) 1300 feet
D) 1500 feet

6. Sarah works at a library and a cafe. In a 30-day period, Sarah worked $\frac{1}{3}$ of the days at the library and did not work $\frac{1}{6}$ of the days. On the remaining days Sarah worked at the cafe. How many days did Sarah work at the cafe during the 30-day period?

A) 15
B) 10
C) 20
D) 5

7. If a climber ascends 25% of a 1,300 ft mountain in a day, how many feet does the climber ascend?

A) 325 ft
B) 25 ft
C) 375 ft
D) 97.5 ft

8. A conveyor belt is currently set to move at a speed of 5.921 meters per minute (MPM). The speed is increased to 6.088 MPM. By how much was the speed increased?

A) 0.167 MPM
B) 1.167 MPM
C) 1.833 MPM
D) 1.967 MPM

9. A faucet fills a bathtub at a rate of 2 gallons per minute. If the bathtub has a capacity of 160 gallons, how long will it take to fill the bathtub?

A) 10 minutes
B) 50 minutes
C) 80 minutes
D) 100 minutes

10. The volume of a cube is given by the formula $V = s^3$, where s is the length of a side of the cube. If the volume of a cube is 64 cubic inches, what is the length of each side?

A) 4 inches
B) 8 inches
C) 16 inches
D) 32 inches

11. Tim's total sales for the first four months of the year were $4500, $5200, $4800, and $5100. If he wants his average monthly sales to be $5000 after the fifth month, how much does he need to sell in the fifth month?

A) $5000
B) $5200
C) $5400
D) $4900

12. A salesman earns a commission of 7% of the total value of merchandise he sells. If he sells $48,000 worth of merchandise in one month, how much money will he earn in commission?

A) $1960
B) $2100
C) $3360
D) $3750

13. It costs $1.20 per square foot to paint a wall. How much will it cost to paint a 12-foot-by-20-foot wall?

A) $288.00
B) $240.00
C) $144.00
D) $200.00

14. A bakery has a monthly overhead of $4,500. It costs $1.50 to make each cupcake, and the cupcakes sell for $3.00 each. How many cupcakes must the bakery sell each month in order to make a profit?

A) 2,500
B) 3,000
C) 4,000
D) 3,500

15. Lily starts walking north at 3 miles per hour (mph) from her house. One hour later, her sister Emma realizes Lily forgot her water bottle and begins jogging after her at 6 miles per hour. How long will it take Emma to catch up with Lily?

A) 1 hour
B) 1.5 hours
C) 2 hours
D) 2.5 hours

Answers and Explanations

1. C) 24. Explanation: $\frac{288}{12} = 24$

2. B) $92. Explanation: $80 + 80 \times \frac{15}{100} = 80 + 12 = 92$

3. A) $12.00. Explanation: Calculate the Number of Bottles Needed: $24 \times \left(1 - \frac{1}{3}\right) = 24 \times \frac{2}{3} = 16$ bottles.

   Then calculate the Cost to Refill the Pack: $16 \times 0.75 = 12.00$.

4. C) 3. Explanation: Let x be the number of pineapples. Then, $x + 2$ is the number of apples.

   Hence, $1(x + 2) + 4x = 17 \implies x + 2 + 4x = 17 \implies 5x + 2 = 17 \implies 5x = 15 \implies x = 3$.

   Thus, Liam bought 3 pineapples.

5. D) 1500 feet. Explanation: Change in elevation $= 1300 - (-200) = 1500$.

6. B) 10. Explanation: Total days $= 30$. Days at the library $= \frac{1}{3} \times 30 = 10$.

   Days not worked $= \frac{1}{6} \times 30 = 5$. Remaining days $= 30 - 10 - 5 = 15$. Days at the cafe $= 15$.

   $$30 - \left(\frac{1}{3} \times 30\right) - \left(\frac{1}{6} \times 30\right) = 10$$

7. A) 325 ft. Explanation: $0.25 \times 1300 = 325$ ft.

8. A) 0.167 MPM. Explanation: $6.088 - 5.921 = 0.167$ MPM

9. C) 80 minutes. Explanation: $\frac{160 \text{ gallons}}{2 \text{ gallons per minute}} = 80$ minutes.

10. A) 4 inches. Explanation: $s^3 = 64 \implies s = \sqrt[3]{64} = 4$.

11. C) $5400. Explanation: The total sales over five months for an average of $5000 would be: $5 \times 5000 = 25000$.

    Now, add up the sales for the first four months: $4500 + 5200 + 4800 + 5100 = 19600$.

    Subtract the current total from the required total to find the amount Tim needs to sell in the fifth month: $25000 - 19600 = 5400$. Thus, $5400 of sales is needed in the 5th month to reach an average of $5000.

12. C) $3360. Explanation: To find the commission the salesman will earn, we calculate 7% of $48,000:

    $0.07 \times 48000 = 3360$. Thus, the salesman will earn $3360 in commission.

13. A) $288.00. Explanation: To find the cost of painting the wall, first calculate the area of the wall:

    $$\text{Area} = 12 \times 20 = 240 \text{ square feet}$$

    Now, multiply the area by the cost per square foot: $240 \times 1.20 = 288.00$.

14. B) 3,000. Explanation:

    Each cupcake sells for $3.00, and it costs $1.50 to make, so the profit per cupcake is: 3.00 - 1.50 = 1.50.

    Now, divide the bakery's monthly overhead by the profit per cupcake: $\frac{4500}{1.50} = 3000$

    Thus, the bakery must sell 3,000 cupcakes each month to make a profit.

15. A) 1 hour. Explanation:

    By the time Emma starts jogging, Lily has already been walking for 1 hour at 3 mph, so Lily is: $3 \times 1 = 3$ miles ahead. Emma is jogging 6 mph while Lily walks at 3 mph, so Emma is closing the gap at: $6 - 3 = 3$ mph.

    To catch up with Lily, Emma must close the 3-mile gap. The time it will take her to do so is: $\frac{3 \text{ miles}}{3 \text{ mph}} = 1$ hour.

CHAPTER 5: GENERAL SCIENCE

INTRODUCTION

The ASVAB General Science (GS) subtest assesses your knowledge of basic scientific concepts across multiple disciplines. It covers life science, physical science, and earth and space sciences, focusing on high school-level material. You'll need to demonstrate an understanding of fundamental principles and how they apply to various scientific scenarios.

What to Expect

The GS subtest evaluates your ability to recall and apply essential scientific knowledge. Key areas include:

Life Science: Expect questions on biology, including cell structure, ecosystems, and human anatomy. You may also encounter topics such as genetics, plant biology, and nutrition.

Physical Sciences: This section covers basic physics and chemistry concepts, such as energy, motion, atomic structure, and the periodic table. You'll need to understand chemical reactions, forces, and laws of motion etc.

Earth and Space Sciences: Be prepared for questions on geology, meteorology, and astronomy. Test questions cover topics such as the structure of the Earth, weather systems, and the solar system, as well as the basics of the universe.

Now, let's dive in!

§1. LIFE SCIENCES

BIOLOGY BASICS AND KEY CONCEPTS

Biology is the study of life and living organisms, encompassing everything from microscopic cells to vast ecosystems. It seeks to understand the structure, function, growth, evolution, and interactions of all forms of life. By grasping the essential principles of biology, we can better comprehend how life operates and interacts within the natural world. Below are the key concepts that provide the foundation for biological understanding.

The Cell as the Fundamental Unit of Life

All living things, regardless of their complexity, are composed of **cells**, the smallest unit of life. Cells perform essential functions that sustain life, including respiration, energy production, and growth. There are two major types of cells: **prokaryotic** cells (which lack a true nucleus and are found in organisms like bacteria) and **eukaryotic** cells (which have a nucleus and are found in plants, animals, and fungi). While some organisms consist of just one cell (unicellular), others, like humans, are made up of trillions of specialized cells (multicellular), each playing a specific role.

DNA: The Genetic Blueprint

At the heart of all living organisms is **DNA (Deoxyribonucleic Acid)**, a long molecule that contains the genetic instructions necessary for growth, development, and reproduction. DNA is organized into structures called **chromosomes**, which are located in the nucleus of eukaryotic cells. Each segment of DNA, known as a **gene**, codes for a specific protein, and these proteins perform essential tasks within the organism. The unique combination of genes inherited from both parents shapes the organism's traits, from eye color to susceptibility to diseases.

Metabolism: The Energy System of Life

Living organisms need a continuous supply of **energy** to carry out their life processes. This energy is obtained from food and is used to fuel **metabolism**, the series of chemical reactions within cells that break down or build up molecules. Metabolism can be divided into **anabolic** processes, which build larger molecules from smaller ones (such as muscle growth), and **catabolic** processes, which break down molecules to release energy (such as digestion). **Cellular respiration** is a key metabolic process that occurs in the **mitochondria**, where glucose is broken down to release energy in the form of **ATP** (adenosine triphosphate), the energy currency of the cell.

Homeostasis: Maintaining Internal Balance

To survive, organisms must regulate their internal environment to remain stable despite changes in the external environment. This process is called **homeostasis**. For example, humans maintain a constant body temperature of about 98.6°F (37°C) by sweating when it's too hot or shivering when it's too cold. Similarly, organisms maintain other crucial conditions like pH, water balance, and glucose levels. This ability to regulate internal processes is vital for maintaining health and function across varying environmental conditions.

Growth, Development, and Reproduction

All living organisms undergo **growth** and **development** as they progress through different stages of life. Growth involves an increase in size and mass, while development refers to changes in an organism's form and function as it matures. For instance, a seed grows into a tree, and a fertilized egg develops into a mature adult. In addition to growth, organisms have the ability to **reproduce**, ensuring the continuation of their species. **Asexual reproduction** involves a single parent producing offspring identical to itself, while **sexual reproduction** requires the fusion of male and female gametes, leading to genetic variation in offspring.

Evolution: Change Over Time

A core principle of biology is **evolution**, the process by which populations of organisms change over generations through inherited genetic variations. This process, driven largely by **natural selection**, explains the vast diversity of life on Earth. Organisms with traits better suited to their environments are more likely to survive and reproduce, passing on those advantageous traits to future generations. Over long periods, these changes can result in the formation of new species. **Evolutionary biology** provides insight into the shared ancestry of all living organisms and the adaptations that have allowed them to thrive in different ecosystems.

Ecological Interdependence

Living organisms do not exist in isolation; they are part of larger systems called **ecosystems**, where they interact with both living (biotic) and non-living (abiotic) elements. **Ecology**, the study of these interactions, examines how organisms affect and are affected by their environment. For example, plants produce oxygen through **photosynthesis**, which animals need to breathe, while animals release carbon dioxide, which plants use to grow. These interrelationships form a web of life, where each species plays a crucial role in maintaining the balance of the ecosystem. Disruptions to this balance, such as habitat destruction or climate change, can have significant consequences for biodiversity and ecosystem health.

Biology, with its focus on understanding the principles of life, forms the basis for exploring the complexities of living organisms. From the cellular level, where DNA and metabolism govern life's processes, to the larger ecological systems that demonstrate the interdependence of organisms, these foundational concepts are critical for understanding biology. As we delve deeper into subjects like cell structure, genetics, and human physiology in the subsequent sections, these core principles will continue to guide our exploration of life.

PLANT AND ANIMAL CELL STRUCTURE

Cells are the basic units of life, and while plant and animal cells share many common structures, they also have key differences that reflect their unique functions within living organisms. Understanding the structure of plant and animal cells is fundamental to the study of biology and helps explain how these cells perform the vital functions necessary for life. In this section, we will explore the similarities and differences between plant and animal cell structures, focusing on the various organelles that contribute to their functions.

Common Features of Plant and Animal Cells

Both plant and animal cells are **eukaryotic**, meaning they have a true nucleus and other membrane-bound organelles. This is in contrast to **prokaryotic** cells, such as bacteria, which lack a nucleus and other complex structures. Below are the key organelles found in both plant and animal cells:

Cell Membrane: The cell membrane, also known as the plasma membrane, is a thin, flexible barrier that surrounds the cell. It is primarily composed of a **phospholipid bilayer** with embedded proteins. The cell membrane plays a critical role in controlling the movement of substances in and out of the cell, maintaining the cell's internal environment (homeostasis), and facilitating communication with other cells. The **selectively permeable** nature of the cell membrane allows essential nutrients to enter while keeping harmful substances out.

Nucleus: The nucleus is the control center of the cell, housing the cell's genetic material in the form of **DNA**. Within the nucleus, DNA is organized into structures called **chromosomes**, which carry the instructions for all cellular activities. The nucleus is surrounded by a **nuclear envelope**, a double membrane that contains **nuclear pores** to regulate the exchange of materials between the nucleus and the cytoplasm. Inside the nucleus, the **nucleolus** is responsible for producing **ribosomes**, which are essential for protein synthesis.

Cytoplasm: The cytoplasm is the jelly-like substance that fills the interior of the cell, where all the organelles are suspended. It consists mainly of water, salts, and proteins and provides a medium for chemical reactions to occur. The cytoplasm helps in the movement of materials within the cell and supports the organelles.

Mitochondria: Often referred to as the "powerhouses" of the cell, mitochondria are responsible for generating the energy that cells need to function. Mitochondria convert **glucose** and **oxygen** into **ATP (adenosine triphosphate)** through a process called **cellular respiration**. This energy is used for various cellular activities, including growth, repair, and movement. Mitochondria have their own DNA, which is inherited maternally, and they can replicate independently within the cell.

Ribosomes: Ribosomes are small, round structures either floating freely in the cytoplasm or attached to the **endoplasmic reticulum (ER)**. They are responsible for assembling proteins by linking together **amino acids** according to instructions provided by messenger RNA (mRNA). These proteins play a crucial role in nearly every cellular function, including enzyme production, structural support, and cell signaling.

Endoplasmic Reticulum (ER): The endoplasmic reticulum (ER) is a network of membrane-bound tubules that extends from the nuclear envelope into the cytoplasm. There are two types of ER: **rough ER** and **smooth ER**. The rough ER is studded with ribosomes, making it the site of protein synthesis and modification. The smooth ER, which lacks ribosomes, is involved in lipid synthesis, detoxification of harmful substances, and storage of ions.

Golgi Apparatus: The Golgi apparatus functions as the cell's packaging and distribution center. After proteins and lipids are synthesized in the ER, they are transported to the Golgi apparatus, where they are further modified, sorted, and packaged into **vesicles**. These vesicles are then sent to their destinations, either within the cell or to the cell membrane for secretion.

Lysosomes: Found predominantly in animal cells, lysosomes are membrane-bound organelles that contain digestive enzymes. They are responsible for breaking down waste materials, old cell parts, and foreign invaders like bacteria. Lysosomes play a key role in **autophagy**, the process by which cells recycle their own components, helping to maintain cellular health.

Cytoskeleton: The cytoskeleton is a network of protein fibers that provides structural support to the cell. It helps maintain the cell's shape, anchors organelles in place, and assists with cell movement and division. The cytoskeleton is composed of three main types of fibers: **microfilaments**, **intermediate filaments**, and **microtubules**, each playing distinct roles in cellular processes.

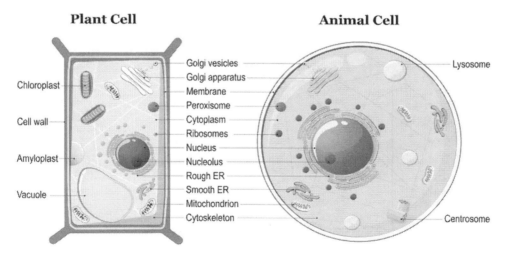

Unique Features of Plant Cells

In addition to the organelles shared with animal cells, plant cells possess several unique structures that allow them to carry out specific functions, such as photosynthesis and maintaining structural integrity.

Cell Wall: Unlike animal cells, plant cells have a cell wall that surrounds the cell membrane. The cell wall is primarily made of **cellulose**, a strong carbohydrate that provides rigidity and support. The cell wall allows plants to maintain their shape and stand upright, which is essential for maximizing exposure to sunlight. Additionally, the cell wall offers protection against mechanical stress and pathogens.

Chloroplasts: One of the most distinctive features of plant cells is the presence of chloroplasts, which are the organelles responsible for **photosynthesis**. Chloroplasts contain the pigment **chlorophyll**, which captures light energy from the sun and converts it into chemical energy in the form of glucose. This process not only provides energy for the plant but also produces oxygen, which is released into the atmosphere. Chloroplasts have their own DNA and replicate independently, similar to mitochondria.

Large Central Vacuole: Plant cells contain a large central vacuole, which is a membrane-bound sac that stores water, nutrients, and waste products. The vacuole plays a crucial role in maintaining **turgor pressure**, the internal pressure exerted by the vacuole against the cell wall. This pressure helps keep the plant upright and prevents wilting. The vacuole also stores important molecules and contributes to the breakdown of waste materials, functioning somewhat like lysosomes in animal cells.

Unique Features of Animal Cells

While plant cells have chloroplasts, cell walls, and large vacuoles, animal cells contain structures that are either absent or not as prominent in plant cells. Below are some key differences:

Centrioles: Animal cells contain structures known as centrioles, which are involved in **cell division**. Centrioles are cylindrical structures made of microtubules that help organize the assembly of the **mitotic spindle** during cell division (mitosis and meiosis). Plant cells typically do not have centrioles, although they still undergo cell division through a slightly different mechanism.

Smaller Vacuoles: While plant cells have a large central vacuole, animal cells contain smaller vacuoles or vesicles. These smaller vacuoles are involved in storage, transport, and waste removal, but they do not play as significant a role in maintaining cell structure as the large vacuole in plant cells.

Comparison of Plant and Animal Cells

Although plant and animal cells share many of the same organelles, their unique structures reflect their differing roles in the natural world. For example, the **cell wall** and **chloroplasts** in plant cells enable them to capture sunlight and perform photosynthesis, a process that animal cells cannot do. On the other hand, **centrioles** and **lysosomes** in animal cells are specialized for tasks related to digestion and cell division, functions that are less emphasized in plant cells.

Both cell types are essential to life on Earth, with plant cells forming the basis of ecosystems by producing energy through photosynthesis, while animal cells play roles in consuming and distributing that energy within the food chain.

Understanding the structures of plant and animal cells is fundamental to the study of biology. While they share many common features, such as the cell membrane, nucleus, mitochondria, and endoplasmic reticulum, they also have unique components that enable them to perform specialized functions. Plant cells, with their cell walls, chloroplasts, and large central vacuole, are optimized for photosynthesis and structural support, whereas animal cells rely on lysosomes, centrioles, and a flexible membrane to support their more dynamic and diverse functions. Together, these cells represent the building blocks of life in plants and animals, each adapted to their environment and role within biological systems.

PLANT PHYSIOLOGY

Plant physiology studies how plants function, including how they grow, reproduce, and respond to their environment. Plants are complex organisms that rely on a variety of processes to survive, such as absorbing water and nutrients, producing food through photosynthesis, and reproducing to create new plants. In this section, we'll explore the main physiological processes that keep plants alive and help them thrive.

Photosynthesis: How Plants Make Their Food

One of the most important processes for plants is **photosynthesis**, which is how they produce their own food. Photosynthesis takes place in the **chloroplasts**, which contain the pigment **chlorophyll**. Chlorophyll allows plants to capture energy from sunlight and use it to convert water and carbon dioxide into glucose (a type of sugar) and oxygen. The glucose provides energy for the plant to grow, while the oxygen is released into the air. Photosynthesis is vital not only for the plant itself but also for the ecosystem, as plants provide oxygen and serve as a food source for many animals.

Respiration: Using Energy for Growth and Survival

While photosynthesis is how plants make food, **respiration** is the process they use to break down that food and turn it into energy. This energy is used for all the plant's activities, including growing, repairing tissues, and transporting nutrients. Respiration takes place in the plant's cells, specifically in the **mitochondria**, and it happens day and night, unlike photosynthesis, which only occurs when there's sunlight.

Water and Nutrient Transport: The Role of Xylem and Phloem

Plants need water and nutrients to grow, and they have special tissues to transport these throughout the plant. These tissues are called **xylem** and **phloem**.

Xylem carries water and minerals from the roots to the rest of the plant. Water enters the roots from the soil and travels upward through the xylem to the stems and leaves, where it's used in photosynthesis. **Phloem** transports sugars made during photosynthesis from the leaves to other parts of the plant, such as the roots, stems, and developing flowers or fruits. This ensures that all parts of the plant have the energy they need to grow and function.

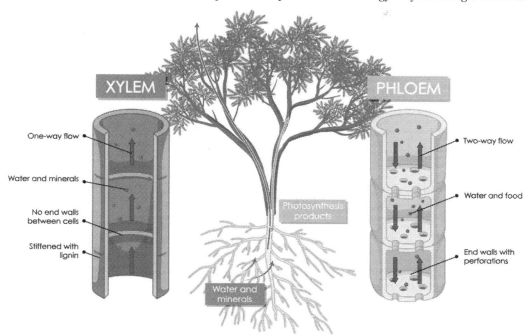

Stomata: Tiny Openings for Gas Exchange

Plants take in carbon dioxide from the air and release oxygen through tiny openings on their leaves called **stomata**. These openings are essential for photosynthesis and respiration. The **guard cells** surrounding the stomata can open or close them depending on the plant's needs. For example, the stomata may close on a hot day to prevent too much water loss through evaporation, helping the plant conserve water.

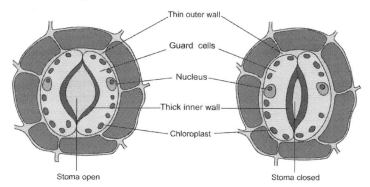

Plant Hormones: How Plants Grow and Respond to Their Environment

Plants produce special chemicals called **hormones** that help regulate their growth, development, and responses to environmental changes. For example, some hormones promote stem and root growth, while others help the plant conserve water during droughts by closing the stomata. Hormones also guide plants to grow toward light or help fruits ripen. These substances ensure plants can adapt to changes in their surroundings and thrive under different conditions.

Plant Reproduction: Sexual and Asexual Methods

Plants have two main ways of reproducing: **sexual reproduction** and **asexual reproduction**.

Sexual reproduction occurs when pollen from the male part of the plant (the anther) is transferred to the female part of the plant (the stigma). This can happen through wind, water, or pollinators like bees. Once the pollen reaches the stigma, fertilization occurs, and seeds are formed. These seeds can then grow into new plants.

Asexual reproduction, or **vegetative reproduction**, happens without seeds. Instead, new plants grow from parts of the parent plant, like stems, roots, or leaves. For example, a potato plant can grow from a single potato tuber, and strawberry plants send out runners that develop into new plants. Asexual reproduction produces plants that are genetically identical to the parent plant.

Plant Responses to the Environment

Plants are sensitive to their surroundings and can change their behavior or growth patterns based on environmental factors. Some of the main ways plants respond to their environment include:

Phototropism: Plants tend to grow toward a light source. This is because they need light for photosynthesis, and growing toward light ensures they can capture as much as possible.

Gravitropism: Plants also respond to gravity. Roots typically grow downward (toward gravity), while stems grow upward (against gravity), helping the plant stay anchored and upright.

Thigmotropism: Some plants, like vines, respond to touch. This is called thigmotropism, and it allows climbing plants to wrap around objects for support as they grow.

Plants can also show **nastic movements**, which are not related to the direction of the stimulus. For example, the Mimosa pudica plant closes its leaves when touched, and some flowers open and close at certain times of the day based on temperature or light.

BASICS OF GENETICS

Genetics studies how traits are passed from one generation to the next in both plants and animals. It explains why offspring resemble their parents and how certain characteristics, like eye color in humans or flower color in plants, are inherited. The basic principles of genetics apply to all living organisms, whether they are plants, animals, or even microorganisms.

DNA: The Genetic Code for Life

At the center of genetics is **DNA (deoxyribonucleic acid)**, which acts as the blueprint for all living organisms. DNA is made up of a double-helix structure composed of four chemical bases: adenine (A), thymine (T), cytosine (C), and guanine (G). These bases pair up in specific ways (A with T, C with G) to form the rungs of the DNA "ladder."

Each segment of DNA that codes for a specific trait is called a **gene**. For example, a gene might determine an animal's fur color or a plant's height. These genes are organized on **chromosomes**, which are long strands of DNA found in the nucleus of every cell.

DNA Structure

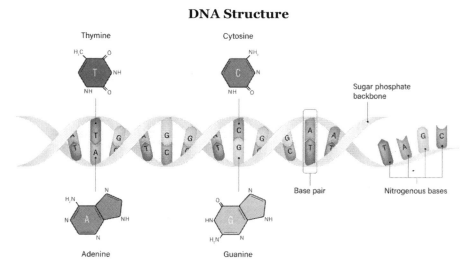

Genes and Inheritance

Genes come in pairs, with one copy inherited from each parent. In both plants and animals, this combination of genes from the mother and father determines the traits of the offspring. The different versions of a gene are known as **alleles**. For example, a gene responsible for flower color in a plant might have a "red" allele and a "white" allele.

If an organism inherits two of the same alleles for a trait (one from each parent), it is said to be **homozygous** for that trait. If it inherits two different alleles, it is **heterozygous**. Dominant alleles can mask the effects of recessive alleles, so even if an organism has one dominant and one recessive allele, it will exhibit the trait of the dominant allele. For example, in humans, brown eyes are dominant over blue eyes, so a person with one brown-eye allele and one blue-eye allele will have brown eyes.

DNA Replication: Copying Genetic Information

For both plants and animals, cells must copy their DNA before they divide to ensure that each new cell has the same genetic information. This process is called **DNA replication**.

During replication, the DNA molecule unwinds, and the two strands separate. Each strand serves as a template for the formation of a new complementary strand, ensuring that each new cell receives an exact copy of the original DNA. This process is essential for growth, repair, and reproduction in living organisms.

Mutations: Changes in Genetic Information

Sometimes, mistakes happen during DNA replication, leading to changes in the genetic code. These changes are called **mutations**. Mutations can be caused by environmental factors like radiation or chemicals, but they can also happen randomly.

Most mutations are harmless, but some can affect the organism's traits. In plants, a mutation might cause a flower to develop a different color, while in animals, it might lead to changes in fur patterns or even health conditions. Occasionally, mutations can be beneficial, providing an advantage that helps an organism survive better in its environment. Over time, beneficial mutations can lead to evolutionary changes in species.

Selective Breeding and Genetics

Humans have long used genetics to improve both plants and animals through **selective breeding**. By choosing individuals with desired traits and breeding them together, we can enhance certain characteristics over generations. For example, farmers might breed plants that produce more fruit, or dog breeders might select for specific coat colors or temperaments.

This practice has been crucial in agriculture, helping to develop crop varieties that are more resistant to pests, drought, or disease. In animals, selective breeding has given rise to the wide variety of dog breeds and livestock that meet specific needs for food or work.

Genetic Variation and Diversity

In both plants and animals, genetic diversity is essential for the survival and adaptation of species. Sexual reproduction increases genetic variation by combining genes from two parents, leading to offspring with unique genetic makeups. This diversity allows species to adapt to changing environments and helps protect against diseases that might otherwise wipe out genetically identical populations.

In summary, genetics provides the blueprint for life, guiding the development, reproduction, and diversity of both plants and animals. From the copying of DNA to the inheritance of traits, the study of genetics helps explain the continuity and variation seen in all living things.

ECOLOGY: FUNDAMENTAL CONCEPTS AND PRINCIPLES

In this section, we'll discuss how living organisms interact with each other and their environment, which is the focus of ecology. Ecology helps us gain insight into how life on Earth is sustained, how ecosystems function, and how humans impact natural systems.

Levels of Ecological Organization

Ecology is often studied at various levels of organization, each representing a different scale of interaction between organisms and their environment. These levels include:

Organism: The individual living being. This level focuses on how a single organism interacts with its environment, including how it obtains food, reproduces, and responds to external conditions.

Population: A group of individuals of the same species living in a specific area. Ecologists study population dynamics, such as growth rates, birth and death rates, and how populations are affected by factors like competition for resources.

Community: A collection of different populations that live in the same area and interact with one another. This level of organization examines how species coexist and the effects of predation, competition, and symbiosis on community structure.

Ecosystem: A community of living organisms and the non-living components of their environment (such as water, soil, and air) that interact as a system. Ecosystem ecology looks at how energy flows through the system and how nutrients cycle between organisms and their environment.

Biosphere: The largest level of organization in ecology, encompassing all ecosystems on Earth. It includes every living organism and the environments they inhabit. The biosphere is essentially the global ecological system.

Energy Flow in Ecosystems

One of the most fundamental principles in ecology is how energy flows through ecosystems. Energy originates from the sun and is captured by producers (usually plants) through photosynthesis. These producers convert sunlight into chemical energy, which is stored in their tissues as food.

Energy then flows through the ecosystem in the following way:

Producers (autotrophs): Plants, algae, and some bacteria that produce their own food by converting sunlight into energy.

Consumers (heterotrophs): Organisms that cannot produce their own food and must consume other organisms to obtain energy. Consumers are further classified into primary consumers (herbivores), secondary consumers (carnivores that eat herbivores), and tertiary consumers (carnivores that eat other carnivores).

Decomposers: Fungi, bacteria, and other organisms that break down dead organic material, returning nutrients back to the soil. This recycling of nutrients is critical for the continuation of life in an ecosystem.

Energy transfer between these levels is not 100% efficient. Typically, only about 10% of the energy from one level is passed on to the next, while the rest is lost as heat. This is known as the **10% rule** and explains why ecosystems typically have fewer large carnivores than herbivores.

Nutrient Cycling

Another key principle in ecology is the cycling of nutrients, such as carbon, nitrogen, and phosphorus, which are essential for life. Unlike energy, which flows in one direction through an ecosystem, nutrients are recycled. The **carbon cycle**, for example, describes how carbon moves between the atmosphere, organisms, and the Earth. Plants take in carbon dioxide during photosynthesis, which is then passed through the food chain when consumers eat plants. Carbon is returned to the atmosphere through respiration, decomposition, and combustion (burning fossil fuels).

Similarly, the **nitrogen cycle** involves nitrogen being fixed from the atmosphere by certain bacteria, made available to plants, passed on to consumers, and eventually returned to the atmosphere or soil through waste and decay. These cycles ensure that essential elements are available for organisms to survive.

Habitat and Niche

A **habitat** is the physical environment where an organism lives, while a **niche** refers to the role an organism plays within its ecosystem. A species' niche includes how it obtains food, its behavior, and how it interacts with other species.

For example, a bird's habitat might be a forest, but its niche could include eating insects from the trees, nesting in tree branches, and contributing to seed dispersal. Understanding niches helps ecologists determine how species coexist and how they affect one another. When two species have overlapping niches, they may compete for the same resources, which can lead to **competitive exclusion**, where one species outcompetes the other.

Population Dynamics

The study of **population dynamics** explores how populations change in size and composition over time. Factors such as birth rates, death rates, immigration, and emigration influence population growth. Populations tend to grow rapidly when resources are abundant, but as resources become limited, growth slows and may eventually reach a stable state, known as **carrying capacity**. Carrying capacity is the maximum population size that an environment can sustainably support.

Populations can experience different growth patterns. **Exponential growth** is rapid population increase under ideal conditions, where resources are unlimited. This type of growth is typically seen in populations introduced to a new environment. **Logistic growth** is the type of growth that slows as resources become limited, eventually stabilizing at the carrying capacity. Natural population fluctuations are common due to environmental changes, predation, disease, and competition for resources.

Species Interactions

Species within an ecosystem interact in various ways, including:

Predation: One organism (the predator) hunts and kills another (the prey). Predation helps regulate population sizes and maintain balance within ecosystems.

Competition: Species compete for the same resources, such as food, water, or space. This competition can be either **interspecific** (between different species) or **intraspecific** (within the same species).

Symbiosis: A close and long-term interaction between different species. There are several types of symbiotic relationships. **Mutualism** refers to the interaction where both species benefit from the interaction (e.g., bees pollinating flowers). **Commensalism** is the interaction when one species benefits, and the other is neither harmed nor helped (e.g., birds nesting in trees). Finally, **parasitism** is when one species benefits at the expense of the other (e.g., ticks feeding on mammals).

Human Impact on Ecosystems

Humans have a profound effect on ecosystems through activities such as deforestation, pollution, and climate change. These actions can disrupt the balance of ecosystems, leading to habitat loss, species extinction, and changes in nutrient cycling and energy flow. Understanding the principles of ecology helps us identify ways to mitigate our impact and promote the sustainability of natural systems.

CLASSIFICATION OF LIVING THINGS

With so many plants and animals in such a diverse ecological system, how do we put them into different categories to better understand the natural world? The answer lies in taxonomy, the science of classifying living things. Taxonomy organizes organisms into groups based on shared characteristics, helping us understand their relationships and how they have evolved over time. This system not only helps scientists study biodiversity but also aids in identifying and categorizing new species as we continue to explore the vast variety of life on Earth.

The Taxonomic Hierarchy

The taxonomic hierarchy categorizes living organisms into increasingly specific groups. The primary levels, from the most general to the most specific, are:

1. **Domain**: The highest rank, which divides all life into three broad categories based on cell structure: Bacteria, Archaea, and Eukarya.

2. **Kingdom**: A broad classification that groups organisms based on their basic characteristics, such as whether they are plants, animals, fungi, or microorganisms.

3. **Phylum**: Organisms in a kingdom are further divided into phyla based on more specific traits.

4. **Class**: Each phylum is divided into classes. For example, mammals and birds are different classes within the animal kingdom.

5. **Order**: Classes are divided into orders based on similarities in body structure and other characteristics.

6. **Family**: Orders are divided into families, grouping organisms with even more closely related characteristics.

7. **Genus**: A genus groups species that are very closely related and often resemble each other.

8. **Species**: The most specific level of classification, a species refers to a group of individuals that can breed and produce fertile offspring.

The Three Domains of Life

All living organisms can be classified into one of the three domains:

1. **Bacteria**: This domain includes prokaryotic, single-celled organisms that lack a nucleus. Bacteria are incredibly diverse and can be found in nearly every environment on Earth.

2. **Archaea**: Like bacteria, archaea are prokaryotic and single-celled, but they differ in their genetic makeup and can often survive in extreme environments, such as hot springs and salt lakes.

3. **Eukarya**: This domain includes all organisms with eukaryotic cells, which have a nucleus and other membrane-bound organelles. Eukarya includes animals, plants, fungi, and protists.

The Five Kingdoms

Within the Eukarya domain, organisms are classified into one of five kingdoms:

1. **Animalia**: Multicellular organisms that obtain food by consuming other organisms (heterotrophs). This kingdom includes mammals, birds, fish, insects, and more.

2. **Plantae**: Multicellular organisms that produce their own food through photosynthesis (autotrophs). This kingdom includes flowering plants, ferns, and mosses.

3. **Fungi**: Organisms that absorb nutrients from decaying organic matter. Fungi include mushrooms, molds, and yeasts.

4. **Protista**: A diverse group of mostly single-celled organisms, such as algae and protozoa, that do not fit into the other kingdoms.

5. **Monera**: This kingdom, often used to classify bacteria, includes single-celled prokaryotes.

As an example, the table below summarizes the classification hierarchy of a human being (Homo sapiens) and a sunflower (Helianthus annuus):

Taxonomic Rank	Human (Homo sapiens)	Sunflower (Helianthus annuus)
Domain	Eukarya	Eukarya
Kingdom	Animalia	Plantae
Phylum	Chordata	Angiosperms
Class	Mammalia	Dicotyledons
Order	Primates	Asterales
Family	Hominidae	Asteraceae
Genus	Homo	Helianthus
Species	Homo sapiens	Helianthus annuus

Binomial Nomenclature

The system of **binomial nomenclature** is used to name species, giving each organism a two-part name based on its genus and species. For example, the scientific name of a human is **Homo sapiens**, where *Homo* is the genus and *sapiens* is the species. This naming system helps avoid confusion, as many organisms may have multiple common names but only one scientific name.

HUMAN BODY SYSTEMS

The human body is an incredibly complex and organized structure, made up of different systems that work together to maintain health, growth, and survival. Each system has specific components and performs vital functions, contributing to the body's overall function and balance, or homeostasis.

Human Body Systems

Body System	Components	Function
Circulatory System	Heart, blood vessels (arteries, veins, capillaries), blood	Transports oxygen, nutrients, and waste throughout the body
Digestive System	Mouth, esophagus, stomach, intestines, liver, pancreas, gallbladder	Breaks down food into nutrients for energy, growth, and cell repair
Respiratory System	Lungs, trachea, bronchi, diaphragm	Facilitates gas exchange (oxygen intake and carbon dioxide release)
Nervous System	Brain, spinal cord, nerves	Controls bodily functions, sends signals between body and brain

Body System	Components	Function
Skeletal System	Bones, cartilage, ligaments, tendons	Provides structure, protects organs, and allows movement
Muscular System	Skeletal muscles, smooth muscles, cardiac muscle	Facilitates movement, maintains posture, and generates heat
Integumentary System	Skin, hair, nails, sweat glands	Protects the body, regulates temperature, and senses external stimuli
Endocrine System	Glands (e.g., thyroid, adrenal, pituitary), hormones	Regulates body functions through hormones
Immune System	White blood cells, lymph nodes, spleen	Defends against pathogens and infections
Urinary System	Kidneys, bladder, ureters, urethra	Removes waste products from the blood and regulates fluid balance
Reproductive System	Male: testes, penis; Female: ovaries, uterus, vagina	Produces offspring and regulates reproductive hormones
Lymphatic System	Lymph nodes, lymphatic vessels, spleen	Maintains fluid levels and supports the immune system

Circulatory System

The **circulatory system**, also known as the cardiovascular system, is responsible for transporting oxygen, nutrients, and waste products throughout the body. This system consists of the heart, blood vessels (including arteries, veins, and capillaries), and blood itself. The heart acts as a pump, propelling blood through a network of vessels to reach every part of the body.

Blood has two primary components: **red blood cells**, which carry oxygen from the lungs to tissues, and **plasma**, the liquid portion that carries nutrients, hormones, and waste products. Oxygen-poor blood returns to the heart through the veins and is sent to the lungs, where it picks up oxygen and releases carbon dioxide. This oxygenated blood then flows back to the heart and is pumped throughout the body via the arteries.

The circulatory system plays a critical role in maintaining **homeostasis**, which is the body's ability to maintain stable internal conditions. For example, it helps regulate body temperature by distributing heat throughout the body and by directing blood to the skin's surface when the body needs to cool down. Additionally, the circulatory system delivers white blood cells and other immune factors to sites of infection, making it a key player in the body's defense mechanisms.

The heart has four chambers: two upper chambers (the **atria**) and two lower chambers (the **ventricles**). The heart beats approximately 100,000 times a day to keep blood circulating. The health of the circulatory system is critical for overall well-being. Conditions like hypertension (high blood pressure), atherosclerosis (narrowing of the arteries), and heart disease can impair its function, leading to serious complications such as heart attacks or strokes.

Digestive System

The **digestive system** is responsible for breaking down the food we consume into nutrients, which are then absorbed and used by the body for energy, growth, and cell repair. It consists of a series of hollow organs that form a long, continuous tube from the mouth to the anus. The main components of the digestive system include the mouth, esophagus, stomach, small intestine, large intestine, liver, pancreas, and gallbladder.

Digestion begins in the mouth, where food is chewed and mixed with saliva. Saliva contains enzymes that start breaking down carbohydrates. The chewed food is then swallowed and travels down the esophagus into the stomach. In the stomach, powerful acids and enzymes continue to break down the food, particularly proteins.

The partially digested food moves into the **small intestine**, where most nutrient absorption takes place. The **pancreas** secretes digestive enzymes into the small intestine to aid in the breakdown of carbohydrates, proteins, and fats. The liver produces bile, which is stored in the gallbladder and released into the small intestine to help digest fats. The walls of the small intestine are lined with tiny, finger-like projections called villi, which increase the surface area for nutrient absorption.

Once the nutrients are absorbed, the remaining indigestible material passes into the large intestine (or colon). Here, water is absorbed, and the waste material is compacted into feces. This waste is eventually eliminated from the body through the anus.

Respiratory System

The **respiratory system** is responsible for exchanging gases between the body and the environment. Its primary function is to bring oxygen into the body and expel carbon dioxide, a waste product of cellular respiration. The main organs involved in this system include the lungs, trachea, bronchi, bronchioles, and diaphragm.

Air enters the body through the nose or mouth and travels down the **trachea**. The trachea divides into two **bronchi**, which lead into each lung. Inside the lungs, the bronchi further divide into smaller tubes called **bronchioles**, which end in tiny air sacs known as **alveoli**. The alveoli are surrounded by **capillaries**, where oxygen from the inhaled air is absorbed into the bloodstream and carbon dioxide from the blood is released into the lungs to be exhaled.

The **diaphragm**, a dome-shaped muscle located below the lungs, plays a key role in breathing. When the diaphragm contracts, it flattens, allowing the lungs to expand and fill with air. When the diaphragm relaxes, the lungs compress, pushing air out.

The respiratory system works closely with the circulatory system to deliver oxygen to the body's tissues and remove carbon dioxide. Oxygen is vital for the process of cellular respiration, which generates the energy cells need to perform their functions.

Nervous System

The **nervous system** is the body's control center, responsible for regulating both voluntary actions, such as movement, and involuntary actions, such as heart rate and digestion. It is made up of two main components: the **central nervous system (CNS)**, which includes the brain and spinal cord, and the **peripheral nervous system (PNS)**, which consists of all the nerves that extend throughout the body.

The brain is the command center of the nervous system. It processes sensory information, controls muscle movements, and manages cognitive functions like memory, thinking, and emotions. The spinal cord acts as a highway for information, transmitting signals between the brain and the rest of the body.

The peripheral nervous system is further divided into the **somatic nervous system**, which controls voluntary movements like walking, and the **autonomic nervous system**, which controls involuntary functions like breathing and heart rate. The autonomic nervous system is further divided into the **sympathetic** and **parasympathetic** systems, which work together to maintain balance in the body's responses to stress and relaxation.

Nerve cells, or **neurons**, are the basic building blocks of the nervous system. Neurons communicate with each other through electrical and chemical signals, allowing the brain and body to respond to stimuli. **Sensory neurons** transmit information from the body to the brain, while **motor neurons** carry instructions from the brain to muscles and organs.

Skeletal System

The **skeletal system** provides the structural framework for the body, protecting vital organs and allowing movement. It consists of bones, cartilage, ligaments, and tendons. Humans have 206 bones, which come in various shapes and sizes to support different functions.

Bones serve several key roles: they provide structure, enable movement by acting as levers for muscles, protect internal organs (like the skull protecting the brain), store minerals (especially calcium and phosphorus), and produce blood cells in the bone marrow.

Cartilage is a flexible, rubbery tissue that cushions the joints and allows smooth movement. It is found in areas such as the nose, ears, and between bones at joints. **Ligaments** are tough bands of tissue that connect bones to other bones, stabilizing joints, while **tendons** attach muscles to bones, enabling movement.

Muscular System

The **muscular system** is responsible for all the movements of the body, from large motions like walking and lifting to small actions like blinking and speaking. There are three types of muscles in the body: skeletal muscles, smooth muscles, and cardiac muscle.

Skeletal muscles are attached to bones by tendons and are under voluntary control, meaning we consciously decide to move them. These muscles work in pairs; when one muscle contracts, the opposing muscle relaxes, allowing for coordinated movement. **Smooth muscles** are found in the walls of internal organs like the stomach, intestines, and blood vessels. They are involuntary muscles, meaning they function automatically without conscious thought. **Cardiac muscle**, found only in the heart, is also involuntary and contracts to pump blood throughout the body.

Muscle contraction occurs when muscle fibers are stimulated by nerve signals. **ATP (adenosine triphosphate)**, the body's energy currency, powers muscle contractions. Muscle function is critical for maintaining posture, generating heat to keep the body warm, and facilitating bodily movements essential for daily life.

Integumentary System

The **integumentary system** includes the skin, hair, nails, and glands (such as sweat and oil glands). It serves as the body's first line of defense against environmental hazards, such as harmful microorganisms and physical injuries, while also helping regulate body temperature and enabling sensory perception.

The **skin** is the body's largest organ, and it consists of three main layers: the epidermis, the dermis, and the subcutaneous layer. The **epidermis** is the outermost layer and acts as a protective barrier. The **dermis** lies beneath the epidermis and contains hair follicles, sweat glands, oil glands, nerves, and blood vessels. The **subcutaneous layer** is the innermost layer, made up of fat and connective tissue, which helps insulate the body and cushion internal organs.

Hair and nails are made of **keratin**, a tough protein that provides strength and protection. Hair helps regulate body temperature and protects the skin, while nails protect the tips of fingers and toes.

Sweat glands in the skin help regulate body temperature by releasing sweat, which cools the body when it evaporates. Oil glands produce **sebum**, an oily substance that lubricates and waterproofs the skin and hair.

Endocrine System

The **endocrine system** regulates various bodily functions through the production and release of hormones. Hormones are chemical messengers that travel through the bloodstream to target organs and tissues, influencing processes like growth, metabolism, and reproduction. The main components of the endocrine system include glands such as the thyroid, pituitary, adrenal glands, and pancreas.

The **thyroid gland** regulates metabolism, controlling how quickly the body uses energy. The **pituitary gland**, often called the "master gland," controls the release of hormones from other glands and regulates functions such as growth and reproduction. The **adrenal glands** produce hormones like adrenaline and cortisol, which help the body respond to stress. The **pancreas** regulates blood sugar levels by releasing insulin and glucagon.

The endocrine system works in concert with the nervous system to maintain balance and stability within the body. Hormonal imbalances can lead to a range of health issues, such as diabetes, hyperthyroidism, or hypothyroidism. Maintaining a healthy lifestyle, managing stress, and getting regular medical check-ups are important for keeping the endocrine system functioning properly.

Immune System

The **immune system** defends the body against harmful pathogens, such as bacteria, viruses, and parasites. It includes various organs and cells, such as white blood cells, the thymus, bone marrow, lymph nodes, and the spleen. The immune system identifies and neutralizes threats before they can cause significant harm.

White blood cells (or leukocytes) play a central role in the immune response. They can be classified into two main types: **phagocytes**, which engulf and digest invading organisms, and **lymphocytes**, which help the body recognize and remember pathogens for future defense. Lymphocytes include **B-cells**, which produce antibodies, and **T-cells**, which destroy infected cells.

The immune system has two main lines of defense: innate immunity and adaptive immunity. **Innate immunity** provides immediate defense against invaders through barriers like the skin and mucous membranes. **Adaptive immunity** develops over time and is more specialized, targeting specific pathogens that the body has encountered before.

When functioning properly, the immune system can prevent infections and diseases. However, when it malfunctions, it can lead to conditions such as autoimmune diseases (where the body attacks its own cells) or immunodeficiencies (where the immune system is weakened). Vaccination is one way to support the immune system by preparing it to recognize and combat specific diseases.

Urinary System

The **urinary system** helps remove waste products from the body and regulates fluid balance. Its main components are the kidneys, ureters, bladder, and urethra. The **kidneys** filter waste products and excess water from the blood, forming urine. The filtered blood returns to the body, while the urine is transported to the bladder via the **ureters**.

The bladder stores urine until it is expelled from the body through the urethra. This system helps maintain the body's fluid and electrolyte balance, regulate blood pressure, and remove harmful waste products.

The urinary system plays a crucial role in maintaining homeostasis. Conditions such as kidney stones, urinary tract infections (UTIs), and chronic kidney disease can affect its function. Drinking plenty of water, maintaining a healthy diet, and practicing good hygiene are important steps in maintaining urinary health.

Reproductive System

The **reproductive system** is responsible for producing offspring and ensuring the continuation of the species. In males, it includes organs such as the testes, which produce sperm, and the penis. In females, it includes the ovaries, which produce eggs, and the uterus, where a fertilized egg can develop into a fetus.

The male reproductive system produces sperm cells, which are essential for fertilizing the female's egg. The process begins in the **testes**, where sperm is produced and stored. During sexual activity, sperm is transported through the vas deferens and mixed with fluids from the prostate gland and seminal vesicles to form semen, which is expelled through the penis.

The female reproductive system produces egg cells and prepares the body for pregnancy. The **ovaries** release eggs during ovulation, and if an egg is fertilized by sperm, it implants itself in the uterus. Hormones like estrogen and progesterone regulate the menstrual cycle and prepare the body for pregnancy.

The reproductive system also produces hormones that regulate reproductive cycles and sexual characteristics. Conditions such as infertility, polycystic ovary syndrome (PCOS), and prostate cancer can affect the reproductive system.

The human body is an intricate network of systems, each of which plays a unique and vital role in maintaining health, supporting growth, and ensuring survival. From the circulatory system that transports oxygen and nutrients, to the nervous system that regulates body functions, to the skeletal and muscular systems that allow movement, every system is interconnected. Proper function of these systems depends on the balance and cooperation among them, creating a harmonious biological environment known as homeostasis.

Understanding the function of each body system helps us appreciate the complexity of the human body and the importance of maintaining its health through proper nutrition, exercise, and regular medical care, which we will cover next.

NUTRITION, HEALTH, AND DISEASES

Nutrition, health, and disease are closely intertwined aspects of human biology. Good nutrition is essential for maintaining the health of the body's systems, while poor nutrition can contribute to poor health and the development of diseases. Understanding the basics of nutrition and how it impacts health is key to preventing many illnesses and promoting overall well-being.

The Importance of Nutrition

Nutrition refers to the intake of food and how the body uses it for energy, growth, and cell repair. The human body needs a variety of nutrients, including **macronutrients** (carbohydrates, proteins, and fats) and **micronutrients** (vitamins and minerals), to function properly.

Carbohydrates provide the primary source of energy for the human body. **Proteins** are necessary for the growth and repair of tissues, as well as the production of enzymes and hormones. **Fats** are essential for energy storage, insulation, and the absorption of fat-soluble vitamins. **Vitamins** and **minerals** play important roles in regulating body processes, such as immune function, bone health, and red blood cell production.

A balanced diet that includes fruits, vegetables, whole grains, lean proteins, and healthy fats is vital for supporting the body's functions and preventing nutritional deficiencies. Poor dietary choices, such as consuming too much sugar, unhealthy fats, or processed foods, can lead to a range of health problems, including obesity, heart disease, and diabetes.

How Nutrition Affects Health

Good nutrition strengthens the immune system, supports healthy body weight, and reduces the risk of chronic diseases. For example, diets rich in fruits and vegetables provide antioxidants that help protect the body from cellular damage. Calcium and vitamin D are important for bone health, reducing the risk of osteoporosis. Omega-3 fatty acids, found in fish and certain plant oils, promote heart health by reducing inflammation and lowering cholesterol levels.

On the other hand, poor nutrition can lead to nutrient deficiencies, weaken the immune system, and increase the likelihood of developing diseases. **Malnutrition** can result from both undernutrition (not getting enough nutrients) and overnutrition (eating too many calories). Both conditions can have serious health consequences, from stunted growth and developmental delays in children to obesity and cardiovascular disease in adults.

Common Diseases Linked to Nutrition

Many common diseases are influenced by poor nutrition and lifestyle choices. For example:

- **Heart disease** is often associated with diets high in saturated fats, cholesterol, and salt. Consuming too much processed and fast food can increase the risk of developing cardiovascular issues.

- **Type 2 diabetes** is linked to excess sugar intake and poor weight management. Consistently high blood sugar levels can lead to insulin resistance, the hallmark of diabetes.

- **Obesity** is caused by an imbalance between calorie intake and energy expenditure. Excessive caloric intake, combined with a lack of physical activity, can lead to unhealthy weight gain and increase the risk of other diseases, such as joint problems, diabetes, and certain cancers.

- **Osteoporosis**, a condition in which bones become weak and brittle, can result from insufficient calcium and vitamin D intake.

Human Pathogens

Human pathogens are microorganisms that cause diseases in humans. These include bacteria, viruses, fungi, and protozoa. Each type of pathogen has unique characteristics, but all can invade the human body, multiply, and disrupt normal functions, leading to illness.

Bacteria are single-celled organisms that can cause diseases such as strep throat, tuberculosis, and urinary tract infections. Some bacteria are beneficial, but pathogenic bacteria can release toxins that harm human tissues.

Viruses are even smaller than bacteria and can only reproduce inside a host's cells. Diseases like influenza, HIV/AIDS, and COVID-19 are caused by viruses. They hijack the body's cells, turning them into virus-producing factories.

Fungi can cause infections, particularly in individuals with weakened immune systems. Athlete's foot and yeast infections are common fungal diseases.

Protozoa are single-celled organisms that cause illnesses like malaria and giardiasis. They are often transmitted through contaminated water, food, or insect bites.

The spread of pathogens can occur through direct contact, airborne droplets, contaminated food or water, or vectors like mosquitoes. Preventive measures such as vaccinations, good hygiene, and proper sanitation are crucial in controlling the spread of human pathogens. Early diagnosis and treatment with medications like antibiotics (for bacterial infections) or antiviral drugs (for viral infections) can help manage diseases caused by pathogens.

Maintaining good health involves more than just avoiding diseases. It requires a proactive approach to managing nutrition, physical activity, and lifestyle habits. A balanced diet, regular exercise, adequate hydration, and sufficient sleep are key components of a healthy lifestyle. In addition, regular medical check-ups and preventive care can catch potential health issues early and help manage existing conditions.

GENERAL AND LIFE SCIENCES PRACTICE QUESTIONS

Select the correct answer from the choices given. Life science questions are part of the ASVAB General Science (GS) subtest.

1. What is the primary function of DNA in living organisms?

A) To provide structural support to cells
B) To transport oxygen through the body
C) To code for proteins and genetic traits
D) To break down food for energy

2. Which of the following is an example of an anabolic process in metabolism?

A) Digestion of food into smaller molecules
B) Cellular respiration to release energy
C) Building muscle tissue from amino acids
D) The release of carbon dioxide from cells

3. In photosynthesis, which substance do plants use to capture sunlight?

A) Glucose
B) Oxygen
C) Chlorophyll
D) Carbon dioxide

4. Which organelle is responsible for producing energy in both plant and animal cells?

A) Nucleus
B) Mitochondria
C) Ribosome
D) Golgi apparatus

5. Which process is primarily responsible for plants producing their own food?

A) Cellular respiration
B) Photosynthesis
C) Fermentation
D) Protein synthesis

6. In humans, what is the primary role of the digestive system?

A) To circulate blood throughout the body
B) To break down food into nutrients
C) To regulate body temperature
D) To store fat for energy

7. Which system is responsible for transporting oxygen and nutrients throughout the body?

A) Respiratory system
B) Digestive system
C) Circulatory system
D) Endocrine system

8. What is the primary function of ribosomes in a cell?

A) To store genetic information
B) To synthesize proteins
C) To produce energy
D) To transport materials within the cell

9. Which type of reproduction involves genetic material from two parents, resulting in genetic variation in offspring?

A) Asexual reproduction
B) Sexual reproduction
C) Binary fission
D) Budding

10. Which of the following is an example of homeostasis in the human body?

A) Increased heart rate during exercise
B) Sweating to cool the body when it's hot
C) Growing taller during adolescence
D) Digesting food in the stomach

11. What is the primary role of the xylem in plants?

A) Transport sugars from leaves to roots
B) Facilitate photosynthesis
C) Transport water and minerals from roots to leaves
D) Release oxygen during photosynthesis

12. Which process ensures that each new cell in plants and animals receives an identical copy of DNA during cell division?

A) Photosynthesis
B) DNA replication
C) Cellular respiration
D) Meiosis

Answers and Explanations

1. C) To code for proteins and genetic traits.   Explanation: DNA contains genetic information in the form of genes, which are segments of DNA that code for specific proteins. These proteins perform essential functions in the body and help determine an organism's traits, such as eye color or susceptibility to certain diseases.

2. C) Building muscle tissue from amino acids.   Explanation: Anabolic processes involve the building up of larger molecules from smaller ones. In this case, the body builds muscle tissue by assembling amino acids into proteins, which is a typical anabolic activity. In contrast, catabolic processes break down molecules, such as in digestion.

3. C) Chlorophyll.   Explanation: Chlorophyll is the green pigment found in plants' chloroplasts that captures sunlight, which is then used to convert carbon dioxide and water into glucose during photosynthesis. This process also releases oxygen as a byproduct.

4. B) Mitochondria.   Explanation: The mitochondria are often called the "powerhouses" of the cell because they generate ATP (energy) through cellular respiration, which is essential for the cell's energy needs in both plants and animals.

5. B) Photosynthesis.   Explanation: Photosynthesis is the process by which plants convert sunlight, carbon dioxide, and water into glucose (a form of sugar) and oxygen. This glucose serves as food for the plant, providing energy for growth and development.

6. B) To break down food into nutrients.   Explanation: The digestive system's primary function is to break down the food we consume into smaller molecules like carbohydrates, proteins, and fats, which are then absorbed and used by the body for energy, growth, and repair.

7. C) Circulatory system.   Explanation: The circulatory system, consisting of the heart, blood vessels, and blood, is responsible for transporting oxygen from the lungs and nutrients from the digestive system to cells throughout the body.

8. B) To synthesize proteins.   Explanation: Ribosomes are responsible for assembling proteins by linking together amino acids based on the instructions provided by messenger RNA (mRNA), which is a crucial step in the production of proteins necessary for cellular functions.

9. B) Sexual reproduction.   Explanation: Sexual reproduction involves the combination of genetic material from two parents (sperm and egg), resulting in offspring with genetic variation. This variation is essential for the evolution and adaptation of species.

10. B) Sweating to cool the body when it's hot.   Explanation: Homeostasis refers to the body's ability to maintain a stable internal environment. Sweating is an example of homeostasis, where the body cools itself by releasing sweat in response to high temperatures to regulate body temperature.

11. C) Transport water and minerals from roots to leaves.   Explanation: Xylem is responsible for carrying water and dissolved minerals from the roots of the plant up through the stems and to the leaves, where it supports photosynthesis and other vital processes.

12. B) DNA replication.   Explanation: DNA replication is the process through which a cell copies its DNA before it divides, ensuring that each new cell has an identical set of genetic instructions. This is essential for growth, repair, and reproduction in living organisms.

§2. PHYSICAL SCIENCES

METRIC SYSTEM OF MEASUREMENT

The metric system, also known as the International System of Units (SI), is the standard system of measurement used in science and most countries around the world. Developed in the late 18th century, it provides a consistent way to measure and compare physical quantities like length, mass, volume, and temperature. This system is based on multiples of ten, making it simple and efficient to use across various scientific disciplines, including physics, chemistry, and biology.

Base Units of the Metric System

In the metric system, there are seven fundamental base units that define all other measurements, which are summarized in the following table.

Seven Fundamental Base Units of the Metric System

Quantity Measured	Base Unit	Symbol
Length	Meter	m
Mass	Kilogram	kg
Time	Second	s
Electric Current	Ampere	A
Temperature	Kelvin	K
Amount of Substance	Mole	mol
Luminous Intensity	Candela	cd

Prefixes in the Metric System

The metric system uses prefixes to indicate multiples or fractions of the base units. Each prefix represents a power of ten, making it easy to convert between larger and smaller quantities. For example:

- Kilo- (k) means 1,000 times the base unit. One kilometer (km) is 1,000 meters.
- Centi- (c) means 1/100th of the base unit. One centimeter (cm) is 0.01 meters.
- Milli- (m) means 1/1,000th of the base unit. One milliliter (mL) is 0.001 liters.
- Micro- (μ) means 1/1,000,000th of the base unit. One micrometer (μm) is 0.000001 meters.

These prefixes are essential in scientific measurements because they allow scientists to work with very large or very small numbers in a manageable way. For example, measuring the distance between stars might require gigameters (Gm), while observing bacteria under a microscope would use micrometers (μm).

One of the key reasons the metric system is preferred in science is its universality. Since the metric system is used worldwide, scientists can collaborate and share their results without needing to convert between different systems of measurement. This eliminates confusion and ensures that scientific data is accurate and comparable regardless of where the research is conducted.

Additionally, the metric system is decimal-based, which simplifies calculations. Converting between units is straightforward: simply move the decimal point. For instance, converting from centimeters to meters requires moving the decimal two places to the left (since there are 100 centimeters in a meter). This simplicity contrasts with non-metric systems like the Imperial system, where conversions between units are more complex (e.g., 12 inches in a foot, 3 feet in a yard).

PHYSICS

Weight vs. mass

Weight and mass are often used interchangeably, but they refer to different concepts. Mass is the amount of matter in an object and remains constant regardless of location. It is measured in kilograms (kg) or grams. Weight, on the other hand, is the force exerted on an object due to gravity and depends on both the object's mass and the gravitational pull acting on it. It is measured in newtons (N). For example, an object's mass stays the same on Earth and the Moon, but its weight would be less on the Moon due to the weaker gravitational pull. Thus, mass is intrinsic, while weight varies with gravity.

Motion: Key Concepts

Motion is the change in position of an object over time, and it is a fundamental concept in physics. Understanding motion requires analyzing several key concepts: **velocity**, **displacement**, **momentum**, and **acceleration**.

Velocity and Displacement

Velocity is the rate at which an object changes its position. It's a vector quantity, meaning it has both magnitude (speed) and direction. Velocity differs from speed because speed only tells us how fast an object is moving, while velocity tells us both how fast and in what direction. For example, if a car is moving at 60 miles per hour north, that's its velocity. The formula for velocity is: $v = \frac{\Delta x}{\Delta t}$, Where v is velocity, Δx is displacement (change in position), and Δt is the time it takes for that displacement to occur.

Displacement refers to an object's overall change in position, considering both the distance and the direction from its starting point to its final position. Unlike distance, which only measures how much ground has been covered, displacement takes direction into account. For example, if you walk 5 meters east and then 5 meters west, your total distance is 10 meters, but your displacement is zero because you ended up in the same place you started.

Momentum

Momentum is a measure of how much motion an object has and is also a vector quantity. It depends on both the mass of an object and its velocity. The more massive an object or the faster it's moving, the more momentum it has. The formula for momentum is: $p = mv$, where p is momentum, m is mass, and v is velocity. For example, a truck moving at 20 m/s will have more momentum than a bicycle moving at the same speed because the truck has much more mass.

Momentum is important in understanding collisions and impacts. When two objects collide, the total momentum before the collision is equal to the total momentum after the collision, provided no external forces act on the system. This principle is known as the conservation of momentum.

Acceleration

Acceleration refers to the rate at which an object's velocity changes over time. It occurs when there's a change in speed, direction, or both. Like velocity, acceleration is a vector quantity, meaning it has both magnitude and direction. The formula for acceleration is: $a = \frac{\Delta v}{\Delta t}$, where a is acceleration, Δv is the change in velocity, and Δt is the time over which this change occurs. Positive acceleration means an object is speeding up, while negative acceleration (often called deceleration) means it's slowing down.

An example of acceleration can be seen when a car speeds up from rest to 60 miles per hour in 10 seconds. The car's velocity is increasing, so it is accelerating. If the car suddenly comes to a stop, it experiences negative acceleration as it slows down to zero.

Work, Force, Energy, and Power

In physics, work, force, energy, and power are fundamental concepts that explain how objects move, interact, and transfer energy in different situations. These terms are closely related, but each has its own specific meaning and application.

Force

Force is any interaction that, when unopposed, changes the motion of an object. It can cause an object to start moving, stop moving, or change its direction. Force is a vector quantity, meaning it has both magnitude and direction. It is measured in newtons (N), and the formula to calculate force is: $F = ma$, where: F is the force, m is the mass of the object, a is the acceleration.

For example, pushing a cart requires a force, and the larger the mass of the cart, the more force is needed to accelerate it.

Work

Work occurs when a force is applied to an object, causing it to move. In physics, work is only done when the force results in movement, and the movement is in the direction of the applied force.

The formula for work is: $W = Fd \cos \theta$, where: W is work (measured in joules (J)), F is the applied force, d is the distance the object moves, θ is the angle between the force and the direction of movement.

If the force is applied in the same direction as the object's movement, $\cos \theta$ equals 1, and the formula simplifies to $W = Fd$. For example, lifting a box vertically requires work because you are applying a force (upward) to move the box over a distance (upward).

If no movement occurs, no work is done—even if a large force is applied. For example, if you push against a wall with all your strength and it doesn't move, you haven't done any physical work in the scientific sense.

Energy

Energy is the capacity to do work. It comes in various forms, including kinetic energy, potential energy, and thermal energy. In physics, the most common forms of energy are: kinetic energy and potential energy.

Kinetic energy (KE): The energy an object possesses due to its motion. The faster an object moves, the more kinetic energy it has. The formula for kinetic energy is: $KE = \frac{1}{2}mv^2$, where: m is the mass of the object, v is its velocity.

Potential energy (PE): The energy stored in an object due to its position in a force field, typically a gravitational field. The formula for gravitational potential energy is: $PE = mgh$, where: m is the mass of the object, g is the acceleration due to gravity, h is the height above a reference point.

For example, a book held above a table has potential energy due to its position. If it falls, that potential energy is converted to kinetic energy.

Energy is measured in joules (J), the same unit as work. This reflects the fact that energy is the ability to perform work.

Example—Energy Calculation: A car with a mass of 1,200 kg is traveling at a velocity of 20 m/s. Calculate the car's kinetic energy.

Solution: The formula for kinetic energy (KE) is: $KE = \frac{1}{2}mv^2$

Step 1: Identify the known values
- Mass of the car, $m = 1{,}200$ kg
- Velocity of the car, $v = 20$ m/s

Step 2: Plug the values into the formula:
$$KE = \frac{1}{2} \times 1{,}200 \,\text{kg} \times (20\,\text{m/s})^2 = \frac{1}{2} \times 1{,}200\,\text{kg} \times 400\,\text{m}^2/\text{s}^2 = 240{,}000\,\text{kg} \cdot \text{m}^2/\text{s}^2$$
Hence, the kinetic energy of the car is 240,000 joules (J).

This example demonstrates how kinetic energy is calculated based on the mass and velocity of an object. In this case, the car's motion provides a significant amount of energy due to its large mass and speed.

Power

Power is the rate at which work is done or the rate at which energy is transferred or transformed. It tells us how quickly work is completed. The formula for power is: $P = \frac{W}{t}$, where: P is power (measured in watts (W)), W is work (in joules), t is the time taken (in seconds).

Power can also be expressed as: $P = \frac{Fd}{t}$. This equation shows that the faster work is done, or the faster energy is transferred, the greater the power output. For example, if two people lift identical boxes to the same height, but one person lifts the box in half the time, that person has exerted more power.

Examples of Work, Energy, and Power in Everyday Life

Work: A person pushing a lawnmower does work because they apply force to move the lawnmower across a distance.

Energy: A moving car has kinetic energy due to its motion. When the car brakes, that kinetic energy is transformed into thermal energy (heat) through friction.

Power: A 100-watt lightbulb uses 100 joules of electrical energy per second to produce light.

To recap, force causes motion, work is done when a force moves an object, energy is the capacity to do work, and power is the rate at which work is performed or energy is transferred. These concepts are fundamental to understanding how objects move and interact with forces in the physical world.

Newton's Three Laws of Motion and the Law of Universal Gravitation

Sir Isaac Newton's three laws of motion and his law of universal gravitation are foundational principles in physics. Together, they describe how objects move and interact with forces, including the force of gravity, which governs the motion of everything from falling apples to orbiting planets.

Newton's First Law of Motion (Law of Inertia)

Newton's first law states that: "An object at rest will remain at rest, and an object in motion will remain in motion at a constant velocity unless acted upon by an external force."

This is also known as the law of inertia, which refers to an object's resistance to changes in its state of motion. If no external force acts on an object, its motion will not change—an object at rest will stay at rest, and a moving object will continue moving in a straight line at constant speed.

Example: A soccer ball lying still on the ground will not move unless someone kicks it (an external force). Once kicked, it will keep moving until forces like friction or a player's foot act to stop it.

Newton's Second Law of Motion (Force and Acceleration)

Newton's second law explains how force and acceleration are related, and is expressed by the formula: $F = ma$, where: F is the force applied to the object (in newtons, N), m is the mass of the object (in kilograms, kg), a is the acceleration of the object (in meters per second squared, m/s^2).

This law states that the acceleration of an object depends on the force applied to it and its mass. A greater force results in greater acceleration, but heavier objects require more force to accelerate at the same rate as lighter ones.

Example: Pushing an empty shopping cart requires less effort (force) than pushing a fully loaded cart. The more mass the cart has, the more force you need to apply to achieve the same acceleration.

Example: Let's assume a car has a mass of 1,200 kg, and it accelerates at a rate of 3 m/s². To find the force required to produce this acceleration, we can apply Newton's Second Law.

$$F = m \cdot a = 1{,}200\,\text{kg} \times 3\,\text{m/s}^2 = 3{,}600\,\text{N}$$

So, the force needed to accelerate the car is 3,600 N (Newtons). This illustrates how the relationship between mass and acceleration dictates the force necessary to move an object, following Newton's Second Law of Motion.

Newton's Third Law of Motion (Action and Reaction)

Newton's third law states: "For every action, there is an equal and opposite reaction."

This means that whenever one object exerts a force on another, the second object exerts an equal force in the opposite direction. These forces are always paired, with both acting simultaneously.

Example: When you jump off a diving board, you push down on the board with your legs (action), and the board pushes you upward with an equal force (reaction), allowing you to leap into the air. Similarly, a rocket launches by expelling gas downward (action), which propels the rocket upward (reaction).

Newton's Law of Universal Gravitation

Newton's law of universal gravitation describes the force of gravity between two objects. The law states that: "Every particle in the universe attracts every other particle with a force directly proportional to the product of their masses and inversely proportional to the square of the distance between their centers."

The formula for this gravitational force is: $F = G\frac{m_1 m_2}{r^2}$, where: F is the gravitational force between two objects, G is the gravitational constant ($6.674 \times 10^{-11}\,\text{Nm}^2/\text{kg}^2$), m_1 and m_2 are the masses of the two objects, r is the distance between the centers of the two objects.

This law explains why objects fall toward Earth and why planets orbit the Sun. Gravity is always present, pulling objects with mass toward one another, though the force weakens as distance increases.

Example: The gravitational pull of Earth keeps the Moon in orbit, and the force between Earth and an apple causes the apple to fall when it is dropped. The larger the masses of the objects, and the closer they are to one another, the stronger the gravitational force.

How These Laws Work Together

Newton's three laws of motion describe how objects behave when forces act on them, and his law of universal gravitation explains the specific force of gravity. For example, when you drop a ball, the force of gravity (as described by the law of gravitation) pulls it toward the Earth. According to Newton's first law, the ball would remain stationary unless acted on by this external force (gravity). As it falls, the ball accelerates due to gravity, following Newton's second law ($F = ma$). When the ball hits the ground, Newton's third law applies—the ball exerts a force on the ground, and the ground exerts an equal and opposite force on the ball, causing it to bounce.

Together, these principles give us a comprehensive understanding of motion, whether it's the motion of everyday objects or the orbits of planets in space. Newton's laws provide the foundation for much of classical physics and are crucial for solving real-world problems involving force, motion, and gravity.

Velocity

Velocity is a vector quantity that describes the speed of an object in a specific direction. It differs from speed, which only accounts for the magnitude (how fast an object is moving) and not the direction. The formula for velocity when an object is accelerating is:

$$v = u + a \cdot t$$

Where:

- v is the final velocity,
- u is the initial velocity (starting speed),
- a is the acceleration (change in velocity over time),
- t is the time over which the acceleration occurs.

Example 1: A car starts from rest (initial velocity $u = 0$ m/s) and accelerates at a rate of $2 \, \text{m/s}^2$ for 5 seconds. What is the car's final velocity?

Solution: Using the formula: $v = u + a \cdot t = 0 \, \text{m/s} + (2 \, \text{m/s}^2 \times 5 \, \text{seconds}) = 10 \, \text{m/s}$

  Final Velocity: The car's velocity after 5 seconds is $10 \, \text{m/s}$.

Example 2: A cyclist is moving with an initial velocity of 10 m/s and accelerates at a rate of $3 \, \text{m/s}^2$ for 8 seconds. What is the final velocity?

Solution: Using the formula: $v = u + a \cdot t = 10 \, \text{m/s} + (3 \, \text{m/s}^2 \times 8 \, \text{seconds}) = 10 \, \text{m/s} + 24 \, \text{m/s} = 34 \, \text{m/s}$

  Final Velocity: The cyclist's final velocity is $34 \, \text{m/s}$.

In both examples, the formula for velocity incorporates the initial velocity, the acceleration, and the time over which acceleration occurs. In the first example, the object starts from rest, making it simpler to calculate. In the second example, the object starts with an initial velocity, requiring the calculation of how much the velocity increases due to the acceleration over time.

Waves

Waves are disturbances that transfer energy from one point to another without transferring matter. They are found in many physical phenomena, including light, water, and sound. Waves can be classified into two main types: mechanical waves and electromagnetic waves. Sound waves are a specific type of mechanical wave that requires a medium, like air, water, or solids, to travel through.

Types of Waves

Mechanical Waves: These waves require a medium (like air, water, or solids) to propagate. Examples include sound waves and water waves. Mechanical waves can be further divided into:

- Transverse waves: In these waves, the motion of the medium is perpendicular to the direction of the wave. For example, in water waves, the water particles move up and down while the wave travels horizontally.

- Longitudinal waves: In these waves, the motion of the medium is parallel to the direction of the wave. Sound waves are an example of longitudinal waves, where the particles of the medium (such as air) move back and forth in the same direction as the wave.

Electromagnetic Waves: These waves do not require a medium and can travel through a vacuum. Light, radio waves, and X-rays are examples of electromagnetic waves. Unlike mechanical waves, electromagnetic waves are transverse waves.

Key Characteristics of Waves

Waves have several key characteristics that define their behavior. The **wavelength** is the distance between two consecutive points in phase on a wave, such as two crests or troughs, and is measured in meters. Another important feature is the **frequency**, which represents the number of waves that pass a given point in a specific period and is measured in hertz (Hz). A higher frequency means more waves pass through a point over time. **Amplitude** refers to the height of the wave from its rest position to its crest in transverse waves, or the maximum displacement in longitudinal waves. The amplitude determines the energy carried by the wave—the greater the amplitude, the more energy it possesses. The **speed of the wave** is how fast the wave travels through a medium and depends on the type of wave and the properties of the medium.

Parts of a Wave

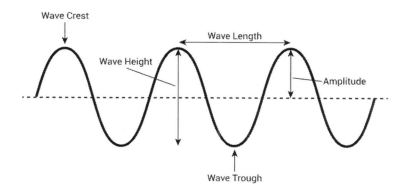

Sound Waves

Sound waves are mechanical, longitudinal waves that propagate through a medium (such as air, water, or solids) by vibrating the particles in that medium. The movement of particles creates areas of compression (where particles are close together) and rarefaction (where particles are spread apart). These compressions and rarefactions travel through the medium, allowing sound to propagate.

Sound waves differ from electromagnetic waves in that they cannot travel through a vacuum because they need a medium to carry the vibrations. The speed of sound varies depending on the medium:

- In air, sound travels at approximately 343 m/s.
- In water, sound travels faster, at about 1,480 m/s.
- In solids, sound travels even faster because the particles are more tightly packed, making it easier for them to transfer vibrations.

Pitch and Volume: The frequency of a sound wave determines its pitch. Higher frequency sound waves produce higher-pitched sounds (like a whistle), while lower frequency sound waves produce lower-pitched sounds (like a drum).

The amplitude of a sound wave is related to its volume. A wave with a greater amplitude will sound louder, while a wave with a smaller amplitude will sound quieter.

The Doppler Effect: One important phenomenon related to sound waves is the Doppler Effect. This occurs when the source of a sound is moving relative to the observer. If the source is moving toward the observer, the sound waves are compressed, resulting in a higher pitch (higher frequency). Conversely, if the source is moving away, the waves are stretched, resulting in a lower pitch (lower frequency). A classic example of the Doppler Effect is the change in pitch of a siren as an ambulance passes by.

Applications of Sound Waves: Sound waves have many practical applications. For example, ultrasound technology uses high-frequency sound waves to create images of structures inside the body, such as unborn babies in prenatal care. Another example is Sonar (Sound Navigation and Ranging), which uses sound waves to detect objects underwater, which is widely used in submarine navigation and fish detection.

In summary, waves are disturbances that transfer energy, and sound waves are a specific type of mechanical wave that propagate through a medium.

Electromagnetic spectrum

The electromagnetic spectrum encompasses all types of electromagnetic radiation, from the low-energy radio waves to the high-energy gamma rays. **Electromagnetic radiation** consists of waves of electric and magnetic fields that travel through space at the speed of light, carrying energy. These waves don't require a medium and can propagate through the vacuum of space, unlike mechanical waves like sound. The spectrum is categorized based on the wavelength and frequency of these waves, with longer wavelengths corresponding to lower frequencies and energy, and shorter wavelengths corresponding to higher frequencies and energy.

At the low-frequency end of the spectrum, **radio waves** have the longest wavelengths and are used extensively in communication technologies, such as radio, television, and cell phones. Moving up the spectrum, **microwaves** have shorter wavelengths and are used in radar technology and microwave ovens. Further along, **infrared radiation** is primarily associated with heat, as objects emit infrared light when they radiate heat. **Visible light**, the only part of the electromagnetic spectrum perceptible to the human eye, occupies a relatively small range within the spectrum, and its wavelengths correspond to the colors we see. Beyond visible light lies **ultraviolet radiation**, which has higher energy and can cause sunburn. The highest-energy waves on the spectrum are **X-rays** and **gamma rays**, both of which are used in medical imaging and cancer treatment due to their ability to penetrate matter.

Two key phenomena related to the behavior of electromagnetic waves are refraction and reflection. **Refraction** occurs when light or other electromagnetic waves pass from one medium into another (such as from air into water) and change speed, causing the wave to bend. The degree to which the wave bends depends on the wavelength of the light and the properties of the two media. This effect is why a straw in a glass of water appears bent or displaced at the surface of the water. Refraction is also responsible for phenomena like the splitting of white light into a rainbow when it passes through a prism, with each color bending by a different amount due to its wavelength.

Reflection, on the other hand, occurs when electromagnetic waves encounter a surface and bounce back rather than passing through it. A common example is the reflection of light off a mirror. The angle at which the light hits the surface, known as the angle of incidence, is equal to the angle at which it reflects off the surface, called the angle of reflection. Reflection is essential in technologies such as optical instruments and communication devices, where mirrors or reflective surfaces direct waves to specific locations.

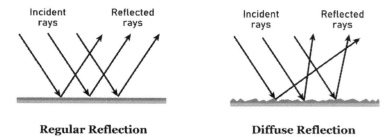

Regular Reflection   **Diffuse Reflection**

The interaction of electromagnetic waves with different materials and surfaces—whether through refraction, reflection, or other processes—enables the wide range of applications and technologies that depend on the electromagnetic spectrum, from wireless communication to medical imaging.

Heat and Phase Change

Heat is a form of energy that flows between objects due to a difference in their temperatures. It is crucial in understanding how matter changes between its three fundamental states: solid, liquid, and gas. The process by which matter transitions from one state to another is known as a **phase change**, and these transitions occur when heat energy is either absorbed or released by a substance.

In a **solid** state, the molecules are tightly packed together and vibrate in place, giving solids a definite shape and volume. As heat is added to a solid, the molecules begin to vibrate more rapidly, and if enough heat is supplied, the substance reaches its **melting point**, the temperature at which it transitions into a **liquid**. In the liquid state, the molecules are still close together but can move around more freely, allowing liquids to take the shape of their container while maintaining a fixed volume.

As more heat is added to a liquid, the molecules gain enough energy to break free from the forces that hold them together, leading to **evaporation** or **boiling**, where the liquid transitions into a gas. In the gaseous state, molecules are far apart and move independently, which allows gases to fill any container they are in. The temperature at which a liquid turns into a gas is called its **boiling point**.

Conversely, when heat is removed from a gas, the molecules lose energy, slow down, and move closer together, eventually condensing into a liquid. This process is called **condensation** and occurs when gas molecules release energy in the form of heat as they return to a liquid state. If even more heat is removed, the liquid can solidify through **freezing**, where the molecules arrange themselves into a rigid structure again, forming a solid.

During these phase transitions, the temperature of the substance remains constant, even though heat is being added or removed. For instance, while ice melts into water, the temperature stays at 0°C (32°F) until all the ice has melted, despite the continuous input of heat. Similarly, when water boils, its temperature stays at 100°C (212°F) until it fully transitions into steam. This constant temperature during phase changes occurs because the added heat energy is used to break molecular bonds rather than increasing the kinetic energy of the molecules.

Heat also plays a critical role in processes like **sublimation**, where a solid transitions directly into a gas without becoming a liquid, and **deposition**, where a gas turns directly into a solid, bypassing the liquid phase. Dry ice, for example, sublimates at room temperature, turning from solid carbon dioxide directly into carbon dioxide gas.

Heat Transfer: How Heat is Conducted Between Objects

Heat transfer is the process by which thermal energy moves from one object to another due to a temperature difference. Heat always flows from a hotter object to a cooler one until both objects reach thermal equilibrium. There are three primary methods of heat transfer: conduction, convection, and radiation.

Conduction is the transfer of heat through direct contact between objects. It occurs when particles in a hot object collide with particles in a cooler object, transferring energy in the form of heat. For example, when you touch a metal spoon in a hot pot, heat is conducted from the spoon to your hand. Materials like metals are good conductors of heat because their particles transfer energy easily. On the other hand, materials like wood or plastic are poor conductors, known as insulators, because they resist the transfer of heat.

In **convection**, heat is transferred through the movement of fluids (liquids or gases). As the fluid heats up, it becomes less dense and rises, while cooler, denser fluid sinks, creating a circulation pattern that transfers heat. This is why warm air rises and cooler air sinks in a room.

Radiation transfers heat through electromagnetic waves without needing a medium. For example, the Sun transfers heat to the Earth through radiation, even though space is a vacuum and there is no physical contact between the Sun and Earth.

Four Laws of Thermodynamics

The study of heat and its role in phase changes leads us naturally to the four laws of thermodynamics, which provide a deeper understanding of energy exchange in physical systems. These laws define the fundamental principles of how energy is conserved, transferred, and transformed, from the heat flowing between objects to the work done by engines or other systems.

Zeroth Law of Thermodynamics: this law establishes the concept of **thermal equilibrium**. It says that if two systems are each in thermal equilibrium with a third system, they are also in equilibrium with each other. This law explains why we can use thermometers to measure temperature—if two objects have the same temperature, no heat will flow between them.

The **First Law of Thermodynamics** states that energy cannot be created or destroyed, only transferred or transformed. The total energy in a system remains constant. For example, when you heat an object, some of the heat is used to raise its temperature, while some may be used to do work. Energy is always conserved.

The **Second Law** introduces the idea of **entropy**, which is the measure of disorder in a system. It states that natural processes tend to increase entropy, meaning energy spreads out and becomes less usable over time. This explains why heat always flows from hot objects to cold ones and why no machine can be 100% efficient.

The **Third Law** states that as a system approaches **absolute zero** (0 Kelvin), its entropy, or disorder, approaches a minimum value. In other words, at absolute zero, particles have minimal motion, and the system reaches its most ordered state. In reality, absolute zero is unreachable, but this law explains the behavior of systems at very low temperatures.

Magnetism and Polarization

Magnetism is a force generated by the movement of electric charges, causing certain materials to attract or repel each other. Magnetic fields are created by electrons moving within atoms, and these fields exert forces on other magnets or magnetic materials like iron. Magnets have two poles, north and south, where the magnetic force is strongest. Opposite poles attract, while like poles repel.

Polarization in magnetism refers to the alignment of the magnetic domains within a material. In unmagnetized materials, these domains are randomly oriented, canceling each other out. However, when exposed to a magnetic field, the domains align in the same direction, creating a magnetic effect. This process is crucial in creating magnets and in technologies like magnetic storage devices.

Magnetism and polarization are essential in many modern applications, from electric motors and generators to data storage in computers, all relying on controlled magnetic fields.

CHEMISTRY

Elements and the Periodic Table

In chemistry, **elements** are the simplest forms of matter, composed of only one type of atom. These atoms are characterized by the number of protons in their nucleus, which defines their **atomic number**. For example, hydrogen has an atomic number of 1 (one proton), while carbon has an atomic number of 6 (six protons). Every element has its unique atomic structure, which gives it specific chemical properties.

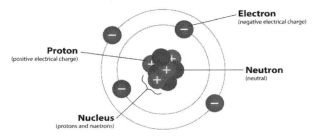

Atoms consist of three subatomic particles:

- **Protons:** These are positively charged particles found in the nucleus (center) of an atom. The number of protons in an atom determines its element and its atomic number on the periodic table.

- **Neutrons:** Neutrons are neutral (no charge) particles also located in the nucleus. They help stabilize the nucleus and, together with protons, contribute to an atom's atomic mass.

- **Electrons:** Electrons are negatively charged particles that orbit the nucleus in various energy levels or shells. They are much smaller than protons and neutrons and are responsible for the chemical reactions and bonding between atoms.

Protons and neutrons make up the dense core of the atom called the nucleus, while electrons orbit the nucleus in various energy levels or shells. The arrangement of these electrons largely determines an element's chemical reactivity.

Overview of the Periodic Table

The Periodic Table of Elements is a systematic arrangement of elements based on their atomic numbers. The table is structured in periods (horizontal rows) and groups (vertical columns). Elements within the same group have similar properties due to the same number of valence electrons, or electrons in their outer shell. The arrangement helps predict how elements behave chemically and how they will react with other elements.

PERIODIC TABLE OF THE ELEMENTS

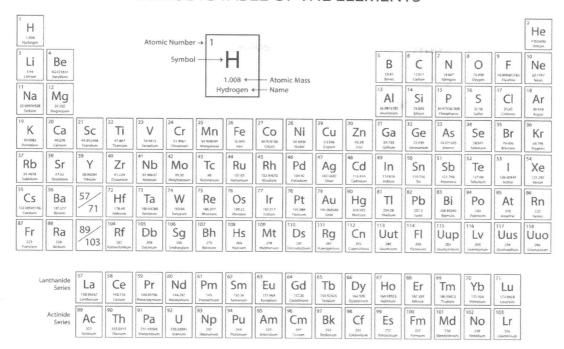

The periodic table contains a great deal of information about the atoms of each known element. Let's use the following figure as an example. This figure presents key information about an element as displayed on the periodic table. Each section of the element's box provides specific details essential for identifying the element and its properties.

Element Name: The full name of the element, in this case, Molybdenum.

Atomic Number: This represents the number of protons in an atom's nucleus. For Molybdenum, it's 42.

Atomic Symbol: The one- or two-letter abbreviation for the element, here it's "Mo."

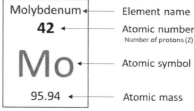

Atomic Mass: This is the average mass of an atom of the element, accounting for all isotopes. For Molybdenum, it is 95.94 atomic mass units (amu).

Groups and Periods

Groups are the vertical columns, numbered from 1 to 18. Elements in the same group tend to have similar chemical behaviors because of their similar electron configurations. For instance, Group 1 consists of the alkali metals, which are highly reactive due to their single valence electron. Group 18, the noble gases, is composed of elements that are generally inert because they have full valence shells.

Periods are the horizontal rows. As you move across a period from left to right, elements transition from metals to nonmetals, and their chemical properties change. For example, elements on the left side (like sodium) are metals, while those on the right (like chlorine) are nonmetals.

Element Categories

Metals: Found on the left and center of the periodic table, metals are typically malleable, conductive, and shiny. Examples include iron (Fe) and copper (Cu).

Nonmetals: Located on the right side of the table, nonmetals are usually poor conductors of heat and electricity. They are often gases or brittle solids at room temperature. Examples include oxygen (O) and carbon (C).

Metalloids: Elements that possess properties of both metals and nonmetals, making them useful in technology and industry. Silicon (Si), for example, is a metalloid often used in semiconductors.

Key Element Groups

Alkali Metals (Group 1): Extremely reactive, especially with water, alkali metals include lithium (Li) and potassium (K). They are soft metals that are highly reactive due to their single valence electron.

Alkaline Earth Metals (Group 2): These metals, such as calcium (Ca) and magnesium (Mg), are less reactive than alkali metals but still react with water and air to form oxides.

Transition Metals (Groups 3-12): Known for their ability to form colorful compounds, transition metals are often used in construction and manufacturing. Examples include iron (Fe) and gold (Au).

Halogens (Group 17): These are reactive nonmetals, such as fluorine (F) and chlorine (Cl), which readily form compounds with metals and other nonmetals.

Noble Gases (Group 18): Known for their lack of reactivity, noble gases like helium (He) and neon (Ne) have full electron shells, making them stable and chemically inert.

Periodic Trends

The periodic table reveals various trends that help predict element behavior:

- **Atomic Radius:** The size of an atom, or atomic radius, increases as you move down a group because additional electron shells are added. However, as you move across a period from left to right, the atomic radius decreases due to increasing positive charge in the nucleus pulling electrons closer.

- **Electronegativity:** This is the ability of an atom to attract electrons. Electronegativity increases across a period from left to right because atoms become more eager to fill their valence shell. Conversely, it decreases as you move down a group.

- **Ionization Energy:** This refers to the energy required to remove an electron from an atom. Ionization energy increases across a period, as atoms hold onto their electrons more tightly, and decreases down a group as the outer electrons are farther from the nucleus and easier to remove.

Importance of the Periodic Table

The periodic table is an indispensable tool in chemistry. By organizing elements based on their atomic structure and properties, it allows scientists and students to predict how elements will interact in chemical reactions. For example, understanding the periodic trends can explain why sodium reacts explosively with water or why noble gases are used in applications where chemical stability is crucial. This systematic arrangement of elements has revolutionized the way we study and understand the building blocks of matter.

Physical vs. Chemical Changes

A **molecule** is a group of two or more atoms chemically bonded together. These atoms can be of the same element, such as in oxygen (O_2), or different elements, like in water (H_2O). Molecules are the basic building blocks of chemical substances and can vary in size, complexity, and function, forming everything from simple gases to complex proteins in living organisms.

Molecules can change in physical or chemical ways. **Physical changes** affect the appearance or state of a substance without altering its chemical structure. For example, melting ice changes its state from solid to liquid, but it remains H_2O.

Chemical changes, on the other hand, involve a transformation at the molecular level. Bonds between atoms are broken and reformed, creating new substances with different properties. A classic example is the rusting of iron, where iron reacts with oxygen to form iron oxide, a completely new compound.

Compound vs. Molecule

A discussion of the difference between molecule and compound is in order here. A **compound** is a substance made up of two or more different types of atoms chemically bonded together in a fixed ratio. For example, water (H_2O) is a compound consisting of two hydrogen atoms and one oxygen atom. In contrast, Oxygen (O_2) is not a compound because it consists of only one type of element—oxygen. A compound, by definition, must contain two or more different elements chemically bonded together.

While **molecules** are groups of atoms bonded together, they can either be compounds (different types of atoms) or elements (same type of atom, like O_2). Therefore, all compounds are molecules, but not all molecules are compounds. Compounds always involve different elements, whereas molecules can consist of the same element.

Compound vs. Mixture

We already know that a compound is a substance formed when two or more different elements are chemically bonded together in fixed proportions. The chemical bonds that hold the elements together give the compound unique properties, distinct from the elements that form it. For example, water(H_2O) is a compound made of hydrogen and oxygen atoms. In a compound, the individual elements lose their original properties to create a new substance with different characteristics.

A **mixture**, on the other hand, consists of two or more substances physically combined but not chemically bonded. Each substance in a mixture retains its original properties and can be separated by physical means. For example, saltwater is a mixture of salt (NaCl) and water (H_2O). Mixtures can be **homogeneous** (uniform composition, like saltwater or wine) or **heterogeneous** (non-uniform, like a salad). Here are a couple of examples of heterogeneous mixture:

- **Oil and water**: When mixed, these liquids do not combine uniformly and instead separate into different layers, forming a heterogeneous mixture.

- **Granite**: A type of rock that is made up of visibly different minerals like quartz, feldspar, and mica, creating a non-uniform composition.

The key distinction between compound and mixture is that no chemical reaction occurs between the components in a mixture, whereas a compound involves a chemical change where bonds are formed or broken.

Acids vs. Bases

Acids are substances that release hydrogen ions (H$^+$) when dissolved in water, making the solution more acidic. Common acids include vinegar (acetic acid) and lemon juice (citric acid). Acids typically taste sour, can corrode metals, and have a pH less than 7. Strong acids like hydrochloric acid (HCl) completely dissociate in water, while weak acids, like acetic acid, only partially dissociate.

Bases, on the other hand, release hydroxide ions (OH$^-$) in water or accept hydrogen ions. Examples include baking soda (sodium bicarbonate) and bleach (sodium hypochlorite). Bases usually feel slippery, taste bitter, and have a pH greater than 7. Strong bases, such as sodium hydroxide (NaOH), fully dissociate, while weak bases only partially ionize.

Comparison: Acids and bases are opposites on the pH scale, with acids having a pH below 7 and bases above 7. While acids donate hydrogen ions, bases either accept them or release hydroxide ions. When mixed, they can neutralize each other, forming water and a salt. Both are essential in various chemical reactions, though they have contrasting properties and uses in everyday life.

Food Acidity and Alkalinity

Many foods and beverages are more acidic or basic than you might think. In fact, to human taste buds, acidic foods taste sour or tart and basic foods taste bitter. Knowing the pH of food and beverages can help you maintain a healthy diet. Research has proven that a highly acidic diet can cause long-term stomach problems such as ulcers or acid reflux, while a highly basic diet can cause digestion problems, due to an increased pH in your stomach. In addition, acidic foods and beverages can have a slow, but dangerous effect on your teeth. Your teeth are composed of a form of calcium phosphate, which can melt under acidic conditions. A list of acidic and basic foods is provided in the following table.

Food	pH
Cake, bread, rice	7.0–7.5
Vegetables (peas, cabbage, etc.)	6.0–6.5
Onions, mushrooms, eggplant	5.3–5.8
Peaches, apples, oranges	3.8–4.3
Grapes, strawberries	3.4–3.7
Soda (Coca-Cola, Sprite, Mountain Dew)	2.8–3.0

PHYSICAL SCIENCE PRACTICE QUESTIONS

Select the correct answer from the choices given. Physical science questions are part of the ASVAB General Science (GS) subtest.

1. What is the base unit of length in the metric system?

A) Gram
B) Meter
C) Kelvin
D) Ampere

2. What does the prefix 'kilo-' represent in the metric system?

A) 100
B) 1,000
C) 10
D) 10,000

3. What is the Second Law of Thermodynamics?

A) Energy can be created from nothing
B) Energy transfers increase the disorder (entropy) of a system
C) Heat naturally flows from colder objects to hotter objects
D) Energy is always conserved in a closed system

4. What is the basic principle of refraction?

A) Light reflects off a surface at an equal angle
B) Light bends as it passes from one medium to another
C) Light travels faster in denser materials
D) Light cannot travel through a vacuum

5. Which of the following is a longitudinal wave?

A) Light wave
B) Sound wave
C) Microwave
D) Radio wave

6. Which phenomenon occurs when sound waves are reflected?

A) Refraction
B) Absorption
C) Echo
D) Polarization

7. What property of a sound wave determines its pitch?

A) Wavelength
B) Amplitude
C) Frequency
D) Speed

8. Which of the following describes convection?

A) Heat transfer through direct contact
B) Heat transfer through fluids moving due to temperature differences
C) Heat transfer through electromagnetic waves
D) Heat transfer through solid materials only

9. Which type of radiation does not require a medium to travel through?

A) Conduction
B) Convection
C) Electromagnetic
D) Thermal

10. What is potential energy?

A) The energy of motion
B) The energy stored due to position
C) The energy transferred by heat
D) The energy transferred by work

11. What determines an element's atomic number?

A) Number of electrons
B) Number of protons
C) Number of neutrons
D) Total mass

12. Which subatomic particle is negatively charged?

A) Proton
B) Neutron
C) Electron
D) Nucleus

13. What are neutrons responsible for in an atom?

A) Chemical bonding
B) Stabilizing the nucleus
C) Conducting electricity
D) Determining reactivity

Answers and Explanations

1. B) Meter. Explanation: The meter is the base unit of length in the metric system, used universally in science to measure distance and displacement.

2. B) 1,000. Explanation: 'Kilo-' means 1,000 times the base unit. For example, one kilometer (km) equals 1,000 meters, and one kilogram (kg) equals 1,000 grams.

3. B) Energy transfers increase the disorder (entropy) of a system. Explanation: The Second Law of Thermodynamics states that natural processes tend to increase the entropy, or disorder, in a system.

4. B) Light bends as it passes from one medium to another. Explanation: Refraction occurs when light changes speed and direction as it moves between different mediums, such as air and water.

5. B) Sound wave. Explanation: Sound waves are longitudinal, meaning the oscillations of particles are parallel to the direction of the wave's travel. Electromagnetic waves, such as light, radio waves, and microwave are transverse waves.

6. C) Echo. Explanation: An echo occurs when sound waves bounce off a surface and return to the listener, creating a reflected sound.

7. C) Frequency. Explanation: The pitch of a sound is determined by its frequency. Higher frequencies produce higher-pitched sounds, while lower frequencies produce lower-pitched sounds.

8. B) Heat transfer through fluids moving due to temperature differences. Explanation: Convection is the transfer of heat through the movement of fluids (liquids or gases) due to temperature-driven density differences.

9. C) Electromagnetic. Explanation: Electromagnetic radiation, such as light and radio waves, does not require a medium and can travel through a vacuum, unlike conduction and convection.

10. B) The energy stored due to position. Explanation: Potential energy is the stored energy an object has due to its position, such as an object elevated above the ground, which has gravitational potential energy.

11. B) Number of protons. Explanation: The atomic number is based on the number of protons in an atom's nucleus, which uniquely identifies the element and defines its chemical behavior.

12. C) Electron. Explanation: Electrons carry a negative charge and orbit the nucleus in various energy levels. Their arrangement affects how atoms interact and bond with others.

13. B) Stabilizing the nucleus. Explanation: Neutrons help stabilize the nucleus by balancing the repulsive forces between positively charged protons, contributing to an atom's stability.

§3. EARTH AND SPACE SCIENCES

GEOLOGY

The ASVAB exam may test your understanding of the fundamentals of geology. Geology is the study of the Earth, including its materials, processes, and history.

Structure of Earth

One key aspect of geology is understanding the structure of the Earth, which consists of four distinct layers: the crust, mantle, outer core, and inner core, each varying in composition and depth.

The **crust** is the outermost layer, extending from 5 to 70 kilometers (3 to 43 miles) deep. It is thinner beneath oceans (oceanic crust) and thicker under continents (continental crust). The crust is where all life exists, and it's composed of solid rocks like granite and basalt.

Beneath the crust lies the **mantle**, which extends from 70 kilometers to about 2,900 kilometers (43 to 1,800 miles) deep. The mantle is semi-solid, composed mainly of silicate minerals, and slowly moves due to convection currents, driving plate tectonics.

Below the mantle is the **outer core**, a liquid layer of iron and nickel, extending from 2,900 to 5,100 kilometers (1,800 to 3,200 miles) deep. The motion in this layer generates Earth's magnetic field.

At the very center is the **inner core**, a solid sphere of iron and nickel, reaching depths of 6,371 kilometers (3,959 miles). Despite extreme temperatures (up to 5,400°C or 9,800°F), the inner core remains solid due to the immense pressure exerted upon it.

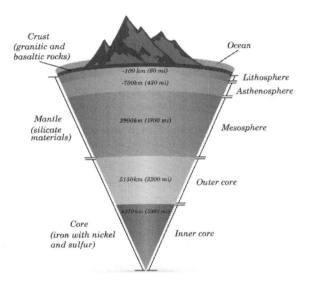

Plate Tectonics

Plate tectonics describes the movement of large, rigid plates that make up Earth's outer layer, or **lithosphere**, which is divided into several major and minor plates. These plates float atop the semi-fluid **asthenosphere**, a part of the upper mantle. The convection currents in the semi-fluid asthenosphere of the mantle allows the plates to move slowly over time.

There are three main types of plate boundaries: **divergent**, **convergent**, and **transform**. At **divergent boundaries**, plates move away from each other, allowing magma from the mantle to rise and form new crust, such as at the mid-Atlantic Ridge. At **convergent boundaries**, plates collide, and one plate may be forced beneath the other in a process called **subduction**, which can form mountain ranges or cause volcanic activity, as seen in the Andes Mountains. **Transform boundaries** occur where plates slide past one another, leading to earthquakes, such as those along California's San Andreas Fault.

Plate tectonics is responsible for shaping Earth's surface over millions of years, leading to the formation of continents, oceans, mountains, and the occurrence of natural phenomena like earthquakes and volcanic eruptions.

Earthquake

Earthquakes occur when stress builds up along **fault lines** or at plate boundaries, causing the Earth's crust to suddenly release energy. This energy travels through the Earth as seismic waves, which can cause the ground to shake. Most earthquakes happen along tectonic plate boundaries, where plates either collide, move apart, or slide past each other. The release of energy happens because the plates get stuck due to friction and then break free, releasing the stored stress in the form of an earthquake.

Earthquakes are measured by their intensity and magnitude. The **Richter scale** is one common method for measuring an earthquake's **magnitude**, which quantifies the amount of energy released during the event. Each number on the Richter scale represents a tenfold increase in amplitude of the seismic waves and roughly 32 times more energy released. A **seismograph** is the instrument used to detect and record seismic waves, helping scientists pinpoint the earthquake's epicenter and strength.

In addition to the Richter scale, the **Modified Mercalli Intensity (MMI) scale** measures the intensity of an earthquake based on its observed effects, such as structural damage and human perception. Earthquakes can cause significant destruction, making understanding their mechanics crucial for preparedness and safety.

Types of Rock

Rocks are classified into three main types based on how they form: igneous, sedimentary, and metamorphic.

Igneous rocks form from the cooling and solidification of molten rock, either magma (beneath the Earth's surface) or lava (on the surface). These rocks are further divided into intrusive and extrusive types. **Intrusive igneous rocks**, such as granite, form when magma cools slowly beneath the Earth's surface, resulting in large crystals. **Extrusive igneous rocks**, like basalt, form when lava cools quickly on the surface, leading to smaller crystals or a glassy texture.

Sedimentary rocks form from the accumulation and compaction of sediments, which can include fragments of other rocks, minerals, and organic materials. Over time, these sediments are deposited in layers and harden into rock. Examples of sedimentary rocks include **limestone** and **sandstone**. These rocks often contain fossils, providing valuable information about Earth's past environments.

Metamorphic rocks are formed when existing rocks—whether igneous, sedimentary, or other metamorphic rocks—are subjected to intense heat, pressure, or chemically active fluids, causing them to transform. This process, known as **metamorphism**, alters the rock's structure and mineral composition. Marble, for instance, is a metamorphic rock formed from limestone, while gneiss is a metamorphic rock that can form from granite.

Each rock type plays a significant role in the rock cycle, contributing to the dynamic processes that shape Earth's surface over time.

Geologic Time Scale

The geologic time scale is a system that geologists use to organize the vast history of Earth into manageable intervals. It divides Earth's 4.6-billion-year history into a series of eons, eras, periods, and epochs based on significant geological and biological events, such as the appearance and extinction of species, continental shifts, and climate changes. This system helps scientists understand the timing and relationships between events in Earth's past.

The **largest division** of time is the **eon**, and Earth's history is split into four eons: the **Hadean**, **Archean**, **Proterozoic**, and **Phanerozoic**. The Phanerozoic Eon is the most recent and is divided into three major **eras**: the **Paleozoic**, **Mesozoic**, and **Cenozoic**. Each era is characterized by major shifts in life forms and Earth's environment.

For example, the **Paleozoic Era** is known for the development of early life forms, including fish and amphibians, while the **Mesozoic Era** is often called the "Age of Reptiles" due to the dominance of dinosaurs. The **Cenozoic Era**, which continues today, is known as the "Age of Mammals" and has seen the rise of humans.

Each era is divided further into **periods**, such as the **Jurassic Period** during the Mesozoic Era, and **epochs** within periods, particularly in the more recent Cenozoic Era. The geologic time scale allows scientists to piece together the events that shaped the Earth and the evolution of life.

Eon	Era	Period	Epoch	Key Events	Time Frame
Phanerozoic	**Cenozoic**	Quaternary	Holocene	Rise of human civilization	11,700 years ago - present
			Pleistocene	Ice ages, early humans	2.58 million - 11,700 years ago
		Neogene	Miocene, Pliocene	Diversification of mammals, first hominids	23 - 2.58 million years ago
	Mesozoic	Cretaceous		Extinction of dinosaurs	145 - 66 million years ago
		Jurassic		Dominance of dinosaurs	201 - 145 million years ago
		Triassic		First dinosaurs, early mammals	252 - 201 million years ago
	Paleozoic	Permian		Mass extinction	299 - 252 million years ago
		Carboniferous		Vast swamp forests, first reptiles	359 - 299 million years ago
		Devonian		Age of fishes	419 - 359 million years ago
		Silurian		First land plants	443 - 419 million years ago
		Ordovician		Marine life flourishes	485 - 443 million years ago
		Cambrian		Explosion of life forms	541 - 485 million years ago
Proterozoic	-	-		First multicellular life	2.5 billion - 541 million years ago
Archean	-	-		First single-celled organisms	4 billion - 2.5 billion years ago
Hadean	-	-		Formation of Earth	4.6 billion - 4 billion years ago

Water Cycle

The water cycle, also known as the hydrologic cycle, is a continuous process that moves water throughout Earth's systems, connecting the atmosphere, land, and oceans. This cycle plays a crucial role in regulating climate, supporting ecosystems, and maintaining the availability of fresh water.

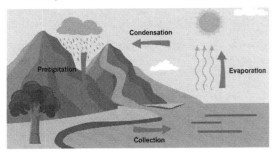

The water cycle consists of several key processes: evaporation, condensation, precipitation, and collection. The cycle begins with **evaporation**, where heat from the Sun causes water from oceans, lakes, and rivers to change from a liquid to a gas (water vapor). Plants also contribute to evaporation through a process called **transpiration**, where water is released from their leaves into the atmosphere.

As water vapor rises and cools in the atmosphere, it undergoes **condensation**, forming clouds. These clouds, when saturated with moisture, eventually lead to **precipitation**, which falls back to the Earth's surface in the form of rain, snow, sleet, or hail.

Once water reaches the ground, it follows different paths. It may flow as **runoff** into rivers, lakes, or oceans, or it may infiltrate into the ground, replenishing groundwater supplies. Groundwater can be stored in underground aquifers, and over time, this water may return to the surface through springs or be drawn up by plants.

The cycle repeats continuously, driven primarily by solar energy and gravity. The water cycle is critical in maintaining Earth's weather patterns, supporting life, and shaping landscapes. It also plays a role in transporting nutrients and minerals throughout ecosystems, making it essential for sustaining life on Earth.

Carbon Cycle

The carbon cycle describes the movement of carbon among the atmosphere, oceans, land, and living organisms. Carbon is a fundamental element in life and plays a significant role in regulating Earth's climate by controlling the concentration of carbon dioxide (CO_2) in the atmosphere.

The cycle begins when carbon dioxide from the atmosphere is absorbed by plants through photosynthesis. During this process, plants convert CO_2 into glucose, a form of organic carbon, which they use for growth. As animals consume plants, carbon is transferred to them and becomes part of their bodies. When plants and animals respire, they release CO_2 back into the atmosphere.

When organisms die, **decomposition** breaks down their bodies, releasing carbon back into the soil or atmosphere. In some cases, organic matter is buried and subjected to intense heat and pressure over millions of years, forming **fossil fuels** like coal, oil, and natural gas. When these fossil fuels are burned, they release stored carbon back into the atmosphere in the form of CO_2, contributing to the **greenhouse effect** and **global warming**.

The oceans also play a key role in the carbon cycle. They absorb large amounts of CO_2 from the atmosphere, where it dissolves and forms carbonic acid. Marine organisms, such as plankton, use dissolved carbon to build their shells. When these organisms die, their shells settle on the ocean floor, where the carbon can be stored for long periods in marine sediments.

Human activities, such as deforestation and the burning of fossil fuels, have significantly altered the natural balance of the carbon cycle, leading to an increase in atmospheric CO_2 levels and contributing to climate change.

PALEONTOLOGY

Paleontology is the scientific study of life that existed in the distant past, primarily through the examination of fossils. **Fossils** are the preserved remains or traces of ancient organisms, including bones, shells, imprints, and even evidence of their behavior, such as footprints or burrows. Paleontology bridges the gap between biology and geology, helping us understand the history of life on Earth and the evolutionary processes that have shaped it.

By studying fossils, paleontologists can reconstruct past ecosystems, track the evolution of species, and investigate how organisms interacted with each other and their environments over millions of years. Fossil evidence is crucial for understanding events like **mass extinctions**, such as the one that wiped out the dinosaurs, as well as the emergence of new species.

Paleontology is not limited to studying animals; it also includes plant fossils, microorganisms, and traces of ancient life forms. Through various dating techniques, including **carbon dating** for younger fossils and **radiometric dating** for older fossils, paleontologists can estimate the age of fossils and their surrounding rocks. This information is vital for constructing a timeline of Earth's biological and geological history, offering invaluable insights into the evolution of life and environmental changes over time

Paleontology is closely linked to **geology** because the remains of ancient organisms are preserved in layers of rock known as **strata**. Geologists study the composition, structure, and processes that have shaped the Earth's crust, while paleontologists analyze the fossils within these rock layers to interpret the history of life. The process of **stratigraphy**, the study of rock layers, is crucial for paleontology. Fossils are often found in sedimentary rocks, which form through the deposition of material over time. By examining different layers of rock, paleontologists can determine the relative ages of fossils and understand the timeline of life on Earth.

Paleontology also helps geologists understand the conditions that shaped ancient environments. For example, the discovery of marine fossils in desert regions suggests that these areas were once covered by oceans. Fossils also reveal information about climate change, mass extinctions, and the migration of species. In this way, paleontology and geology complement each other, with geology providing the context in which paleontologists interpret the fossil record. Together, they offer a detailed history of life and Earth's geological changes over time.

METEOROLOGY

Meteorology is the scientific study of the atmosphere and the processes that produce weather and climate. It involves understanding various elements of the Earth's atmosphere, the impact of fronts, cloud formation, and interpreting temperature changes. Meteorology plays a vital role in predicting weather patterns, studying climate, and understanding how atmospheric conditions influence life on Earth.

Earth's Atmosphere

The Earth's atmosphere is a layer of gases surrounding the planet, held by Earth's gravity. It extends about 10,000 kilometers (6,200 miles) above Earth and is composed of several layers, each with distinct characteristics. The atmosphere is mainly made up of nitrogen (78%), oxygen (21%), and trace gases such as carbon dioxide and argon. These layers include:

- **Troposphere**: This is the lowest layer where all weather occurs. It extends from Earth's surface to about 8-15 kilometers (5-9 miles). The temperature decreases with altitude in this layer, and it contains most of the atmosphere's water vapor, which forms clouds and precipitation.

- **Stratosphere**: Extending from the top of the troposphere to about 50 kilometers (31 miles) above Earth, this layer contains the ozone layer, which absorbs and scatters ultraviolet solar radiation.

- **Mesosphere**: Located above the stratosphere, the mesosphere extends from 50 kilometers to 85 kilometers (31 to 53 miles) and is where most meteors burn up upon entering the atmosphere.

- **Thermosphere**: This layer extends up to 600 kilometers (373 miles) and is where auroras occur. Temperatures increase significantly with altitude due to the absorption of high-energy solar radiation.

- **Exosphere**: The outermost layer, extending from the thermosphere up to 10,000 kilometers (6,200 miles). It gradually fades into space, and its particles are sparse, often escaping into space.

Magnetosphere

The magnetosphere is the region surrounding Earth where its magnetic field dominates. Earth's magnetic field is generated by the movement of molten iron in the outer core and extends far into space. The magnetosphere protects the planet from harmful solar wind and cosmic radiation by deflecting charged particles from the Sun. When some particles are trapped in the magnetosphere, they collide with gases in the upper atmosphere, creating the natural phenomenon known as the **auroras** (Northern and Southern Lights).

The magnetosphere is crucial for life on Earth because it shields the planet from solar radiation that could otherwise strip away the atmosphere and make Earth uninhabitable. Understanding the magnetosphere helps scientists track space weather and predict disruptions caused by solar storms, which can affect satellites, GPS systems, and power grids on Earth.

Fronts

In meteorology, a front is the boundary between two air masses of different temperatures and densities. Fronts are responsible for a variety of weather conditions, including precipitation, storms, and temperature changes. There are four main types of fronts:

Cold front: This occurs when a cold air mass moves into a region occupied by warmer air. Cold fronts often lead to rapid temperature drops, strong winds, and thunderstorms. After a cold front passes, the air is usually cooler and drier.

Warm front: A warm front forms when a warm air mass slides over a cooler air mass. Warm fronts move more slowly than cold fronts and typically bring steady rain or snow over a large area. The temperature increases gradually as the warm front passes.

Stationary front: When neither a cold air mass nor a warm air mass has the strength to replace the other, a stationary front forms. This front can result in prolonged cloudy, rainy weather that may last for several days.

Occluded front: This occurs when a cold front overtakes a warm front, lifting the warm air mass off the ground. Occluded fronts can bring a mix of weather patterns, including precipitation and changing temperatures.

Fronts are essential in meteorology because they often trigger significant weather events, including storms, changes in wind direction, and varying levels of precipitation.

Clouds

Clouds are a visible collection of tiny water droplets or ice crystals suspended in the atmosphere. Clouds form when moist air rises and cools, causing water vapor to condense into liquid droplets. Clouds are classified into different types based on their appearance and altitude:

- **Cumulus clouds**: Puffy, white clouds with flat bases, often associated with fair weather. However, when they grow taller, they can develop into cumulonimbus clouds, which bring thunderstorms.

- **Stratus clouds**: These are uniform, gray clouds that often cover the entire sky and resemble fog. They are typically associated with overcast conditions and light rain or drizzle.

- **Cirrus clouds**: High-altitude clouds made of ice crystals, appearing wispy or feather-like. Cirrus clouds are usually a sign of fair weather, but they can indicate that a change in the weather is coming.

- **Nimbus clouds**: Clouds that bring precipitation. When combined with other cloud types (like cumulonimbus or nimbostratus), these clouds produce rain, snow, or thunderstorms.

Cloud formation plays a critical role in Earth's weather systems, as clouds regulate the distribution of sunlight and heat and are the source of precipitation.

Temperature Conversions

In meteorology, temperature is an important variable that influences weather conditions. Temperature is typically measured in degrees Celsius (°C) or Fahrenheit (°F), depending on the region. To convert between these two units, use the following formulas:

Celsius to Fahrenheit:
$T(°F) = T(°C) \times \frac{9}{5} + 32$. For example, to convert 25°C to Fahrenheit: $T(°F) = 25 \times \frac{9}{5} + 32 = 77°$.

Fahrenheit to Celsius:
$T(°C) = (T(°F) - 32) \times \frac{5}{9}$. For example, to convert 77°F to Celsius: $T(°C) = (77 - 32) \times \frac{5}{9} = 25°$.

ASTRONOMY

Astronomy is the study of the universe beyond Earth, exploring celestial objects such as stars, planets, galaxies, and the vast expanse of space. It is one of the oldest sciences, as humans have long looked to the skies to understand their place in the cosmos. Astronomy seeks to explain the origins, evolution, and structure of the universe and the various phenomena observed in space.

The universe itself is an incredibly vast and expanding space filled with billions of **galaxies**, each containing countless stars, planets, and other celestial objects. It began approximately 13.8 billion years ago with the **Big Bang**, a massive explosion that marked the origin of space and time. Since then, the universe has been expanding, creating the complex structures and celestial bodies we observe today.

The Milky Way

Among the billions of galaxies in the universe, we live in the Milky Way Galaxy, a large, spiral-shaped galaxy that contains our solar system. The Milky Way is estimated to be about 100,000 light-years in diameter and has four main spiral arms. At the center of the Milky Way is a dense region thought to contain a supermassive black hole.

Our solar system is located in one of the outer spiral arms, called the Orion Arm, about 27,000 light-years from the galactic center. The Milky Way is part of a local group of galaxies, which includes neighboring galaxies like Andromeda. From Earth, we can see the Milky Way as a faint, milky band of light across the night sky, which is made up of the light from countless stars too distant to distinguish individually.

The Sun

The Sun is the central star of our solar system and the primary source of energy for life on Earth. It is classified as a G-type main-sequence star or a yellow dwarf, though it appears white from space. The Sun is an enormous ball of hydrogen and helium undergoing **nuclear fusion**, where hydrogen atoms fuse to form helium, releasing vast amounts of energy in the process. This energy radiates outward in the form of light, heat, and solar wind, driving weather systems on Earth and supporting photosynthesis in plants.

The Sun has a diameter of about 1.39 million kilometers (865,000 miles) and accounts for about 99.86% of the total mass of the solar system. The surface temperature of the Sun is approximately 5,500°C (9,932°F), while its core reaches temperatures of about 15 million°C (27 million°F), where nuclear fusion occurs.

The Sun is about 4.6 billion years old and is expected to remain stable for another 5 billion years before evolving into a **red giant** and eventually shedding its outer layers to form a **white dwarf**. The Sun influences everything in the solar system, from planetary orbits to space weather, and supports all forms of life on Earth.

The Solar System

The solar system consists of the Sun, eight planets, and a variety of other celestial objects that orbit around it. The Sun's gravitational pull keeps everything in the solar system in orbit. Surrounding the Sun are the planets, dwarf planets, moons, asteroids, comets, and other small bodies.

The eight planets of the solar system are divided into two groups: terrestrial planets and gas giants. The four **terrestrial planets**—Mercury, Venus, Earth, and Mars—are rocky and have solid surfaces. Mercury is the closest planet to the Sun and has extreme temperatures. Venus has a thick, toxic atmosphere and is the hottest planet. Earth is the only planet known to support life, and Mars is often called the Red Planet due to its iron oxide surface.

Beyond Mars lies the **asteroid belt**, a region filled with rocky debris. Past the asteroid belt are the gas giants—Jupiter and Saturn—and the ice giants—Uranus and Neptune. Jupiter is the largest planet, with a strong magnetic field and dozens of moons. Saturn is famous for its stunning ring system. Uranus and Neptune are colder and have atmospheres rich in hydrogen, helium, and methane, giving them a bluish tint.

Beyond Neptune is the **Kuiper Belt**, home to dwarf planets like Pluto and other icy objects. Farther still lies the **Oort Cloud**, a distant region filled with comets that marks the outermost boundary of the solar system.

The solar system also contains numerous moons orbiting the planets, asteroids, and comets. These objects, along with the planets and Sun, make up a dynamic and interconnected system that has existed for billions of years, continually evolving and influencing each other through gravitational forces.

Meteors, Comets, and Asteroids

Meteors, comets, and asteroids are small celestial bodies with distinct characteristics. A **meteor** is the flash of light seen when a **meteoroid** (a small space rock) enters Earth's atmosphere and burns up due to friction. If a meteoroid survives the atmosphere and reaches Earth's surface, it's called a **meteorite**.

Comets are icy bodies from the outer solar system that develop a glowing coma and a tail as they approach the Sun and their ice vaporizes. They follow long, elliptical orbits and are visible from Earth periodically. The tail always points away from the Sun due to solar wind.

Asteroids are rocky remnants mostly found in the asteroid belt between Mars and Jupiter. Unlike comets, they don't develop tails because they are made of rock and metal. While most asteroids remain in the belt, some can be nudged into Earth's path, with rare impacts throughout history.

These celestial bodies provide valuable insight into the early solar system and its formation.

The Seasons on Earth

The seasons on Earth are a result of the planet's 23.5-degree axial tilt and its elliptical orbit around the Sun. This tilt causes different areas of Earth to receive varying amounts of sunlight at different times of the year, which leads to the familiar cycle of seasons: spring, summer, fall (autumn), and winter.

As Earth orbits the Sun, the tilt of its axis means that one hemisphere is tilted toward the Sun while the other is tilted away. This is what causes the seasons to change. For instance, during the **summer solstice** (around June 21), the Northern Hemisphere is tilted toward the Sun, experiencing more direct sunlight and longer days, which marks the beginning of summer. At the same time, the Southern Hemisphere is tilted away from the Sun, receiving less sunlight and shorter days, resulting in winter. Six months later, during the **winter solstice** (around December 21), the roles reverse: the Northern Hemisphere tilts away from the Sun, entering winter, while the Southern Hemisphere enjoys summer.

In between the solstices are the **equinoxes** (around March 21 and September 21), when Earth's tilt is such that both hemispheres receive nearly equal amounts of sunlight. This balance between day and night length marks the transition into spring or fall, depending on the hemisphere.

The degree of seasonal change varies with latitude. Regions near the equator experience little seasonal variation because they consistently receive strong sunlight throughout the year. In contrast, areas near the poles endure extreme seasonal differences, with long, cold winters and short, cool summers. These seasonal cycles influence weather patterns, ecosystems, and human behavior worldwide.

Phases of the Moon

The phases of the Moon occur as the Moon orbits Earth, changing the portion illuminated by the Sun. This cycle takes approximately 29.5 days and includes eight main phases:

1. New Moon: The Moon is between the Earth and the Sun, making it invisible from Earth.
2. Waxing Crescent: A small crescent of the Moon becomes visible.
3. First Quarter: Half of the Moon's right side is illuminated.
4. Waxing Gibbous: More than half of the Moon is visible but not yet full.
5. Full Moon: The entire face of the Moon is illuminated.
6. Waning Gibbous: The visible portion begins to shrink after the full moon.
7. Last Quarter: Half of the Moon's left side is illuminated.
8. Waning Crescent: A small crescent is visible before transitioning back to a new moon.

These phases repeat in a regular cycle, influencing Earth's tides and human culture.

Solar and Lunar Eclipses

Solar and lunar eclipses occur when the Sun, Earth, and Moon align in specific ways, temporarily blocking sunlight.

A **solar eclipse** happens when the Moon passes between the Earth and the Sun, blocking some or all of the Sun's light. The following is an illustration of how a solar eclipse occurs.

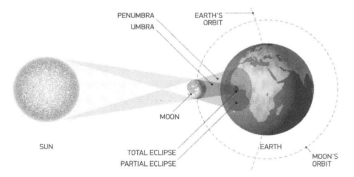

In the above figure, umbra is the darkest part of the shadow where the Sun is completely obscured. In a solar eclipse, observers within the umbra experience a total eclipse. Penumbra is the partially shaded outer region of the shadow. In a solar eclipse, observers in the penumbra experience a partial eclipse.

There are three types of solar eclipses:

- Total solar eclipse: The Moon completely covers the Sun, casting a shadow on Earth, and the sky darkens as if it were night. This occurs in a narrow path where the Moon's shadow falls.

- Partial solar eclipse: The Moon only partially covers the Sun, creating a visible crescent of sunlight.

- Annular solar eclipse: The Moon is farther from Earth and doesn't completely cover the Sun, leaving a ring of sunlight visible around the Moon.

Solar eclipses are rare and only occur during the new moon phase.

A **lunar eclipse** occurs when the Earth passes between the Sun and the Moon, casting Earth's shadow on the Moon. There are two types:

- Total lunar eclipse: The Earth completely blocks sunlight from reaching the Moon, and the Moon takes on a reddish color, often called a "blood moon".

- Partial lunar eclipse: Only part of the Moon enters Earth's shadow, and the rest remains illuminated.

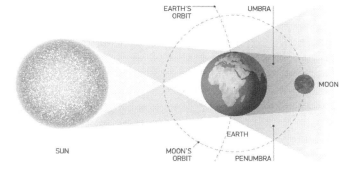

In a lunar eclipse, observers within the umbra experience a total eclipse, while observers in the penumbra experience a partial or penumbral lunar eclipse.

Lunar eclipses can occur only during a full moon and are visible from anywhere on Earth where the Moon is above the horizon. Unlike solar eclipses, lunar eclipses are safe to watch without eye protection.

EARTH AND SPACE SCIENCES PRACTICE QUESTIONS

Select the correct answer from the choices given. Earth and space sciences questions are part of the ASVAB General Science (GS) subtest.

1. What is the outermost layer of the Earth called?

A) Mantle
B) Inner core
C) Crust
D) Outer core.

2. Which layer of the Earth is responsible for generating the planet's magnetic field?

A) Crust
B) Outer core
C) Mantle
D) Inner core

3. What is the primary cause of earthquakes?

A) Solar flares
B) Tectonic plate movements
C) Volcanic eruptions
D) Ocean tides

4. Which type of tectonic plate boundary is associated with the formation of mountains?

A) Divergent boundary
B) Convergent boundary
C) Transform boundary
D) Subduction zone

5. What type of rock is formed from cooling lava or magma?

A) Sedimentary
B) Metamorphic
C) Igneous
D) Organic

6. What is the primary factor responsible for the Earth's seasons?

A) Distance from the Sun
B) Earth's axial tilt
C) Solar radiation
D) Moon's gravitational pull

7. Which geologic period is known for the dominance of dinosaurs?

A) Cambrian
B) Jurassic
C) Devonian
D) Silurian

8. Which process in the water cycle involves water changing from a gas to a liquid?

A) Evaporation
B) Precipitation
C) Condensation
D) Transpiration

9. What drives the movement of tectonic plates?

A) Earth's rotation
B) Solar energy
C) Mantle convection
D) Magnetic field

10. What scale is commonly used to measure the magnitude of an earthquake?

A) Mercalli scale
B) Fujita scale
C) Richter scale
D) Kelvin scale

11. Which rock type often contains fossils?

A) Igneous
B) Metamorphic
C) Sedimentary
D) Volcanic

12. What is the term for the continuous movement of carbon between the atmosphere, oceans, land, and living organisms?

A) Hydrologic cycle
B) Tectonic cycle
C) Carbon cycle
D) Rock cycle

13. Which type of front typically leads to thunderstorms and rapid temperature drops?

A) Warm front
B) Cold front
C) Stationary front
D) Occluded front

Answers and Explanations

1. C) Crust. Explanation: The crust is the Earth's outermost layer, where all life exists, and it extends from 5 to 70 kilometers deep.

2. B) Outer core. Explanation: The outer core, composed of liquid iron and nickel, generates Earth's magnetic field through its motion. Remember that the outer core is below the crust and mantle and is a liquid layer of iron and nickel, extending from 2,900 to 5,100 kilometers (1,800 to 3,200 miles) deep. The motion in this layer generates Earth's magnetic field. In contrast, earth's inner core is at the center of the earth and is a solid sphere of iron and nickel and cannot move, and hence cannot generate a magnetic field.

3. B) Tectonic plate movements. Explanation: Earthquakes occur when stress builds along fault lines or at tectonic plate boundaries, causing the Earth's crust to release energy.

4. B) Convergent boundary. Explanation: At convergent boundaries, plates collide, and one plate may be forced under the other, forming mountain ranges.

5. C) Igneous. Explanation: Igneous rocks form from the cooling and solidification of molten rock, either magma (intrusive) or lava (extrusive).

6. B) Earth's axial tilt. Explanation: Earth's tilt on its axis (23.5 degrees) causes different parts of the planet to receive varying amounts of sunlight, leading to the changing seasons as the earth rotates around the sun.

7. B) Jurassic. Explanation: The Jurassic Period is famous for the dominance of dinosaurs during the Mesozoic Era. Remember this fact by recalling Steven Spielberg's movie *Jurassic Park*.

8. C) Condensation. Explanation: Condensation occurs when water vapor in the atmosphere cools and changes into liquid water, forming clouds.

9. C) Mantle convection. Explanation: Tectonic plates move due to convection currents in the semi-fluid asthenosphere of the mantle. Mantle convection is the very slow creep of Earth's solid silicate mantle as convection currents carry heat from the interior to the planet's surface.

10. C) Richter scale. Explanation: The Richter scale measures an earthquake's magnitude, quantifying the amount of energy released during the event.

11. C) Sedimentary. Explanation: Sedimentary rocks form from compacted sediments, often containing fossils, which provide clues about Earth's past environments. Any fossils would likely have been largely or entirely destroyed in Igneous, volcanic, or metamorphic rocks.

12. C) Carbon cycle. Explanation: The carbon cycle describes the movement of carbon through various Earth systems, regulating climate and supporting life.

13. B) Cold front. Explanation: Cold fronts occur when cold air moves into a region of warm air, often causing thunderstorms and rapid temperature decreases.

GENERAL SCIENCE PRACTICE SET

Time: 12 minutes for 15 questions

Select the correct answer from the choices given. This practice subtest reflects the number of questions and time limits you'll encounter on the CAT-ASVAB General Science subtest without any tryout questions.

1. What is the basic unit of life in all living organisms?

A) Atom
B) Cell
C) Organ
D) Molecule

2. Which organelle is responsible for producing energy in the cell?

A) Nucleus
B) Mitochondria
C) Ribosome
D) Chloroplast

3. Which type of cells lack a true nucleus?

A) Eukaryotic cells
B) Prokaryotic cells
C) Plant cells
D) Animal cells

4. What process allows plants to make their own food?

A) Cellular respiration
B) Digestion
C) Photosynthesis
D) Fermentation

5. Which process is responsible for the breakdown of glucose into energy in cells?

A) Photosynthesis
B) Cellular respiration
C) Transcription
D) Translation

6. What is the primary function of the endocrine system?

A) Transport nutrients
B) Produce hormones
C) Regulate temperature
D) Fight infections

7. Which part of a plant cell stores water, nutrients, and waste?

A) Mitochondria
B) Vacuole
C) Chloroplast
D) Ribosome

8. Which system is responsible for removing waste from the body?

A) Circulatory system
B) Immune system
C) Respiratory system
D) Urinary system

9. What is the gravitational potential energy of a 10 kg object raised to a height of 5 meters? (Assume $g = 9.8\,\text{m/s}^2$)

A) 98 J
B) 49 J
C) 490 J
D) 980 J

10. How is power defined in physics?

A) The rate at which work is done
B) The amount of energy stored in a system
C) The force applied over a distance
D) The total energy in a system

11. What is the base unit for mass in the metric system?

A) Pound
B) Kilogram
C) Gram
D) Ton

12. Which of the following describes a metalloid?

A) Highly reactive .
B) Only conducts electricity at high temperatures
C) Exhibits properties of both metals and nonmetals
D) Completely nonreactive

13. What happens to atomic radius as you move across a period from left to right?

A) It increases
B) It decreases
C) It stays the same
D) It fluctuates

14. Which type of rock forms from pre-existing rocks undergoing heat and pressure?

A) Igneous
B) Sedimentary
C) Metamorphic
D) Organic

15. What is the cause of Earth's magnetic field?

A) Motion in the outer core
B) Rotation of the Earth
C) Movement of the tectonic plates
D) Solar radiation

Answers and Explanations

1. B) Cell. Explanation: The cell is the smallest unit of life and is responsible for carrying out all life processes.

2. B) Mitochondria. Explanation: Mitochondria are known as the powerhouses of the cell because they generate energy in the form of ATP through cellular respiration.

3. B) Prokaryotic cells. Explanation: Prokaryotic cells, such as bacteria, lack a true nucleus, while eukaryotic cells, like those in plants and animals, have a defined nucleus.

4. C) Photosynthesis. Explanation: Photosynthesis is the process by which plants convert sunlight into glucose, their food source.

5. B) Cellular respiration. Explanation: Cellular respiration converts glucose into usable energy (ATP) within the mitochondria of cells.

6. B) Produce hormones. Explanation: The endocrine system consists of glands that release hormones, which regulate bodily functions.

7. B) Vacuole. Explanation: The large central vacuole in plant cells stores water, nutrients, and waste products, helping maintain cell structure.

8. D) Urinary system. Explanation: The urinary system, which includes the kidneys and bladder, filters and removes waste from the blood and expels it as urine.

9. C) 490 J. Explanation: Gravitational potential energy is calculated as $PE = mgh = 10\,\text{kg} \times 9.8\,\text{m/s}^2 \times 5\,\text{m} = 490\,\text{J}$.

10. A) The rate at which work is done. Explanation: Power is the rate at which work is performed or energy is transferred, and is measured in watts (W). It is calculated as $P = \dfrac{W}{t}$.

11. B) Kilogram. Explanation: The kilogram is the SI base unit for mass. It is commonly used in scientific and everyday measurements, with 1 kilogram equal to 1,000 grams.

12. C) Exhibits properties of both metals and nonmetals. Explanation: Metalloids have mixed properties, making them useful in electronics. For example, silicon is a semiconductor, conducting electricity under specific conditions.

13. B) It decreases. Explanation: As you move across a period, the increasing positive charge in the nucleus pulls the electrons closer, resulting in a smaller atomic radius.

14. C) Metamorphic. Explanation: Metamorphic rocks are created when igneous or sedimentary rocks are subjected to intense heat and pressure, altering their structure and mineral composition.

15. A) Motion in the outer core. Explanation: Earth's magnetic field is generated by the movement of liquid iron and nickel in the outer core.

CHAPTER 6: ELECTRONICS INFORMATION

INTRODUCTION

The Electronics Information (EI) subtest of the ASVAB evaluates your knowledge of basic electrical concepts, circuits, devices, and electronic systems. It is designed to assess your understanding of how electricity works and how various electronic components function together. This subtest is essential for individuals seeking military careers in technical fields such as communications, avionics, and electrical engineering, where a strong foundation in electronics is crucial.

The questions on the Electronics Information subtest cover a range of topics, including basic electrical theory, resistors, capacitors, semiconductors, and various tools used in electronics work. Familiarity with Ohm's law, electrical measurements, and different types of circuits (such as series and parallel) is key to performing well on this portion of the test.

In this chapter, we will break down these core concepts, starting with the basics of electricity and moving through more complex topics like circuits and electronic devices. Understanding these principles will not only help you succeed on the ASVAB but also provide a foundation for a variety of technical and engineering roles in the military.

UNDERSTANDING ELECTRICITY

Electricity is a form of energy that results from the movement of electrons, which are subatomic particles found in atoms. At its most fundamental level, electricity is the flow of electrical charge, typically through a conductor, which allows electrons to move easily.

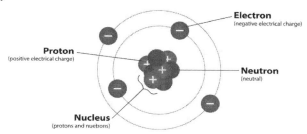

To understand how electricity exists, we must first look at the structure of an atom. Atoms are the basic building blocks of all matter and consist of three primary particles: protons, neutrons, and electrons. **Protons** have a positive charge, **neutrons** have no charge (they are neutral), and **electrons** carry a negative charge. Protons and neutrons are found in the **nucleus**, or center, of the atom, while electrons orbit the nucleus in shells or energy levels.

Electricity forms when electrons are freed from their orbits around the nucleus and flow from one atom to another. This flow of electrons is what we refer to as an electric current. In materials like metals, certain electrons, called **free electrons**, are loosely bound to atoms, making them easier to move. When a voltage (electrical force) is applied, these free electrons move in a directed way, creating an electrical current.

The ability of a material to conduct electricity depends on how easily its electrons can move. Materials fall into three main categories based on their electrical conductivity: conductors, insulators, and semiconductors.

Conductors are materials that allow electrons to flow freely. Metals, such as copper, aluminum, and silver, are good conductors because they have many free electrons that can easily move from atom to atom. This is why metals are commonly used in electrical wiring and circuits.

Insulators are materials that do not allow electrons to move freely, making them poor conductors of electricity. Examples of insulators include rubber, glass, and plastic. In these materials, electrons are tightly bound to their atoms, making it difficult for an electric current to flow. Insulators are important in preventing electrical currents from flowing where they are not wanted, such as in the protective coatings around electrical wires.

Semiconductors fall between conductors and insulators. They do not conduct electricity as well as metals, but under certain conditions (such as the introduction of heat or the addition of certain impurities), they can become conductive. Silicon and germanium are common semiconductor materials, and they are crucial in the manufacture of electronic devices like transistors and integrated circuits. Semiconductors are the foundation of modern electronics, allowing devices like computers and smartphones to function.

Electric Current

Electric current refers to the flow of electric charge through a conductor, typically measured in the movement of electrons. When a voltage is applied across a conductor, it creates an electric field that drives the flow of electrons from a region of higher potential to lower potential. This movement of electrons constitutes what we call an electric current. Essentially, electric current is how electric energy travels through circuits to power devices, from small electronics like smartphones to large machines.

There are two primary types of electric current:

- **Direct Current (DC):** In this type of current, electrons flow in a single, constant direction. DC is commonly found in batteries, where current flows from the positive terminal to the negative terminal through a device.

- **Alternating Current (AC):** In AC, the direction of electron flow periodically reverses. This type of current is used in homes and businesses, as it is more efficient for transmitting electricity over long distances.

An **elementary charge** is the smallest unit of electric charge that is carried by a single proton or electron. It is a fundamental constant in physics, representing the basic quantum of electric charge. Electric current is measured in amperes (A), commonly referred to as "amps." One ampere represents the flow of one **coulomb** of charge per second through a point in a circuit. A coulomb (C) is the standard unit of electric charge in the International System of Units (SI), and one coulomb is equivalent to approximately 6.242×10^{18} **elementary charges**. To measure electrical current in a circuit, one needs an **ammeter** or a multimeter set to the current (ampere) mode.

Voltage

Electric voltage, often referred to simply as voltage, is a measure of the **electric potential difference** between two points in an electric circuit. Voltage can be thought of as the "pressure" that pushes electric charges through a conductor, such as a wire. It is a critical concept in understanding how electrical energy moves through a circuit, powering devices and allowing them to operate.

At its core, voltage represents the **electric potential energy** per unit charge at a point in a circuit. This electric potential can be thought of as the ability of a charge to do work, like moving through a circuit to power a device. When there is a difference in electric potential between two points, this creates an electrical potential difference, which is what drives the movement of electrons, or electric current.

In some contexts, the term **electromotive force (EMF)** is used to describe the voltage generated by a source, such as a battery or a generator. Although it includes the word "force," EMF is actually a type of voltage and not a physical force. It represents the energy provided to each charge as it moves through the source of the voltage.

To measure voltage, an instrument called a **voltmeter** is used. This device is connected across two points in a circuit and provides a reading of the electrical potential difference between them. Voltage is measured in units called **volts** (V), and it is one of the most important parameters in any electrical system, dictating how much energy is available to move charges through a circuit.

Resistance

Electric resistance is a measure of how much a material or component opposes the flow of electric current. It determines how difficult it is for the current to pass through a conductor. In simpler terms, resistance can be thought of as the "friction" that electric charges experience as they move through a circuit.

Different materials have different levels of resistance. **Conductors**, like copper or aluminum, have very low resistance, allowing current to flow easily through them. On the other hand, **insulators**, such as rubber or glass, have high resistance, which prevents the flow of current. Resistance is a key factor in controlling the amount of current that flows through a circuit.

Several factors affect the resistance of a material. The type of material plays a significant role, as metals generally have lower resistance than non-metals. The length of the conductor also matters; the longer the conductor, the higher the resistance. Similarly, the cross-sectional area of the material affects its resistance; a thinner wire has more resistance than a thicker one. Temperature also influences resistance, as most materials increase in resistance as their temperature rises.

Devices called **resistors** are specifically designed to introduce a known amount of resistance into a circuit. Resistors are used to control current, protect components, and adjust signal levels.

Electrical Effects

Electrical energy, when applied to different components or materials, can lead to various electrical effects, primarily chemical, heat, and magnetic effects. These effects form the basis of many everyday applications and devices. Here is a discussion of each type:

1. Chemical Effect

When an electric current is passed through certain liquids, it can cause chemical changes. This process is known as electrolysis. The chemical effect of electricity is used in various applications, such as:

- Electroplating: A process in which a layer of metal is deposited onto a surface using an electric current. For example, gold-plating jewelry.

- Battery Operation: In rechargeable batteries, chemical energy is converted to electrical energy when discharging and vice versa when charging.

2. Heating Effect

When electric current flows through a conductor with resistance, heat is generated due to the resistance opposing the current flow. This is known as the Joule heating effect or resistive heating. Applications of the heating effect include:

- Electric Heaters: Devices like electric stoves and room heaters convert electrical energy into heat to warm a space.

- Incandescent Bulbs: Current passes through a thin tungsten filament, heating it up until it glows and produces light.

- Fuses: The heating effect is used in fuses to break the circuit when excessive current flows, protecting electrical appliances.

3. Magnetic Effect

When electric current flows through a conductor, it creates a magnetic field around it. This is the basis of the magnetic effect of electricity, and it is used in several important applications:

- Electromagnets: Electric current through a coil produces a magnetic field, and this effect is used in lifting heavy metallic objects in junkyards.

- Electric Motors: Current passing through coils in motors generates magnetic fields that create motion, allowing devices like fans, washing machines, and drills to operate.

- Transformers: Magnetic fields produced by alternating current in coils allow transformers to step up or step down voltages in power systems.

These electrical effects are fundamental to various technologies and devices and understanding them allows for their practical and safe use in electrical and electronic systems.

CIRCUITS

An electric circuit is a path through which electric current flows, enabling the transfer of energy from a source to a device or load. At its core, a circuit consists of a few fundamental elements, including a voltage source, conductors (wires), loads (such as resistors or light bulbs), and switches.

In the image provided, the circuit features a battery as the **voltage source**, supplying the electrical energy needed to push electrons through the system. A voltage source creates an electric potential difference, which drives current through the circuit.

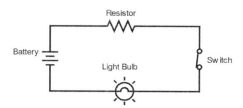

The **load** in this case includes a resistor and a light bulb. The resistor limits the current, protecting the components and ensuring that they operate within safe parameters. The light bulb serves as an example of an electrical load, converting electrical energy into light and heat. Loads in circuits consume the energy provided by the source to perform useful work.

A **switch** is also present in the circuit. When the switch is open, it creates an open circuit, meaning the path for the current is interrupted, and no current flows. In contrast, when the switch is closed, it completes the circuit, creating a closed circuit where current can flow uninterrupted from the voltage source through the components.

Electric circuits can vary in complexity, but the basic principles remain the same: energy flows from the source, passes through the circuit's components, and returns to the source. The flow of electricity can be indicated using two different notations: electron flow notation and conventional current notation. **Electron flow notation** depicts the actual physical movement of electrons, which flow from the negative terminal to the positive terminal. This notation reflects the fact that electrons, which are negatively charged, are responsible for carrying electric current through conductive materials.

Conventional current notation represents the flow of current as moving from the positive terminal to the negative terminal of a power source. This direction was assumed before the discovery of electrons and is based on the movement of positive charges. Conventional current notation is typically used in diagrams today.

Ohm's Law

Ohm's Law is a fundamental principle that describes the relationship between voltage, current, and resistance in an electrical circuit. It states that the current flowing through a conductor is directly proportional to the voltage applied across it and inversely proportional to the resistance.

The formula for Ohm's Law is: $V = I \times R$, where: V represents the voltage (measured in volts), I is the current (measured in amperes), R is the resistance (measured in ohms).

This equation allows you to calculate any one of the three variables if the other two are known. For instance, if you know the voltage and resistance in a circuit, you can calculate the current using: $I = \frac{V}{R}$.

Example: Imagine you have a simple circuit with a resistor, and the voltage across it is 12 volts, while the resistance is 4 ohms. To find the current flowing through the circuit, you can apply Ohm's Law: $I = \frac{12\,\text{V}}{4\,\Omega} = 3$ A. So, the current in the circuit is 3 amperes.

Series Circuits

A series circuit is one of the simplest types of electrical circuits where components are connected end-to-end, providing only one path for the current to flow. In a series circuit, all the components, such as resistors, are arranged in a single loop. This means that the same electric current flows through each component without branching. The image provided shows a battery connected to three resistors — Resistor 1, Resistor 2, and Resistor 3 — in a series configuration.

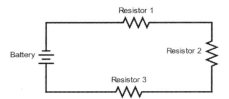

Characteristics of Series Circuits

Current: One of the defining characteristics of a series circuit is that the current (I) is the same at all points in the circuit. Since the current has only one path to take, it must pass through each resistor in turn. This means that if you were to measure the current at any point along the circuit — before Resistor 1, after Resistor 3, or anywhere in between — the current would be the same.

Resistance: In a series circuit, the total resistance (R) is the sum of the individual resistances of the components. As you add more resistors in series, the total resistance of the circuit increases, making it harder for the current to flow. In the example image, the total resistance R_{total} is the sum of the three resistors:

$$R_{\text{total}} = R_1 + R_2 + R_3$$

Because the resistances add up, increasing the number of resistors will reduce the overall current, given a constant voltage. This is important in designing circuits where controlling the current is necessary.

Voltage: Unlike the current, the voltage (V) in a series circuit is not the same across all components. The voltage from the battery is divided across each resistor, depending on its resistance. The total voltage across all the resistors must add up to the total voltage provided by the battery. This is known as **voltage drop**.

For example, if the battery provides 12 volts, and the resistors have different values, the voltage drop across each resistor will be different but will sum up to 12 volts. The voltage drop across each resistor depends on its resistance, with larger resistances experiencing a larger voltage drop.

Example: Given a series circuit as the one in the above image, a battery with a voltage of 18 V is connected to three resistors in series. Resistor 1 is 2 ohms, Resistor 2 is 3 ohms, and Resistor 3 is 5 ohms. What is the total resistance, the current flowing through the circuit, and the voltage drop across Resistor 2?

Solution:

Step 1: Calculate the Total Resistance.

To find the total resistance in the circuit, simply add the individual resistances:

$$R_{\text{total}} = R_1 + R_2 + R_3 = 2\,\Omega + 3\,\Omega + 5\,\Omega = 10\Omega$$

Step 2: Calculate the Total Current Using Ohm's Law

With the total resistance known, we can calculate the current flowing through the circuit using Ohm's Law:

$$I = \frac{V}{R_{\text{total}}} = \frac{18\,V}{10\,\Omega} = 1.8\,A$$

So, the current in the circuit is 1.8A and this current is the same through each resistor.

Step 3: Calculate the Voltage Drop Across Resistor 2

In a series circuit, the voltage drop across each resistor can be calculated using Ohm's Law: $V_{\text{drop}} = I \times R$

For Resistor 2, with a resistance of 3 ohms and the current $I = 1.8$A, the voltage drop is:

$$V_{\text{drop, R2}} = I \times R_2 = 1.8\,A \times 3\,\Omega = 5.4\,V$$

Step 4: Conclusion:

- Total Resistance: 10 ohms
- Current in the Circuit: 1.8 amperes
- Voltage Drop Across Resistor 2: 5.4 volts

This means that out of the total 18 volts provided by the battery, 5.4 volts are dropped across Resistor 2. You could similarly calculate the voltage drop across Resistor 1 and Resistor 3 using the same method.

In summary, a series circuit provides a single path for current to flow. The current is the same at all points, but the total resistance is the sum of all individual resistances. Voltage is divided across each component, with each resistor experiencing a voltage drop proportional to its resistance. Understanding these concepts is key for solving typical series circuit problems that might appear on the ASVAB or other exams.

Parallel Circuits

A parallel circuit is a type of electrical circuit where components are connected across the same voltage source in such a way that there are multiple paths for the current to flow. Unlike in series circuits where there is just one path, each component in a parallel circuit lies on a separate branch, and the total current from the source is divided among these branches.

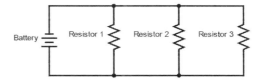

Characteristics of Parallel Circuits

Voltage: In a parallel circuit, the voltage across each component (resistor, light bulb, etc.) is the same. This means that each resistor in the attached diagram experiences the same voltage drop as provided by the battery, regardless of its resistance or the current flowing through it.

Current: The total current flowing from the source (battery) is split among the branches. The amount of current flowing through each branch depends on the resistance of the branch. A lower resistance draws more current, and vice versa.

Resistance: The total resistance in a parallel circuit is less than the resistance of the least resistive branch. This is because the presence of multiple paths allows more current to flow through the circuit than would be possible through a single resistor.

Calculating Parameters in Parallel Circuits

In parallel circuits, the formula for total resistance (R_{total}) is not simply the sum of the resistances. Instead, the total resistance is determined by the reciprocal of the sum of the reciprocals of each individual resistance:

$$\frac{1}{R_{\text{total}}} = \frac{1}{R_1} + \frac{1}{R_2} + \frac{1}{R_3}$$

This formula shows that adding more resistors in parallel decreases the total resistance.

Example: A battery provides a voltage of 12 V to a parallel circuit consisting of three resistors. Resistor 1 has a resistance of 6 ohms, Resistor 2 has a resistance of 3 ohms, and Resistor 3 has a resistance of 2 ohms. Calculate the total resistance of the circuit and the current through each resistor.

Solution:

Step 1: Calculate Total Resistance: The total resistance R_{total} can be calculated by the reciprocal formula for parallel circuits. Using the provided resistances:

$$\frac{1}{R_{\text{total}}} = \frac{1}{6} + \frac{1}{3} + \frac{1}{2} = \frac{1}{6} + \frac{2}{6} + \frac{3}{6} = \frac{6}{6} = 1$$

Step 2: Calculate Current through Each Resistor: Using Ohm's Law $I = \frac{V}{R}$ and knowing the voltage is 12 V for each resistor:

$$I_1 = \frac{12\,V}{6\,\Omega} = 2\,A$$
$$I_2 = \frac{12\,V}{3\,\Omega} = 4\,A$$
$$I_3 = \frac{12\,V}{2\,\Omega} = 6\,A$$

The total current from the battery is $I_{\text{total}} = I_1 + I_2 + I_3 = 2\,A + 4\,A + 6\,A = 12\,A$

This example shows how voltage remains constant across each resistor in a parallel circuit while the current varies depending on the resistance.

Series-Parallel Circuits

A series-parallel circuit is a type of electrical circuit that combines elements of both series and parallel configurations. This allows different components in the circuit to exhibit characteristics of both series and parallel circuits, leading to a more complex behavior of current, voltage, and resistance. The figure here shows an example of a series-parallel circuit where Resistor 1 is in series with the parallel combination of Resistors 2 and 3. We'll use this figure throughout this section to discuss Series-Parallel Circuits.

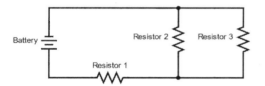

In a series-parallel circuit, some components are connected in series, while others are connected in parallel:

Series components: Components that share the same current, as there is only one path for current to flow through them. In the image, Resistor 1 is in series with the parallel section of the circuit (Resistors 2 and 3).

Parallel components: Components that are connected across the same voltage, but the current splits between them. In this case, Resistor 2 and Resistor 3 are connected in parallel.

Characteristics of Series-Parallel Circuits

Current: In a series-parallel circuit, the current behaves differently in the series and parallel portions. In the series portion of the circuit (the part that includes Resistor 1), the current is the same through all components because there is only one path for the current to follow.

In the parallel portion of the circuit (the part that includes Resistor 2 and Resistor 3), the current splits between the branches. The amount of current in each branch depends on the resistance of the individual components in that branch. Components with lower resistance will carry more current.

Resistance: Calculating the total resistance in a series-parallel circuit involves combining the rules for both series and parallel resistances:

1. First, calculate the equivalent resistance of the components in parallel (Resistors 2 and 3). The formula for parallel resistances is: $\frac{1}{R_{\text{parallel}}} = \frac{1}{R_2} + \frac{1}{R_3}$

2. Once the equivalent resistance of the parallel section is known, add it to the resistance of the series component (Resistor 1) to find the total resistance of the circuit: $R_{\text{total}} = R_1 + R_{\text{parallel}}$

Voltage: Voltage behaves differently in the series and parallel portions of the circuit. In the series portion, the voltage drop is proportional to the resistance of each component. The voltage across Resistor 1 will depend on its resistance and the total current flowing through the circuit.

In the parallel portion, the voltage across each parallel branch (Resistors 2 and 3) is the same and equal to the voltage applied to that portion of the circuit.

Example: A battery supplies 24 volts to a series-parallel circuit. Resistor 1 has a resistance of 4 ohms, Resistor 2 has a resistance of 6 ohms, and Resistor 3 has a resistance of 12 ohms. What is the total resistance of the circuit, the current through Resistor 1, and the voltage across Resistor 2?

Solution:

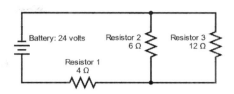

Step 1: Calculate the Equivalent Resistance of the Parallel Section. First, find the combined resistance of Resistor 2 and Resistor 3, which are in parallel:

$$\frac{1}{R_{parallel}} = \frac{1}{6\,\Omega} + \frac{1}{12\,\Omega} = \frac{2}{12} + \frac{1}{12} = \frac{3}{12}$$
$$R_{parallel} = \frac{12}{3} = 4\Omega$$

Step 2: Find the Total Resistance. The total resistance of the circuit is the resistance of Resistor 1 (which is in series with the parallel section) plus the equivalent resistance of the parallel section:

$$R_{total} = R_1 + R_{parallel} = 4\,\Omega + 4\,\Omega = 8\Omega$$

Step 3: Calculate the Total Current. Using Ohm's Law $I = \frac{V}{R}$ the total current in the circuit is: $I = \frac{24\,V}{8\,\Omega} = 3\,A$

Step 4: Find the Voltage Across Resistor 2. The voltage across the parallel section (Resistors 2 and 3) is the same as the voltage drop across each resistor in that section. The voltage drop across Resistor 1 is:

$$V_1 = I \times R_1 = 3\,A \times 4\,\Omega = 12\,V$$

The remaining voltage is across the parallel section: $V_{parallel} = 24\,V - 12\,V = 12\,V$

So, the voltage across Resistor 2 is 12V.

As illustrated in the above example, series-parallel circuits combine the characteristics of both series and parallel circuits, making them versatile and more complex than purely series or parallel circuits.

Measuring Electric Power

Electric power is the rate at which electrical energy is transferred in a circuit. It is measured in **watts** (W), where one watt equals one joule of energy transferred per second. The basic formula to calculate electric power is: $P = V \times I$, where: P is the power in watts, V is the voltage in volts, I is the current in amperes.

Power increases as either the voltage or current increases. This formula applies to all electrical devices, from small household items to large industrial machines. For larger power measurements, we often use **kilowatts** (kW) and **megawatts** (MW). 1 kilowatt (kW) is equal to 1,000 watts. This unit is commonly used to measure the power output of household appliances and small machines. 1 megawatt (MW) is equal to 1,000 kilowatts or 1,000,000 watts. Megawatts are used to measure large-scale power generation, such as power plants or large industrial equipment.

Example: A light bulb operates with a current of 2 A and a voltage of 120 V. What is the power consumed by the light bulb?

Solution: Using the formula $P = V \times I$: $P = 120\,V \times 2\,A = 240\,W$. The power consumed is 240 watts or 0.24 kW.

ELECTRICAL AND ELECTRONIC SYSTEMS

Electrical and electronic systems are fundamental to modern life, powering everything from household appliances to sophisticated digital devices. **Electrical systems** are designed to generate, transmit, and use electrical energy, focusing on large-scale power distribution and consumption. In contrast, **electronic systems** deal with controlling the flow of electrons through smaller circuits, used in devices such as computers, mobile phones, and many automated control systems. Together, these systems form the backbone of modern infrastructure and technology.

AC vs. DC

Alternating Current (AC) and Direct Current (DC) are the two main types of electric current used in electrical and electronic systems.

Alternating Current (AC): In AC, the direction of the flow of electrons alternates periodically. This means that the current changes direction at regular intervals, typically many times per second. The frequency of AC is measured in hertz (Hz), which indicates the number of cycles per second. AC is primarily used for power transmission and distribution because it can be easily transformed to higher or lower voltages, making it efficient for transmitting electricity over long distances. Most of the electricity supplied to homes and businesses is AC.

Direct Current (DC): In DC, the flow of electrons is unidirectional, meaning it moves in a constant direction from the negative terminal to the positive terminal. DC is commonly used in batteries, electronic devices, and automotive systems. It is preferred for applications requiring stable and consistent voltage, such as charging mobile phones or powering electronic circuits.

The key difference between AC and DC is how they deliver electrical energy. AC is ideal for efficiently transmitting power over long distances, while DC is more suited for low-voltage, portable applications.

Grounding

Grounding is an essential safety practice in electrical systems that involves creating a direct physical connection between electrical devices or circuits and the earth. The purpose of grounding is to prevent electrical shock, protect equipment, and ensure the safe operation of electrical systems by providing a controlled path for excess or stray electrical current.

In any electrical system, unintended faults or malfunctions can cause electrical current to flow in unintended ways, potentially leading to dangerous situations. Grounding directs these currents safely into the earth, reducing the risk of electric shock or fire. For example, if an exposed wire accidentally touches a metal part of an appliance, grounding ensures that the excess current flows to the ground instead of energizing the appliance's casing and posing a shock hazard to anyone touching it.

Chassis Ground   Earth Ground   Signal Ground

There are two primary types of grounding in electrical systems:

System Grounding: This involves grounding the neutral point of electrical power systems, such as transformers or generators. It stabilizes voltage during normal operation and ensures that the power system has a reference point, which helps in maintaining consistent voltage throughout the circuit.

Equipment Grounding: This involves connecting the metal parts of appliances and devices to the ground to protect users. The grounding wire carries away excess current in case of a fault, preventing damage and shock.

Grounding systems typically involve ground rods or other conductors driven into the earth, providing a low-resistance path for electricity. **Ground fault circuit interrupters (GFCIs)** are often used alongside grounding to provide an additional layer of safety, especially in wet environments like kitchens or bathrooms, where the risk of electric shock is higher.

Proper grounding is a crucial part of any electrical installation, making it safer for both people and equipment by reducing the risks associated with electrical faults.

Impedance

Impedance is the measure of opposition that an alternating current (AC) experiences in a circuit, similar to resistance but with additional complexities that come from components like capacitors and inductors. Unlike resistance, which only affects direct current (DC) by reducing current flow, impedance considers both resistance and the effects of changing current and voltage in AC circuits.

Capacitive Reactance: Capacitive reactance refers to the opposition created by a capacitor in an AC circuit. Capacitors are components that store energy in the form of an electric field and tend to resist changes in voltage. The opposition offered by capacitors decreases as the frequency of the AC signal increases. This means that at higher frequencies, capacitors allow more current to pass through, making them effective for filtering and managing low-frequency signals. Essentially, the faster the current alternates, the less the capacitor opposes it.

Inductive Reactance: Inductive reactance is the opposition provided by an inductor in an AC circuit. Inductors store energy in the form of a magnetic field, and they resist changes in current. In contrast to capacitors, the opposition presented by an inductor increases as the frequency of the AC signal rises. This means that inductors are more effective at blocking high-frequency signals while allowing lower-frequency signals to pass. As the current alternates more rapidly, inductors create greater opposition to the flow of current.

Impedance in AC Circuits: In an AC circuit, impedance combines the effects of resistance, capacitive reactance, and inductive reactance. Resistance affects both AC and DC in the same way, while capacitive and inductive reactance change based on the frequency of the AC signal. Together, these factors determine how much opposition the current faces in the circuit. Capacitors and inductors cause a phase difference between the current and voltage, meaning the two are not perfectly in sync—sometimes the current leads or lags behind the voltage depending on the component. This phase relationship is a crucial aspect of how AC circuits behave.

Electric and Electronic Components

Electric and electronic components are the building blocks of all electrical and electronic circuits, enabling the functionality of devices ranging from simple household appliances to complex communication systems. These components help control, direct, and transform electrical energy to perform tasks like switching, amplifying signals, or storing energy. Below is a list of common components.

Power Supply

A power supply is a crucial component that provides the necessary electrical energy to power electronic devices and circuits. It converts electrical energy from a source, such as a wall outlet, into the appropriate voltage, current, and type (AC or DC) required by the system. Power supplies can be linear or switching types, with linear power supplies providing a stable output voltage and switching power supplies being more energy efficient.

Battery single-cell   Battery multi-cell   AC voltage source

Wire

A wire is a conductor that provides a pathway for electrical current to flow through a circuit. Typically made of copper or aluminum, wires are chosen for their excellent conductivity and ability to carry current with minimal resistance. Wires are insulated with materials like plastic or rubber to prevent accidental contact with other conductive surfaces and to protect users from electric shock.

Wires come in various **gauges**, which refer to the thickness or diameter of an electrical wire, which is measured using standards like the American Wire Gauge (AWG) system. In AWG, a smaller number indicates a thicker wire, while a higher number indicates a thinner wire.

Wire gauge affects both the current-carrying capacity and the resistance of the wire. Thicker wires can carry more current with less resistance, making them suitable for high-power applications, while thinner wires are used for lower current needs. Choosing the correct gauge is essential for safety and efficiency, as using a wire with too small a gauge could lead to overheating and potential fire hazards.

Electrical wires are **color-coded** to indicate their specific functions, ensuring safety and proper connections during installation and maintenance. The color-coding of wires varies slightly between regions, but certain standards are widely recognized.

- Black, Red, or Blue wires are typically used for live (hot) wires, carrying current from the power source to devices or appliances.

- White or Gray wires are used as neutral wires, providing the return path for current and completing the circuit.

- Green, Green with Yellow Stripes, or Bare Copper wires are used as ground wires, which connect the system to the earth to prevent electrical shock in case of faults.

Color codes may differ slightly in different countries or regions, so it is important to follow local electrical standards.

In an electrical diagram, different notations are used to indicate whether wires are connected or not connected.

- Connected Wires: A solid dot is placed at the intersection of wires to indicate they are electrically connected.

- Not Connected Wires: Wires that cross without connecting are shown without a dot, often with one wire having a small arc over the other to indicate they are not joined.

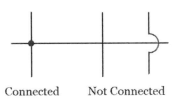

Connected   Not Connected

These symbols ensure clear interpretation of electrical pathways and prevent errors in circuit construction.

Switch

A switch is an electromechanical component that controls the flow of electrical current in a circuit. It works by opening or closing the circuit, effectively turning devices on or off. When the switch is open, the circuit is incomplete, and no current flows; when it is closed, the circuit is complete, allowing current to pass through. Switches come in various types, including toggle switches, push-button switches, and rotary switches, each designed for different applications and levels of current.

Switch, single-pole single-throw   Switch, single-pole double-throw

In addition to controlling devices manually, switches are also used in automation systems to respond to certain conditions, such as temperature or pressure changes, making them versatile in both simple and complex electrical systems.

Fuse and Circuit Breaker

Fuses and circuit breakers are safety devices designed to protect electrical circuits from excessive current that could cause damage or create a fire hazard.

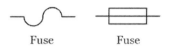

Fuse   Fuse

A fuse is a component containing a metal wire that melts when the current exceeds a specified level, breaking the circuit and stopping the current flow. Fuses are inexpensive and simple but need to be replaced once blown.

A circuit breaker is a switch that automatically opens when it detects an overload or short circuit, interrupting the current. Unlike fuses, circuit breakers can be reset and used again. Circuit breakers are often used in residential and industrial electrical panels to protect wiring and equipment.

Both fuses and circuit breakers are crucial for preventing damage to electrical systems and ensuring safety by stopping the flow of excess current before it causes harm. They play a critical role in protecting both people and equipment from the risks associated with electrical faults.

Amplifier

An amplifier is an electronic device that increases the power, voltage, or current of an input signal. Its main purpose is to make a weak signal stronger, allowing it to drive a larger load, such as a speaker, or to be processed by other components in an electronic system. Amplifiers are found in various applications, from audio systems, where they amplify sound signals, to radio transmitters, where they boost the power of signals for long-distance communication.

Amplifier

There are different types of amplifiers depending on their application and the signals they process. Audio amplifiers are used in sound systems to enhance audio signals, allowing music and voice to be heard loudly through speakers. Radio frequency (RF) amplifiers are used in communication systems to boost high-frequency signals for transmission. There are also operational amplifiers (op-amps), which are versatile components used in signal processing, filtering, and analog computation.

Amplifiers are characterized by their gain, which is the ratio of the output signal strength to the input signal strength. A higher gain means a more substantial amplification effect. However, amplifiers must maintain signal quality, so distortion and noise are crucial factors in determining amplifier performance.

Semiconductor

A semiconductor is a material that has electrical conductivity between that of a conductor (like copper) and an insulator (like glass). The conductivity of a semiconductor can be manipulated by adding impurities, a process known as **doping**, which creates either an excess of electrons (n-type) or a shortage of electrons (p-type). This makes semiconductors highly versatile for controlling current.

Semiconductors are the foundation of most electronic components, including diodes, transistors, and integrated circuits (ICs). Common materials used in semiconductors are silicon and germanium, with silicon being the most widely used due to its abundance and favorable properties.

The key advantage of semiconductors is their ability to control electrical behavior with precision. By combining n-type and p-type materials, components can be made to amplify signals, switch currents, or regulate voltage. The p-n junction formed in diodes and transistors is a core aspect of their functionality.

Semiconductors are the backbone of the electronics industry, enabling the development of computers, smartphones, and virtually all modern electronic devices.

Resistor

A resistor opposes the flow of electric current, allowing control over the amount of current passing through a circuit. Resistors are used to limit current, divide voltage, and protect components from excess current. They are available in variable and non-variable (fixed) types.

Resistor   Rheostat   Potentiometer

Fixed resistors have a specific resistance value that does not change. They are used where a constant level of resistance is required, such as setting current in a circuit. **Variable resistors**, also known as potentiometers or rheostats, allow the user to adjust the resistance value manually. Potentiometers are often used as volume controls in audio devices, while rheostats are used for adjusting the brightness of lights or motor speeds.

The resistance value of a resistor is measured in ohms (Ω), and its power-handling capacity determines how much energy it can dissipate as heat. Resistors are typically color-coded to indicate their resistance value, making them easy to identify and use in circuit design.

Whether fixed or variable, resistors are crucial in controlling and stabilizing current and voltage, ensuring that circuits operate safely and effectively.

Diodes

A diode is an electronic component that allows current to flow in only one direction, acting as a one-way valve for electrical current. Diodes are used to protect circuits by blocking reverse currents that could damage components, and they are also fundamental in **rectification**, which converts alternating current (AC) into direct current (DC).

Diode

Diodes are made from semiconductor materials, typically silicon, and have two terminals: the **anode** (positive side) and the **cathode** (negative side). Current flows from the anode to the cathode when a forward voltage is applied, but it is blocked if a reverse voltage is applied. This directional behavior makes diodes useful in power supplies and signal processing.

There are different types of diodes designed for specific purposes. **Light Emitting Diodes (LEDs)** emit light when current flows through them and are used for displays and indicators. **Zener diodes** are used for voltage regulation, allowing current to flow in the reverse direction when a specific breakdown voltage is reached.

Rectifier and Inverter

A rectifier is an electrical device that converts alternating current (AC) into direct current (DC). This process, called **rectification**, is fundamental in power supply systems, where many electronic devices require DC power to operate, even though the electricity available from the power grid is AC. Rectifiers are used in devices like phone chargers, power adapters, and other power supplies that convert household AC into usable DC.

The key component used in a rectifier is a diode. In a basic rectification process, the diode is used to block the negative portion of the AC signal, allowing only the positive portion to pass, effectively creating a pulsating DC signal. There are different types of rectifiers:

- **Half-wave rectifiers** use a single diode to convert half of the AC cycle, resulting in DC output that pulses.

- **Full-wave rectifiers** use multiple diodes (often four in a bridge rectifier) to convert both the positive and negative halves of the AC cycle, resulting in a smoother DC output.

In short, a diode is the core component that makes rectification possible, and a rectifier is a circuit that uses one or more diodes to achieve the conversion from AC to DC, crucial for powering electronic devices.

An **inverter** is an electrical device that converts direct current (DC) into alternating current (AC). It is used in various applications where AC power is needed but only a DC source, such as a battery or solar panel, is available.

The primary function of an inverter is to provide AC power for devices like home appliances, tools, or grid systems from DC sources. Inverters are commonly used in renewable energy systems, uninterruptible power supplies (UPS), and electric vehicles, ensuring that the generated DC can power standard AC devices efficiently.

Transistor

A transistor is a semiconductor device used to amplify or switch electronic signals. It has three terminals: the emitter, base, and collector. By applying a small input current to the base, a transistor can control a much larger current flowing between the collector and emitter. This ability makes transistors fundamental in both analog and digital circuits.

PNP BJT   NPN BJT
Transistor   Transistor

Transistors come in two main types: **Bipolar Junction Transistors (BJTs)** and **Field-Effect Transistors (FETs)**. BJTs use both electron and hole charge carriers, while FETs control current flow using an electric field. FETs are widely used in integrated circuits due to their efficiency and small size.

Transistors are used as amplifiers to increase signal strength and as switches in digital circuits, such as those found in microprocessors. Their switching capability allows them to represent binary states (on and off), making them essential for building logic gates and digital devices. The invention of the transistor revolutionized electronics, enabling the miniaturization and integration of complex circuits.

Transformer

A transformer is an electrical device used to transfer electrical energy between two or more circuits through the principle of electromagnetic induction. Its primary function is to change the voltage levels, either stepping up (increasing) or stepping down (decreasing) the voltage, depending on the requirement. Transformers consist of two coils, known as the primary and secondary windings, which are wound around a magnetic core. When alternating current (AC) flows through the primary winding, it creates a changing magnetic field, which induces a voltage in the secondary winding.

Transformer

The ratio of the number of turns in the primary coil to the secondary coil determines whether the transformer steps up or steps down the voltage. For example, if the secondary winding has more turns than the primary, the transformer will increase the voltage, making it a step-up transformer. Conversely, if the primary has more turns, the transformer will reduce the voltage, making it a step-down transformer.

Transformers are widely used in power distribution systems to efficiently transmit electricity over long distances. High-voltage transmission reduces energy loss, and step-down transformers are then used to bring the voltage to safer, usable levels for homes and businesses. They are also used in electronic devices, such as power adapters and chargers, to convert the high-voltage supply to a lower voltage suitable for the device.

Transistor vs Amplifier: Compared with a transistor, an **amplifier** is a circuit or device that increases the power, current, or voltage of an input signal. It usually consists of multiple components, including transistors, resistors, and capacitors, which work together to boost a signal. For example, in an audio system, an amplifier increases the weak input signal from a microphone or music player so that it can drive a speaker. In essence, a transistor is a component that can be used within an amplifier circuit, but an amplifier itself is a broader assembly designed for the specific purpose of boosting signals. Transistors are thus building blocks, while amplifiers are complete systems that perform a defined task.

Capacitor

A capacitor is an electrical component that stores energy in an electric field and releases it when needed. It consists of two conductive plates separated by an insulating material called the **dielectric**. When voltage is applied across the plates, an electric charge builds up, storing energy that can be quickly released.

Capacitors are used in a variety of applications, such as filtering (removing unwanted frequencies from signals), energy storage (providing power in short bursts), and timing circuits (creating delays). A capacitor handles AC (alternating current) and DC (direct current) differently due to its ability to store and release energy in an electric field.

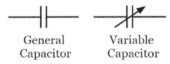

General Capacitor   Variable Capacitor

Capacitor with DC: When DC is applied, a capacitor initially allows current to flow as it charges up to the applied voltage. Once fully charged, the capacitor blocks further current because there is no changing voltage across its terminals. Essentially, after charging, a capacitor acts like an open circuit for DC, meaning no current flows after the capacitor is fully charged.

Capacitor with AC: When AC is applied, the voltage across the capacitor is constantly changing direction. This causes the capacitor to continuously charge and discharge, which allows current to flow through the circuit. As the voltage changes in each cycle, the capacitor opposes these changes, creating a phase difference between the voltage and current. It effectively allows AC to pass while blocking DC.

In summary, a capacitor blocks DC after charging, acting like an open circuit, while it allows AC to pass by continuously charging and discharging in response to the alternating voltage.

There are different types of capacitors, such as electrolytic capacitors, which have high capacitance values and are often used in power supplies, and ceramic capacitors, which are smaller and used in signal processing. A capacitor is measured by its **capacitance**, which indicates the capacity to store electrical charge. The unit of capacitance is the farad (F), named after the English scientist Michael Faraday.

Inductor

An inductor is a passive electrical component that stores energy in the form of a magnetic field when electric current flows through it. It typically consists of a coil of wire, often wound around a core made of magnetic material, such as iron. When current passes through the coil, it creates a magnetic field, and the energy is stored in that magnetic field. The property that defines an inductor is called inductance, measured in henrys (H), which indicates how effectively the inductor can store energy.

Inductor

Inductors resist changes in current, meaning they oppose a rapid increase or decrease in the current flowing through them. This property makes inductors useful in applications such as filters, tuning circuits, and energy storage. They are often used in conjunction with capacitors to create oscillators or in power supplies to smooth out voltage changes.

Inductors play a critical role in AC circuits, where their inductive reactance depends on the frequency of the alternating current. They are commonly found in transformers, motors, and electrical chokes.

A key fact to remember is that a capacitor stores energy in an electric field, while an inductor stores energy in a magnetic field:

- A capacitor stores energy in an electric field between its plates when a voltage is applied across it.
- An inductor stores energy in a magnetic field that is generated around it when current flows through the coil.

Transducer

A transducer is a device that converts one form of energy into another. In electronics, transducers are used to convert physical quantities, like pressure, temperature, or light, into electrical signals or vice versa. Examples include microphones (which convert sound waves into electrical signals) and speakers (which convert electrical signals into sound).

Transducers are classified based on the type of energy they convert. **Sensors** are transducers that convert physical conditions into electrical signals, such as thermistors for temperature measurement. **Actuators**, on the other hand, convert electrical signals into mechanical motion, such as in motors.

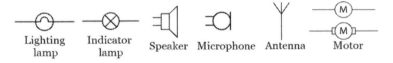

Lighting lamp   Indicator lamp   Speaker   Microphone   Antenna   Motor

Transducers are essential in a wide range of applications, including automation, measurement, and control systems. They enable machines to interact with the physical world, making them crucial for applications ranging from medical instruments to industrial robots.

ELECTRICITY AND MAGNETISM

Electricity Generation and Distribution

Electricity generation is the process of converting various forms of energy into electrical energy, which powers homes, industries, and cities. The most common method involves using turbines, which are rotated by steam, wind, or water. For instance, in a thermal power plant, fossil fuels like coal, natural gas, or oil are burned to produce steam, which drives a turbine connected to an electric generator.

In **hydroelectric power plants**, falling or flowing water turns turbines, while in wind farms, wind spins the blades of wind turbines. **Nuclear power plants** use nuclear reactions to produce heat that creates steam to turn turbines. **Renewable energy sources** like solar panels convert sunlight directly into electricity using photovoltaic cells, while geothermal power taps the heat from beneath the Earth's surface.

The generator in each of these processes uses **electromagnetic induction** to convert mechanical energy into electrical energy. Inside the generator, a coil of wire rotates within a magnetic field, inducing an electric current. Once generated, electricity is transmitted over the power grid to reach consumers. Different generation methods vary in efficiency, environmental impact, and availability, providing a diverse mix of energy sources for reliable electricity production.

Electricity is distributed through a complex network called the **power grid**, which ensures that power generated at power plants reaches homes, businesses, and industries. The distribution process begins with electricity generation at power stations, which produce high-voltage electricity. To minimize energy loss during transmission, the voltage is significantly increased using step-up transformers.

The high-voltage electricity then travels through **transmission lines**, which carry power over long distances. Transmission lines connect to substations, where step-down transformers reduce the voltage to safer levels for local distribution.

From the **substations**, electricity flows into a network of distribution lines that deliver power to neighborhoods and individual buildings. These local lines further lower the voltage to the levels suitable for residential and commercial use. Finally, **service transformers** near homes and businesses step down the voltage to a level that can be safely used by electrical appliances and equipment.

Throughout the grid, switches and circuit breakers are used to manage and protect the flow of electricity. The power grid is monitored and controlled to ensure a consistent and reliable supply, responding to changes in demand and rerouting electricity in case of faults or maintenance needs. This system makes modern, reliable electricity supply possible.

Electric Generator and Motor

Electric generators and motors are essential devices that operate on the principle of electromagnetic induction. Although their purposes are opposite, they share similar components and working principles.

An **electric generator** converts mechanical energy into electrical energy. It works based on Faraday's **law of electromagnetic induction**, which states that a changing magnetic field within a coil of wire induces an electric current. Generators typically consist of a rotor (the rotating part) and a stator (the stationary part). When a turbine or another mechanical force rotates the rotor inside a magnetic field, it creates a flow of electricity in the coils. Generators are widely used in power plants, including thermal, hydro, wind, and nuclear, to produce the electricity that powers homes and industries.

On the other hand, an electric motor performs the reverse function—converting electrical energy into mechanical energy. Motors rely on the interaction between a magnetic field and electric current to generate torque, which then produces rotational motion. Motors are composed of similar components to generators, with a rotor and stator, but instead of producing electricity, they use it to create movement. Electric motors are found in various applications, from household appliances to industrial machinery and electric vehicles.

In essence, electric generators and motors are closely related, with generators supplying the electricity needed for motors to perform useful mechanical tasks. Both are integral to energy production, consumption, and numerous everyday applications, contributing significantly to modern technology and convenience.

ELECTRONICS INFORMATION PRACTICE SET

Time: 10 minutes for 15 questions

Select the correct answer from the choices given. This practice subtest reflects the number of questions and time limits you'll encounter on the CAT-ASVAB Electronics Information subtest without any tryout questions.

1. A circuit breaker with a rating higher than recommended for a circuit

A) ensures longer device lifespan
B) provides no protection against overcurrent
C) prevents any circuit malfunction
D) is ideal for all loads

2. In a residential circuit, the hot wire is usually

A) green
B) black
C) blue
D) whitish

3. To measure electrical current in a circuit, you would use a(n)

A) ohmmeter
B) ammeter
C) voltmeter
D) wattmeter

4. A capacitor whose capacitance can be adjusted is called a

A) fixed capacitor
B) variable capacitor
C) variable resistor
D) potentiometer

5. A step-up transformer is used to

A) increase voltage
B) decrease resistance
C) reduce voltage
D) increase capacitance

6. Which of the following circuit components is least affected by a direct current?

A) —⋀⋀⋀—

B) —||—

C) —⎍⎍⎍—

D) —▷|—

7. An inductor stores

A) electric charge
B) magnetic energy
C) heat
D) light

8. Which of the following describes a conductor?

A) Prevents the flow of current
B) Amplifies voltage
C) Allows easy flow of electrical current
D) Stores magnetic energy

9. Electrons have a ____ charge, and neutrons are ____ charged.

A) negative, neutral
B) positive, negative
C) neutral, positive
D) positive, neutral

10. What type of circuit has multiple paths for current to flow?

A) open circuit
B) series circuit
C) parallel circuit
D) short circuit

11. In the power formula, $P = V \times I$, the V represents

A) current
B) resistance
C) voltage
D) power

12. The N-type material in a diode is associated with

A) holes
B) free electrons
C) positive charge carriers
D) current amplification

13. In the given circuit, a 24V battery is connected across two parallel elements: a resistor of 10 ohms and a light bulb of 10 ohms. What is the total current supplied by the battery?

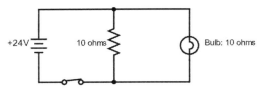

A) 1.2 A
B) 2.4 A
C) 3.6 A
D) 4.8 A

14. The addition of impurities to germanium to improve conductivity is called

A) annealing
B) doping
C) diffusion
D) oxidation

15. What type of circuit does the following show?

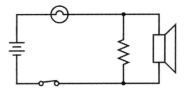

A) Series Circuit
B) Parallel Circuit
C) Series-Parallel Circuit
D) Short Circuit

Answers and Explanations

1. B) provides no protection against overcurrent. Explanation: Using a higher-rated circuit breaker means it may not trip when necessary, failing to protect against overcurrent. A), C), and D) are incorrect because they misstate the effect of a higher-rated breaker.

2. B) black. Explanation: The hot wire is typically black in residential wiring. A) is incorrect; green represents ground. C) is incorrect; blue is used for specific phases. D) is incorrect; whitish represents neutral.

3. B) ammeter. Explanation: An ammeter measures current flowing through a circuit. A) measures resistance. C) measures voltage. D) measures power.

4. B) variable capacitor. Explanation: A variable capacitor allows the capacitance to be adjusted. A) is incorrect as a fixed capacitor has a set value. C) and D) are unrelated to capacitors.

5. A) increase voltage. Explanation: A step-up transformer is used to increase voltage from the primary winding to the secondary winding. B), C), and D) are incorrect, as they do not describe the function of a step-up transformer.

6. A) ⎓⎓⎓⎓⎓⎓. Explanation:

> A) Resistor: A resistor opposes the flow of current and will behave the same regardless of whether the current is AC (alternating current) or DC (direct current) or the direction of the DC. It simply converts electrical energy into heat, and there is no significant change in its operation with DC, making it the least affected.

> B) Capacitor: A capacitor stores energy in an electric field. With DC, it will charge up to the applied voltage and then block further current flow once fully charged. Its behavior is significantly different with DC compared to AC, where it continuously charges and discharges.

> C) Inductor: An inductor stores energy in a magnetic field and resists changes in current. With DC, once the initial change occurs, the inductor will allow the steady flow of current, but its behavior depends on current change, making it more affected by DC than a resistor.

> D) Diode: A diode allows current to flow in only one direction. It significantly changes its behavior with DC depending on the direction of the current, either allowing it to pass or blocking it entirely.

> Thus, the resistor is the component least affected by direct current, making option A the correct answer.

7. B) magnetic energy. Explanation: An inductor stores magnetic energy when current flows through it. A) is incorrect, as electric charge is stored by capacitors. C) and D) are unrelated to an inductor's function.

8. C) Allows easy flow of electrical current. Explanation: A conductor is a material that allows current to flow easily. A) and B) are incorrect; they describe an insulator and an amplifier, respectively. D) refers to an inductor.

9. A) negative, neutral. Explanation: Electrons are negatively charged, and neutrons are neutral (having no charge). B) is incorrect; electrons are not positively charged. C) and D) are incorrect as they mix up the charges.

10. C) parallel circuit. Explanation: A parallel circuit has multiple paths for current to flow. A) does not allow current to flow. B) has only one path. D) indicates a faulty condition where the current bypasses the load.

11. C) voltage. Explanation: In the formula $P = V \times I$, V represents voltage.

12. B) free electrons. Explanation: N-type material has free electrons that contribute to conductivity. A) describes P-type material. C) is incorrect because N-type carries negative charges. D) is not directly related to diode conductivity.

13. D) 4.8 A. Explanation: 1. The two elements (resistor and bulb) are in parallel, each with 10 ohms of resistance.

> 2. The equivalent resistance of the two parallel resistances R_{eq} can be found using the formula for parallel resistors: $\frac{1}{R_{eq}} = \frac{1}{R_1} + \frac{1}{R_2} \implies \frac{1}{R_{eq}} = \frac{1}{10} + \frac{1}{10} = \frac{2}{10} = \frac{1}{5}$. Hence, $R_{eq} = 5\,\Omega$.

> 3. Using Ohm's Law to find the total current supplied by the battery: $I = \frac{V}{R_{eq}} = \frac{24\,V}{5\,\Omega} = 4.8\,A$

14. B) doping. Explanation: Doping is the process of adding impurities to a semiconductor to enhance conductivity. A) and C) are unrelated to the introduction of impurities. D) is a process for creating an insulating layer, not for improving conductivity.

15. C) Series-Parallel Circuit. Explanation: The given diagram shows a combination of both series and parallel elements: The battery, switch, and lamp are in a series connection. The resistor and speaker are connected in parallel with each other. This combination of series and parallel components within the same circuit indicates that it is a series-parallel circuit.

CHAPTER 7: AUTOMOTIVE INFORMATION

The ASVAB Automotive Information subtest evaluates your knowledge of vehicle systems, such as the engine, transmission, brakes, and electrical components. This section tests your understanding of car maintenance, vehicle operations, and general automotive concepts.

In the Computer-Based ASVAB (CAT-ASVAB), the Automotive Information and Shop Information sections are separate, allowing for more focused assessment of each area. In contrast, the Paper-Based ASVAB (P&P-ASVAB) combines Automotive and Shop Information into a single test, covering both automotive mechanics and shop practices.

This book will follow the computer-based ASVAB format, with separate chapters for the Automotive and Shop subtests, ensuring thorough coverage and preparation for each specific area.

An automobile is a complex machine designed to transport people or cargo from one place to another. It operates by converting fuel energy into mechanical energy to produce movement. An automobile comprises multiple systems that work together to ensure safety, performance, and comfort. These systems include the engine, transmission, brakes, steering, and electrical systems, among others. Each system has a specific role that contributes to the overall operation and efficiency of the vehicle.

These components and systems form the foundation of automotive technology and allow the automobile to perform its basic function—safe and efficient transportation. We will cover these systems in the following sections.

ENGINE AND IGNITION

Engines are classified based on the type of fuel they use and the technology they employ to convert energy into movement. The main types of engines found in modern vehicles are:

Gasoline Engines: These engines use spark ignition to ignite a mixture of gasoline and air, creating a controlled explosion that drives the pistons. They are common in most cars and are known for their smooth operation and relatively low emissions.

Diesel Engines: Diesel engines use compression ignition, where air is compressed to a high temperature before fuel is injected, causing spontaneous combustion. Diesel engines are more fuel-efficient than gasoline engines, especially under heavy loads, making them popular in trucks and large vehicles.

Hybrid Engines: A hybrid engine combines a gasoline or diesel engine with an electric motor. The electric motor assists in powering the vehicle at low speeds or when accelerating, which improves fuel efficiency and reduces emissions. Hybrid engines are popular for city driving where fuel efficiency is important.

Electric Engines: Electric engines use electric power from a battery pack to generate movement. They are extremely efficient, produce no emissions, and provide instant torque, leading to quick acceleration. They require charging from an external power source and are becoming increasingly common with the push for more environmentally friendly transportation.

Internal Combustion Engine

The internal combustion engine (ICE) is one of the most common types of engines in vehicles today. It works by burning fuel within the engine itself, converting the energy stored in the fuel into mechanical energy. In an ICE, a mixture of air and fuel is compressed and then ignited, producing a rapid expansion of gases that pushes pistons. This up-and-down movement of the pistons is then converted into rotary motion that turns the wheels.

Internal combustion engines are classified based on the number of cylinders (e.g., 4-cylinder, 6-cylinder), the layout (e.g., inline, V-type, horizontally opposed), and the stroke cycle they use (commonly four-stroke). The internal combustion engine powers the majority of vehicles on the road today.

Key Parts of the ICE Engine

An ICE engine generally needs the following key parts:

Pistons: The pistons are cylindrical components that move up and down inside the engine's cylinders. They are driven by the expansion of gases created during combustion. The pistons are connected to the crankshaft, and their movement is responsible for converting the energy of combustion into useful mechanical work.

Piston Rings: Metal rings fitted around the piston, providing a seal between the piston and cylinder wall. They prevent fuel mixture and combustion gases from leaking into the crankcase and ensure proper lubrication.

Camshaft: The camshaft is responsible for controlling the opening and closing of the engine's valves. It rotates in synchronization with the crankshaft and ensures that the intake and exhaust valves open and close at the right times during the engine cycle. Proper timing of these valves is crucial for engine performance and efficiency.

Intake Valve: A valve that opens to allow the air-fuel mixture into the combustion chamber during the intake stroke and closes during compression.

Exhaust Valve: A valve that opens to release the burned exhaust gases after combustion, allowing them to exit the combustion chamber and pass through the exhaust system.

Crankshaft: The crankshaft is connected to the pistons via connecting rods. It transforms the up-and-down motion of the pistons into rotary motion, which is used to turn the vehicle's wheels. The crankshaft ensures the power generated by the combustion process is efficiently transmitted to the drivetrain.

Cylinders: The hollow tubes where the pistons move up and down during the engine cycle. They are integral to the combustion process, and their number determines the engine's power and configuration.

Combustion Chamber: The space at the top of the cylinder where the air-fuel mixture is compressed and ignited, resulting in an explosion that pushes the piston down and produces power.

Connecting Rods: Rods that connect the pistons to the crankshaft, converting the up-and-down motion of the pistons into rotary motion, which powers the vehicle's drivetrain.

Carburetor: A device that mixes air and fuel in the correct ratio before it enters the combustion chamber. Common in older vehicles, it has largely been replaced by fuel injection systems for better efficiency.

Fuel Injector: An electronically controlled component that precisely sprays fuel into the intake manifold or combustion chamber, ensuring optimal fuel-air mixture for efficient combustion.

Flywheel: the flywheel stores rotational energy generated during combustion and releases it when no combustion is occurring to maintain smooth engine operation. By balancing power fluctuations, the flywheel ensures steady rotation and helps reduce engine vibrations, improving overall efficiency and performance.

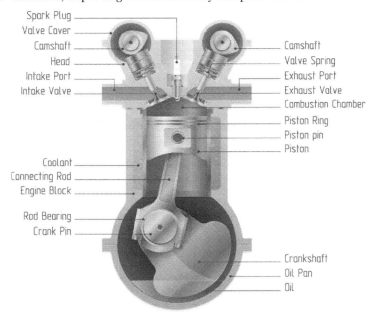

Engine Cycles

Most internal combustion engines use a four-stroke cycle, which includes the intake, compression, power, and exhaust strokes. This cycle is repeated continuously to keep the engine running:

1. Intake Stroke: The intake valve opens, allowing a mixture of air and fuel to enter the cylinder. The piston moves downward, drawing the mixture in, similar to how a syringe draws in liquid.

2. Compression Stroke: Once the intake valve closes, the piston moves back up, compressing the air-fuel mixture. Compression makes the mixture more explosive, which increases the power produced during combustion.

3. Power Stroke: At the top of the compression stroke, the spark plug ignites the compressed air-fuel mixture (in a gasoline engine), causing it to combust and rapidly expand. The expansion of the gases pushes the piston down, which is the main source of power for the engine.

4. Exhaust Stroke: After the power stroke, the exhaust valve opens, and the piston moves back up to expel the burnt gases from the cylinder. These gases are then directed out of the vehicle through the exhaust system.

The four-stroke cycle is efficient and reliable, making it the most common engine cycle for automotive use. Each of these four strokes contributes to the smooth running of the engine.

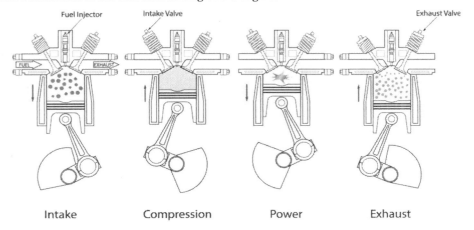

Intake   Compression   Power   Exhaust

Ignition System

The ignition system is essential for igniting the air-fuel mixture in a gasoline engine's combustion chamber at precisely the right moment, ensuring efficient combustion and engine performance. It all starts with the **battery**, which supplies the initial electrical energy needed to power the ignition system. When the driver turns the **ignition switch**, this energy is directed through the **ignition circuit** to initiate the starting process.

The **ignition coil** plays a crucial role by transforming the low voltage from the battery (usually 12 volts) into a much higher voltage, typically thousands of volts, required to create a spark. This high voltage is then sent to the **spark plugs**, which generate a spark across a small gap in each cylinder. This spark ignites the compressed air-fuel mixture, causing combustion, which pushes the pistons down and produces the mechanical energy necessary to drive the vehicle.

Modern ignition systems are controlled electronically rather than mechanically. The **ignition control module (ICM)** or **engine control unit (ECU)** regulates the precise timing of the spark, ensuring that it occurs at the optimal point in the engine cycle for maximum efficiency. Sensors, such as the crankshaft position sensor, provide critical data to the ECU, which adjusts the spark timing to suit the current engine speed and load conditions.

This precise control ensures that the ignition system delivers reliable performance, better fuel efficiency, and lower emissions compared to older mechanical ignition systems. If the spark timing is off or components like the ignition coil or spark plugs fail, it can lead to misfires, poor engine performance, or increased emissions.

A modern car's digital start system allows the vehicle to be started electronically, often without the need for a physical key. Instead, it uses a key fob or proximity sensor to start the engine with the push of a button. These systems rely on advanced electronics and are common in newer vehicles.

TRANSMISSION AND DRIVETRAIN

The **transmission** of an automobile transfers power from the engine to the wheels, allowing the vehicle to change speed and move efficiently. The transmission adjusts the torque (rotational force) and speed, ensuring that the engine operates within its optimal range under varying driving conditions. The **drivetrain** refers to the system that transmits power from the transmission to the wheels, which includes components like the differential, drive axles, and driveshaft. Together, the transmission and drivetrain work to provide the right balance of speed and power for smooth and controlled movement.

There are two main types of transmission systems: manual and automatic, each with distinct features and benefits.

Manual Transmission: In a manual transmission, the driver is responsible for selecting the gears using a gear stick and a clutch pedal. The clutch pedal allows the driver to disconnect the engine from the gearbox, change gears, and then reconnect them. Manual transmissions are known for offering better control, increased fuel efficiency, and simpler construction compared to automatic transmissions.

Automatic Transmission: Automatic transmissions do not require the driver to manually change gears. Instead, they use a **torque converter** or other automatic shifting mechanisms to handle gear changes automatically based on vehicle speed, load, and engine conditions. This makes them more convenient, especially for urban driving and heavy traffic. Automatic transmissions have become more sophisticated over the years, and modern systems often include features like continuously variable transmissions (CVTs), which provide smooth and seamless acceleration without distinct gear shifts.

Components: Clutch, Gearbox, Driveshaft

The **clutch** is a critical component of manual transmission systems. It is responsible for engaging and disengaging the engine from the gearbox, allowing for smooth gear changes. The clutch uses friction plates that press against each other to transmit power or disengage when the driver presses the clutch pedal. In an automatic transmission, the clutch is replaced by a **torque converter** that performs a similar function automatically.

The **gearbox** contains gears of different sizes that control the vehicle's speed and torque. By shifting gears, the gearbox adjusts the ratio between engine speed and wheel speed, allowing the vehicle to accelerate smoothly and efficiently handle different driving conditions. In manual transmissions, the gears are selected by the driver, whereas automatic transmissions use sensors and hydraulic systems to determine the appropriate gear.

The **driveshaft** is a long, rotating shaft that transmits power from the transmission to the differential in vehicles with rear-wheel drive or all-wheel drive. It converts the rotational energy produced by the gearbox and directs it to the differential, which then distributes power to the wheels. Front-wheel-drive vehicles typically do not use a long driveshaft but instead have half-shafts connecting the transmission to the front wheels.

Differential and Drive Axles

The differential is a component that splits the power from the driveshaft between the wheels, allowing them to rotate at different speeds. This is essential when turning, as the wheels on the inside of a turn need to rotate slower than the wheels on the outside. The differential ensures that power is distributed properly, enhancing vehicle stability and traction.

The **drive axles** connect the differential to the wheels. In front-wheel drive (FWD) vehicles, the drive axles are connected to the front wheels, while in rear-wheel drive (RWD) vehicles, they connect the rear wheels to the differential. In all-wheel drive (AWD) and four-wheel drive (4WD) vehicles, drive axles are present on both the front and rear wheels.

Front-Wheel Drive, Rear-Wheel Drive, and All-Wheel Drive Systems

In an FWD system, power is sent to the front wheels, which are responsible for both steering and driving the vehicle. FWD systems are efficient, offer good traction in wet conditions, and provide more space within the vehicle due to the absence of a rear driveshaft. They are popular in compact and midsize cars.

In an RWD system, power is delivered to the rear wheels. This setup allows for better weight distribution and handling, making it ideal for sports cars and trucks. RWD systems provide good performance under normal driving conditions but may have reduced traction on slippery surfaces compared to FWD.

AWD and 4WD systems provide power to all four wheels, enhancing traction and stability, especially on rough or slippery surfaces. AWD systems are typically always engaged, automatically adjusting the power distribution between the front and rear wheels as needed. 4WD systems, on the other hand, often allow the driver to engage and disengage four-wheel drive manually. These systems are commonly used in off-road vehicles and trucks designed for rough terrain.

FUEL AND EXHAUST SYSTEMS

The fuel system is responsible for delivering the correct amount of fuel to the engine, where it mixes with air for combustion. There are two main types of fuel delivery systems used in vehicles: carburetors and fuel injection.

Carburetors: Carburetors were widely used in vehicles before the 1980s. They function by creating a vacuum that draws fuel into the air stream and mixes it in the right proportions for combustion. While they are simple and effective, they are less precise compared to modern systems, often resulting in less efficient fuel usage and higher emissions.

Fuel Injection: Fuel injection systems have replaced carburetors in modern vehicles. In a fuel injection system, fuel is injected directly into the intake manifold or combustion chamber in precise amounts. These systems use electronic sensors to monitor engine conditions and deliver the right amount of fuel at the right time, leading to better fuel efficiency, improved performance, and reduced emissions. Port fuel injection and direct fuel injection are two common types of fuel injection used in modern vehicles.

Fuel Tank, Fuel Pump, and Fuel Lines

The fuel system starts with the fuel tank, which stores gasoline or diesel until it is needed by the engine. From the fuel tank, fuel is delivered through fuel lines to the engine. The fuel pump pumps fuel from the tank to the fuel injectors at the correct pressure.

The fuel tank is typically located at the rear of the vehicle and is designed to safely store fuel until it is needed. It has safety features, such as a venting system, to handle changes in pressure as the fuel is used.

The fuel pump is responsible for maintaining the correct fuel pressure. In modern vehicles, an electric fuel pump located inside the tank is the most common type. It ensures that fuel is delivered consistently to the fuel injectors.

Fuel lines transport fuel from the tank to the engine, while the fuel filter removes any impurities that may be in the fuel. This helps to protect the fuel injectors and other engine components from potential damage due to contaminants.

Exhaust System Components

After combustion, the exhaust gases need to be removed from the engine. The exhaust system manages these gases, reducing harmful emissions, and ensuring the engine runs smoothly.

The **exhaust manifold** collects exhaust gases from each cylinder and directs them into the exhaust pipe. It is typically made of cast iron or stainless steel to withstand the high temperatures of the exhaust gases.

The **catalytic converter** is designed to reduce harmful emissions. It uses chemical reactions to convert pollutants such as carbon monoxide, nitrogen oxides, and unburned hydrocarbons into less harmful substances like carbon dioxide and water vapor. The catalytic converter is crucial for meeting environmental emission standards.

Oxygen sensors are placed in the exhaust system before and after the catalytic converter. They measure the amount of oxygen in the exhaust gases and send this information to the engine control unit (ECU). The ECU then adjusts the air-fuel ratio to optimize combustion, improve fuel efficiency, and reduce emissions. Proper functioning of oxygen sensors is vital for maintaining fuel economy.

The **muffler** is designed to reduce the noise produced by the exhaust gases as they exit the vehicle. It contains chambers and perforated tubes that cancel out sound waves, allowing for quieter operation. The muffler also plays a role in directing the exhaust gases safely out of the vehicle.

Emission Control Systems

Modern vehicles are equipped with various emission control systems to reduce the release of harmful pollutants into the environment. These systems include:

Positive Crankcase Ventilation (PCV): The PCV valve recycles unburned gases that escape from the combustion chamber into the crankcase back into the engine to be burned again, reducing emissions.

Evaporative Emission Control (EVAP) System: The EVAP system prevents fuel vapors from escaping the fuel tank and fuel system into the atmosphere. It captures these vapors and routes them back to the engine for combustion.

EGR (Exhaust Gas Recirculation): The EGR system reduces nitrogen oxide emissions by recirculating a portion of the exhaust gases back into the intake manifold, lowering the combustion temperature.

The fuel and exhaust systems are essential to the functioning of an automobile. The fuel system ensures that the right amount of fuel is delivered to the engine for efficient combustion, while the exhaust system manages and treats the by-products of combustion. Advances such as fuel injection have improved the efficiency of the fuel system, while components like the catalytic converter and oxygen sensors have made vehicles cleaner and more environmentally friendly.

COOLING AND LUBRICATION SYSTEMS

The cooling system in an engine maintains an optimal temperature, preventing overheating, and ensuring efficient performance. It circulates coolant throughout the engine to absorb and remove excess heat generated during combustion. The main components of the cooling system are:

Radiator: The radiator is responsible for dissipating the heat absorbed by the coolant. As the hot coolant passes through the radiator's thin tubes, air flowing over these tubes cools the fluid before it recirculates back into the engine.

Water Pump: The water pump circulates coolant through the engine and the radiator. It ensures continuous coolant flow, which is essential for maintaining consistent engine temperatures. The pump is usually driven by a belt connected to the engine.

Thermostat: The thermostat controls the flow of coolant based on the engine's temperature. It remains closed when the engine is cold to allow faster warm-up, then opens as the engine reaches the desired operating temperature to regulate the cooling process.

Coolants

Coolants, also known as antifreeze, are specially formulated liquids designed to absorb heat and prevent freezing or overheating. There are different types of coolants: Ethylene Glycol Coolant (most common), Propylene Glycol Coolant, Hybrid Organic Acid Technology (HOAT).

Coolants typically come pre-mixed or as concentrates that need to be mixed with water, and the correct coolant type and mixture are essential for effective cooling.

Lubrication System

The lubrication system ensures that all engine components are properly lubricated, reducing friction and preventing wear. It also helps cool the engine by dissipating heat from the moving parts.

The **oil pump** circulates engine oil through the lubrication system. It draws oil from the oil pan and sends it to the various parts of the engine that need lubrication, ensuring consistent oil flow.

The **oil pan** is located at the bottom of the engine and serves as a reservoir for engine oil. It stores the oil that is not currently circulating in the system.

Oil Filter

The **oil filter** removes contaminants from the engine oil before it circulates through the engine. Clean oil ensures that the engine parts remain lubricated and that abrasive particles do not cause wear.

Maintaining the correct engine temperature is critical for efficient performance and longevity. Overheating can cause severe damage, including warped cylinder heads and engine failure, while running too cold can reduce fuel efficiency and increase emissions. The cooling system prevents overheating, while the lubrication system reduces friction between moving parts, preventing wear and tear. Proper lubrication also reduces the amount of heat generated by friction, contributing to overall temperature control and the health of the engine. Regular maintenance of both systems is vital to keep the engine operating smoothly and efficiently.

ELECTRICAL AND CHARGING SYSTEMS

Battery

The battery is the heart of the vehicle's electrical system, providing the energy needed to start the engine and power all electrical components when the engine is not running. It stores chemical energy and converts it into electrical energy to supply power. The battery is also used to stabilize voltage to protect the vehicle's electrical system. Proper battery maintenance is crucial to avoid unexpected breakdowns. This includes regularly checking the battery terminals for corrosion, ensuring the connections are tight, and testing the battery charge periodically to confirm that it holds a sufficient charge. In colder climates, ensuring the battery is fully charged is especially important, as lower temperatures reduce battery efficiency.

If your car battery is drained of electricity for any reason, you will need to **jump-start** it. Jump-starting transfers power from a well charged battery, either from another vehicle or a portable jump starter, to your dead battery. This process will provide enough power to start your engine, allowing the alternator to recharge the battery as the car runs.

To begin, park the car with the working battery close to your vehicle with the dead battery, ensuring they don't touch. Both cars should be turned off before you proceed. Once ready, attach the red (positive) jumper cable to the positive terminal of the dead battery, then connect the other end of the red cable to the positive terminal of the charged battery. Next, connect the black (negative) cable to the negative terminal of the good battery, and finally, attach the other end of the black cable to an unpainted metal surface on the dead vehicle, such as the engine block.

After securing the cables, start the car with the good battery and let it run for a few minutes. Then, attempt to start the car with the drained battery. If successful, remove the jumper cables in reverse order and keep the car running to allow the battery to recharge.

Alternator

Once the engine is running, the alternator takes over from the battery as the primary source of electrical power. The alternator is a generator that converts mechanical energy from the engine into electrical energy, supplying power to all electrical components and recharging the battery. The alternator works as part of the charging system, which ensures that the battery remains charged and that the vehicle has sufficient power for components such as the headlights, radio, and air conditioning. The charging system also includes a voltage regulator, which controls the alternator's output to maintain a consistent voltage, preventing damage to electrical components from voltage spikes.

Starter Motor and Starting the Engine

The starter motor is responsible for getting the engine running. When you turn the ignition key or press the start button, the battery sends electrical current to the starter motor, which engages the flywheel connected to the engine's crankshaft. The starter motor's powerful torque initiates the engine's initial rotation, allowing it to start the combustion cycle. Once the engine begins running, the starter motor disengages. A properly functioning starter motor is essential for the vehicle to start smoothly, and any issues, such as a worn-out starter or faulty electrical connections, can lead to starting problems.

Electrical Components

The electrical system of a vehicle also includes several essential components that ensure proper functioning and safety:

Fuses protect the electrical circuits from overcurrent. If an electrical component or circuit draws too much current, the fuse blows, breaking the circuit and preventing damage or fire. Fuses are typically located in fuse boxes that are accessible for easy replacement.

Relays are electrically operated switches that allow a low-current circuit to control a high-current circuit. They are used for components such as the headlights, cooling fan, or fuel pump, allowing the electrical system to control powerful devices safely and efficiently.

The **wiring harness** is a collection of wires and connectors that routes electrical power and signals throughout the vehicle. It acts as the central nervous system of the vehicle's electrical system, connecting all the components and ensuring they function together seamlessly.

The electrical and charging systems are essential for starting the vehicle and ensuring all electrical components function correctly. The battery provides initial power, while the alternator maintains power when the engine is running. The starter motor initiates engine operation, and components like fuses, relays, and the wiring harness ensure the system operates safely and efficiently.

CHASSIS, STEERING AND SUSPENSION

Chassis

The chassis of a vehicle is the structural framework that supports and holds all the major components of the vehicle together. It is essentially the vehicle's skeleton, providing strength, stability, and rigidity. The chassis is responsible for ensuring that all parts of the vehicle are securely attached and aligned properly, and it must be designed to withstand the stresses and loads generated during driving. The chassis can include components such as the frame, suspension system, steering system, and drivetrain.

The chassis system forms the backbone of a vehicle, providing the framework upon which all other systems and components are mounted. The chassis system plays a vital role in determining a vehicle's handling characteristics, overall safety, and ability to withstand different driving conditions. Chassis systems are engineered to manage stress loads, distribute weight evenly, and ensure proper alignment of the suspension and steering components for a safe and comfortable ride.

Steering System: Rack and Pinion, Power Steering

The steering and suspension systems are critical to the control, stability, and comfort of a vehicle. These systems work together to provide a smooth driving experience while ensuring that the vehicle responds accurately to the driver's inputs and maintains proper contact with the road.

The steering system is responsible for translating the driver's inputs into the movement of the vehicle's wheels. The two primary types of steering systems used in modern vehicles are rack and pinion and power steering.

Rack and Pinion Steering is a common steering mechanism found in modern vehicles. It consists of a rack, which is a long metal bar, and a pinion gear that engages with the rack. When the driver turns the steering wheel, the pinion gear moves along the rack, causing the front wheels to turn. This system provides precise and responsive steering, making it ideal for passenger cars.

Rack and Pinion Steering

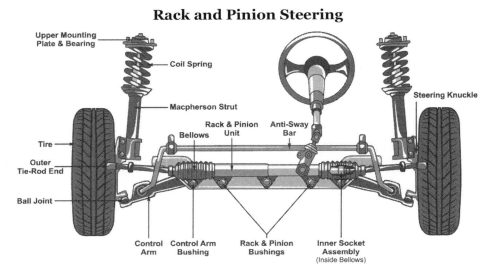

Power steering uses hydraulic or electric assistance to reduce the amount of effort needed to turn the steering wheel, particularly at low speeds or when parking. In hydraulic power steering, a pump driven by the engine provides hydraulic pressure to assist the driver. Electric power steering (EPS), on the other hand, uses an electric motor to provide the assistance, which is more energy-efficient and provides greater control over steering dynamics.

Suspension System Overview: Springs, Shock Absorbers, Struts

The suspension system ensures that the vehicle's wheels maintain constant contact with the road, providing a smooth ride and enhancing control over the vehicle. Key components of the suspension system include springs, shock absorbers, and struts.

Springs are designed to absorb and distribute the energy generated when the vehicle travels over bumps or uneven surfaces. Common types of springs include coil springs and leaf springs. Coil springs are used in most modern vehicles for their compact design and ability to absorb vertical motion.

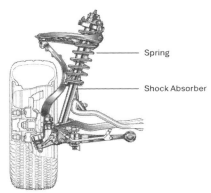

Shock absorbers, also known simply as shocks, work alongside the springs to dampen the energy produced by the movement of the springs. They prevent excessive bouncing by converting the kinetic energy of suspension movement into heat, which is then dissipated.

Struts are a combination of a shock absorber and a coil spring in a single unit. They support the weight of the vehicle while providing damping and stability. Struts are commonly used in front suspension systems for their ability to save space and provide structural support.

Types of Suspension: Independent vs. Solid Axle

In an **independent suspension** system, each wheel moves independently of the others. This setup allows for better handling, improved ride comfort, and enhanced road contact. Most passenger cars use independent front suspension for precise control, and many modern vehicles also use independent rear suspension for added comfort.

In a **solid axle** (or live axle) suspension, the left and right wheels are connected by a single solid axle. This means that movement in one wheel affects the other. Solid axles are commonly used in trucks and off-road vehicles because Solid axles are more durable and capable of handling heavy loads, but they tend to provide a rougher ride compared to independent suspension.

Steering Alignment

Steering alignment refers to the adjustment of the angles of the wheels to ensure they are set to the manufacturer's specifications. Proper alignment is essential for several reasons:

1. Tire Wear: Correct alignment prevents uneven tire wear, extending the life of the tires and ensuring safe driving.

2. Vehicle Handling: Proper alignment improves handling and ensures that the vehicle travels straight without pulling to one side. This is particularly important for maintaining control at high speeds and when driving on winding roads.

3. Fuel Efficiency: Misaligned wheels create additional friction between the tires and the road, which forces the engine to work harder, reducing fuel efficiency.

4. Driver Comfort and Safety: Proper alignment ensures a smooth and comfortable ride, reducing strain on both the driver and the suspension components. Misalignment can lead to excessive vibrations, making the ride uncomfortable and potentially unsafe.

To sum up, the steering and suspension systems are essential for vehicle stability, handling, and comfort. The rack and pinion steering system and power steering work together to ensure precise control of the vehicle. The suspension system, consisting of springs, shock absorbers, and struts, absorbs road impacts and maintains traction. Different suspension types—independent and solid axle—serve specific purposes, with independent suspension offering better comfort and handling, and solid axle providing durability under heavy loads. Proper steering alignment is crucial for tire longevity, handling, and overall safety.

BRAKING SYSTEM

The braking system is one of the most critical safety features of any vehicle, designed to slow down or stop the vehicle effectively under various driving conditions. It works by converting the vehicle's kinetic energy into heat energy, which is then dissipated. The braking system allows the driver to control the vehicle's speed, prevent accidents, and maintain safety on the road. The main types of braking systems found in vehicles are disc brakes and drum brakes, each with distinct advantages and applications.

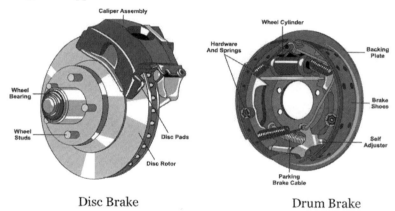

Disc Brake   Drum Brake

Disc brakes are commonly used in most modern vehicles, especially on the front wheels. They consist of a brake disc (or rotor) attached to the wheel, a caliper, and brake pads. When the driver presses the brake pedal, hydraulic fluid forces the caliper to squeeze the brake pads against the disc, creating friction that slows the wheel's rotation. Disc brakes are preferred for their superior stopping power, excellent heat dissipation, and consistent performance, even under demanding conditions. They are highly effective at providing strong braking force and are commonly used in performance vehicles.

Drum brakes, on the other hand, are often found on the rear wheels of many vehicles. They consist of a brake drum attached to the wheel, along with brake shoes that press against the inside of the drum to create friction. While not as efficient as disc brakes in terms of heat dissipation, drum brakes are still effective and are often used in applications where cost savings and durability are a priority. Drum brakes are also commonly used for the parking brake mechanism, as they have a self-energizing effect, which helps to hold the vehicle in place.

The braking system operates using hydraulic pressure, which means that when the driver presses the brake pedal, a **master cylinder** pushes brake fluid through the brake lines to activate the brakes at each wheel. The brake fluid is vital because it transfers the force from the brake pedal to the brakes. Proper maintenance of the brake fluid, such as checking for leaks and replacing the fluid periodically, is crucial to ensure that the brakes work effectively and safely.

The **brake booster** plays a crucial role in enhancing the efficiency of a car's hydraulic braking system by reducing the amount of force the driver needs to apply on the brake pedal. It works in tandem with the hydraulic system, which relies on brake fluid to transmit force from the master cylinder to the brake calipers or drum brakes.

When the driver presses the brake pedal, the brake booster uses vacuum pressure generated by the engine to amplify the force applied to the master cylinder. The master cylinder then converts this amplified force into hydraulic pressure, pushing brake fluid through the brake lines to engage the brakes at each wheel. This amplified force makes the hydraulic system more responsive and efficient, enabling the driver to stop or slow the vehicle with minimal effort. Without the brake booster, significantly more force would be required to engage the hydraulic system and achieve the same braking effect, making braking harder and less responsive.

Another important feature in modern braking systems is the **anti-lock braking system (ABS)**. ABS prevents the wheels from locking up during hard braking, which helps maintain steering control and avoid skidding. This system uses sensors to monitor wheel speed and modulates brake pressure to ensure that the wheels continue to rotate rather than locking up. ABS has become a standard feature in most vehicles today, significantly enhancing safety, especially on wet or slippery surfaces.

TIRES AND WHEELS

The tires and wheels system is a crucial component of any vehicle, providing support, traction, and the ability to move over various surfaces safely and smoothly. Tires and wheels work together to ensure stability, control, and safety, as they are the only contact point between the vehicle and the road.

Tires are designed to provide traction, absorb road shocks, and support the vehicle's weight. They are made of multiple layers, including rubber, fabric, and steel, and have a tread pattern that varies depending on their intended use. **Tread** is the part of the tire that makes contact with the road, and it is responsible for providing grip, channeling water away in wet conditions, and improving overall traction. Proper tire maintenance, including checking the tread depth, ensures that the vehicle remains safe to drive. Worn-out tires with low tread can lead to loss of control, especially in wet or slippery conditions.

The type of tire chosen significantly impacts vehicle performance. **All-season tires** are the most common type, providing balanced performance in various weather conditions. **Summer tires** offer enhanced grip and handling for warm, dry conditions, while **winter tires** have specific tread designs and rubber compounds to enhance performance in cold weather and on snow-covered roads. Specialized tires like off-road tires are designed for vehicles that frequently drive on uneven terrain, providing better traction on loose surfaces like mud or gravel.

Tire pressure is another critical factor affecting the performance of the tires and wheels system. Maintaining the correct tire pressure, as specified by the vehicle manufacturer, ensures even tire wear, improved fuel efficiency, and optimal traction. Over-inflated or under-inflated tires can lead to uneven tread wear, reduced handling capability, and increased risk of tire failure. Regularly checking tire pressure with a pressure gauge and adjusting as needed is vital to the health of the tires.

Wheels serve as the mounting structure for the tires and help in supporting the vehicle's weight and transferring power from the drivetrain to the road. Wheels are made from various materials, such as steel or aluminum alloy, with alloy wheels being lighter and often offering better heat dissipation. Proper wheel maintenance, including balancing and alignment, is essential for ensuring smooth operation, preventing vibrations, and promoting even tire wear.

Wheel alignment refers to the adjustment of the wheels' angles to meet the manufacturer's specifications. Proper alignment is essential for keeping the vehicle stable, preventing the car from pulling to one side, and reducing unnecessary wear on the tires. Misaligned wheels can lead to uneven tire wear and a decrease in fuel efficiency. Routine alignment checks help maintain optimal driving performance and extend tire life.

Wheel balancing is also important, as imbalanced wheels can lead to vibrations at higher speeds and uneven tire wear. Balancing involves adjusting the weight distribution of the wheel and tire assembly to ensure smooth rotation, which promotes better ride quality and longer-lasting tires.

Overall, the tires and wheels system plays an essential role in the vehicle's overall safety, efficiency, and performance. Regular tire inspection, maintaining correct tire pressure, and ensuring proper alignment and balancing are key practices that help prolong the life of the tires and enhance the vehicle's handling, fuel efficiency, and safety.

SAFETY AND CONTROL SYSTEMS

Vehicle safety and control systems are designed to protect passengers and enhance driver control, particularly in challenging driving conditions. These systems have evolved significantly, incorporating modern technologies to minimize the risk of accidents and injuries.

Airbags and seatbelts are fundamental components of vehicle safety. Seatbelts are the primary line of defense in an accident, designed to keep passengers securely restrained in their seats, preventing them from being ejected or thrown against the dashboard or windshield. Modern vehicles are equipped with three-point seatbelts that distribute the force of a collision across the chest, shoulders, and pelvis, reducing the risk of injury.

Airbags complement seatbelts by providing additional protection during a crash. Airbags deploy instantly upon impact, creating a cushion that reduces the force on occupants and prevents direct contact with the steering wheel, dashboard, or side structures of the vehicle. Advanced airbag systems now include front, side, curtain, and knee airbags to offer comprehensive protection from all angles. Proper use of seatbelts is necessary for airbags to function effectively, as they work together to reduce injury in the event of a collision.

The **Traction Control System (TCS)** is designed to prevent the loss of traction between the vehicle's tires and the road surface, particularly during acceleration. TCS monitors wheel speed using sensors, and if it detects that one or more wheels are spinning faster than others, it reduces engine power or applies braking force to the affected wheel(s). This helps the vehicle maintain grip, especially on slippery or uneven surfaces, improving stability and preventing skidding. TCS is especially useful in wet or icy conditions where tires are more prone to losing traction.

Electronic Stability Control (ESC) is an advanced system that helps maintain vehicle stability by reducing the risk of skidding or sliding during sudden maneuvers. ESC uses sensors to monitor the vehicle's steering input, speed, and lateral movement, comparing the driver's intended direction with the vehicle's actual movement. If the system detects that the vehicle is losing control, it automatically applies braking force to individual wheels and adjusts engine power to help bring the vehicle back on course. ESC is particularly effective in emergency situations, such as avoiding obstacles or taking sharp turns, and is proven to significantly reduce the risk of rollovers and accidents.

Modern vehicles are equipped with multiple computer systems, often referred to as **Electronic Control Units (ECUs)**, that control various aspects of vehicle operation. These systems manage everything from engine performance and fuel injection to transmission control, climate systems, and safety features like TCS and ESC. The integration of computers allows for real-time data analysis and precise control, resulting in improved performance, better fuel efficiency, and enhanced safety. Computers also enable features like adaptive cruise control, collision warning systems, and automatic emergency braking.

Vehicle safety standards are regulations designed to ensure that vehicles meet specific safety requirements to protect passengers and reduce accidents. These standards are set by regulatory bodies, such as the National Highway Traffic Safety Administration (NHTSA) in the United States, which mandates that vehicles must be equipped with safety features like airbags, seatbelts, ESC, and ABS. The development and enforcement of safety standards have been crucial in reducing the severity of injuries and fatalities in traffic accidents.

PRACTICE SET

Time: 7 minutes for 10 questions

Select the correct answer from the choices given. This practice subtest reflects the number of questions and time limits you'll encounter on the CAT-ASVAB Automotive Information subtest without any tryout questions.

1. What is the primary purpose of a flywheel in an internal combustion engine?

(A) To regulate engine temperature
(B) To store rotational energy and smooth out engine operation
(C) To increase the engine's horsepower
(D) To control fuel injection timing

2. A clutch in a manual transmission is responsible for

(A) engaging and disengaging the engine from the drivetrain.
(B) regulating the speed of the vehicle.
(C) cooling the engine during long drives.
(D) controlling the fuel flow to the engine.

3. What is the primary purpose of the radiator in a car's engine cooling system?

(A) To increase engine horsepower
(B) To prevent the engine from overheating by dissipating heat
(C) To regulate the oil pressure in the engine
(D) To charge the car's battery

4. What is the correct order of steps to safely jump-start a car with a dead battery?

A) Connect the positive and negative cables to the dead battery first, then to the working battery, and start both cars.
B) Connect the positive cable to the dead battery, then connect the negative cable to the dead battery. Start the working car and then the dead car.
C) Connect the positive cable to the dead battery, then to the working battery; connect the negative cable to the working battery, and the other end to an unpainted metal surface on the dead car. Start the working car first, then the dead car.
D) Connect the negative cable to the working battery first, then connect the positive cable to the dead battery, and start the dead car.

5. An alternator in a car functions to

(A) provide spark for combustion.
(B) convert mechanical energy into electrical energy.
(C) supply hydraulic power to brakes.
(D) store electrical energy.

6. Which of the following components helps to prevent engine overheating?

(A) Fan belt
(B) Water pump
(C) Brake booster
(D) Spark plug

7. Identity this engine component the arrow points to:

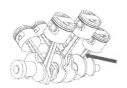

A) Piston
B) Serpentine Belt (Fan Belt)
C) Rod
D) Crankshaft

8. Which of the following engines uses compression ignition to burn fuel and is known for higher fuel efficiency, especially under heavy loads?

A) Gasoline Engine
B) Diesel Engine
C) Hybrid Engine
D) Electric Engine

9. Which of the following strokes in a four-stroke engine cycle is responsible for igniting the air-fuel mixture to generate power?

A) Intake Stroke
B) Compression Stroke
C) Power Stroke
D) Exhaust Stroke

10. Which component of an internal combustion engine is responsible for converting the up-and-down motion of the pistons into rotary motion that drives the vehicle's wheels?

A) Camshaft
B) Crankshaft
C) Piston Rings
D) Fuel Injector

Answers and Explanations

1. (B) To store rotational energy and smooth out engine operation. Explanation: A flywheel in an internal combustion engine serves to store rotational energy during the power stroke and release it during other strokes, helping to smooth out the engine's operation. The flywheel helps maintain a steady rotation by compensating for the engine's inherent fluctuations in power output, especially during times when no combustion is occurring. This contributes to a more consistent, balanced operation.

2. (A) engaging and disengaging the engine from the drivetrain. Explanation: The clutch's primary function in a manual transmission system is to engage or disengage the engine from the drivetrain, allowing the vehicle to either move or stop without killing the engine. Regulating speed is incorrect, as that is primarily done through acceleration and brakes. Cooling the engine is the job of the radiator, and controlling the fuel flow is managed by fuel injection or carburetor systems.

3. (B) To prevent the engine from overheating by dissipating heat. Explanation: The radiator is designed to cool the engine by dissipating excess heat. It works by circulating coolant through the engine and then releasing the heat absorbed from the engine into the atmosphere. This prevents the engine from overheating. Options A, C, and D are incorrect because they are unrelated to the radiator's function in temperature regulation.

4. C) Connect the positive cable to the dead battery, then to the working battery; connect the negative cable to the working battery, and the other end to an unpainted metal surface on the dead car. Start the working car first, then the dead car.

Explanation: Option C is the correct procedure for jump-starting a car. You always begin by connecting the positive cable to the dead battery and then the working battery. After that, connect the negative cable to the working battery and attach the other end of the negative cable to an unpainted metal surface on the dead car (not the battery itself, which reduces the risk of sparks near the battery). The working vehicle should be started first, allowing it to charge the dead battery before starting the other car.

5. (B) convert mechanical energy into electrical energy. Explanation: The alternator converts the mechanical energy from the engine into electrical energy to recharge the car battery and power electrical systems when the engine is running. Providing a spark for combustion is the role of the ignition system. Supplying hydraulic power is incorrect as that involves the braking system, and storing electrical energy is the role of the battery, not the alternator.

6. (B) Water pump. Explanation: The water pump circulates coolant through the engine to prevent overheating by transferring excess heat to the radiator. The fan belt powers accessories like the alternator but doesn't directly prevent overheating. The brake booster assists with braking, and the spark plug ignites the air-fuel mixture in the engine but does not control temperature.

The term "fan belt" originates from older car designs where the belt was primarily responsible for driving the engine's cooling fan. In modern vehicles, the cooling fan is usually electrically powered, and the belt—now often referred to as the serpentine belt—drives other components such as the alternator, power steering pump, and air conditioning compressor. Although the belt no longer directly drives a fan in most modern cars, the name "fan belt" has persisted as a holdover from earlier designs.

7. C) Rod. Explanation: The rod, also known as the connecting rod, connects the piston to the crankshaft in an engine. Its primary function is to convert the up-and-down (reciprocating) motion of the piston into the rotational motion of the crankshaft, which drives the vehicle. The Piston (A) in the illustration is above the rod. The serpentine belt (B) is not shown. The Crankshaft (D) is connected to and is below the rod. Therefore, the correct answer is the rod.

8. B) Diesel Engine. Explanation: Diesel engines use compression ignition, where air is compressed to a high temperature, and fuel is injected, causing spontaneous combustion. This process makes diesel engines more fuel-efficient, particularly under heavy loads, compared to gasoline engines, which rely on spark ignition. Hybrid engines combine a gasoline or diesel engine with an electric motor, while electric engines run solely on battery power.

9. C) Power Stroke. Explanation: During the power stroke, the compressed air-fuel mixture is ignited by the spark plug, causing combustion. The resulting expansion of gases pushes the piston downward, generating the engine's main source of power. The intake stroke brings in the air-fuel mixture, the compression stroke compresses it, and the exhaust stroke expels the burnt gases.

10. B) Crankshaft. Explanation: The crankshaft is connected to the pistons via connecting rods and is responsible for converting the up-and-down motion of the pistons into rotary motion. This rotary motion drives the vehicle's wheels. The camshaft controls the opening and closing of the valves, piston rings provide a seal, and the fuel injector ensures proper fuel delivery, but none of these components convert piston motion into rotary motion like the crankshaft does.

CHAPTER 8: SHOP INFORMATION

The Shop Information subtest of the ASVAB evaluates your knowledge of basic tools, materials, and practices commonly used in various trades, such as woodworking, metalworking, plumbing, and automotive repair. This section is particularly useful for individuals considering careers in mechanical or technical fields, as it provides insight into your aptitude for hands-on tasks and shop environments.

In the Shop Information subtest, you can expect questions covering a wide range of topics, such as the types and uses of hand tools and power tools, safety practices, materials commonly used in workshops, and basic shop terminology. You will also encounter questions about the functions of various shop tools, how to perform different tasks safely, and the properties of materials like wood and metal. The test aims to assess not only your theoretical knowledge but also your ability to apply basic principles in real-world situations.

Questions in this subtest might involve identifying tools from pictures, selecting the best tool for a specific task, understanding how to measure and cut materials, and knowing which safety precautions to follow. You will need to recognize the difference between tools like wrenches, saws, drills, chisels, and sanders, as well as understand how these tools are used in practical settings. Additionally, some questions may cover processes like joining materials, working with finishes, or operating machinery safely and effectively.

This chapter will provide you with valuable information to help you prepare for the Shop Information subtest. By understanding the fundamental concepts and familiarizing yourself with the tools, materials, and practices that are tested, you will be better equipped to answer the questions confidently.

MEASURING AND MARKING TOOLS

Measuring Tools

Measuring tools are essential in any shop environment, ensuring that materials are accurately measured, and cuts are precisely made. Below is an overview of some common measuring tools used in the shop.

Ruler

A ruler is a basic measuring tool that is commonly used to measure length or distance. It is often made of wood, metal, or plastic, and has markings in both metric and imperial units. Rulers are great for making small, straight measurements and are frequently used in tasks like woodworking or metalworking to draw straight lines or verify the dimensions of smaller objects.

Tape Measure

A tape measure is a flexible measuring tool used to measure longer distances or larger surfaces. It is typically made of metal and housed in a retractable casing, making it compact and easy to use. Tape measures are marked in inches and centimeters, and they can easily measure curves or irregular surfaces, making them versatile for a wide range of applications.

Calipers

Calipers are tools used for more precise measurements, especially when determining the internal or external dimensions of an object. They come in different forms, such as vernier calipers or digital calipers, and are commonly used in metalworking and mechanical engineering. Calipers are ideal for measuring distances, depths, and thicknesses that require a higher degree of accuracy than a ruler or tape measure can provide.

An **Inside caliper** is designed to measure the internal dimensions of an object, such as the diameter of a hole or the inside width of a slot. It has outward-bent legs that fit into the interior of the object being measured.

An **Outside caliper** is used to measure the external dimensions of an object, like the thickness or outside diameter of a pipe or rod. Its legs curve inward to grasp the outer surface of the object.

A **vernier caliper** is a precise measuring tool used to measure internal and external dimensions, as well as depths, with high accuracy. It consists of a main scale and a sliding vernier scale, which allows measurements to be read down to fractions of a millimeter or inch. Commonly used in mechanical engineering and manufacturing, it provides more accurate readings than a regular ruler or tape measure.

Micrometer

A micrometer is a precision measuring tool used to take highly accurate measurements of small objects, often to within thousandths of an inch or hundredths of a millimeter. It is commonly used in engineering and machining to measure components such as screws, bearings, or other small parts.

A micrometer consists of a frame, anvil, spindle, and a thimble with a graduated scale. The object being measured is placed between the anvil and spindle, and the thimble is turned to move the spindle toward the object until it lightly touches. The measurement is then read from the graduated scale on the thimble and the sleeve, providing a highly accurate reading of the object's size. Micrometers are often used to ensure parts meet specific tolerances, making them an invaluable tool in quality control and precision engineering.

Protractor

A protractor is a measuring tool used to measure angles. It is usually a half-circle or full-circle tool made of plastic or metal, marked with degrees from 0° to 180° or 0° to 360°. Protractors are used in both woodworking and metalworking to ensure that the angles being cut or assembled are correct, ensuring precision in projects requiring specific angles, such as framing or miter joints.

Square

A square is used to measure and check for right angles (90°) in projects. There are different types of squares, such as carpenter's squares and try squares, which are used to ensure that edges and corners are accurately aligned. Squares are also useful for marking out lines perpendicular or parallel to an edge, making them an essential tool in maintaining accuracy in construction and fabrication.

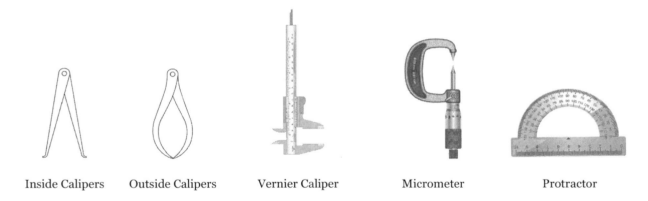

| Inside Calipers | Outside Calipers | Vernier Caliper | Micrometer | Protractor |

Marking Tools

Marking tools are used to create lines, points, or guides on a material to help ensure accuracy during cutting, drilling, or assembling. Below is an overview of some common marking tools found in a shop environment.

Chalk Line

A chalk line is a tool used to create long, straight lines on large surfaces, such as wood, drywall, or concrete. It consists of a string coated in colored chalk, which is pulled tight across the surface and then snapped to leave a visible line. This tool is often used for layout work, such as marking reference lines before making cuts or aligning components. Chalk lines are especially useful for ensuring that long cuts or installations are straight.

Scriber

A scriber is a metal tool used to make fine, precise lines on hard surfaces like metal or plastic. It has a pointed tip, usually made of hardened steel, carbide, or another durable material, which is used to scratch a mark onto the surface. Scribers are typically used in metalworking to create reference marks that will not be erased or smudged during the work process. They are ideal for making accurate lines before cutting or drilling metal parts.

Punch

A punch is a tool used to create an indentation or mark at a specific point on a material, usually metal or wood. There are different types of punches, such as center punches and pin punches. A **center punch** is commonly used to mark the location of a hole before drilling. The indentation made by the punch helps prevent the drill bit from wandering, ensuring that the hole is drilled in the correct location.

A **dot punch** is a marking tool used to create small indentations on surfaces, usually metal or wood, as a guide for drilling. The indentation helps keep the drill bit from wandering, ensuring that holes are drilled accurately. Unlike a center punch, which makes deeper indentations, the dot punch is designed for lighter marks, often used in precise layout work.

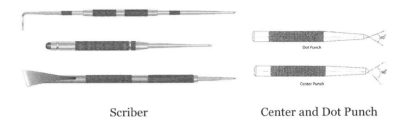

Scriber   Center and Dot Punch

GRIPPING TOOLS

Gripping tools are essential in any shop environment, used to hold materials securely in place, providing the stability needed for tasks such as cutting, drilling, or assembling. They ensure that workpieces do not move during operations, which helps achieve accuracy and safety.

Pliers are among the most versatile hand tools used for gripping, bending, and manipulating small objects. Different types of pliers serve specific purposes. **Slip-joint pliers** are adjustable and can grip objects of various sizes, making them ideal for general-purpose tasks in the workshop. **Needle-nose pliers**, with their long, slender jaws, are perfect for reaching into tight spaces or holding small objects that require precision. They are especially useful in electrical work or intricate mechanical tasks. **Locking pliers**, also known as **vise-grips**, can be locked into place, providing a secure and stable hold on objects that need to be held firmly over a longer period. This feature makes them particularly useful for heavy-duty tasks or when extra force is needed to hold materials in place.

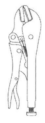

Slip-joint Plier   Needle-nose Plier   Cutting Plier   Linesman Plier   Locking Plier

Clamps are used when materials need to be held securely while being worked on, ensuring that they remain stationary during cutting, sanding, or assembling. **C-clamps** are shaped like the letter "C" and have a threaded screw that adjusts the clamping pressure. These clamps are commonly used in both woodworking and metalworking for holding smaller items in place. **Bar clamps** consist of a long metal bar with adjustable jaws, making them suitable for clamping larger items like wooden boards or panels. **Pipe clamps** are similar to bar clamps but use a pipe for added versatility and length, making them particularly useful in cabinetry and furniture making, where large items need to be secured.

Vises are mechanical devices mounted to a workbench to hold workpieces securely in place while they are being drilled, sawed, or otherwise worked on. The **bench vise** is one of the most common types and is used to secure objects during tasks like sawing or filing. It features two jaws—one fixed and one adjustable—to hold the workpiece firmly. **Woodworking vises** are specifically designed for woodworkers and are mounted on a woodworking bench. They are used to hold wooden pieces securely during tasks such as planing or sanding, ensuring the material stays in place for accurate results.

Gripping tools, such as pliers, clamps, and vises, are crucial for maintaining stability and precision in various tasks. They allow workers to manipulate, hold, and secure materials effectively, which contributes to both safety and the quality of the work produced in any shop environment.

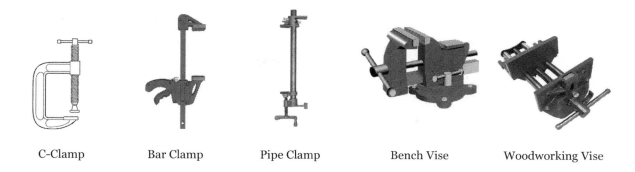

C-Clamp   Bar Clamp   Pipe Clamp   Bench Vise   Woodworking Vise

CUTTING AND DRILLING TOOLS

Cutting and drilling tools are essential in the shop for shaping, resizing, or creating openings in various materials. These tools can be either manual or powered, each suited for different tasks depending on the material and level of precision required.

Manual saws are non-powered tools used to cut materials like wood, metal, or plastic. The **hand saw** is the most common type, used primarily for cutting wood. It features a straight blade with serrated teeth, making it suitable for general-purpose cutting in woodworking. For cutting metal or plastic, the **hacksaw** is often preferred. It has a fine-toothed blade held in a U-shaped frame, allowing for precision cutting of harder materials. When intricate shapes or curves need to be cut in wood, the **coping saw** is an ideal choice. It has a thin, replaceable blade held under tension by a metal frame, making it effective for detailed work in tight spaces where precision is crucial.

Powered saws make cutting tasks more efficient, especially for larger projects or tougher materials. The **circular saw** is a versatile power tool that uses a round, toothed blade to make straight cuts in wood, metal, or other materials. It is portable and well-suited for cutting lumber, plywood, and similar materials on construction sites. The **jigsaw** is another type of powered saw, featuring a reciprocating blade that allows for curved or intricate cuts in wood, metal, or plastic. This makes it useful for applications requiring more detailed cuts. Finally, the **reciprocating saw** operates with a push-and-pull motion, making it ideal for demolition work and quickly cutting through various materials, including wood, metal, and plastic.

Hand Saw   Hacksaw   Coping Saw   Circular Saw   Jigsaw   Reciprocating Saw

DRILLING AND BORING TOOLS

Drilling and boring tools are used to create round holes or enlarge existing holes in a workpiece. These tools can be operated manually or powered.

Brace and Bit

A brace is a hand-operated tool used in conjunction with a bit to bore holes. It has a U-shaped handle that allows the user to apply torque by twisting the brace back and forth, while the bit creates the hole. Brace and bit tools are often used in woodworking for larger holes, providing better control compared to a hand drill.

Power Drill

A power drill is an electric or battery-powered tool that uses rotating drill bits to create holes quickly and accurately. Corded and cordless power drills are available, and they are widely used for drilling holes and driving screws. Power drills can also be fitted with various attachments to accommodate different tasks.

Auger

An auger is a tool used for boring larger holes, particularly in wood. It features a helical shaft that removes material as it cuts, making it efficient for creating deep holes in materials like wood, soil, or ice. Augers are commonly used in woodworking or construction for drilling through beams and posts.

Drill Bits

Drill bits are the cutting tools that are attached to drills for creating holes. They come in various shapes and sizes, each designed for a specific material, such as wood, metal, plastic, or masonry. Common types of drill bits include twist bits, spade bits, and masonry bits.

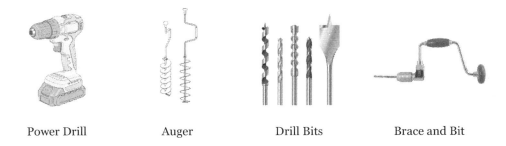

Power Drill   Auger   Drill Bits   Brace and Bit

TURNING TOOLS

Turning tools are used in the workshop to tighten or loosen fasteners such as screws, nuts, and bolts. They are crucial for assembling and disassembling various parts in both woodworking and metalworking.

Screwdriver

Screwdrivers are essential tools for driving or removing screws, and they come in several types, each suited for different applications. The **flathead screwdriver** is one of the most basic tools, featuring a flat, straight blade that fits into screws with a single slot. It is versatile and can be used in a variety of tasks, ranging from carpentry to electrical work. On the other hand, the **Phillips screwdriver** has a cross-shaped tip, which fits into corresponding cross-slotted screws. This design offers better grip and torque, reducing the risk of slipping, making it suitable for tasks requiring precision and a secure fit. The **Torx screwdriver** has a star-shaped tip that is commonly used with Torx screws. This design allows for better torque transfer, making it especially useful in automotive and electronic applications where a strong and secure fit is necessary.

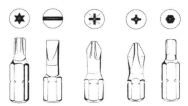

Torx Slotted Pozidriv Phillips Hex

Wrenches

Wrenches are used to tighten or loosen nuts and bolts, and there are different types available, each serving specific purposes. The **box-end wrench** features a closed loop at both ends, designed for specific nut or bolt sizes. This type of wrench provides a secure grip, minimizing the risk of rounding off the edges of the fastener. For situations where the fastener must be approached from the side, the **open-end wrench** is ideal. It has U-shaped ends, making it easy to apply to bolts or nuts, especially in tight spaces where a full rotation is not possible. The **adjustable wrench** offers versatility, featuring a movable jaw that can be adjusted to fit various bolt and nut sizes. It is a convenient tool to have on hand for many situations where a specific size wrench is not available, making it an indispensable addition to any toolbox.

Socket Wrench

A socket wrench is used with detachable sockets that fit over a bolt or nut, allowing for efficient tightening or loosening. The key feature of a socket wrench is its ability to attach to a variety of socket sizes, allowing it to fit many different fasteners. The socket wrench applies direct torque to the fastener, which can be in either direction, depending on how the handle is manipulated. Socket wrenches are ideal for working on cars or machinery where bolts need to be tightened or loosened in confined spaces.

Socket wrenches are commonly used with a ratchet, which allows continuous turning without needing to remove and reposition the tool.

Ratchet

A ratchet is a tool that usually works in combination with a socket wrench. A ratchet has a gear mechanism inside that allows it to move freely in one direction while engaging the fastener in the other direction, making the work more efficient by reducing the need to lift and reposition the tool after every partial rotation. It makes tightening or loosening fasteners much faster, especially in spaces where a full rotation is not possible. The ratchet mechanism allows for easy and efficient operation in repetitive tasks.

Socket wrenches can be used without a ratchet in cases where there is ample space to make full rotations. However, when space is tight, the ratchet's back-and-forth motion makes it much easier to operate.

Hex Key (Allen Wrench)

A hex key, also known as an Allen wrench, is a small, L-shaped tool used to drive bolts or screws with hexagonal sockets. Hex keys are commonly used in furniture assembly and mechanical applications where screws are recessed for a flush finish.

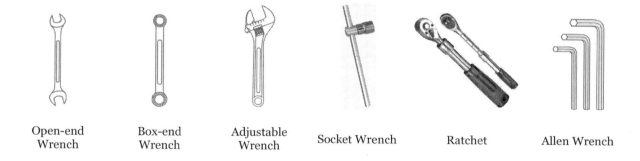

| Open-end Wrench | Box-end Wrench | Adjustable Wrench | Socket Wrench | Ratchet | Allen Wrench |

STRIKING TOOLS

Striking tools are used to deliver force to a workpiece, typically for driving fasteners or breaking apart materials. These tools are essential for many construction, metalworking, and demolition tasks.

Hammer

The **claw hammer** is the most common type of hammer, featuring a flat face for driving nails and a claw on the opposite side for pulling nails out. This versatility makes it a go-to tool in carpentry and general construction work, allowing users to both drive and remove nails efficiently. Its ergonomic design and dual functionality make it an essential tool in almost every toolkit.

The **ball-peen hammer** is specifically designed for metalworking. It has a rounded end opposite the flat face, which is ideal for shaping metal, setting rivets, and other metal fabrication tasks. It is often used in conjunction with chisels and punches, making it a staple in both machinists' and metalworkers' toolkits. The rounded "peen" helps shape metal without causing excessive damage.

The **sledgehammer** is a large, heavy hammer used primarily for breaking apart hard materials like concrete or stone. Its long handle provides significant leverage, allowing the user to apply considerable force, which makes it effective for demolition tasks. Due to its size and weight, the sledgehammer is typically reserved for jobs that require a substantial amount of power and force.

Chisel Hammer

A chisel hammer is used in conjunction with a chisel to apply force for cutting or shaping materials. It has a flat face that provides controlled force, making it ideal for precise tasks like carving wood or metal.

Mallet

A mallet is a soft-headed striking tool used when a softer impact is needed. Unlike metal hammers, mallets are made of wood or rubber to prevent damage to the material being worked on. They are often used in woodworking to tap chisels or join parts without marring the surface.

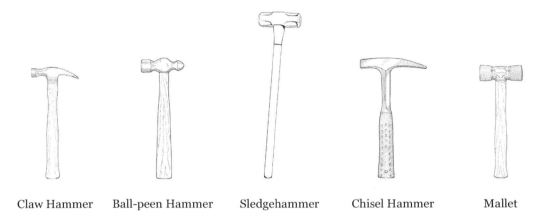

Claw Hammer   Ball-peen Hammer   Sledgehammer   Chisel Hammer   Mallet

Punch

We introduced punches a marking tools earlier, but they can be striking tools as well. A **center punch** is used to create an indentation in a material before drilling, which helps guide the drill bit and ensures it stays in place without wandering. This small mark provides stability and accuracy when starting to drill.

A **dot punch** is also used to create small indentations on surfaces, usually metal or wood, as a guide for drilling. Unlike a center punch, which makes deeper indentations, the dot punch is designed for lighter marks, often used in precise layout work.

A **pin punch**, on the other hand, is used to drive out or insert pins in mechanical assemblies. Its straight shank allows it to fit into holes precisely, making it effective for pushing or removing pins during disassembly or repair. Both tools are essential for ensuring accuracy and precision in metalworking tasks.

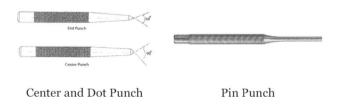

Center and Dot Punch   Pin Punch

PRYING TOOLS

Prying tools are essential in various construction, demolition, and repair tasks, providing the leverage needed to separate materials or remove fasteners like nails. These tools are designed to help lift, pry, and dismantle components efficiently without causing excessive damage.

A **crowbar** is a long metal bar with one or both ends flattened and curved, used primarily for prying apart objects or removing nails. Its significant length provides excellent leverage, making it particularly useful in demolition and heavy construction work where a large force is needed to separate materials or lift heavy objects. Crowbars are ideal for tasks like dismantling wooden structures or lifting large panels, as the increased leverage allows for significant force with minimal effort.

A **pry bar** functions similarly to a crowbar but is typically smaller and more versatile. It is used for prying apart objects, removing molding, or lifting components during repair tasks. Pry bars come in various shapes and sizes, making them well-suited for fitting into tight spaces or providing more precise leverage in delicate operations. They are often used for lighter jobs where control is more important than brute force.

The **nail puller** is specifically designed for removing nails, especially those that are deeply embedded or difficult to extract. It features a V-shaped notch at one end that can slide under the nail head, allowing the user to leverage and pull the nail out from wood or other materials. Nail pullers are particularly useful when a **claw hammer** cannot effectively remove the nail, either due to depth or angle. This tool is essential for reducing damage to the surrounding material while removing stubborn nails.

Crowbar   Pry Bar   Nail Puller

FASTENING TOOLS AND FASTENERS

Fastening tools and fasteners are used to join two or more materials securely. Different types of fasteners serve different purposes, depending on the materials involved and the strength required.

Ring Fasteners

Ring fasteners, also known as snap rings or circlips, are used to hold components, such as gears or bearings, onto a shaft or inside a bore. They fit into a groove and provide a secure hold, preventing lateral movement. Special snap ring pliers are used to install and remove these fasteners.

Nails

Nails are simple, versatile fasteners that are primarily used for joining pieces of wood. They are driven into materials using a hammer or a nail gun. Nails come in different types, such as common nails, finishing nails, and brads, depending on their application. Common nails are used in framing, while finishing nails are used in trim work where the nail head should not be visible.

Screws and Bolts

Screws and bolts are threaded fasteners used to assemble parts. Screws are commonly used to fasten materials such as wood, metal, and plastic. They can be driven directly into the material or into pre-drilled holes. Bolts, on the other hand, are used with nuts and washers to secure two or more parts together. Screws can be installed using a screwdriver or power drill, while bolts require the use of wrenches or socket wrenches.

Nuts and Washers

Nuts are used with bolts to secure materials, creating a strong joint. Different types of nuts, such as hex nuts, locknuts, and wing nuts, serve different purposes. Washers are placed between the nut and the surface to distribute pressure, prevent damage, and improve the stability of the joint. Flat washers and lock washers are commonly used in various assemblies.

Rivet Gun and Rivets

A rivet gun is used to install rivets, which are permanent mechanical fasteners. Rivets are used when welding or screwing is not suitable, often in sheet metal work, such as attaching metal panels. The rivet is inserted through the materials, and the rivet gun deforms the end, creating a secure hold that is ideal for load-bearing applications.

Soldering Tools

Soldering tools are used to join metal components, particularly in electronics. Soldering irons melt solder, which is a fusible metal alloy used to create a connection between two components. Soldering is typically used to connect wires or attach components to circuit boards.

Welding Tools

Welding tools are used to join metals by heating them to their melting point and fusing them together. Common welding tools include welders, welding torches, and welding helmets. Welding requires intense heat, which makes proper safety gear essential to protect against burns and sparks.

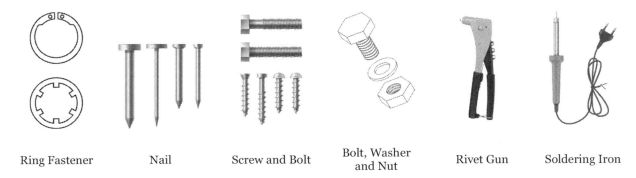

| Ring Fastener | Nail | Screw and Bolt | Bolt, Washer and Nut | Rivet Gun | Soldering Iron |

SHAPING AND FINISHING TOOLS

Shaping and finishing tools are used to refine materials, giving them their final form and achieving a smooth, polished surface. These tools are crucial in woodworking, metalworking, and other trades where precision and quality of the finished product matter.

A **plane** is one of the most common shaping tools in woodworking. It is used to smooth and flatten wooden surfaces, shaving off thin layers to achieve an even and level finish. Planes are ideal for removing rough spots, reducing wood thickness, and creating perfectly flat surfaces. **Wood chisels** are also frequently used, especially for more detailed shaping tasks like carving joints or decorative details. Chisels are applied with either hand pressure or struck with a mallet, providing precision in removing small amounts of material to create intricate shapes or notches.

Files and **rasps** are shaping tools that are useful for refining both wood and metal surfaces. Files have fine teeth that are designed to create smooth finishes and are used for precision shaping, while rasps are coarser and are better suited for rapid material removal when rough shaping is required. Both tools are valuable for achieving specific contours and ensuring parts fit together as intended.

The **grinder** is a powerful tool used primarily in metalworking to remove excess material and create a smooth edge or surface. It utilizes a rotating abrasive wheel to grind down metal, shape pieces, and remove burrs, making it essential in metal fabrication. Finally, **sandpaper** is a finishing tool used to smooth surfaces in preparation for painting or sealing. It comes in a variety of grits, from coarse for initial smoothing to fine for a polished finish.

Shaping and finishing tools are essential for achieving the precise dimensions and surface quality required in professional craftsmanship, ensuring that the final product is both functional and aesthetically pleasing

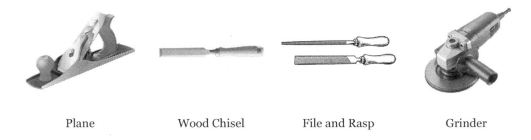

| Plane | Wood Chisel | File and Rasp | Grinder |

ELECTRICAL TOOLS

Electrical tools are crucial for safely managing electrical installations, repairs, and maintenance in any workshop setting. These tools help ensure that electrical components are connected securely and function properly, preventing potential hazards.

A commonly used electrical tool is the **wire stripper**, which removes insulation from wires without damaging the conductor inside. Properly stripped wires are necessary for making secure electrical connections, whether they are to be twisted, crimped, or soldered. Wire strippers feature notches for different wire sizes, making them versatile for a variety of tasks.

Another essential tool is the **multimeter**, used for measuring voltage, current, and resistance. It is indispensable for diagnosing electrical issues, such as locating faulty components or verifying that circuits function as intended. A multimeter helps troubleshoot problems like short circuits or incorrect voltage levels, which can prevent equipment damage or ensure safety.

The **soldering iron** is used to create permanent connections in wiring and electronic components by heating and melting solder. This tool is vital for assembling circuit boards, repairing broken connections, or splicing wires. Proper soldering technique ensures that electrical connections are secure and reliable over time.

Lastly, the **crimping tool** is used to attach connectors to the ends of wires by compressing them, providing a strong mechanical and electrical connection. Crimping is often used in automotive and networking applications to create quick and secure terminations without the need for solder.

These electrical tools are essential for ensuring that wiring systems are well-constructed, safe, and functional, making them an important part of any technician's toolkit.

Wire Stripper   Multimeter   Crimping Tool

SAFETY TOOLS

Safety tools are fundamental in any workshop or job site to protect workers from the various hazards they face during tasks like cutting, welding, drilling, or handling materials. Using the proper safety tools helps minimize risks and ensures that individuals can work efficiently without compromising their health or well-being.

Goggles are one of the most crucial safety tools, providing eye protection from dust, flying debris, sparks, and harmful chemicals. Whether working with power tools, welding, or handling caustic substances, wearing goggles can prevent severe eye injuries. It's important that goggles fit well and provide full coverage to avoid any materials reaching the eyes.

Gloves are equally essential, protecting hands from cuts, abrasions, burns, and exposure to harmful chemicals. Depending on the task, different types of gloves may be used. For instance, heat-resistant gloves are worn when welding, while cut-resistant gloves are used when handling sharp tools or materials. Gloves not only protect against physical harm but also ensure a better grip, reducing the likelihood of accidents.

Ear protection, such as **earplugs** or **earmuffs**, is critical in environments where loud machinery is being operated. Prolonged exposure to high noise levels can cause permanent hearing damage. Wearing ear protection helps prevent hearing loss and reduces the overall strain on the worker, allowing them to remain focused on the task at hand.

Dust masks are used to protect the respiratory system from airborne particles, such as sawdust, fumes, or chemical vapors. Breathing in these particles over time can lead to respiratory issues and other health complications. A dust mask helps filter out harmful particles, ensuring that workers can breathe safely, especially when sanding, grinding, or working with materials that produce fine dust.

Using appropriate safety tools not only reduces the risk of injury but also ensures that workers can perform their tasks more effectively and confidently. Incorporating these tools into everyday practices is essential for creating a safer, more productive workshop environment.

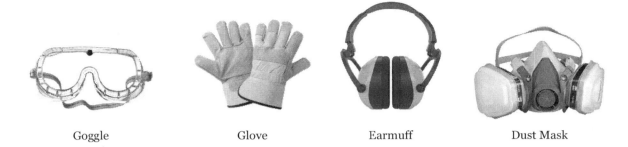

| Goggle | Glove | Earmuff | Dust Mask |

PRACTICE SET

Time: 6 minutes for 10 questions

Select the correct answer from the choices given. This practice subtest reflects the number of questions and time limits you'll encounter on the CAT-ASVAB Shop Information subtest without any tryout questions.

1. What is a tape measure best suited for?

A) Measuring internal diameters
B) Measuring angles
C) Measuring long, flexible surfaces
D) Measuring small, flat objects

2. Which tool is used to create long, straight lines on large surfaces like wood or drywall?

A) Scriber
B) Chalk Line
C) Punch
D) Slip-joint Pliers

3. What is the name of the tool shown here?

A) Wire Cutter
B) Wire Stripper
C) Pliers
D) Crimping Tool

4. Which tool is most commonly used for boring deep, large holes in wood or soil?

A) Power Drill
B) Brace and Bit
C) Auger
D) Hand Drill

5. Which screwdriver is designed with a cross-shaped tip to provide better grip and torque?

A) Flathead screwdriver
B) Phillips screwdriver
C) Torx screwdriver
D) Hex key (Allen wrench)

6. Which tool is essential for protecting your ears from prolonged exposure to loud machinery?

A) Earmuffs
B) Goggles
C) Gloves
D) Dust mask

7. What is the primary purpose of a center punch?

A) To drive out pins from mechanical assemblies
B) To create an indentation for guiding a drill bit
C) To shape metal surfaces
D) To join wood components without damage

8. What type of plier is shown below is a slip-joint plier?

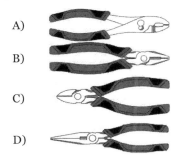

A)

B)

C)

D)

9. What is the primary function of a scriber in a shop environment?

A) To grip small objects in tight spaces
B) To punch starter holes before drilling
C) To make fine, precise lines on hard surfaces
D) To snap lines on drywall or wood

10. What is a ruler typically used for in a shop environment?

A) Measuring long, curved surfaces
B) Measuring internal dimensions
C) Drawing straight lines and measuring small distances
D) Measuring angles

Answers and Explanations

1. C) Measuring long, flexible surfaces

Explanation: Tape measures are flexible and housed in a retractable case, making them ideal for measuring longer distances, curved surfaces, or larger objects. Unlike rulers, tape measures can adapt to irregular shapes and cover greater lengths. They are not suitable for precise internal measurements or angles, as described by the incorrect choices.

2. B) Chalk Line

Explanation: A chalk line is specifically designed to mark long, straight lines on large surfaces such as wood, drywall, or concrete. The string is coated in chalk and snapped to leave a visible line. The other options, like the scriber or punch, are used for more detailed or precise marking on smaller surfaces, while slip-joint pliers are for gripping, not marking.

3. B) Wire Stripper

Explanation: The tool shown in the image is a wire stripper. It is designed to remove the insulation from electrical wires without damaging the wire itself, which is crucial for making secure electrical connections. A wire cutter (A) is used for cutting wires, pliers (C) are used for gripping and manipulating materials, and a crimping tool (D) is used to attach connectors to the ends of wires.

4. C) Auger

Explanation: An auger is specifically designed for creating large, deep holes in materials such as wood or soil. Its helical design efficiently removes material as it cuts. While power drills (A) and hand drills (D) are great for smaller, quicker holes, and brace and bit (B) are suited for manual drilling, the auger is the ideal tool for deeper, larger holes.

5. B) Phillips screwdriver

Explanation: A Phillips screwdriver is designed with a cross-shaped tip that fits into cross-slotted screws, providing more torque and reducing the chance of slipping compared to flathead or other screwdrivers. The flathead (A) has a single, flat tip, while Torx (C) has a star-shaped tip, and a hex key (D) is L-shaped and used for hexagonal screws.

6. A) Earmuffs

Explanation: Earmuffs are designed to protect your ears from prolonged exposure to loud noises, which can cause permanent hearing damage. Goggles (B) protect the eyes from dust or debris, gloves (C) protect hands from cuts and burns, and dust masks (D) protect the respiratory system from inhaling harmful particles.

7. B) To create an indentation for guiding a drill bit

Explanation: A center punch is used to create a small indentation in a material before drilling, ensuring that the drill bit does not wander. A pin punch (A) is used to drive out pins from mechanical assemblies. Option C describes a function of a ball-peen hammer, and D refers to a mallet's function in woodworking.

8. A). Explanation: The plier shown in option A is a slip-joint plier. This type of plier has an adjustable pivot point, allowing the user to change the size of the jaw opening. The jaws can open wider or narrower depending on the task, making them versatile for gripping objects of different sizes. B) is a linesman plier, typically used for electrical work involving cutting and twisting wires. C) is a cutting plier used for cutting wire, not for gripping or adjusting. D) is a needle-nose plier, used for precision work in tight spaces, such as bending or holding small objects.

9. C) To make fine, precise lines on hard surfaces

Explanation: A scriber is a sharp tool used to create precise lines on hard materials like metal or plastic, ensuring accuracy in tasks like cutting or drilling. It scratches the surface to make marks that won't rub off. Pliers (A) grip, punches (B) create indentations, and chalk lines (D) mark long, straight lines on larger surfaces, which are different functions.

10. C) Drawing straight lines and measuring small distances

Explanation: A ruler is a basic tool used for measuring short, straight distances, typically marked in both metric and imperial units. It is ideal for smaller measurements and tasks like drawing straight lines in woodworking or metalworking. Rulers are not designed for measuring curved surfaces, internal dimensions, or angles, as suggested by the other options.

CHAPTER 9: MECHANICAL COMPREHENSION

The Mechanical Comprehension subtest of the ASVAB evaluates your understanding of fundamental mechanical and physical principles. This subtest is designed to measure your ability to comprehend and apply concepts related to mechanics, machinery, and physical laws—knowledge that is crucial for a variety of technical and mechanical roles in the military. Whether you are aiming to become a technician, engineer, or work in other roles requiring an aptitude for mechanics, this section helps determine your suitability for those positions.

In the Mechanical Comprehension subtest, you can expect to see questions covering a wide range of topics such as simple machines, forces and motion, energy, fluid dynamics, and thermodynamics. You will be tested on how well you understand the operation of mechanical devices like levers, pulleys, gears, and springs, as well as your grasp of basic concepts like work, power, and energy conservation. Questions may also include practical scenarios, such as how gears interact, how forces are distributed, or how to calculate mechanical advantage in different systems.

The questions will often include illustrations of machines or diagrams to help you visualize the scenario. You may need to determine how a force is applied, predict the direction of movement, or understand how changing one component affects the rest of the system. This subtest is not only about memorizing definitions—it requires logical thinking and the ability to apply mechanical concepts to solve problems effectively.

This chapter will provide you with the key concepts you need to excel, ensuring that you are well-prepared for this part of the ASVAB exam.

BASIC MECHANICAL CONCEPTS AND PRINCIPLES

Forces and Motion

Understanding **forces and motion** is fundamental to grasping how mechanical systems function. Forces are what cause objects to move, stop, or change direction, and they play an essential role in how machines and structures operate. In this section, we will explore Newton's Laws of Motion, the forces of gravity and friction, different types of forces such as tension, compression, and shear, and the concepts of equilibrium and balance in force interactions.

Newton's Laws of Motion

Chapter 5 (General Science) of this book has more detailed coverage on Newton's Laws of Motion. Below is a brief review.

Newton's Laws of Motion form the foundation of classical mechanics and describe how objects respond to forces. These three laws explain why objects move the way they do, and understanding them is critical for analyzing mechanical systems.

Newton's First Law of Motion, often called the **law of inertia**, states that an object will remain at rest or continue moving in a straight line at constant speed unless acted upon by an external force. In simpler terms, an object will keep doing what it's doing—whether staying still or moving—until something else interferes.

To explain this using a bowling ball, imagine rolling the ball down a perfectly smooth and level bowling lane. As you push the ball, it starts rolling and would ideally keep rolling indefinitely in a straight line at a constant speed. This is because, according to Newton's First Law, the ball has inertia, which means it will continue in its state of motion unless an external force acts upon it. In reality, however, several forces eventually cause the bowling ball to stop. **Friction** between the ball and the lane surface slows the ball down gradually, while **air resistance** also plays a minor role in reducing its speed. If the lane were perfectly frictionless, the bowling ball would keep moving without ever stopping. In this example, the initial push gives the bowling ball its motion, but friction acts as the external force that eventually stops it, demonstrating Newton's First Law.

Newton's Second Law states that the acceleration of an object is directly proportional to the net force acting on it and inversely proportional to its mass. This is often expressed as the equation $F = ma$, where F represents force, m represents mass, and a represents acceleration. In practical terms, if you apply more force to an object, it will accelerate faster. For example, when pushing a shopping cart, the harder you push (force), the faster it accelerates. Likewise, if the cart is loaded with heavy items (greater mass), you need more force to achieve the same acceleration. This principle is widely used in engineering to determine how much force is required to move an object or control the speed of machinery.

Newton's Third Law states that for every action, there is an equal and opposite reaction. This means that when one object exerts a force on another, the second object exerts an equal force in the opposite direction. This law is evident when you jump off a small boat: as you push down on the boat to leap, the boat moves backward in reaction to your force. Similarly, in mechanical systems, the action-reaction principle can be seen in the recoil of a gun or the lift generated by an airplane's wings as air pushes against them.

Gravity and Friction

Gravity and friction are two of the most significant forces that affect the movement of objects.

Gravity

Gravity is the force that pulls objects toward the center of the Earth. It gives weight to objects and causes them to fall when dropped. In mechanical systems, gravity can be both a benefit and a hindrance. For example, gravity helps water flow in pipelines and can aid in the movement of conveyor belts going downhill. On the other hand, it can also make lifting and supporting heavy loads challenging. Engineers design cranes, elevators, and other lifting devices specifically to overcome the gravitational pull, allowing heavy materials to be moved with less effort.

Weight is the force exerted on an object due to gravity, and it can be calculated using Newton's Second Law of Motion. Newton's Second Law states that the force (F) acting on an object is the product of its mass (m) and its acceleration (a): $F = m \cdot a$

When dealing with weight, the acceleration in question is the gravitational acceleration (g). On Earth, this gravitational acceleration is approximately $9.8 \, \text{m/s}^2$. Therefore, we can express weight (W) as the force due to gravity by using Newton's Second Law: $W = m \cdot g$, where: W is the weight (in Newtons, N), m is the mass (in kilograms, kg), g is the gravitational acceleration, which on Earth is about $9.8 \, \text{m/s}^2$. This formula shows that weight is the gravitational force acting on an object's mass.

Example 1: Consider an object with a mass of 15 kg. To calculate its weight on Earth, we use the formula:

$$W = m \cdot g = 15 \, \text{kg} \times 9.8 \, \text{m/s}^2 = 147 \, \text{N}$$

Thus, the object weighs 147 Newtons on Earth.

Example 2: Weight on Other Planets

Newton's Second Law also explains why an object weighs less on the Moon or more on a planet with stronger gravity. On the Moon, where the gravitational acceleration is only $1.62 \, \text{m/s}^2$, the weight of the same 15 kg object would be:

$$W = 15 \, \text{kg} \times 1.62 \, \text{m/s}^2 = 24.3 \, \text{N}$$

This example demonstrates that weight is a force determined by the mass of the object and the local gravitational field, in line with Newton's Second Law. The object's mass remains the same, but its weight changes based on the gravitational acceleration acting upon it.

Friction

Friction is a force that resists the motion of objects or surfaces sliding past each other. It plays a vital role in many everyday activities, from walking to driving, by providing the necessary force to prevent slipping. Frictional forces can be categorized into two types: static friction and kinetic friction.

Static friction acts between surfaces that are at rest relative to each other. This type of friction must be overcome to initiate movement. It is usually stronger than kinetic friction.

Kinetic friction (also called sliding friction) acts between surfaces that are moving relative to each other. Once the object is in motion, this frictional force slows it down or prevents further acceleration unless a force continues to act on it.

Both types of friction depend on the normal force and the coefficient of friction. The **normal force** is the force exerted by a surface perpendicular to the object resting on it (typically equivalent to the object's weight when on a flat surface). The **coefficient of friction** is a dimensionless number that characterizes the interaction between two surfaces. A **dimensionless number** is a quantity that has no physical units associated with it. In other words, it is a pure number that does not depend on any system of measurement (such as meters, kilograms, or seconds). These numbers represent ratios or comparisons between quantities that cancel out any units during their calculation.

In the context of friction, the coefficient of friction (μ) is dimensionless because it is the ratio of the frictional force to the normal force. Since both forces are measured in the same unit (Newtons, for example), their units cancel out, leaving just a pure number. The coefficient of friction essentially describes how "sticky" or "slippery" two surfaces are relative to each other, without needing to refer to any specific units of measurement. For example, a coefficient of friction of $\mu = 0.5$ means that the frictional force is half the value of the normal force, regardless of the actual units involved.

The coefficient of friction is typically different for static friction (μ_s) and kinetic friction (μ_k). Different surfaces usually have different coefficients of friction. Rougher surfaces generally have higher coefficients of friction than smoother surfaces.

The force of friction F_f is calculated using the following formula: $F_f = \mu F_n$, where μ is the coefficient of friction (static or kinetic), F_n is the normal force, usually calculated as the weight of the object.

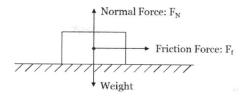

For static friction: $F_{f,static} \leq \mu_s F_n$

Static friction prevents motion until a certain threshold (equal to $\mu_s F_n$) is exceeded.

For kinetic friction: $F_{f,kinetic} = \mu_k F_n$

Once an object is in motion, kinetic friction remains constant and is typically less than static friction, i.e., $\mu_k < \mu_s$

Static friction is generally greater than kinetic friction because it takes more force to initiate the movement of an object than to keep it moving. Once an object is in motion, less force is needed to overcome the kinetic friction.

Example: Let's say we have a box weighing 100 N (Newtons) resting on a horizontal surface. The coefficients of static and kinetic friction between the box and the surface are $\mu_s = 0.4$ and $\mu_k = 0.3$ respectively. We want to know the static friction and kinetic friction.

Solution:

    Step 1: Calculate the normal force

    On a flat surface, the normal force F_n is equal to the weight of the object: $F_n = 100\,N$

    Step 2: Calculate the maximum static friction

    Using the coefficient of static friction $\mu_s = 0.4$ and the normal force $F_n = 100\,N$, the maximum static friction is:

$$F_{f,static} = \mu_s F_n = 0.4 \times 100\,N = 40\,N$$

    Therefore, the box will not move unless a force greater than 40 N is applied.

    Step 3: Calculate the kinetic friction

    If a force greater than 40 N is applied and the box starts moving, the kinetic friction will be calculated using $\mu_k = 0.3$:

$$F_{f,kinetic} = \mu_k F_n = 0.3 \times 100\,N = 30\,N$$

    Hence, once the box is moving, a force of 30 N will continuously resist its motion.

In this example, static friction (40 N) is greater than kinetic friction (30 N), reflecting the general principle that more force is required to overcome static friction and initiate motion than to overcome kinetic friction and maintain motion.

Types of Forces: Tension, Compression, and Shear

There are different types of forces that act on objects in mechanical systems, including **tension**, **compression**, and **shear**. Each type of force affects materials differently, and understanding these effects helps engineers design structures that can withstand various loads.

Tension is a force that pulls or stretches a material. It occurs when forces act in opposite directions, trying to elongate the material. For example, the force in a rope during a game of tug-of-war is a form of tension. In mechanical systems, tension is often experienced in cables, chains, or belts used to transmit force. Suspension bridges, for instance, rely on tension in their cables to support the weight of the bridge deck. Materials under tension need to have high tensile strength to resist stretching and breaking.

Compression is the force that pushes or squeezes a material. It occurs when forces act toward each other, compressing the material. A common example is the force experienced by the legs of a chair when someone sits on it. Compression is also present in columns and beams that support heavy loads, such as in buildings or bridges. Materials under compression need to be strong enough to resist buckling or crushing.

Shear is a force that causes one part of a material to slide past another. Shear forces act parallel to the surface and can cause deformation or failure when the material cannot resist the sliding action. An example of shear force is when scissors cut through paper, as the blades apply a shearing force that causes the paper to separate. In mechanical systems, shear forces can occur in bolts, rivets, and beams subjected to opposing forces.

Equilibrium and Balance of Forces

Equilibrium is a state in which all the forces acting on an object are balanced, resulting in no net force and, consequently, no acceleration. In mechanical systems, equilibrium is vital for ensuring that structures and machines remain stable and function as intended. There are two main types of equilibrium: static equilibrium and dynamic equilibrium.

Static equilibrium occurs when an object is at rest, and the forces acting on it are balanced. For example, a book lying on a table is in static equilibrium because the downward force of gravity is balanced by the upward normal force exerted by the table. In mechanical systems, static equilibrium is essential for stability. Structures like bridges and buildings must be designed to remain in static equilibrium under various loads, ensuring that they do not collapse or shift.

Dynamic equilibrium occurs when an object is moving at a constant velocity, and the forces acting on it are balanced. For instance, a car moving at a constant speed on a straight road is in dynamic equilibrium because the driving force provided by the engine is balanced by the opposing forces of friction and air resistance. In mechanical systems, maintaining dynamic equilibrium is crucial for consistent performance. For example, conveyor belts and rotating machinery need to operate in dynamic equilibrium to ensure smooth and efficient operation without sudden changes in motion.

The concept of **balance of forces** is crucial in designing mechanical systems that can handle various loads without failing. When forces are balanced, the system remains stable, and the risk of damage or failure is minimized. For instance, in a bridge, the downward force of gravity acting on the bridge deck must be balanced by the upward tension in the supporting cables and the compressive forces in the pillars. If these forces are not balanced, the bridge may collapse.

In mechanical systems, achieving equilibrium often requires the use of **counterweights**, **springs**, or **adjustable components** to ensure stability. For example, cranes use counterweights to balance the load being lifted, preventing the crane from tipping over. Springs are used in vehicle suspensions to balance the forces acting on the wheels, ensuring a smooth ride and preventing excessive bouncing or tipping.

Another critical aspect of equilibrium is the concept of **center of gravity**. The center of gravity is the point at which the entire weight of an object can be considered to act. For an object to be stable, its center of gravity must be positioned in such a way that the forces acting on it are balanced. In mechanical systems, keeping the center of gravity low and well-distributed helps maintain stability. For example, vehicles are designed with a low center of gravity to prevent them from tipping over during sharp turns or sudden maneuvers.

Energy and Power

In this section, we will explore potential and kinetic energy, conservation of energy, calculating work, power, and energy, and different types of power sources, including electrical, hydraulic, and mechanical power.

Potential and Kinetic Energy

Energy is the capacity to do work, and in mechanical systems, energy often comes in two primary forms: potential energy and kinetic energy.

Potential energy is the energy an object possesses due to its position or configuration. Essentially, it is the energy stored within an object that has the potential to be converted into another form of energy or to do work. For example, a boulder sitting at the top of a hill has gravitational potential energy because of its height above the ground. This potential energy is a result of the force of gravity acting on the boulder and the height at which it is positioned. The greater the height and mass of an object, the greater its potential energy. Springs also store energy, called **elastic potential energy**, when they are compressed or stretched.

Kinetic energy, on the other hand, is the energy of motion. Any object in motion possesses kinetic energy, which depends on its mass and velocity. For instance, a car driving down a road or a hammer hitting a nail both have kinetic energy. The faster an object moves, or the greater its mass, the more kinetic energy it will have. The relationship between kinetic energy and velocity is exponential, meaning that if you double the speed of an object, its kinetic energy will quadruple. In mechanical systems, kinetic energy is crucial for performing tasks such as driving machinery, moving parts, or transmitting force between components.

The relationship between potential energy and kinetic energy is often demonstrated by a pendulum. When the pendulum is raised to one side, it has maximum potential energy and zero kinetic energy. As it swings downward, the potential energy is converted into kinetic energy, and the pendulum gains speed. At the bottom of the swing, the potential energy is at its minimum, and kinetic energy is at its maximum. This continuous conversion between potential and kinetic energy illustrates the dynamic nature of energy in mechanical systems.

Conservation of Energy in Mechanical Systems

The **law of conservation of energy** states that energy cannot be created or destroyed, only transformed from one form to another. In mechanical systems, this principle means that the total amount of energy remains constant, even though it may change forms—such as from potential to kinetic energy, or into other forms like thermal energy.

Consider a roller coaster as an example. At the top of the track, the roller coaster car has a large amount of potential energy due to its height. As the car begins to descend, that potential energy is converted into kinetic energy, and the car gains speed. At the bottom of the hill, most of the energy is in the form of kinetic energy. As the car climbs another hill, some of that kinetic energy is converted back into potential energy. This energy conversion continues throughout the ride, with the car's speed and height changing continuously. However, the total energy remains constant, assuming we neglect losses due to **friction** and **air resistance**.

In reality, mechanical systems do experience **energy losses**, primarily due to friction and other forms of resistance. These losses convert some of the system's energy into **thermal energy** (heat). For example, in a car engine, the chemical potential energy of the fuel is converted into kinetic energy to move the car, but some of that energy is also lost as heat due to friction between the engine components. Lubrication and design optimizations are used to reduce these losses and make the system more efficient. Despite these losses, the principle of conservation of energy still holds—energy is not destroyed but rather transformed into less useful forms, such as heat.

Calculating Work, Power, and Energy

To understand the role of energy in mechanical systems, it is essential to understand how **work** and **power** are calculated.

Work is defined as the product of force and the distance over which that force is applied. In mathematical terms, work is expressed as:

$$Work = Force \times Distance$$

For work to be done, the force must be applied in the direction of the movement. If an object is not moved, no work is done, regardless of the force applied. For instance, if you push against a wall with all your strength, no work is done if the wall doesn't move, even though you are exerting a force.

Power is the rate at which work is done. It measures how quickly energy is being transferred or converted from one form to another. Power is calculated as:

$$Power = \frac{Work}{Time}$$

The unit of power is the **watt (W)**, which is equivalent to one joule per second. In practical applications, power helps us determine how efficiently a machine can perform a task. For example, an electric motor with more power can perform work faster than a less powerful motor. In mechanical systems, **horsepower (hp)** is also a common unit of power, especially in automotive applications, where it indicates the engine's ability to perform work over time. One horsepower (hp) is equivalent to 746 watts (W).

Energy can be calculated in various forms, depending on whether we are dealing with potential energy or kinetic energy. **Gravitational potential energy (PE)** is calculated as:

$$Potential\ Energy = m \times g \times h$$

where m is mass, g is the acceleration due to gravity, and h is the height above the ground.

Kinetic energy (KE) is calculated as:

$$Kinetic\ Energy = \frac{1}{2}m \times v^2$$

where m is mass and v is velocity. These equations help quantify the amount of energy in a mechanical system, allowing for more precise calculations in engineering and physics.

Example 1— Gravitational Potential Energy: A rock with a mass of 10 kg is lifted to a height of 5 meters. Calculate its gravitational potential energy.

Solution: $PE_g = 10\,kg \times 9.8\,m/s^2 \times 5\,m = 490\,Joules$

The gravitational potential energy of the rock is 490 Joules.

Example 2: Calculating the speed of a rock (with no initial speed) after it has fallen freely for 5 meters.

Solution: Let's use the conservation of energy principle to solve this problem. This principle states that the total mechanical energy in a system remains constant in the absence of external forces (like air resistance). Specifically, the gravitational potential energy at the start will be entirely converted into kinetic energy at the end of the fall.

Step 1: Establish Relationship Between Potential and Kinetic Energy

The potential energy (PE_g) at a height is converted into kinetic energy (KE) as the object falls: $PE_g = KE$

The formulas for gravitational potential energy and kinetic energy are: $PE_g = m \cdot g \cdot h$, and $KE = \frac{1}{2}mv^2$

Since $PE_g = KE$ we can equate these: $m \cdot g \cdot h = \frac{1}{2}mv^2$.

Notice that the mass (m) appears on both sides of the equation, so we can cancel it out: $g \cdot h = \frac{1}{2}v^2$

Now, rearrange the equation to solve for v (the final velocity): $v^2 = 2 \cdot g \cdot h$

Taking the square root of both sides: $v = \sqrt{2 \cdot g \cdot h}$

Step 2: Plug in the Known Values

For this example, we are given: $g = 9.8 \, \text{m/s}^2$ (the acceleration due to gravity), $h = 5$ meters. Substitute these values into the formula:

$$v = \sqrt{2 \cdot 9.8 \, \text{m/s}^2 \cdot 5 \, \text{m}} = \sqrt{98} \approx 9.9 \, \text{m/s}$$

Hence, the rock's speed just before hitting the ground is approximately 9.9 meters per second. This method shows that by using the conservation of energy, we can calculate the final velocity of a falling object without needing to know its mass. The only factors that influence the speed are the height from which it falls and the acceleration due to gravity. The mass cancels out, simplifying the calculation.

Example 3—Speed and Kinetic Energy of a Falling Object: Assume the object has a mass of 10 kg, calculate its speed and kinetic energy after 5 seconds of free fall.

Solution: The velocity of a falling object after time t is given by the formula:

$$v = u + g \cdot t$$

Where:

- v is the final velocity (in meters per second),
- u is the initial velocity (in meters per second, usually 0 if the object is dropped from rest),
- g is the acceleration due to gravity ($9.8 \, \text{m/s}^2$),
- t is the time the object has been falling (in seconds).

Step 1: Given that $u = 0 \, \text{m/s}$ (since it's dropped from rest), $g = 9.8 \, \text{m/s}^2$, $t = 5$ seconds, using the above formula:

$$v = 0 + 9.8 \, \text{m/s}^2 \times 5 \, \text{seconds} = 49 \, \text{m/s}$$

So, the speed of the object after 5 seconds of falling is 49 meters per second. Since mass does not appear in the above formula, it does not affect the falling speed of the object.

Step 2: Calculate the Kinetic Energy after 5 seconds. The kinetic energy (KE) of an object is calculated using the formula:

$$KE = \frac{1}{2}mv^2 = \frac{1}{2} \times 10 \, \text{kg} \times (49 \, \text{m/s})^2 = \frac{1}{2} \times 10 \times 2401 \text{J} = 5 \times 2401 \text{J} = 12005 \, \text{J}$$

Conclusion: The kinetic energy of the object after 5 seconds of falling is 12,005 Joules. This energy is the result of the object's mass and the velocity it has gained due to gravity.

Types of Power Sources: Electrical, Hydraulic, and Mechanical

Mechanical systems often rely on different types of power sources to function. These sources provide the energy required to perform work, and each type has its unique characteristics, advantages, and applications.

Electrical Power is one of the most commonly used power sources in mechanical systems. Electrical power is generated by converting other forms of energy—such as mechanical energy from wind turbines or chemical energy from burning fossil fuels—into electricity. This electricity can then be used to power electric motors, lights, and other devices. **Electric motors** are popular in various applications, including household appliances, industrial machinery, and electric vehicles. The primary advantage of electrical power is its convenience and the ability to control power output precisely.

Hydraulic Power is used in systems that require significant force over short distances. Hydraulic systems operate based on **Pascal's Law**, which states that pressure applied to a confined fluid is transmitted equally in all directions. Hydraulic power is generated by using a **hydraulic pump** to pressurize a fluid (usually oil), which is then directed through hoses to **actuators** or **cylinders**. This pressurized fluid creates force that can move heavy loads. Hydraulic systems are widely used in construction machinery, such as excavators, cranes, and forklifts, because they provide high power output and precise control. The major advantage of hydraulic systems is their ability to generate large amounts of force efficiently, even in compact designs.

Mechanical Power refers to power generated directly by a mechanical system, often involving gears, pulleys, levers, and rotating shafts. In mechanical power transmission, energy is transferred from one component to another through direct contact, such as gears transmitting torque from a motor to a wheel. **Mechanical advantage** is achieved by using simple machines to reduce the force needed to perform work, such as a lever that multiplies the input force. Mechanical power systems are found in many machines, including bicycles, where pedaling produces mechanical power to turn the wheels, and in windmills, where the wind's kinetic energy is converted into rotational motion to generate power.

Each type of power source has specific advantages and limitations, making them suitable for different applications. Electrical power is efficient for small and precise tasks, offering easy control and versatility. Hydraulic power excels in situations requiring massive amounts of force in compact spaces, making it ideal for heavy machinery. Mechanical power provides direct and efficient energy transfer, commonly used in applications where simple and robust designs are needed.

Torque

Torque refers to the rotational equivalent of force. While force causes linear movement, torque causes rotational movement about a pivot point or axis. Torque is critical in understanding how machines and mechanical systems work, particularly those involving rotating parts such as engines, wheels, gears, and levers.

In simple terms, torque measures how much a force acting on an object causes that object to rotate. The force must be applied at a certain distance from the pivot point, and this distance is called the "lever arm." The longer the lever arm and the greater the applied force, the more torque is generated.

The mathematical expression for torque is given by:

$$\tau = r \cdot F \cdot \sin(\theta)$$

Where: τ (tau) is the torque, r is the distance (lever arm) from the pivot point to where the force is applied, F is the magnitude of the applied force, and θ is the angle between the force vector and the lever arm.

In situations where the force is applied perpendicular to the lever arm ($\theta = 90°$), the sine of $90°$ is 1, so the formula simplifies to:

$$\tau = r \cdot F$$

This is the most common scenario in basic torque problems, where the force is applied at a right angle to the lever arm.

Example 1: Imagine you are tightening a bolt using a wrench. The wrench is 0.25 meters long, and you apply a force of 20 Newtons at the end of the wrench, perpendicular to the handle. To calculate the torque generated, you use the simplified torque formula:

$$\tau = r \cdot F = 0.25\,\text{m} \times 20\,\text{N} = 5\,\text{Nm}$$

Force

The torque generated is 5 Newton-meters (Nm). This means that you are applying a rotational force of 5 Nm to the bolt, which will cause it to rotate and tighten.

If you were to increase the length of the wrench (lever arm) to 0.5 meter, keeping the force the same, the torque would increase: $\tau = 0.5\,\text{m} \times 20\,\text{N} = 10\,\text{Nm}$

In this case, doubling the lever arm doubles the torque, making it easier to tighten the bolt with less effort.

Example 2: Consider a door that is hinged on one side. Suppose you push on the door with a force of 15 Newtons at a point 0.8 meters from the hinge, perpendicular to the door. The torque exerted on the door is:

$$\tau = r \cdot F = 0.8\,\text{m} \times 15\,\text{N} = 12\,\text{Nm}$$

This torque will cause the door to rotate about its hinges and swing open.

However, if you apply the force closer to the hinge, say at 0.2 meters, the torque will be smaller:

$$\tau = 0.2\,\text{m} \times 15\,\text{N} = 3\,\text{Nm}$$

In this scenario, even though the force is the same, the shorter lever arm reduces the torque, making it harder to open or close the door. This is why it is easier to push a door open by applying force at the handle, which is farthest from the hinge, rather than near the hinge.

From the above examples, it's clear that torque depends on both the force applied and the distance from the pivot point. Larger forces or longer lever arms generate greater torque. The direction of the applied force also matters. If the force is not applied perpendicular to the lever arm, you need to account for the angle using $\sin(\theta)$ in the torque formula. Only the component of the force that is perpendicular to the lever arm contributes to torque.

Torque is a crucial concept in various fields, including automotive engineering (e.g., tightening bolts, engine mechanics), construction (e.g., using levers and pulleys), and even sports (e.g., the torque generated when swinging a bat or golf club). In summary, torque is a measure of rotational force and is calculated by multiplying the force by the lever arm distance. The longer the lever arm or the greater the force, the more torque is generated, leading to more efficient rotational movement.

HYDRAULIC AND PNEUMATIC SYSTEMS

Fluid power systems use fluids—either liquids or gases—to transmit power. **Hydraulic systems** utilize liquids, typically oil, while **pneumatic systems** use compressed air. Hydraulics are ideal for applications that require high force with precision, such as lifting heavy objects, whereas pneumatics are used for tasks that require fast, lightweight, and repetitive power.

Pressure is a measure of the amount of force exerted per unit area. It tells us how much force is applied on a surface and is usually measured in units such as Pascals (Pa), pounds per square inch (psi), or atmospheres (atm), depending on the context. The formula for calculating pressure is:

$$Pressure = \frac{Force}{Area}, \text{ or } P = \frac{F}{A}$$

where Pressure (P) is measured in Pascals (Pa) or other units like psi, Force (F) is measured in Newtons (N) or pounds (lbs), Area (A) is measured in square meters (m²) or square inches (in²).

Example 1: Let's say you are applying a force of 100 Newtons on a surface that has an area of 2 square meters. To find the pressure exerted on the surface, you would use the formula: $P = \frac{F}{A} = \frac{100\,\text{N}}{2\,\text{m}^2} = 50\,\text{Pa}$.

Example 2: Imagine you need to apply a pressure of 200 Pascals (Pa) on a surface that has an area of 4 square meters. What amount of force is required to generate this pressure?

To calculate the force, we rearrange the pressure formula to solve for force: $Force = Pressure \times Area$

Now, plug in the known values: $Force = 200\,Pa \times 4\,m^2 = 800\,N$

A key concept in hydraulic systems is **Pascal's Law**, which states that when pressure is applied to a confined fluid, it is transmitted equally in all directions. This means that if you apply force to one part of the system, that pressure is transferred throughout the entire fluid, which can then be used to create movement elsewhere. For example, in a **hydraulic jack**, a small force applied to a pump piston creates pressure that is transmitted through the fluid, allowing a larger piston to lift a heavy load, such as a car. The hydraulic jack effectively multiplies the input force, making it possible to lift large weights with minimal effort.

The figure below illustrates a simple hydraulic system. The relationship between the two pistons is governed by the following formula:

$$\frac{F_1}{A_1} = \frac{F_2}{A_2}$$

Where:

F_1 is the force applied on the smaller piston.
A_1 is the area of the smaller piston.
F_2 is the force exerted on the larger piston.
A_2 is the area of the larger piston.

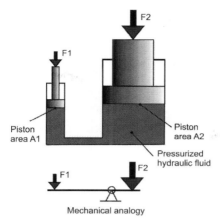

Example: Let's go through an example using Pascal's Law.

Suppose James applies 200 pounds of force to the smaller piston, and the area of the larger piston is 5 times that of the smaller piston. What's the force exerted on the larger piston?

Solution: We can calculate the force exerted on the larger piston using the formula: $F_2 = F_1 \times \frac{A_2}{A_1}$

Given: $F_1 = 200$ pounds, $A_2 = 5 \times A_1$, substituting into the formula: $F_2 = 200 \times \frac{5A_1}{A_1}$

The A_1 terms cancel out: $F_2 = 200 \times 5 = 1000$ pounds. So, the force exerted on the larger piston is 1000 pounds.

This example demonstrates how a hydraulic system can multiply force. In this case, applying 200 pounds of force on the smaller piston results in 1000 pounds of force being exerted on the larger piston.

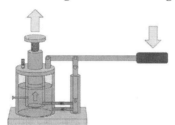

Structure of a Typical Hydraulic Jack

Hydraulic and pneumatic systems are used in many types of machinery. Hydraulic systems are seen in applications like car brakes and heavy machinery such as cranes, where high force is required. On the other hand, pneumatic systems are often used in assembly lines for tasks that need quick and repetitive actions, such as pressing or packaging. For example, a **pneumatic jackhammer** uses compressed air to generate powerful blows for breaking concrete.

PROPERTIES OF MATERIALS

Different materials respond differently under various forces, and knowing their properties can help determine which material will provide the desired performance and safety in mechanical systems. In this section, we will discuss material strength, elasticity vs. plasticity, and common materials used in mechanical systems.

Understanding Material Strength: Tensile, Compressive, and Shear

Material strength refers to the ability of a material to withstand different types of forces without breaking or deforming. Three key types of material strength are tensile strength, compressive strength, and shear strength.

Tensile Strength: This is the ability of a material to withstand pulling forces or forces that try to elongate the material. Materials with high tensile strength, like steel, are used in applications where they need to resist stretching or pulling forces. For instance, suspension bridges use steel cables because they have to bear the tensile forces created by the weight of the bridge and vehicles.

Compressive Strength: Compressive strength is the ability of a material to withstand pushing forces or forces that try to shorten it. It is the opposite of tensile strength. Concrete, for example, has excellent compressive strength and is widely used in constructing columns, foundations, and other structural elements that need to bear heavy loads without buckling.

Shear Strength: Shear strength refers to a material's ability to resist forces that cause layers of the material to slide past each other. It is crucial in applications involving bolts, rivets, and other fasteners. When a bolt holds two plates together, shear forces act parallel to the bolt's length, and the bolt must resist these forces to prevent failure. Metals like steel are often used for bolts due to their high shear strength.

Elasticity vs. Plasticity: How Materials Deform Under Load

Materials can deform in different ways under load, which brings us to the concepts of elasticity and plasticity.

Elasticity is the ability of a material to return to its original shape after the load is removed. This behavior is seen in materials like rubber or spring steel, which can undergo deformation and then recover their shape. For example, when you pull on a rubber band, it stretches (deforms elastically) and then returns to its original length once released. Elastic materials are commonly used in applications where flexibility and recoverable deformation are needed, such as in springs, seals, and gaskets.

Plasticity refers to the ability of a material to undergo permanent deformation without breaking when a load is applied. Once a material exceeds its **elastic limit**, it deforms plastically, meaning it will not return to its original shape. Metals like copper and aluminum exhibit plastic behavior when bent or shaped. Plastic deformation is useful in processes like forging, where metals are shaped under pressure, or in metal forming techniques, such as stamping and bending, to create specific parts.

The difference between elasticity and plasticity is crucial when selecting materials for mechanical systems. Elastic materials are chosen for applications requiring flexibility, while plastic materials are selected for shaping and forming processes where permanent deformation is necessary.

Common Materials Used in Mechanical Systems

In mechanical systems, selecting the appropriate material is essential for ensuring durability, efficiency, and safety. Let's explore some of the most commonly used materials and their properties:

Steel is one of the most widely used materials in mechanical systems due to its high tensile strength, toughness, and versatility. It is used in structures like beams, columns, gears, and shafts. Steel alloys can be adjusted to achieve specific properties, such as improved resistance to wear, corrosion, or high temperatures.

Aluminum is known for being lightweight while still offering good strength. It also has excellent resistance to corrosion, making it suitable for aerospace applications, automotive components, and lightweight machinery. Aluminum's high strength-to-weight ratio makes it ideal for applications where minimizing weight is critical.

Copper is highly ductile, has good tensile strength, and is an excellent conductor of electricity and heat. It is widely used in electrical components, such as wiring and connectors, as well as in heat exchangers and plumbing. Copper's plasticity allows it to be easily bent into shape, making it a preferred material for complex piping systems.

Cast iron is known for its high compressive strength, making it ideal for use in heavy machinery bases, engine blocks, and pipes. It is brittle compared to other metals, which limits its use in applications involving tensile forces or impact loads. However, its excellent damping properties make it well-suited for use in machinery bases to reduce vibrations.

Plastics are increasingly being used in mechanical systems due to their versatility, lightweight nature, and corrosion resistance. Thermoplastics, such as PVC and polyethylene, are used for their flexibility and moldability, while thermosetting plastics, such as epoxy, are used for structural components that require rigidity and durability. Plastics are commonly found in components like gears, bearings, and seals, particularly where low friction and wear resistance are desired.

Composite Materials combine two or more materials to create a product with superior properties. For example, fiber-reinforced polymers (FRP) use fibers like carbon or glass embedded in a plastic matrix to create a strong yet lightweight material. Composites are used in aerospace, automotive, and sporting goods due to their strength-to-weight ratio and resistance to fatigue.

Effects of Heat on Materials (Expansion and Contraction)

Heat affects materials by causing them to expand when heated and contract when cooled. **Thermal expansion** is a significant consideration in mechanical design. For example, railway tracks have small gaps between sections to allow for expansion in hot weather without warping or buckling. In engines, **pistons** expand when heated, and this expansion must be accommodated to ensure they move smoothly within the cylinder. Proper material selection and allowances for expansion and contraction help prevent damage and maintain system efficiency.

In some cases, temperature changes can also affect material properties, such as **ductility** (ability to deform under tensile stress without breaking) and **strength**. Materials can become brittle when subjected to extreme cold, reducing their ability to withstand stress without fracturing. This is why designing mechanical systems must account for the specific operating temperature range to ensure optimal performance.

SIMPLE MACHINES

Simple machines are fundamental mechanical devices that help make work easier by providing a mechanical advantage—allowing users to apply less force over greater distances to move or lift loads. These simple tools form the basis of many complex machines and are key concepts in mechanical engineering and physics. Below, we explore the different types of simple machines, their properties, and their applications.

Lever

A lever is a simple machine consisting of a rigid bar that rotates around a fixed point called the **fulcrum**. Levers help move or lift loads by converting a small applied force into a larger output force, making work easier.

There are three types of levers, each distinguished by the position of the **fulcrum**, **load**, and **effort**:

1. **First-Class Lever**: In a first-class lever, the fulcrum is positioned between the load and the effort. Examples include seesaws and crowbars. By adjusting the distance between the fulcrum and the points of force application, first-class levers can either increase force or speed, depending on the requirements of the task.

2. **Second-Class Lever**: In a second-class lever, the load is positioned between the fulcrum and the effort. Examples include wheelbarrows and nutcrackers. These levers always increase force but decrease speed. By applying effort at a greater distance from the fulcrum than the load, the user can move heavier loads with less effort.

3. **Third-Class Lever**: In a third-class lever, the effort is applied between the fulcrum and the load. Examples include tweezers and baseball bats. These levers are designed to increase the speed of the output rather than force. They require more input effort but allow for greater output distance and speed, making them useful in situations like swinging a bat.

Three Lever Classes

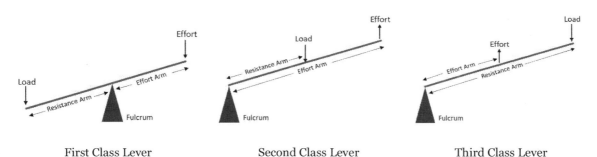

First Class Lever   Second Class Lever   Third Class Lever

Levers are extensively used in everyday applications, such as lifting objects, prying open boxes, and even in muscle movements in the human body. Understanding the types of levers and their applications helps to optimize the amount of force required in different situations.

Example: A person uses a second class lever as shown above to lift a 100 N load. The distance from the fulcrum to the load is 1 meter, and the distance from the fulcrum to the point of effort is 4 meters. How much effort is needed to lift the load?

Solution: To determine the amount of effort needed to lift the load, we use the principle of levers, which is:

$$Effort \times Length\ of\ Effort\ Arm = Load \times Length\ of\ Load\ Arm$$

Rearrange to solve for the effort:

$$Effort = \frac{Load \times Length\ of\ Load\ Arm}{Length\ of\ Effort\ Arm}$$

Substituting the values from the question:

$$Effort = \frac{100 \, N \times 1 \, m}{4 \, m} = \frac{100 \, N}{4} = 25 \, N$$

Thus, effort need is 25 N. By using a longer effort arm compared to the load arm, the force required to lift the load is reduced, demonstrating the mechanical advantage of a lever system.

Pulley

A pulley is a simple machine consisting of a wheel with a groove along its edge through which a rope or cable can pass. Pulleys change the direction of the applied force and can also provide mechanical advantage, making it easier to lift heavy objects.

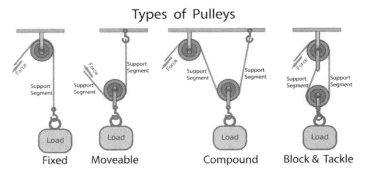

The foregoing figure shows four types of pulley systems: Fixed Pulley, Moveable Pulley, Compound Pulley, and Block & Tackle. Each type of pulley helps reduce the effort required to lift a load by redistributing or multiplying the force, making it easier to lift or move heavy objects. Let's discuss how each type of pulley reduces force needed.

1. Fixed Pulley: A fixed pulley has a wheel attached to a fixed support, such as a ceiling or beam. The rope passes through the wheel, and the load is on one end, while force is applied at the other end.

A fixed pulley does not reduce the amount of force needed to lift the load, but it changes the direction of the force. Instead of lifting the load directly upward, you pull the rope downward, which is often more convenient. As illustrated, there is only one rope segment supporting the load. The road segment to the left-hand side of the pulley does not directly support the load, and it is NOT counted as a supporting rope segment. The mechanical advantage of a fixed pulley is 1, meaning the force required to lift the load is the same as the load itself.

2. Moveable Pulley: A moveable pulley is attached directly to the load itself, and the pulley moves with the load as it is lifted.

A moveable pulley reduces the amount of force needed to lift the load by distributing the weight between two supporting segments of the rope. This effectively halves the effort required. For example, if the load weighs 100 N, the force needed to lift it would be 50 N. The mechanical advantage of a moveable pulley is 2.

Note that the mechanical advantage is equal to the number of supporting rope segments.

3. Compound Pulley: A compound pulley system is a combination of both fixed and moveable pulleys. It allows for a significant reduction in the effort required to lift a load.

By combining fixed and moveable pulleys, a compound pulley provides a higher mechanical advantage. The force needed is reduced based on the number of pulleys in the system, allowing the load to be lifted with much less effort. For instance, with multiple pulleys, the effort needed may be only a fraction of the load's weight. The mechanical advantage can be calculated by counting the number rope segments supporting the load, which, in the figure above is 2. Hence, if the load is 100 N, one will only need to apply a downward force of 50 N to pull it up using the compound pulley as shown.

4. Block & Tackle: A block and tackle system uses multiple pulleys in both fixed and moveable blocks, increasing the mechanical advantage. The **block** refers to the set of pulleys that are housed together in a casing. A block can contain one or more pulleys, and there are usually two blocks in a block and tackle system—one **fixed block** (attached to a support) and one **movable block** (attached to the load). The **tackle** refers to the ropes or cables that are threaded through the pulleys. The tackle is what transfers the force applied by the user to the load.

In a block and tackle system, the load's weight is distributed across multiple sections of the rope, significantly reducing the effort required. The mechanical advantage is equal to the number of rope segments supporting the load. In the figure given before, there are 2 rope segments in this particular block and tackle system. So, the force required is reduced to 1/2 of the load's weight. With a number of pulleys in the block and tackle system, the system allows a user to lift very heavy loads with minimal effort, making it ideal for heavy-duty lifting applications.

Example: The image on the right shows a block and tackle pulley system. If the weight being lifted is 120 Newtons, how much force is needed to pull the load up?

Solution: This pulley system has three supporting ropes, which means the mechanical advantage is 3. The mechanical advantage tells us that the force required to lift the load is divided by the number of ropes supporting it.

To calculate the force needed: $Force = \frac{Load}{Mechanical\ Advantage}$ Given that the load is 120 N and the mechanical advantage is 3: $Force = \frac{120\ N}{3} = 40\ N$.

Wheel and Axle

The wheel and axle is another simple machine that helps reduce friction and makes movement more efficient. It consists of a larger wheel attached to a smaller cylindrical axle, allowing both to rotate together.

The mechanical advantage of a wheel and axle comes from the difference in radius or diameter between the wheel and the axle. When a force is applied to the wheel, it is transferred to the axle, allowing it to exert a larger force over a shorter distance. This principle allows the wheel and axle to convert a small input force into a greater output force, which is useful for tasks such as moving heavy loads or generating rotational movement.

For example, in a car, the steering wheel acts as a wheel and axle system. Turning the large steering wheel requires minimal effort but generates enough force to move the smaller axle, effectively turning the car's wheels. Similarly, a doorknob is a wheel and axle, where the larger knob allows the user to exert less force while applying enough torque to move the latch.

Wheel and axle systems are commonly used in vehicles, pulleys, gears, and tools like screwdrivers. By reducing the effort needed and minimizing friction, this simple machine helps increase efficiency in various applications.

Example: Imagine you have a wheel with a diameter of 50 cm and an axle with a diameter of 10 cm. You apply a force of 20 N to the edge of the wheel. What is the mechanical advantage of this wheel and axle system, and what force is exerted on the axle?

Solution: The formula for mechanical advantage in a wheel and axle system is:

$$MA = \frac{\text{diameter of the wheel}}{\text{diameter of the axle}}$$

Now, calculate the mechanical advantage: $MA = \frac{50}{10} = 5$

Now, Calculate the force exerted on the axle. We know that mechanical advantage can also be written as the ratio of the output force (force on the axle) to the input force (force on the wheel):

$$MA = \frac{\text{Output force (on axle)}}{\text{Input force (on wheel)}}$$

We are given the input force on the wheel as 20 N. Now, let's solve for the output force:

$$5 = \frac{\text{Output force}}{20\ N}$$

$$\text{Output force} = 5 \times 20 = 100\ N$$

Hence, the mechanical advantage of the wheel and axle system is 5, and the output force exerted on the axle is 100 N. This example shows how a wheel and axle system amplifies force, making it easier to lift or move heavy objects.

Inclined Plane: Calculating Effort and Load Relationships

An inclined plane is a flat surface set at an angle, used to facilitate the movement of heavy objects from a lower to a higher elevation or vice versa. The mechanical advantage of an inclined plane comes from spreading the effort needed to move the load over a longer distance, reducing the force required.

The relationship between effort and load on an inclined plane depends on the length of the plane and the height it rises. The longer the length of the inclined plane relative to its height, the less force is needed to move the load. For example, if you need to load a heavy box onto a truck, using a long ramp requires less force than lifting the box directly. However, while less force is needed, the distance over which the box must be moved is increased.

The mechanical advantage of an inclined plane can be calculated by dividing the length of the plane by its height:

$$Mechanical\ Advantage = \frac{Length\ of\ Inclined\ Plane}{Height}$$

Inclined planes are found in many everyday situations, such as wheelchair ramps, loading docks, and roadways on hills. By reducing the required effort to move an object, inclined planes make it possible to accomplish tasks that would otherwise be challenging.

Wedge: Application of Force and Use in Everyday Life

A **wedge** is a type of inclined plane that moves. It consists of two inclined planes joined back-to-back, forming a sharp edge that can be used to split or cut objects. The wedge converts a force applied to its blunt end into forces perpendicular to its inclined surfaces, effectively amplifying the input force to perform tasks like cutting, splitting, or holding materials in place.

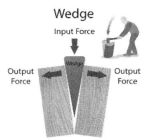

The mechanical advantage of a wedge depends on its angle. The thinner and sharper the wedge, the greater the mechanical advantage. For example, an **axe** used to chop wood is a wedge. When force is applied to the axe head, the sharp edge splits the wood with greater force than was applied by the user. Similarly, **chisels** and **knives** are examples of wedges that amplify the force applied to cut or shape materials.

Wedges are used in a variety of everyday tools, from kitchen knives to doorstops. They are indispensable for many tasks, such as cutting, carving, splitting, and even holding objects in place, highlighting their versatility and efficiency in transferring and amplifying force.

Screw

A screw is a simple machine that consists of an inclined plane wrapped around a cylinder, forming a spiral. The **threads** of the screw help convert **rotational force (torque)** into linear motion, allowing it to move through or hold objects in place.

The **pitch** of a screw refers to the distance between the threads. The smaller the pitch, the more force can be generated with each rotation, as the inclined plane wraps more tightly, effectively reducing the required input force. This is why screws with finer threads are easier to turn but take more rotations to fully insert compared to screws with coarser threads.

In practical applications, screws are used to fasten objects together or lift heavy loads. For example, a **car jack** uses a screw mechanism to lift the vehicle with relatively little effort. By turning the screw, the rotational force is converted into upward linear movement, lifting the car. Similarly, **wood screws** are used to securely join materials, as the threads create friction that resists removal, ensuring a tight and lasting connection.

Screws are one of the most widely used simple machines in the modern world, offering versatility in fastening, lifting, and securing applications, all while providing a mechanical advantage through the conversion of rotational force into linear movement.

Gears

Gears are mechanical components used to transfer power and change the speed or direction of motion between machine parts. There are different types of gears for various applications. **Spur gears** have straight teeth and are the most common type, used in applications requiring simple, parallel movement like clocks or conveyor systems. **Bevel gears** have angled teeth, allowing them to transfer power between shafts at different angles, making them useful in car differentials. **Worm gears** consist of a screw-like worm and a matching gear, which provide high reduction ratios and are used in applications requiring large torque, like elevators.

Spur Gear   Bevel Gear   Worm Gear

The **gear ratio** determines how gears affect the output speed and torque in a mechanical system. The gear ratio is determined by the number of teeth on the gears involved, not by their diameter. Specifically, it is calculated by dividing the number of teeth on the **driven gear** by the number of teeth on the **driving gear**.

If the gear ratio is greater than 1:1, it means that the driven gear has more teeth than the driving gear. As a result, the driven gear rotates more slowly compared to the driving gear, which leads to an increase in torque and a decrease in speed. For instance, if the driving gear has 20 teeth and the driven gear has 80 teeth, the gear ratio is: $Gear\ Ratio = \frac{80}{20} = 4:1$. This means that for every four rotations of the driving gear, the driven gear rotates only once. Such a configuration is ideal when more force is needed, such as in the first gear of a car to provide more power for starting from a stop.

Conversely, if the gear ratio is less than 1:1, the driven gear has fewer teeth than the driving gear. In this scenario, the driven gear rotates faster, resulting in increased speed but reduced torque. For example, if the driving gear has 60 teeth and the driven gear has 20 teeth, the gear ratio is: $Gear\ Ratio = \frac{20}{60} = 1:3$. This means that for every rotation of the driving gear, the driven gear will rotate three times. This setup is useful when speed is more important than force, such as when a cyclist shifts to a higher gear on flat terrain to move faster with less pedaling effort.

It is important to note that while diameter may affect the physical design and placement of gears, it does not determine the gear ratio. The number of teeth alone determines how speed and torque are modified. When the gear ratio is greater than 1:1, the system produces more torque but moves more slowly. When the gear ratio is less than 1:1, the system moves faster but generates less torque.

Example 1: If a motor with a driving gear of 15 teeth turns a driven gear of 45 teeth, what is the gear ratio and how does it affect the output?

A) 1:3, increases speed and decreases torque
B) 1:3, decreases speed and increases torque
C) 3:1, decreases speed and increases torque
D) 3:1, increases speed and decreases torque

Answer: C) 3:1, decreases speed and increases torque.

Explanation: In this example, the driven gear has three times as many teeth as the driving gear, resulting in a 3:1 gear ratio. This means the driven gear will rotate slower than the driving gear, but it will produce three times the torque, making it more effective for tasks requiring additional force.

Example 2: Two gears are in contact with each other. Gear A has 20 teeth and is rotating at 120 RPM (clockwise). Gear B has 40 teeth and is driven by Gear A. What is the rotational speed and direction of Gear B?

A) 60 RPM, counterclockwise
B) 60 RPM, clockwise
C) 240 RPM, counterclockwise
D) 240 RPM, clockwise

Answer: A) 60 RPM, counterclockwise.

Explanation: When two gears are in contact, their teeth interlock, causing them to rotate in opposite directions. This means that if Gear A is rotating clockwise, then Gear B must rotate counterclockwise.

To determine the rotational speed of Gear B, we use the relationship between the number of teeth on the gears and their rotational speeds.

$$Speed\ of\ Gear\ B\ (RPM) \times Number\ of\ Teeth\ on\ Gear\ B = Speed\ of\ Gear\ A\ (RPM) \times Number\ of\ Teeth\ on\ Gear\ A$$

Hence, $Speed\ of\ Gear\ B\ (RPM) = Speed\ of\ Gear\ A\ (RPM) \times \frac{Number\ of\ Teeth\ on\ Gear\ A}{Number\ of\ Teeth\ on\ Gear\ B}$. Given that Speed of Gear A = 120 RPM, Number of Teeth on Gear A = 20, Number of Teeth on Gear B = 40, we have:

$$Speed\ of\ Gear\ B = 120 \times \frac{20}{40} = 120 \times 0.5 = 60\ RPM$$

Thus, the correct answer is: A) 60 RPM, counterclockwise.

PRACTICE SET

Time: 22 minutes for 15 questions

Select the correct answer from the choices given. This practice subtest reflects the number of questions and time limits you'll encounter on the CAT-ASVAB Mechanical Information subtest without any tryout questions.

1. Gear A, B, C, D, E drives Gear B, C, D, E, F respectively, as shown. If Gear A rotates clockwise, what is the rotational direction of Gear E?

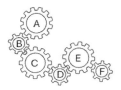

A) Clockwise
B) Counterclockwise
C) Both directions
D) Does not rotate

2. To calculate the efficiency of a machine, you should:

A) Multiply the input force by the output force.
B) Divide the output work by the input work.
C) Multiply the output work by the input work.
D) Subtract the input force from the output force.

3. In the pulley system shown, how much effort is needed to lift a 100-pound load?

A) 50 pounds
B) 100 pounds
C) 200 pounds
D) 25 pounds

4. If Gear 1 has 50 teeth and Gear 2 has 20 teeth, how many revolutions does Gear 2 make for every 10 revolutions Gear 1 makes?

A) 5
B) 12
C) 25
D) 30

5. Two cars with different weights collide head-on while moving at the same speed. What most likely will happen to the heavier car upon impact?

(A) It will be thrown backward.
(B) It will stay in place.
(C) It will keep moving forward.
(D) It will flip over the smaller car.

6. A person is pulling a cart weighing 400 pounds up a ramp that is 20 feet long. If 100 pounds of force is used, how tall is the ramp?

(A) 4 feet
(B) 5 feet
(C) 6 feet
(D) 10 feet

7. The force required to sustain pushing a box across a rough surface is the same as

(A) the weight of the box times the static friction coefficient
(B) the force required to overcome friction while the box is being pushed
(C) the potential energy of the box
(D) the mass of the box divided by gravity

8. How much force is required to lift a 60-pound load using a lever system where the effort arm is 3 times longer than the resistance arm?

(A) 20 lbs
(B) 30 lbs
(C) 60 lbs
(D) 180 lbs

9. A car stuck in the sand requires 1,500 N of force to be pushed 6 m. How much work is done to push the car?

(A) 250 J
(B) 9,000 J
(C) 1,500 J
(D) 6,000 J

10. A machine lifts parts with a weight of 30 N from the ground to a height of 4 meters. If it takes 3 seconds to lift 10 parts, how much power is used?

(A) 120 watts
(B) 400 watts
(C) 40 watts
(D) 160 watts

11. A block and tackle pulley system has 4 segments supporting the load. Ignoring friction, what is the mechanical advantage of the system?

(A) 4
(B) 3
(C) 2
(D) 1

12. A hydraulic lift has a smaller piston area of 10 square inches and a larger piston area of 50 square inches. If you apply 100 pounds of force to the smaller piston, how much force is exerted on the larger piston?

(A) 500 pounds
(B) 1,000 pounds
(C) 2,000 pounds
(D) 10 pounds

13. If a copper rod, a plastic rod, and a wooden rod are left in the sun, which will heat up the fastest?

A) Copper
B) Plastic
C) Wood
D) All will heat up at the same rate

14. In a playground seesaw, one child weighing 40 pounds sits 4 feet on the left side of the fulcrum, and another child weighing 80 pounds sits 2 feet on the left side of the fulcrum. How far must an 80-pound child sit on the right-hand side of the fulcrum to balance the seesaw?

(A) 3 feet
(B) 4 feet
(C) 6 feet
(D) 2 feet

15. A constant force of 5 N is applied to a 10 kg box at rest. Assuming no friction, what is the velocity of the box after 4 seconds?

(A) 0.5 m/s
(B) 2.0 m/s
(C) 10.0 m/s
(D) 20.0 m/s

Answers and Explanations

1. A) Clockwise. Explanation: In systems of gears, when one rotates, it causes the gear it drives to rotate in the opposite direction. If Gear A turns clockwise, Gear B will turn counterclockwise, and Gear C will again rotate opposite to Gear B, which means Gear C rotates clockwise. Hence, Gear A, C, E all rotate clockwise, while Gear B, D, F rotates counterclockwise.

2. B) Divide the output work by the input work. Explanation: Efficiency is determined by dividing the output work by the input work and is often expressed as a percentage.

3. A) 50 pounds. Explanation: This is a moveable pulley system with two support segments. The mechanical advantage is equal to the number of support segments, which is 2. Therefore, the effort needed to lift the load is the load divided by the mechanical advantage: $\text{Effort} = \frac{\text{Load}}{\text{Mechanical Advantage}} = \frac{100 \text{ pounds}}{2} = 50$ pounds.

4. C) 25. Explanation: The number of revolutions Gear 2 makes is inversely proportional to the number of teeth. Gear 1 has 50 teeth, and Gear 2 has 20 teeth. For every revolution of Gear 1, Gear 2 makes $\frac{5}{2}$ revolutions. Therefore, for 10 revolutions of Gear 1, Gear 2 will make: $10 \times \frac{5}{2} = 25$ revolutions.

5. (C) It will keep moving forward. Explanation: when two cars collide, the one with more mass/weight will continue moving forward because it has greater momentum. The smaller car, having less mass/weight, will likely be pushed backward. The laws of motion, particularly the conservation of momentum, dictate that the car with more mass/weight retains more of its forward motion.

6. (B) 5 feet. Explanation: The mechanical advantage of the inclined plane is determined by the length of the ramp divided by its height. With 100 pounds of force used to move a 400-pound object, the mechanical advantage is 4. Therefore, the height of the ramp is 20/4=5 feet.

7. (B) the force required to overcome friction while the box is being pushed. Explanation: When pushing an object across a rough surface, the force that needs to be applied is primarily to overcome the friction between the object and the surface. Friction depends on the surface roughness and the normal force, which is typically the weight of the object. The correct force is the one that counteracts the friction, allowing the object to move. The other choices are not correct because the force needed to push the box does not directly depend on the object's potential energy or mass in isolation. The weight of the object and the static coefficient of friction together define the force needed to make the object move initially; it is usually bigger than the force is needed to actually move the object across a surface once the movement is under way.

8. (A) 20 lbs. Explanation: The mechanical advantage (MA) of a lever is calculated as the ratio of the length of the effort arm to the length of the resistance arm. In this case, the effort arm is 3 times longer than the resistance arm, so: MA = 3. The mechanical advantage tells us how much the force is reduced. Therefore, the effort required to lift the 60-pound load is:

$$\text{Effort} = \frac{\text{Load}}{\text{MA}} = \frac{60 \text{ lbs}}{3} = 20 \text{ lbs}$$

This means only 20 lbs of force is needed to lift the 60-lb load, thanks to the lever's mechanical advantage.

9. (B) 9,000 J. Explanation: Work is the product of force and distance, calculated using the formula: $W = F \times d$

In this case, the force F is 1,500 N and the distance d is 6 m. Hence: $W = 1,500 \, N \times 6 \, m = 9,000 \, J$

10. (A) 120 watts. Explanation: Power is calculated using the formula: $P = \frac{W}{t}$, where W is the work done and t is the time taken. Work $W = F \times d = 30 \, N \times 4 \, m = 120 \, J$. Since the machine lifts 10 parts, the total work is $120 \, J \times 10 = 1,200 \, J$. The time is 3 seconds, so the power is:

$$P = \frac{1,200 \, J}{3 \, s} = 400 \, W$$

11. (A) 4. Explanation: The mechanical advantage in a block and tackle pulley system is equal to the number of rope segments supporting the load. Here, 4 segments give a mechanical advantage of 4.

12. (B) 500 pounds. Explanation: The force on the larger piston is proportional to the area difference between the two pistons. Using Pascal's Law, the formula to calculate the force exerted on the larger piston is: $F_2 = F_1 \times \frac{A_2}{A_1}$

Where: F_1 is the force applied to the smaller piston, A_1 is the area of the smaller piston, A_2 is the area of the larger piston, F_2 is the force exerted on the larger piston.

Given: $F_1 = 100$ pounds, $A_1 = 10$ square inches, $A_2 = 50$ square inches

Substitute the values into the formula: $F_2 = 100 \times \frac{50}{10} = 100 \times 5 = 500$ pounds. So, the force exerted on the larger piston is 500 pounds.

13. A) Copper. Explanation: Copper is a metal and an excellent conductor of heat, meaning it absorbs and transfers heat faster than other materials.

B (Plastic) and C (Wood) are poor heat conductors compared to metals, so they will heat up more slowly.

D is incorrect because the materials have different thermal properties and will not heat up at the same rate.

14. Correct (B) 4 feet. Explanation: To balance the seesaw, the moments (weight × distance) on both sides must be equal. The side with the 40 and 80-pound children has a total moment of $(40 \times 4) + (80 \times 2) = 320\ foot - pounds$. To balance this with a 80-pound child, we set $80 \times$ distance $= 320$, which gives a distance of 4 feet.

15. (B) 2.0 m/s. Explanation: The relationship between force and acceleration is given by Newton's second law:

$F = ma$, where F is the applied force, m is the mass, and a is the acceleration. Solving for a we have:

$$a = \frac{F}{m} = \frac{5\,\text{N}}{10\,\text{kg}} = 0.5\,\text{m/s}^2$$

To find the velocity after 4 seconds, we use the formula: $v = u + at$, where u is the initial velocity (which is 0 because the object starts from rest), $a = 0.5\,\text{m/s}^2$ and $t = 4$ seconds.

Hence: $v = 0 + (0.5\,\text{m/s}^2)(4\,\text{s}) = 2.0\,\text{m/s}$. Thus, the box reaches a velocity of 2.0 m/s.

CHAPTER 10: ASSEMBLING OBJECTS

The Assembling Objects subtest on the ASVAB measures your ability to understand how different objects fit together, a skill important in mechanical and technical fields. In this subtest, you will be asked to visualize how separate pieces come together to form a complete object. This requires strong spatial reasoning skills, which are valuable in many jobs related to construction, engineering, and maintenance.

There are typically two types of problems you may encounter in this subtest: puzzle problems and connection problems. In **puzzle problems**, you will need to determine how different jigsaw-puzzle like pieces fit together, much like assembling an actual puzzle. You will be presented with parts, and you must visualize which configuration will create a complete shape. In **connection problems**, you will need to determine how different objects connect at the indicated points shown on these objects.

In both types of problems, you will be presented with five drawings. The first drawing shows the unconnected or unassembled objects, while the next four drawings are possible options for how the objects would look once they are connected or assembled. Your task is to choose the correct assembled or connected version from the given choices.

Whether or not spatial skills are your strong suit, the abilities tested in this subtest are learnable. In this chapter, we will cover the right tactics to help you solve these types of problems quickly and accurately. With practice, you will be able to improve your visualization skills and tackle these questions with confidence.

PUZZLE PROBLEMS

Puzzle problems are a common type in the Assembling Objects subtest of the ASVAB. These questions assess your ability to visualize how separate pieces come together to correctly form a complete shape. They are similar to traditional jigsaw puzzles, but instead of fitting curved puzzle pieces, you may encounter various geometric shapes that need to be assembled logically.

Example: Imagine you are presented with a drawing that contains four different shapes: a triangle, a rectangle, and two trapezoids. Each of these pieces must be put together to form a recognizable object, such as an abstract geometric pattern. Next to this drawing, you will be provided with four potential assembled versions of how these pieces could be arranged.

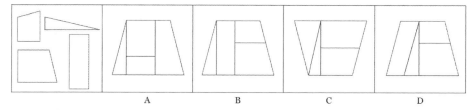

| A | B | C | D |

A Methodical Way to Solve Puzzle Problems

There are hard ways and there are easy ways to solve this problem. Those with gifted spatial abilities may naturally solve such problems with ease. For the rest of us, we believe the following is the most methodical and efficient way that require no special abilities.

1. **Observe the first object**: Look at the top left corner of the first box and temporarily commit it to your memory.

2. **Compare with each choice**: Go through each choice—A, B, C, and D—to see if they include this object. Remember, this object may appear in a rotated form. If you cannot find this object in one of the choices, eliminate that choice.

3. **Proceed to the next object**: Pick the second object in the first box. Going clockwise from the top left corner makes this step easy to follow. Repeat what you did in Step 2. Pick the third, fourth, and remaining objects and repeat the process until you've eliminated three of the four choices.

4. **Confirm the remaining choice**: For the last remaining answer choice, ensure that it contains all the objects in the first box. If it does, that's the correct answer. If not, you may have made a mistake during Steps 1 to 3. Start over.

Now, let's apply this method to the above example:

1. Top left corner object: Pick the small trapezoid at the top left corner of the first box and compare it with the four choices. We see that **A** and **C** do not have this element, so they can be eliminated. Notice that in **B** and **D**, the small trapezoid was rotated clockwise by 90 degrees.

2. Second object: Now we move on to the smaller triangle in the first box. Both **B** and **D** have this element, so we are not able to eliminate either of them.

3. Third object: Next, compare the rectangle in the first box with the elements in **B** and **D**. **B** contains the rectangle, but **C** does not. So, **C** is eliminated, and we are left with **B** as the possible answer.

4. Final check: Go through each of the four elements in the first box one by one, in a clockwise direction, and see if you can find the corresponding element in **C**. The answer is yes—**C** has all four elements, even though the small trapezoid and the triangle have different orientations compared to the original box.

Voilà! We are able to find and confirm that **C** is the correct answer.

Now, let's try this method on the following example.

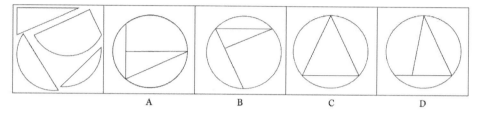

The correct answer is A, and it should be pretty fast to figure that out, isn't it? Let's examine the connection problems next.

CONNECTION PROBLEMS

Connection problems are another type of question you will face in the Assembling Objects subtest of the ASVAB. These questions assess your ability to understand how various components are linked or assembled based on given features, such as matching slots, holes, and tabs. In these problems, you might be asked to connect pieces that resemble mechanical parts, such as blocks with pegs, panels with slots, or various interlocking shapes.

These problems have some common features:

1. There are typically two separate objects to be connected. Each object has a dot indicating the point of connection. The dot can be anywhere on the objects. Typically, though, they are on the edge or at the center.

2. Additionally, a connection line is always present, with a dot at each end. These dots indicate where each object should be attached.

Below is an example of a connection problem.

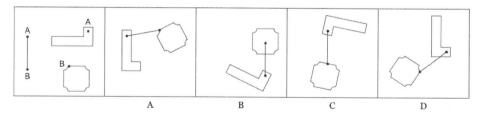

Solve Connection Problems

The method to solve the connection problems is similar to the one we presented above to solve puzzle problems, with some modifications.

1. **Observe the first object**: Ignore the connection line and pick the first object on top or on the left-hand side, and temporarily commit it to your memory.

2. **Compare with each choice**: Go through each choice—A, B, C, and D—to see if they include this object, and make sure the point of connection should be exactly as indicated in the first box. Remember, this object may appear in a rotated form. If you cannot find this object with the connection point exactly at the right location in one of the choices, eliminate that choice.

3. **Proceed to the next object**: Pick the second object in the first box. Repeat what you did in Step 2. This should leave you with only one choice out the four available.

4. **Confirm your final choice**: For the last remaining answer choice, ensure that it contains all the objects in the first box. Also, make sure the point of connection on an object is located exactly at the point indicated in the first box. If both of these requirements are met, then that's the correct answer. If not, you may have made a mistake during Steps 1 to 3. Start over.

Now, let's apply this method to the above example:

1. Pick the object with connection point **A** first (ignore the connection line), and compare it with all four choices. The exact replica of this object appears in **B**, **C**, and **D**. But in **A**, the connection point is at the wrong end of this object. Hence, **A** is eliminated.

2. Second object: Now we move on to the object with connection point B. The exact replica of this object appears in **D** only. In **B**, the connection point is at the center of the object, so **B** is eliminated. In **C**, the connection point is also wrong, so **C** is eliminated. Hence, we're left with **D** as the likely correct answer.

3. Final check: Go through both of the objects in the first box again and see if you can find the corresponding object in **D**. The answer is yes. Do the objects in **D** have the connection points at the right place? Again, this can be verified. Hence, we are able to find and confirm that **D** is the correct answer.

Now, let's try this method on another example.

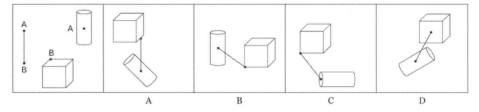

Following the steps outlined above, one will find that the correct answer is B.

NO FLIPPING!

Here is an important caveat: in the Assembling Objects subtest of the ASVAB, it is important to remember that you cannot flip the pieces over—you can only rotate them. This means that you can rotate the objects whichever way you want, but you cannot flip them left to right or top to bottom. This follows the same rule as when you put together a jigsaw puzzle: you can rotate the pieces, but you will never flip it over, as the back side of a jigsaw puzzle is blank!

The following two figures show the difference between rotation and flipping. In the first figure, a curved arrow rotates clockwise for various degrees. In the second figure, the same curved arrow is flipped left to right and top to bottom.

Rotating A Curved Arrow Clockwise

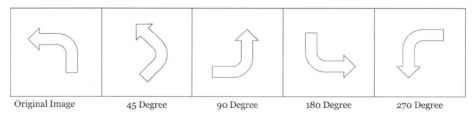

| Original Image | 45 Degree | 90 Degree | 180 Degree | 270 Degree |

Flipping A Curved Arrow

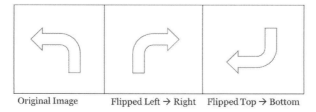

| Original Image | Flipped Left → Right | Flipped Top → Bottom |

Here is a key observation: an image cannot be rotated in such a way that it becomes its own mirror image (or flipped version), unless the original image already has left-to-right or top-to-bottom symmetry.

Hence, when you take the Assembling Objects subtest and think that a piece would fit if it were flipped, remember that this is not allowed in this subtest. You must instead find a way to rotate the piece—either clockwise or counterclockwise—so that it fits appropriately. This applied to both the puzzle problems and the connection problems.

Below is an additional example that compares a rotated and flipped triangle.

Rotating A Triangle Clockwise

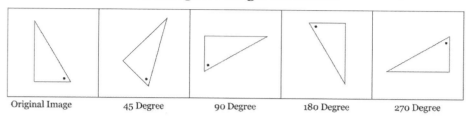

| Original Image | 45 Degree | 90 Degree | 180 Degree | 270 Degree |

Flipping A Triangle

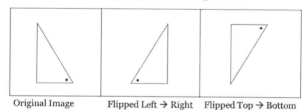

| Original Image | Flipped Left → Right | Flipped Top → Bottom |

We go through these exercises to give you a handy **rule of thumb**: If during the test, you see the original image being flipped in one of the choices instead of being rotated (0° to 360°), and the original image does not have left-to-right or top-to-bottom symmetry to start with, then you can quickly eliminate that choice.

PRACTICE SET

Time: 18 minutes for 15 questions

Select the correct answer from the choices given. This practice subtest reflects the number of questions and time limits you'll encounter on the CAT-ASVAB Assembling Objects subtest without any tryout questions.

1.

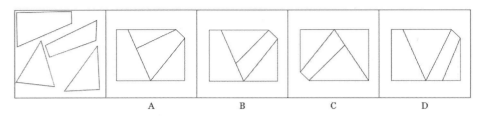

        A   B   C   D

2.

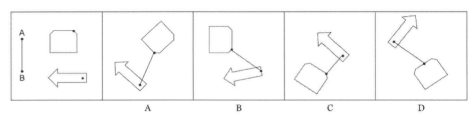

        A   B   C   D

3.

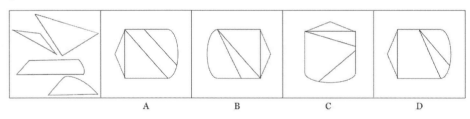

        A   B   C   D

4.

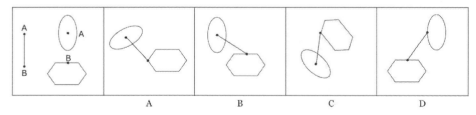

        A   B   C   D

5.

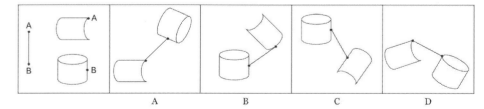

        A   B   C   D

6.

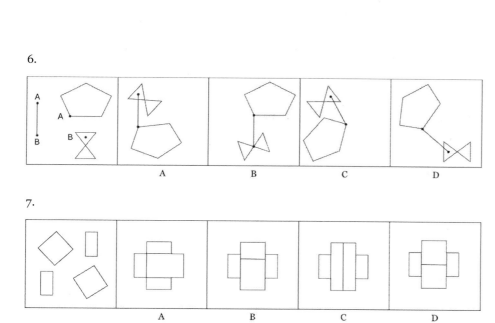

7.

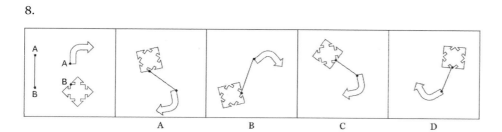

8.

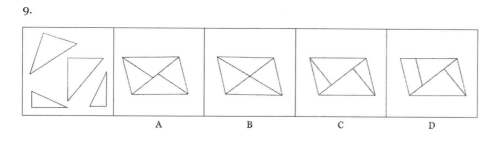

9.

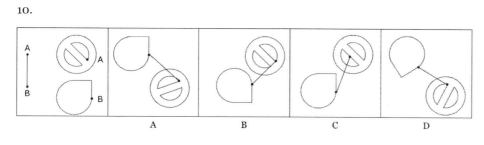

10.

11.

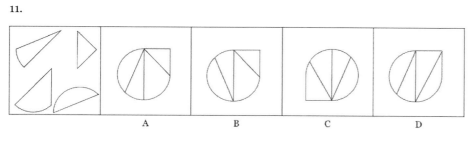

12.

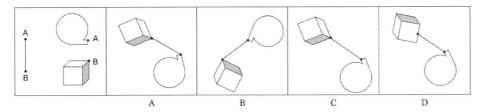

13.

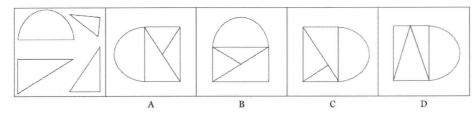

14.

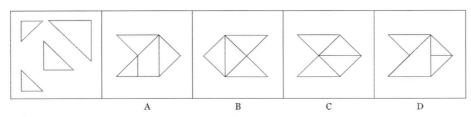

15.

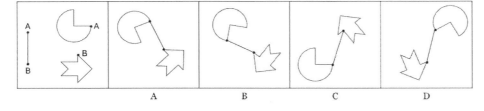

Answers and Explanations

1. B

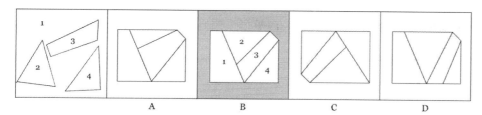

2. C

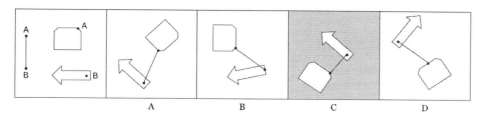

3. A

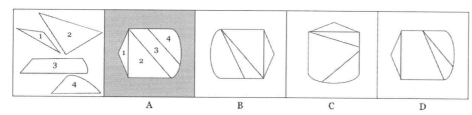

4. B

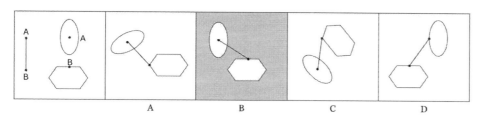

5. A

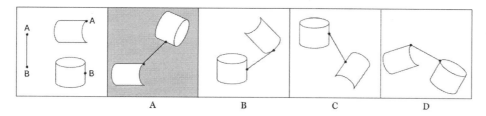

6. D

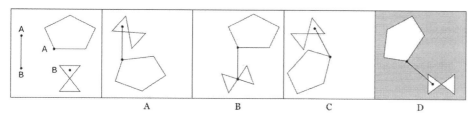

7. D

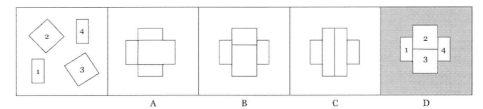

8. B

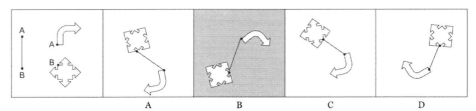

9. C

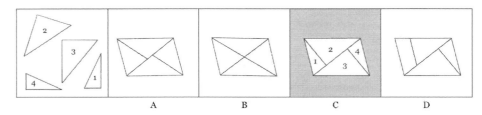

10. A

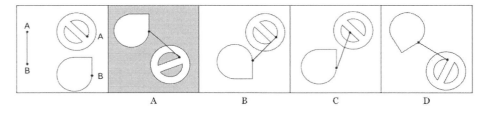

11. A

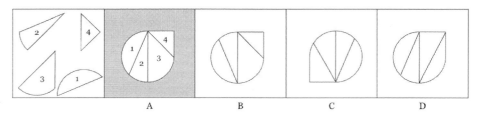

12. C

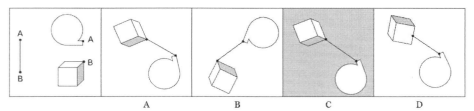

13. C

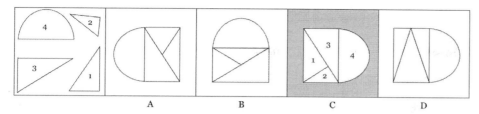

14. D

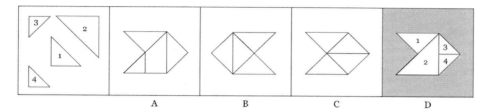

15. D

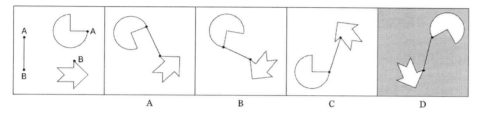

ASVAB PRACTICE TEST 1

PART 1: GENERAL SCIENCE (GS)

Time: 12 minutes for 15 questions

Select the correct answer from the choices given. This practice subtest reflects the number of questions and time limits you'll encounter on the CAT-ASVAB General Science subtest without any tryout questions.

1. Which process allows plants to release oxygen and absorb carbon dioxide?

A) Cellular respiration
B) Transpiration
C) Photosynthesis
D) Fermentation

2. Which molecule is known as the "energy currency" of the cell?

A) Glucose
B) DNA
C) ATP
D) RNA

3. Which nutrient is considered the primary source of energy for the human body?

A) Proteins
B) Carbohydrates
C) Fats
D) Vitamins

4. Which part of the cell is responsible for controlling what enters and leaves the cell?

A) Mitochondria
B) Ribosome
C) Cell membrane
D) Nucleus

5. How is work defined in physics?

A) Force applied over a distance
B) Energy transferred per unit time
C) Mass times velocity
D) Energy stored in an object

6. Which of the following best defines reflection?

A) The bending of light as it passes through a prism
B) Light bouncing off a surface
C) The slowing of light in a medium
D) The absorption of light into a material

7. What is a wave's frequency measured in?

A) Joules
B) Watts
C) Hertz
D) Newtons

8. What property of a sound wave affects its volume?

A) Amplitude
B) Frequency
C) Wavelength
D) Velocity

9. What is electronegativity?

A) Ability of an atom to gain neutrons
B) Ability of an atom to attract electrons
C) Amount of protons in the nucleus
D) Mass of an atom

10. What is the pH range for bases?

A) Below 7
B) Exactly 7
C) Above 7
D) Between 5 and 7

11. What is a heterogeneous mixture?

A) A mixture where substances are evenly distributed
B) A mixture where substances are not uniformly distributed
C) A mixture of elements
D) A compound made of different atoms

12. Which process is responsible for weathering rocks into smaller particles?

A) Tectonic activity
B) Chemical reactions
C) Erosion
D) Weathering

13. What is the main difference between a meteor and a meteorite?

A) A meteorite burns in the atmosphere
B) A meteor reaches Earth's surface
C) A meteorite reaches Earth's surface
D) A meteor is larger than a meteorite

14. What natural phenomenon is caused by the refraction of light in Earth's atmosphere?

A) Solar eclipse
B) Aurora borealis
C) Rainbow
D) Lunar eclipse

15. Which planetary body in the solar system is known for its prominent ring system?

A) Jupiter
B) Mars
C) Uranus
D) Saturn

PART 2: ARITHMETIC REASONING (AR)

Time: 55 minutes for 15 questions

Select the correct answer from the choices given. This practice subtest reflects the number of questions and time limits you'll encounter on the CAT-ASVAB Arithmetic Reasoning subtest without any tryout questions.

1. Jack bought a sedan with a $1,500 down payment and monthly payments of $400 for 4 years. How much in total will Jack pay?

A) $20,700
B) $19,200
C) $23,000
D) $24,000

2. A chef baked 24 slices of cakes. A customer buys one-third of the slices, a party host buys one-fourth of the slices, and a neighbor buys one-sixth of the slices. How many slices of cake does the chef have left?

A) 6
B) 8
C) 12
D) 4

3. Jake needs to buy 6 cans of paint for his house. Normally, each can of paint costs $30.00, but due to a sale, he was able to buy each can for $27. How much money did Jake save on his entire purchase?

A) $12.00
B) $15.00
C) $18.00
D) $20.00

4. Jake's monthly grocery bill used to be $200. Due to inflation, his bill has increased by 15%. What is Jake's new monthly grocery bill?

A) $220
B) $230
C) $240
D) $250

5. Andrew's utility bills for the first three months of the year were $150.75 in January, $142.50 in February, and $146.25 in March. What was Andrew's average monthly utility bill for these three months?

A) $146.50
B) $147.00
C) $149.00
D) $146.75

6. The area of a rectangle is 60 square meters. The length is 4 meters longer than the width. What is the width of the rectangle?

A) 6 meters
B) 8 meters
C) 7 meters
D) 9 meters

7. A train travels 200 miles in 4 hours. What is the average speed of the train?

A) 40 miles per hour
B) 45 miles per hour
C) 50 miles per hour
D) 60 miles per hour

8. Jane is driving from New York to Chicago, a distance of 800 miles. If Jane drives at an average speed of 60 miles per hour, roughly how long will it take her to complete the trip?

A) 10 hours
B) 12 hours
C) 13 hours
D) 15 hours

9. The population of Pine Valley grew by 240,000 people between 2010 and 2020, which was one-third more than what the city planners predicted. How much growth did the city planners originally predict?

A) 160,000
B) 180,000
C) 200,000
D) 150,000

10. A bakery needs 90 pounds of flour for baking. The owner wants to buy the flour at the lowest possible cost. Which of the following options should the bakery choose?

A) Three 30-pound bags at $75 each
B) Six 15-pound bags at $38 each
C) Nine 10-pound bags at $26 each
D) Ninety 1-pound bags at $4 each

11. Tim harvested 300 more apples than Sara. After Tim sells 100 apples, he now has twice as many apples as Sara. How many apples does Sara have?

A) 200
B) 250
C) 300
D) 350

12. A juice company needs to fill 550 bottles with juice. Each bottle holds 8 fluid ounces of juice, and the company has 40 gallons of juice. After filling as many bottles as possible, how many ounces of juice will be left? (There are 128 fluid ounces in every gallon.)

A) 160 ounces
B) 620 ounces
C) 720 ounces
D) 832 ounces

13. Jenny brought 75 snacks to a class trip. There are 20 children, including Jenny, and 15 snacks were left after the trip. What is the average number of snacks each child ate?

A) 2
B) 3
C) 6
D) 7

14. A TV's screen is 40 inches wide and 30 inches tall. What is the length of the diagonal?

A) 50 inches
B) 48 inches
C) 45 inches
D) 55 inches

15. A dog drinks $\frac{3}{4}$ of a gallon of water each day. If you have 12 gallons of water, how many days will the water last for the dog?

A) 16 days
B) 15 days
C) 18 days
D) 12 days

PART 3: WORD KNOWLEDGE (WK)

Time: 9 minutes for 15 questions

Each question below includes an underlined word. You may be asked to determine which one of the four answer choices most closely matches the meaning of the underlined word, or which choice has the opposite meaning. If the word is used within a sentence, your task is to select the option that most accurately reflects its meaning in the context of that sentence. This practice subtest reflects the number of questions and time limits you'll encounter on the CAT-ASVAB Word Knowledge subtest without any tryout questions.

1. The soldier was underlined undaunted by the challenge ahead.

   A) fearful
   B) discouraged
   C) brave
   D) confused

2. The judge's decision was immutable, and there was no chance of an appeal.

   A) flexible
   B) final
   C) changeable
   D) undecided

3. The witness gave a lucid description of the events.

   A) vague
   B) confused
   C) clear
   D) incomprehensible

4. The word enervate most nearly means:

   A) energize
   B) weaken
   C) strengthen
   D) support

5. The word cognizant most nearly means:

   A) unaware
   B) aware
   C) distracted
   D) forgetful

6. The word sagacious most nearly means:

   A) foolish
   B) wise
   C) reckless
   D) uninformed

7. The word benign most nearly means:

   A) harmful
   B) gentle
   C) aggressive
   D) severe

8. His tenacity in pursuing his goals impressed everyone.

   A) determination
   B) laziness
   C) hesitation
   D) confusion

9. The manager had to mitigate the negative effects of the company's policy change.

   A) worsen
   B) reduce
   C) emphasize
   D) hide

10. The manager was known for his meticulous attention to detail.

   A) careless
   B) lazy
   C) precise
   D) forgetful

11. The word assiduous most nearly means:

   A) lazy
   B) diligent
   C) indifferent
   D) inconsistent

12. The word most opposite in meaning to sagacious is:

   A) foolish
   B) wise
   C) prudent
   D) thoughtful

13. The word ominous most nearly means:

   A) threatening
   B) optimistic
   C) cheerful
   D) encouraging

14. The word capacious most nearly means:

   A) small
   B) spacious
   C) crowded
   D) cramped

15. The word precarious most nearly means:

   A) secure
   B) dangerous
   C) stable
   D) reliable

PART 4: PARAGRAPH COMPREHENSION (PC)

Time: 27 minutes for 10 questions

This section presents reading paragraphs followed by questions or incomplete statements. Your task is to read the paragraph and choose the option that best completes the statement or answers the question. This practice subtest simulates the number of questions and time constraints you'll face on the CAT-ASVAB Paragraph Comprehension subtest, without any tryout questions.

The primary objective of the dog teams was to return Scott and his companions to McMurdo Sound in time to catch the departing ship, allowing them to relay news of reaching the South Pole without delay. Scott was anxious to ensure the world knew of their achievement and to communicate their safe return to family members. However, Scott's instructions for the dog teams were vague, leaving them uncertain about how far to proceed. This confusion placed the leaders of the dog teams in a difficult position, as the season was rapidly closing, and clear guidance was not available for how to proceed with the return journey.

1. Which choice best describes the purpose of the passage?

A) To explain how the dog teams were selected for the journey
B) To describe the challenges of navigating McMurdo Sound
C) To explain the goal of the dog-teams and highlight the difficulties they faced due to unclear instructions
D) To discuss the ship's departure and its impact on the team's return

Next morning I started out after the horse thieves. The mule track was easily found, and with very little difficulty I followed it for about two miles into the timber and came upon a place where, as I could plainly see from numerous signs, quite a number of head of stock had been tied among the trees and kept for several days. This was evidently the spot where the thieves had been hiding their stolen stock until they had accumulated quite a herd. From this point it was difficult to trail them, as they had taken the stolen animals out of the timber one by one and in different directions, thus showing that they were experts at the business and experienced frontiersmen.

2. The passage most strongly suggests which characteristics of the horse thieves?

A) They were inexperienced and careless.
B) They were familiar with the local area.
C) They were cunning and skilled at covering their tracks.
D) They were frequently caught by authorities.

And so we came back to our comfortable hut. Whatever merit there may be in going to the Antarctic, once there you must not credit yourself for being there. To spend a year in the hut at Cape Evans because you explore is no more laudable than to spend a month at Davos because you are on vacation, or to spend an English winter at the Berkeley Hotel. It is just the most comfortable thing and the easiest thing to do under the circumstances.

In our case the best thing was not at all bad, for the hut, as Arctic huts go, was as palatial as is the Ritz, as hotels go. Whatever the conditions of darkness, cold and wind, might be outside, there was comfort and warmth and good cheer within.

3. In the passage, the use of "Davos", "Berkeley Hotel" and "Ritz" is to emphasize

A) the importance of luxury in exploration
B) the discomfort of living conditions in the Antarctic
C) the contrast between different types of accommodations
D) the comfort and ease provided by the hut in the Antarctic

Ike Clanton, unable to read the signs and portents of impending tragedy, drove alone into Tombstone on the afternoon of October 25th. Rash, blundering fellow, thus to venture single-handed into the stronghold of his enemies. But he believed in his soul the Earps were secretly afraid of him, would not dare to molest him. How quickly and cruelly was this proud freebooter to be stripped of his foolish illusions. So confident of his own safety was he that, as a law-abiding gesture, he left his Winchester rifle and six-shooter behind the bar at the Grand Hotel and strolled to the saloons and gambling halls.

4. The mention of the Winchester rifle and six-shooter in the passage conveys which of the following?

A) Ike Clanton's desire to show off his weapons
B) Ike Clanton's attempt to appear non-threatening
C) Ike Clanton's plan to attack his enemies
D) Ike Clanton's overconfidence in his safety

Our adventures and our troubles were alike over. We now experienced the incalculable contrast between descending a known and travelled river, and one that is utterly unknown. We hired a man to go with us as guide. We knew exactly what channels were passable when we came to the rapids. It was all child's play compared to what we had gone through. We made long days' journeys, for at night we stopped at some palm-thatched house, inhabited or abandoned, and therefore the men were spared the labor of making camp; and we bought ample food for them, so there was no further need of fishing and chopping down palms for the palm-tops.

5. Which of the following does the author offer as evidence to support the point that his adventures and troubles were over?

A) The river they were traveling on was known and traveled.
B) They encountered numerous rapids and had to unload the canoes.
C) They had to make camp every night.
D) They were frequently chopping down palms for food.

The difference of natural talents in different men is, in reality, much less than we are aware of, and the very different genius which appears to distinguish men of different professions when grown up to maturity is not upon many occasions so much the cause, as the effect of the division of labor. The difference between the most dissimilar characters, between a philosopher and a common street porter, for example, seems to arise not so much from nature, as from habit, custom, and education. When they came into the world, and for the first six or eight years of their existence, they were, perhaps, very much alike, and neither their parents nor playfellows could perceive any remarkable difference.

6. Which of the following statements would the author most likely agree with?

A) Natural talents are the primary reason for the differences in professions.
B) Education and environment play a significant role in shaping a person's abilities.
C) Differences in professions are mostly due to inherent genius.
D) Parents can easily distinguish the talents of their children from birth.

Truth, rather than being an end in itself, is a means to practical outcomes. For example, if someone is lost in the woods and follows a cow-path thinking it leads to a house, the truth is useful because the house can save them. The value of true ideas lies in their practical relevance, though not all truths are important all the time. However, it's useful to maintain knowledge of potential truths for future situations where they may become relevant.

7. What argument does the author make in this passage?

A) The possession of truth is always the ultimate goal.
B) Practical utility determines the value of true ideas.
C) All truths are equally important at all times.
D) Truths should be discarded if they are not immediately useful.

The traveler, though seeking refuge from the harsh landscape, encountered constant obstacles. The sun scorched the barren terrain, and the sparse vegetation did little to offer comfort. Among the few plants, a small but vibrant flower appeared to thrive, despite the malign influence of the dry winds and nutrient-poor soil. However, the winds carried more than just dust—they also spread rumors of danger, warning all who dared to continue their journey deeper into the unknown.

8. In this passage, *malign* most nearly means:

A) Supportive
B) Harmful
C) Innocent
D) Beneficial

True liberty requires restraint, as complete freedom for one person can result in oppression for others. The first condition of a free government is rule by laws, not arbitrary decisions. While law limits individual actions, it protects everyone from arbitrary coercion and aggression, ensuring freedom for all. In this way, liberty and law are not opposing forces; instead, law is necessary for securing true liberty for an entire community.

9. What is the author's view on the relationship between liberty and law?

A) Law is opposed to liberty and should be minimized.
B) Law and liberty are inherently contradictory.
C) Law is essential to achieving true liberty.
D) Liberty can only exist without any form of law.

While crowds may employ reasoning, their arguments are of an inferior kind, relying on superficial associations rather than logical connections. Crowds reason through weak analogies, such as assuming that because ice and glass are both transparent, glass should melt like ice. Similarly, they may believe that consuming the heart of a brave enemy would grant them bravery. The reasoning of crowds is fundamentally flawed, based on apparent but illogical connections.

10. How did the author illustrate a crowd's ability to reason?

A) By showing that crowds use logical arguments similar to those of individuals.
B) By comparing the reasoning of crowds to that of highly educated people.
C) By using examples of flawed reasoning based on superficial associations.
D) By demonstrating that crowds cannot be influenced by any reasoning.

PART 5: MATHEMATICS KNOWLEDGE (MK)

Time: 31 minutes for 15 questions

Select the correct answer from the choices given. This practice subtest reflects the number of questions and time limits you'll encounter on the CAT-ASVAB Mathematics Knowledge subtest without any tryout questions.

1. $\frac{84}{28} =$

A) 2
B) 3
C) 4
D) 5

2. What is the product of 17 and 8?

A) 120
B) 136
C) 124
D) 138

3. Which of the following is equivalent to $\frac{68}{15}$?

A) $4\frac{2}{15}$
B) $4\frac{8}{15}$
C) $3\frac{13}{15}$
D) $3\frac{8}{15}$

4. $\frac{7}{10} - \frac{2}{3} =$

A) $\frac{1}{30}$
B) $\frac{11}{30}$
C) $\frac{5}{30}$
D) $\frac{11}{21}$

5. Which of the following is equivalent to $\frac{2}{5} \div \frac{4}{5}$?

A) $\frac{1}{2}$
B) $\frac{2}{4}$
C) $\frac{5}{4}$
D) $\frac{5}{2}$

6. A rocket traveled 160 kilometers in 360 seconds. On average, how much time did the rocket take to travel each 100 kilometers? (1 minute = 60 seconds)

A) 3 minutes and 45 seconds
B) 4 minutes and 30 seconds
C) 3 minutes and 40 seconds
D) 3 minutes and 45 seconds

7. A jar contains 12 marbles, each marble containing a different number from 1 to 12. If you pull a marble at random from the jar, what's the probability that this number will be less than 5?

A) $\frac{1}{4}$
B) $\frac{1}{3}$
C) $\frac{1}{2}$
D) $\frac{5}{12}$

8. $2(x + 5)x^2 =$

A) $2x^3 + 5x^2$
B) $2x^3 + 10x^2$
C) $2x^3 + 5x$
D) $2x^3 + 10x$

9. Which expression is equivalent to $3x^2 + 7x + 4$?

A) $(3x + 4)(x + 1)$
B) $(3x + 2)(x + 4)$
C) $(2x + 4)(x + 1)$
D) $(x + 4)(3x + 1)$

10. Which expression is equivalent to $8x^{\frac{1}{3}}$?

A) $2\sqrt[3]{x}$
B) $4\sqrt[3]{x}$
C) $8\sqrt[3]{x}$
D) $\frac{1}{\sqrt[3]{8x}}$

11. Which expression is a factor of both $x^2 - 16$ and $x^2 + x - 12$?

A) $x + 4$
B) $x - 4$
C) $x - 3$
D) $x + 2$

12. What is the solution (x, y) to the given system of equations?

$$x + 2y = 9$$
$$2x - y = 3$$

A) $(-1, 6)$
B) $(2, 3.5)$
C) $(0, 4.5)$
D) $(3, 3)$

13. $12x^2 + 5x - 2 = 0$

What are the solutions to the given quadratic equation?

A) $\frac{1}{3}, -2$

B) $-\frac{2}{3}, \frac{1}{4}$

C) $-\frac{5}{4}, \frac{2}{3}$

D) $\frac{1}{2}, -\frac{2}{3}$

14. The table gives the population of the 5 largest cities in a state in the year 2020. Which of the following is closest to the mean population of these cities?

City	Approximate population (thousands)
City A	1,200
City B	800
City C	1,500
City D	900
City E	600

A) 1,200

B) 1,000

C) 800

D) 600

15. In a right triangle, the two legs' length is 6 and 8. What's the value of AD, where AD is perpendicular to BC.

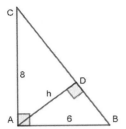

A) 6

B) 5.5

C) 4.8

D) 4

PART 6: ELECTRONICS INFORMATION (EI)

Time: 10 minutes for 15 questions

Select the correct answer from the choices given. This practice subtest reflects the number of questions and time limits you'll encounter on the CAT-ASVAB Electronics Information subtest without any tryout questions.

1. According to Ohm's law, which formula correctly defines the relationship between current, voltage, and resistance?

A) Resistance = Voltage / Current
B) Current = Resistance × Voltage
C) Power = Current + Resistance
D) Voltage = Current - Resistance

2. Current can also be expressed in terms of which unit?

A) volts
B) resistance
C) amperes
D) capacitance

3. A transistor is often used for

A) voltage regulation
B) amplification
C) rectification
D) energy storage

4. Which of the following is the unit of power?

A) Henry
B) Volt
C) Watt
D) Ampere

5. In an inductor, energy is stored in the form of

A) an electric field
B) a magnetic field
C) heat energy
D) electrostatic charge

6. Which of the following controls the current level in a circuit.

A) capacitor
B) resistor
C) inductor
D) transformer

7. In the given circuit, a 50V battery is connected across two series components: a resistor of 20 ohms and a light bulb of 10 ohms. What is the total current flowing through the circuit?

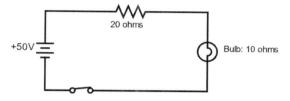

A) 1.33 A
B) 1.50 A
C) 1.67 A
D) 2.0 A

8. Which component is used to convert alternating current (AC) into direct current (DC) by allowing current to pass in only one direction?

A) resistor
B) transistor
C) diode
D) capacitor

9. In electrical systems, AC and DC are abbreviations for

A) alternative conductivity and dynamic charge
B) absolute current and differential charge
C) alternating current and direct current
D) adjustable capacity and DC inverter

10. A device that stores electrical energy in an electric field is called a

A) inductor
B) capacitor
C) transistor
D) relay

11. What is the unit used to measure electrical energy consumption?

A) Watt
B) Kilowatt-hour
C) Volt
D) Ohm

12. The neutral wire in residential wiring is typically colored

A) green
B) white
C) black
D) red

13. Which of the following shows an AC voltage source?

A)

B)

C)

D)

14. Which of the following materials is a poor conductor of electricity?

A) silver
B) rubber
C) gold
D) copper

15. A heater is rated at 1,500 watts. At 120 volts, how much current does it draw?

A) 0.8 amps
B) 12.5 amps
C) 15 amps
D) 20 amps

PART 7: AUTO INFORMATION (AI)

Time: 7 minutes for 10 questions

Select the correct answer from the choices given. This practice subtest reflects the number of questions and time limits you'll encounter on the CAT-ASVAB Auto Information subtest without any tryout questions.

1. In a hydraulic braking system, which of the following is responsible for increasing the force applied to the brakes?

(A) Master cylinder
(B) Hydraulic pump
(C) Radiator
(D) Exhaust system

2. Which engine component is responsible for controlling the opening and closing of the intake and exhaust valves in synchronization with the crankshaft?

A) Carburetor
B) Camshaft
C) Fuel Injector
D) Piston Rings

3. What is the primary function of the pistons in an internal combustion engine?

A) To mix air and fuel for combustion
B) To seal the combustion chamber and prevent leaks
C) To move up and down in the cylinder, converting combustion energy into mechanical work
D) To control the flow of exhaust gases from the engine

4. What is the primary function of a vehicle's transmission?

A) To engage and disengage the engine from the gearbox
B) To transmit power from the driveshaft to the differential
C) To transfer power from the engine to the wheels and adjust speed and torque
D) To allow the differential to distribute power between the wheels

5. Which drivetrain system provides power to the front wheels and is known for offering good traction in wet conditions and more space within the vehicle?

A) Rear-Wheel Drive (RWD)
B) Front-Wheel Drive (FWD)
C) All-Wheel Drive (AWD)
D) Four-Wheel Drive (4WD)

6. What is the primary difference between carburetors and fuel injection systems in vehicles?

A) Carburetors inject fuel directly into the combustion chamber, while fuel injection systems use a vacuum to mix fuel with air.
B) Carburetors create a vacuum to draw fuel into the air stream, while fuel injection systems deliver fuel directly and precisely into the engine.
C) Fuel injection systems are less precise than carburetors in delivering fuel to the engine.
D) Carburetors were used after the 1980s, while fuel injection systems were used earlier.

7. What is the function of the catalytic converter in the exhaust system?

A) It measures oxygen levels in the exhaust gases to adjust the air-fuel ratio.
B) It reduces harmful emissions by converting pollutants into less harmful substances.
C) It filters impurities out of the fuel before it reaches the engine.
D) It recirculates a portion of exhaust gases back into the engine for combustion.

8. The image below shows a brake disc system. Which of the following components is responsible for housing the piston and applying pressure to the brake pads?

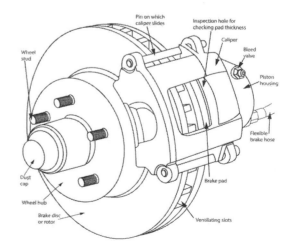

A) Brake Disc
B) Caliper
C) Wheel Hub
D) Ventilating Slots

9. What is the purpose of a vehicle's differential?

A) To automatically change gears based on vehicle speed
B) To transmit power from the engine to the front wheels
C) To allow wheels to rotate at different speeds during turns
D) To disengage the driveshaft from the gearbox

10. In the four-stroke engine cycle, what happens during the compression stroke?

A) The piston moves down, drawing the air-fuel mixture into the cylinder.
B) The piston moves up, compressing the air-fuel mixture to increase its explosive potential.
C) The spark plug ignites the air-fuel mixture, causing it to combust and expand.
D) The piston moves up, expelling burnt gases from the cylinder through the exhaust valve.

PART 8: SHOP INFORMATION (SI)

Time: 6 minutes for 10 questions

Select the correct answer from the choices given. This practice subtest reflects the number of questions and time limits you'll encounter on the CAT-ASVAB Shop Information subtest without any tryout questions.

1. Which tool is typically used to create an indentation before drilling, ensuring the drill bit stays in place?

A) Scriber
B) Punch
C) Needle-nose Pliers
D) Calipers

2. Which tool is best for removing thin layers of wood to smooth and flatten a surface?

A) File
B) Plane
C) Grinder
D) Sandpaper

3. What are calipers primarily used for?

A) Measuring small internal and external dimensions with precision
B) Measuring large, flexible surfaces
C) Drawing straight lines
D) Checking right angles in projects

4. Which tool is adjustable and can grip objects of various sizes?

A) Needle-nose Pliers
B) Locking Pliers
C) Slip-joint Pliers
D) Vise

5. Which of the following tools can be used to most accurately measure the internal diameter of a pipe?

A)

B)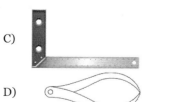

C)

D)

6. Which hammer is typically used for driving nails and also has a feature for pulling nails out?

A) Ball-peen hammer
B) Mallet
C) Claw hammer
D) Sledgehammer

7. Which tool is designed to remove deeply embedded nails that cannot be removed by a claw hammer?

A) Claw Hammer
B) Crowbar
C) Mallet
D) Nail Puller

8. Which of the following screwdriver bits is the correct one for this screw head?

A)

B)

C)

D)

9. What is the function of inside calipers?

A) To measure the external thickness of objects
B) To measure the internal dimensions of objects
C) To measure angles in tight spaces
D) To measure small surface lengths

10 . Which type of wrench provides a secure grip around a bolt or nut by fully enclosing it?

A) Open-end wrench
B) Box-end wrench
C) Adjustable wrench
D) Locking pliers

PART 9: MECHANICAL COMPREHENSION (MC)

Time: 22 minutes for 15 questions

Select the correct answer from the choices given. This practice subtest reflects the number of questions and time limits you'll encounter on the CAT-ASVAB Mechanical Comprehension subtest without any tryout questions.

1. In the pulley system shown, if the weight being lifted is 200 pounds, how much force must be applied to lift the weight?

A) 50 pounds
B) 100 pounds
C) 200 pounds
D) 400 pounds

2. If a metal wrench, a plastic cup, a wool scarf, and a rubber ball are all the same temperature on a cold day, which one will feel the coldest?

A) Wrench
B) Paper cup
C) Scarf
D) Soccer ball

3. An electric motor operates by converting electrical energy into:

A) heat.
B) magnetism.
C) sound.
D) light.

4. If a first-class lever has a resistance arm of 3 feet and an effort arm of 9 feet, what is the mechanical advantage?

A) 2
B) 3
C) 4
D) 1

5. Two equally weighted children are sitting on either side of a seesaw. If one child jumps off, what will happen to the other child?

A) The child will remain stationary.
B) The child will hit the ground hard.
C) The child will rise in the air.
D) The child will stay balanced.

6. Five gears are connected in a series. If Gear #1 turns counterclockwise, which direction will Gear #5 turn?

(A) Clockwise
(B) Counterclockwise
(C) No direction, it stays still.
(D) Faster than Gear #1

7. A ball is dropped from a height of 10 meters. Ignoring air resistance, what will be its approximate speed when it hits the ground?

(A) Cannot be determined because the mass is unknown
(B) Cannot be determined because the time is unknown
(C) 14 m/s
(D) 5 m/s

8. If Gear A has 10 teeth and Gear B has 50 teeth, how many revolutions does Gear B make if Gear A makes 10 revolutions?

(A) 2
(B) 5
(C) 10
(D) 50

9. Two wheels are attached to a shared axle. If the smaller wheel has a diameter of 0.2 m and the larger wheel has a diameter of 0.8 m, what is the mechanical advantage for a force applied to the larger wheel?

(A) 2:1
(B) 4:1
(C) 5:1
(D) 6:1

10. A pair of scissors is based on which simple machine?

(A) Wedge
(B) Pulley
(C) First-class lever
(D) Wheel and axle

11. A boy is using a lever to lift a rock weighing 60 pounds. How much effort is needed if the lever's effort arm is 6 feet while the resistance arm is 2 feet?

A) 60-pound effort
B) 180-pound effort
C) 20-pound effort
D) 30-pound effort

12. The gravitational acceleration on a fictional planet is 4 m/s². If an object weighs 200 N on Earth, which of the following most closely approximates the object's weight on this fictional planet?

(A) 50 N
(B) 80 N
(C) 100 N
(D) 200 N

13. If 100 J of work is done to move an object 5 meters, what was the net force that was applied?

(A) 5 N
(B) 10 N
(C) 20 N
(D) 40 N

14. A person tries to push a heavy box across a rough floor, but the box doesn't move. Which of the following must be true about the applied force and the force of friction?

(A) The applied force is less than the force of static friction.
(B) The applied force is greater than the force of kinetic friction.
(C) The applied force is equal to the force of static friction.
(D) The applied force is equal to the force of kinetic friction.

15. A 600 g block is suspended by two ropes, each positioned equally from the center of the block. What is the approximate tension in each rope?

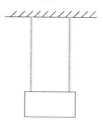

(A) 2.9 N
(B) 3.0 N
(C) 5.9 N
(D) 6.0 N

PART 10: ASSEMBLING OBJECTS (AO)

Time: 18 minutes for 15 questions

Select the correct answer from the choices given. This practice subtest reflects the number of questions and time limits you'll encounter on the CAT-ASVAB Assembling Objects subtest without any tryout questions.

1.

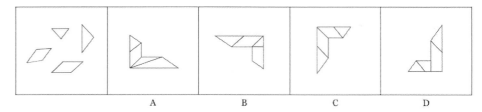

A   B   C   D

2.

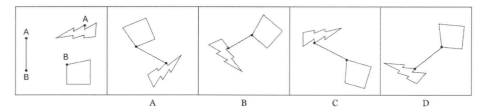

A   B   C   D

3.

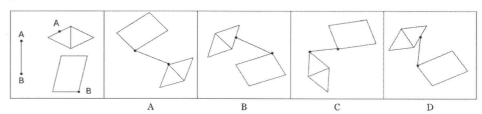

A   B   C   D

4.

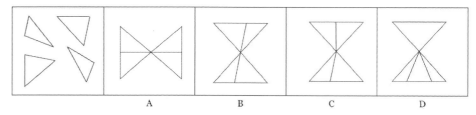

A   B   C   D

5.

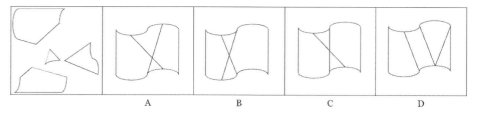

A   B   C   D

6.

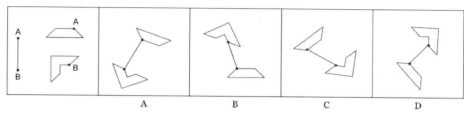

A   B   C   D

7.

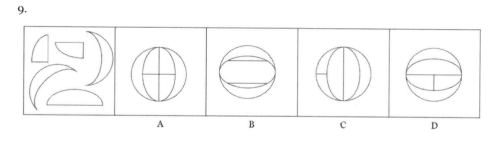

A   B   C   D

8.

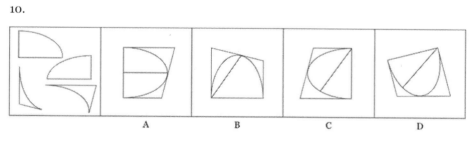

A   B   C   D

9.

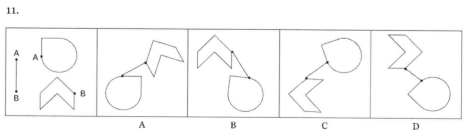

A   B   C   D

10.

A   B   C   D

11.

A   B   C   D

12.

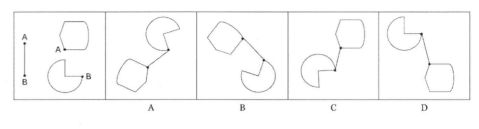

13.

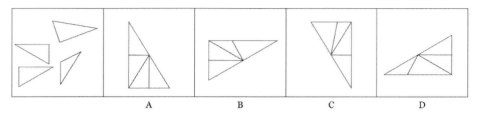

14.

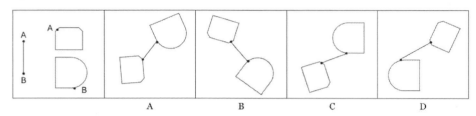

15.

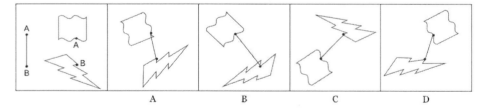

ANSWERS AND EXPLANATIONS—PRACTICE TEST 1

Part 1: General Science (GS)

1. C) Photosynthesis. Explanation: During photosynthesis, plants use carbon dioxide and release oxygen as a byproduct.

2. C) ATP. Explanation: ATP (Adenosine Triphosphate) is the primary molecule that stores and transfers energy in cells.

3. B) Carbohydrates. Explanation: Carbohydrates are the body's primary source of energy, broken down into glucose during digestion, which is used to fuel cellular activities.

4. C) Cell membrane. Explanation: The cell membrane is a semi-permeable barrier that surrounds the cell, controlling the movement of substances in and out of the cell, thereby maintaining the cell's internal environment.

5. A) Force applied over a distance. Explanation: Work is done when a force is applied to an object, causing it to move. It is calculated as $W = Fd$.

6. B) Light bouncing off a surface. Explanation: Reflection happens when light hits a surface and bounces back at the same angle it hit, like when light reflects off a mirror.

7. C) Hertz. Explanation: Frequency is measured in Hertz (Hz), which represents the number of wave cycles that pass a point per second.

8. A) Amplitude. Explanation: The amplitude of a sound wave determines its loudness. Greater amplitude results in louder sounds, while smaller amplitude results in softer sounds.

9. B) Ability of an atom to attract electrons. Explanation: Electronegativity refers to how strongly an atom attracts electrons in a chemical bond. Elements on the right side of the periodic table typically have higher electronegativity.

10. C) Above 7. Explanation: Bases have a pH greater than 7 and release hydroxide ions (OH^-) in water. Strong bases like sodium hydroxide can have pH values near 14.

11. B) A mixture where substances are not uniformly distributed. Explanation: In heterogeneous mixtures, components remain distinct and can be physically separated, such as oil and water or a salad.

12. D) Weathering. Explanation: Weathering refers to the breaking down of rocks into smaller particles through physical, chemical, or biological processes.

13. C) A meteorite reaches Earth's surface. Explanation: A meteor burns up in Earth's atmosphere, while a meteorite is what remains if it reaches the earth's surface.

14. C) Rainbow. Explanation: Rainbows occur when light is refracted and dispersed through water droplets in the atmosphere.

15. D) Saturn. Explanation: Saturn is well-known for its bright and extensive system of rings, composed of ice and rock particles.

Part 2: Arithmetic Reasoning (AR)

1. A) $20,700. Explanation: First, calculate the total amount paid through monthly payments. Since the payments last 4 years, and there are 12 months in a year, the total number of payments is: $4 \times 12 = 48$ months.

   Now, calculate the total from the monthly payments: $48 \times 400 = 19,200$.

   Finally, add the down payment: $19,200 + 1,500 = 20,700$.

2. A) 6. Explanation: To find out how many slices are left, we first calculate how many slices each person bought:

   The customer buys $\frac{1}{3} \times 24 = 8$ slices. The party host buys $\frac{1}{4} \times 24 = 6$ slices. The neighbor buys $\frac{1}{6} \times 24 = 4$ slices. Now, add up the slices bought: $8 + 6 + 4 = 18$. So the chef is left with 24 - 18 = 6 slices.

3. C) $18.00. Explanation: The saving on each can of paint is: 30.00 - 27.00 = 3.00. Since Jake bought 6 cans of paint, the total amount saved is: $3.00 \times 6 = 18.00$.

4. B) $230. Explanation: To calculate the percentage increase, find 15% of $200: $0.15 \times 200 = 30$.

Now, add the increase to the original amount: $200 + 30 = 230$. Thus, Jake's new monthly grocery bill is $230.

5. A) $146.50. Explanation: First, calculate the total amount: $150.75 + 142.50 + 146.25 = 439.50$.

Now, divide the total by 3 to find the average: $\frac{439.50}{3} = 146.50$.

6. A) 6 meters. Explanation: Let the width be x. The length is then $x + 4$.

The area of the rectangle is given by: Area = length × width.

Substitute the values into the equation: $60 = (x + 4) \times x$. Expand and simplify the equation:

$$60 = x^2 + 4x$$
$$x^2 + 4x - 60 = 0$$
$$(x - 6)(x + 10) = 0$$

Thus, x = 6 or x = -10. Since a width cannot be negative, x = 6. Therefore, the width is 6 meters.

7. C) 50 miles per hour. Explanation: To calculate the speed, use the formula $\text{speed} = \frac{\text{distance}}{\text{time}}$. The distance is 200 miles, and the time is 4 hours, so: $\text{speed} = \frac{200}{4} = 50$ miles per hour.

8. C) 13 hours. Explanation: To calculate the time it will take, use the formula: $\text{time} = \frac{\text{distance}}{\text{speed}} = \frac{800}{60} \approx 13.33$ hours.

Thus, it will take Jane approximately 13 hours to complete the trip.

9. B) 180,000. Explanation: Let the original prediction be x. So: $x + \frac{1}{3}x = 240{,}000$. This simplifies to: $\frac{4}{3}x = 240{,}000$.

Hence: $x = \frac{240{,}000 \times 3}{4} = 180{,}000$. The original predicted population would is 180,000.

10. A) Three 30-pound bags at $75 each. Explanation:

- Option A: $3 \times 75 = 225$
- Option B: $6 \times 38 = 228$
- Option C: $9 \times 26 = 234$
- Option D: $90 \times 4 = 360$

The cheapest option is Option A.

11. A) 200. Explanation: Let Sara's apples be x. Tim initially has $x + 300$.

After selling 100 apples, we have the following relationship: $(x + 300) - 100 = 2x$, or $x + 200 = 2x$.

Subtract x from both sides: $200 = x$. Thus, Sara has 200 apples.

12. C) 720 ounces. Explanation: First, convert the 10 gallons to ounces: 40 gallons = $40 \times 128 = 5120$ ounces.

Next, calculate how much juice will be used for the 550 bottles: $550 \times 8 = 4400$ ounces.

Now, subtract the amount used from the total: $5120 - 4400 = 720$ ounces.

13. B) 3. Explanation: First, subtract the snacks left from the total to find how many snacks were eaten: $75 - 15 = 60$.

Now, divide the number of snacks eaten by the number of children: $\frac{60}{20} = 3$. Thus, each child ate 3 snacks on average.

14. A) 50 inches. Explanation: Use the Pythagorean Theorem: $a^2 + b^2 = c^2$, where a and b are the two legs of a right-angle triangle, and the c is the hypotenuse. Substitute the values:

$$40^2 + 30^2 = c^2 \implies 1600 + 900 = c^2 \implies 2500 = c^2 \implies c = \sqrt{2500} = 50$$

Thus, the diagonal length is 50 inches.

15. A) 16 days. Explanation: To find how many days the water will last, divide the total amount of water by the amount the dog rinks each day: $\frac{12}{\frac{3}{4}} = 12 \times \frac{4}{3} = 16$. Thus, the water will last 16 days.

Part 3: Word Knowledge (WK)

1. C) brave. "Undaunted" means not intimidated or discouraged by difficulty, making "brave" the best synonym.

2. B) final. "Immutable" means unchanging or permanent, so "final" is the closest synonym.

3. C) clear. "Lucid" means expressed clearly and easily understood, making "clear" the best choice.

4. B) weaken. "Enervate" means to sap or drain someone of energy, making "weaken" the correct choice.

5. B) aware. "Cognizant" refers to being aware or mindful of something.

6. B) wise. "Sagacious" describes someone who is wise, discerning, or knowledgeable.

7. B) gentle. "Benign" refers to something that is harmless and gentle, the opposite of harmful or aggressive.

8. A) determination. "Tenacity" means the quality of being determined or persistent.

9. B) reduce. "Mitigate" means to make something less severe or reduce its impact.

10. C) precise. "Meticulous" means very careful and precise, particularly about details.

11. B) diligent. "Assiduous" describes someone who is hardworking and persistent.

12. A) foolish. "Sagacious" means wise or showing good judgment, so the antonym is "foolish."

13. A) threatening. "Ominous" suggests something bad or threatening is likely to happen.

14. B) spacious. "Capacious" describes something that has a lot of space or room.

15. B) dangerous. "Precarious" refers to something that is unstable or risky.

Part 4: Paragraph Comprehension (PC)

1. C) To explain the goal of the dog teams and highlight the difficulties they faced due to unclear instructions.

Explanation: The passage primarily outlines the goal of the dog teams, which was to bring Scott and his companions back in time. It then shifts focus to the challenge caused by unclear instructions, which placed the leaders of the dog teams in a difficult position. Therefore, option C best captures the purpose of the passage.

2. C) They were cunning and skilled at covering their tracks.

Explanation: The passage indicates that the horse thieves demonstrated expertise and cunning in hiding and moving the stolen animals in different directions to cover their trail, making it difficult to track them.

3. D) Comfort and ease provided by the hut in the Antarctic

Explanation: The passage uses "Davos", "Berkeley Hotel" and "Ritz" to draw a comparison, emphasizing that the hut at Cape Evans, although in the Antarctic, provides comfort and ease similar to well-known luxurious accommodations.

4. D) Ike Clanton's overconfidence in his safety

Explanation: Ike Clanton left his weapons behind because he believed that he was safe and that the Earps would not dare to attack him. This action shows his overconfidence and false sense of security.

5. A) The river they were traveling on was known and traveled.

Explanation: The author contrasts the current situation with the previous hardships by noting that they were now on a known and traveled river, making navigation easier and reducing the challenges they faced.

6. B) Education and environment play a significant role in shaping a person's abilities.

Explanation: The author argues that the differences in talents and abilities among individuals are largely due to habit, custom, and education rather than natural talents, suggesting that environment and upbringing significantly shape one's abilities.

7. B) Practical utility determines the value of true ideas.

Explanation: The author argues that the value of truth is determined by its practical usefulness in specific situations. If an idea helps in a particular circumstance, like finding a house to save someone, it holds value. Therefore, B is the correct choice.

8. B) Harmful

Explanation: "Malign" refers to something that is harmful or destructive, in this case, describing the influence of the winds on the environment. The word's negative connotation is evident from the context, making "harmful" the correct answer.

9. C) Law is essential to achieving true liberty.

Explanation: The author argues that law is crucial to achieving liberty for everyone in a society. While law may restrain individuals, it also protects them from arbitrary oppression, ensuring a broader sense of freedom. Therefore, C is the correct choice.

10. C) By using examples of flawed reasoning based on superficial associations.

Explanation: The author illustrates that crowds reason through weak analogies and flawed logic, as shown in examples like equating transparency with melting or thinking bravery can be acquired by eating a heart. These examples demonstrate reasoning based on superficial associations, making C the correct answer.

Part 5: Mathematics Knowledge (MK)

1. B) 3. Explanation: $\frac{84}{28} = 3$

2. B) 136. Explanation: $17 \times 8 = 136$

3. B) $4\frac{8}{15}$. Explanation: $\frac{68}{15} = 4\frac{8}{15}$

4. A) $\frac{1}{30}$. Explanation: The least common denominator (LCD) of 10 and 3 is 30.

$$\frac{7}{10} = \frac{7 \times 3}{10 \times 3} = \frac{21}{30}. \quad \frac{2}{3} = \frac{2 \times 10}{3 \times 10} = \frac{20}{30}.$$ Subtract the Fractions: $\frac{21}{30} - \frac{20}{30} = \frac{1}{30}.$

5. A) $\frac{1}{2}$. Explanation: $\frac{2}{5} \div \frac{4}{5} = \frac{2}{5} \times \frac{5}{4} = \frac{2 \times 5}{5 \times 4} = \frac{2}{4} = \frac{1}{2}.$

6. A) 3 minutes and 45 seconds. Explanation: Average speed $= \frac{160 \text{ kilometers}}{360 \text{ seconds}} = \frac{4}{9}$ km/second.

Convert average speed to time taken to travel 100 kilometers:

$$\text{Time for 100 km} = \frac{100 \text{ kilometers}}{\frac{4}{9} \text{ km/second}} = 225 \text{ seconds}$$

Convert 225 seconds into minutes and seconds: the integer portion of 225/60 is 3.

Seconds remaining $= 225 - (3 \times 60) = 45$. Therefore, the average time to travel 100 kilometers is: 3 minutes and 45 seconds.

7. B) $\frac{1}{3}$ Explanation: Numbers less than 5: 1,2,3,4 (4 numbers).

Total numbers: 12. Probability $= \frac{4}{12} = \frac{1}{3}.$

8. B) $2x^3 + 10x^2$. Explanation: $2(x + 5)x^2 = 2x \cdot x^2 + 2 \cdot 5 \cdot x^2 = 2x^3 + 10x^2.$
9. A) $(3x + 4)(x + 1)$. Explanation: Factor $3x^2 + 7x + 4 \Longrightarrow 3x^2 + 7x + 4 = (3x + 4)(x + 1).$

10. C) $8\sqrt[3]{x}$. Note that $(8x)^{\frac{1}{3}} = 2\sqrt[3]{x}$ while $8x^{\frac{1}{3}} = 8\sqrt[3]{x}.$

11. A) $x + 4$. Explanation: Factor $x^2 - 16$: $x^2 - 16 = (x - 4)(x + 4)$.

Factor $x^2 + x - 12$: $x^2 + x - 12 = (x - 3)(x + 4)$. The common factor is $x + 4$.

12. D) (3, 3). Explanation: Solve for y in the second equation: $2x - y = 3 \Rightarrow y = 2x - 3$

Substitute y into the first equation: $x + 2(2x - 3) = 9 \Rightarrow x + 4x - 6 = 9$
$$\Rightarrow 5x - 6 = 9 \Rightarrow 5x = 15 \Rightarrow x = 3$$

Substitute x back into the equation for y: $y = 2(3) - 3 \Rightarrow y = 3$. Solution: $(x, y) = (3,3)$.

13. B) $-\frac{2}{3}, \frac{1}{4}$. Explanation: Use formula: $x = \frac{-b \pm \sqrt{b^2 - 4ac}}{2a}$, where $a = 12$, $b = 5$, $c = -2$.

$x = \frac{-5 \pm \sqrt{5^2 - 4 \cdot 12 \cdot (-2)}}{2 \cdot 12} = \frac{-5 \pm \sqrt{25 + 96}}{24} = \frac{-5 \pm \sqrt{121}}{24} = \frac{-5 \pm 11}{24}$. Hence, $x = \frac{1}{4}$ or $x = -\frac{2}{3}$.

14. B) 1,000. Explanation: Mean population $= \frac{1,200 + 800 + 1,500 + 900 + 60}{5} = \frac{5,000}{5} = 1,000$.

15. C) 4.8. Explanation: First, determine the hypotenuse BC of the right triangle ABC using the Pythagorean theorem: $BC = \sqrt{6^2 + 8^2} = \sqrt{36 + 64} = \sqrt{100} = 10$. Now, use the area approach to find the length of AD. The area of $\triangle ABC$ can be calculated in two ways.

1. Using the legs: $Area = \frac{1}{2} \times 6 \times 8 = \frac{1}{2} \times 48 = 24$.

2. Using the hypotenuse and altitude AD : $Area = \frac{1}{2} \times BC \times AD$. Since $BC = 10$, we know $24 = \frac{1}{2} \times 10 \times AD$. Hence, $24 = 5 \times AD \Rightarrow AD = 4.8$.

Part 6: Electronics Information (EI)

1. A) Resistance = Voltage / Current. Explanation: Ohm's Law defines the relationship between voltage (V), current (I), and resistance (R) as $V = I \times R$. Rearranging this formula gives us $R = V / I$. This makes Option A correct.

2. C) amperes. Explanation: Current is measured in amperes (A), which represents the flow of electric charge per unit time. Volts is incorrect, as volts measure voltage, not current. Resistance is measured in ohms (Ω). Capacitance is measured in farads (F).

3. B) amplification. Explanation: A transistor is often used for amplification of signals. A) is incorrect because transistors are not primarily used for voltage regulation. C) and D) do not describe the main functions of transistors.

4. C) Watt. Explanation: Power is measured in watts (W). A) measures inductance, B) measures voltage, D) measures current.

5. B) a magnetic field. Explanation: An inductor stores energy in a magnetic field when current flows through it. A) and D) are incorrect, as inductors do not store energy in electric fields or charges. C) describes energy dissipation, not storage.

6. B) resistor. Explanation: A resistor is designed to limit or control the flow of electrical current.
A) Capacitor stores electrical energy and does not limit current. C) Inductor stores energy in a magnetic field and opposes changes in current, but not in the same way as a resistor. D) Transformer changes voltage levels and does not limit current directly.

7. C) 1.67 A. Explanation:

1. The two components (resistor and bulb) are in series, so the total resistance (R_{total}) is the sum of both resistances: $R_{\text{total}} = R_1 + R_2 = 20\,\Omega + 10\,\Omega = 30\,\Omega$

2. Using Ohm's Law to find the total current in the circuit: $I = \frac{V}{R_{\text{total}}} = \frac{50\,V}{30\,\Omega} \approx 1.67\,A$

8. C) diode. Explanation: A diode is a semiconductor device that allows current to flow in only one direction, making it suitable for rectification (converting AC to DC). A) Resistor: Incorrect; it limits current but does not allow unidirectional flow. B) Transistor: Incorrect; it controls and amplifies current rather than rectifying AC. D) Capacitor stores energy and does not perform rectification.

9. C) alternating current and direct current. Explanation: AC stands for alternating current, where the direction of flow changes periodically, and DC stands for direct current, where the flow is unidirectional.

10. B) capacitor. Explanation: A capacitor stores electrical energy in an electric field. A) stores energy in a magnetic field. C) is used for amplification or switching. D) is a type of switch.

11. B) Kilowatt-hour. Explanation: Kilowatt-hour (kWh) is the unit for measuring electrical energy consumption. A) measures power. C) and D) measure voltage and resistance, respectively.

12. B) white. Explanation: The neutral wire is typically white. A) Green is for ground. C) Black is for hot/live. D) Red is also used as a live wire in some applications.

13. C) ⊘. Explanation:

   A) ⊣⊢ represents a DC voltage source, usually shown with a longer line (positive) and a shorter line (negative) to indicate polarity.
   B) ⊣⊢ also represents a DC voltage source without the positive and negative markings.
   C) ⊘ represents an AC voltage source, typically shown with a sine wave symbol, which indicates alternating current.
   D) ⊣⊬ is a variable capacitor symbol, not a voltage source.

14. B) rubber. Explanation: B) Rubber is a poor conductor of electricity. A) Silver, C) Gold, and D) Copper are all good conductors of electricity, which allow current to pass through them easily.

15. B) 12.5 amps. Explanation: Using the power formula $P = V \times I$:

$$I = \frac{P}{V} = \frac{1,500\,W}{120\,V} = 12.5\,A$$

Part 7: Auto Information (AI)

1. (A) Master cylinder. Explanation: The master cylinder in a hydraulic braking system increases the force applied to the brakes by converting the mechanical force from the brake pedal into hydraulic pressure. The hydraulic pump, while important in hydraulic systems, is not directly involved in braking. The radiator cools the engine, and the exhaust system removes waste gases from the combustion process.

2. B) Camshaft. Explanation: The camshaft controls the timing of the intake and exhaust valves, ensuring they open and close at the correct times during the engine cycle. This synchronization with the crankshaft is critical for efficient engine performance. The carburetor (in older vehicles) and fuel injectors manage the air-fuel mixture, while piston rings seal the piston and cylinder, but they do not control valve timing like the camshaft does.

3. C) To move up and down in the cylinder, converting combustion energy into mechanical work

Explanation: The pistons in an internal combustion engine move up and down inside the cylinders. They are driven by the expansion of gases during combustion, and this movement is then converted into mechanical work that powers the crankshaft and, ultimately, the vehicle. The other options describe the roles of different components, but the pistons' primary function is converting combustion energy into mechanical motion.

4. C) To transfer power from the engine to the wheels and adjust speed and torque

Explanation: The transmission is responsible for transferring power from the engine to the wheels, adjusting the torque and speed to ensure the engine operates within its optimal range. This allows the vehicle to accelerate and move efficiently under different driving conditions.

5. B) Front-Wheel Drive (FWD). Explanation: In a Front-Wheel Drive (FWD) system, power is sent to the front wheels, which are responsible for both steering and driving the vehicle. FWD systems offer good traction in wet conditions and provide more interior space because they do not require a rear driveshaft.

6. B) Carburetors create a vacuum to draw fuel into the air stream, while fuel injection systems deliver fuel directly and precisely into the engine.

Explanation: Carburetors use a vacuum to mix fuel with air and are less efficient than fuel injection systems, which use sensors and electronically control fuel delivery to optimize performance, improve efficiency, and reduce emissions. Fuel injection systems have replaced carburetors in modern vehicles.

7. B) It reduces harmful emissions by converting pollutants into less harmful substances.

Explanation: The catalytic converter is responsible for reducing harmful emissions by using chemical reactions to convert pollutants like carbon monoxide and nitrogen oxides into less harmful substances such as carbon dioxide and water vapor. This is crucial for meeting environmental emission standards.

8. B) Caliper. Explanation: In the brake disc system, the caliper houses the piston and applies pressure to the brake pads when the brake pedal is pressed. This pressure forces the pads against the brake disc (rotor), creating friction to slow or stop the vehicle. The other components, such as the brake disc and ventilating slots, have different roles in the braking process.

9. C) To allow wheels to rotate at different speeds during turns

Explanation: The differential splits the power from the driveshaft between the wheels and allows them to rotate at different speeds, especially important when turning. This ensures smooth handling and traction, as the inside wheels need to rotate slower than the outside wheels.

10. B) The piston moves up, compressing the air-fuel mixture to increase its explosive potential.

Explanation: During the compression stroke, the intake valve closes, and the piston moves back up, compressing the air-fuel mixture. This compression makes the mixture more volatile, increasing the power produced when it's ignited in the power stroke.

Part 8: Shop Information (SI)

1. B) Punch. Explanation: A punch is designed to create a small indentation on a material like wood or metal, helping the drill bit stay in the correct spot. A scriber (A) makes fine lines on metal or plastic, needle-nose pliers (C) are used for gripping small objects, and calipers (D) are precision tools for measuring dimensions, but none of these are used to create indentations for drilling.

2. B) Plane. Explanation: A plane is designed specifically for removing thin layers of wood, smoothing, and flattening surfaces. It is ideal for tasks like evening out rough spots or reducing the thickness of wood. A grinder (C) is typically used for metalworking and shaping metal surfaces, while a file (A) is for precision shaping and finishing. Sandpaper (D) is used for fine smoothing but doesn't remove material as efficiently as a plane.

3. A) Measuring small internal and external dimensions with precision. Explanation: Calipers are precision instruments used to measure the internal or external dimensions of objects with a high degree of accuracy. They are commonly used in metalworking and engineering for tasks that require precise measurements. They are not suitable for measuring large surfaces or for checking angles, as indicated in the incorrect options.

4. C) Slip-joint Pliers. Explanation: Slip-joint pliers have an adjustable pivot point, allowing them to grip objects of different sizes, making them versatile for a range of tasks. Needle-nose pliers (A) are for precise gripping, locking pliers (B) can hold objects tightly in place, and a vise (D) is a stationary tool used to secure objects, but none are as adjustable as slip-joint pliers.

5. A) Vernier caliper. Explanation: The Vernier caliper (A) is the correct tool for accurately measuring the internal diameter of a pipe. It is designed for precise measurements of both internal and external diameters, as well as depths. The sliding scale on the caliper allows for exact readings, making it ideal for detailed work like pipe measurement.

   B) A ruler is less accurate and cannot measure internal diameters effectively due to its flat design.

   C) A square is primarily used for checking angles and squareness, not for measuring diameters.

   D) Outside calipers is designed to measure external diameters, not internal diameters. Even an internal caliper is less precise than a Vernier caliper since an internal caliper requires manual adjustment and estimation for the final measurement.

6. C) Claw hammer. Explanation: The claw hammer is a versatile tool that features a flat face for driving nails and a claw on the opposite side for pulling them out. This dual-purpose functionality makes it ideal for carpentry and general construction work. A ball-peen hammer (A) is designed for metalwork, a mallet (B) is used for soft strikes, and a sledgehammer (D) is for heavy-duty demolition tasks.

7. D) Nail Puller. Explanation: A nail puller is specifically designed with a V-shaped notch to remove deeply embedded nails, especially when a claw hammer cannot reach or grip them effectively. A claw hammer (A) is often

used to remove nails, but when nails are embedded too deeply, a nail puller is more efficient. A crowbar (B) is used for prying materials apart, and a mallet (C) is for softer strikes.

8. C) Torx bit. Explanation: The screw head shown is a Torx head, characterized by its six-point star shape. The Torx bit (A) is the correct tool for this type of screw. Torx screws provide better torque transfer and reduce the risk of stripping.

> A) is a Phillips bit, designed for cross-shaped screws, making it incompatible with a Torx screw head.

> B) is a flathead bit, used for slotted screws, which would not fit a star-shaped screw.

> D) is a hex bit, used for hexagonal screws, and also not suitable for a Torx screw.

9. B) To measure the internal dimensions of objects. Explanation: Inside calipers are designed specifically to measure the internal dimensions of objects, such as the diameter of holes or the inside width of slots. They are not meant for external measurements, angles, or simple length measurements, which are handled by other tools like outside calipers, protractors, and rulers.

10. B) Box-end wrench. Explanation: A box-end wrench has a closed loop that completely encloses a nut or bolt, reducing the risk of rounding off the edges and providing a more secure grip. An open-end wrench (A) has U-shaped ends that allow access to the fastener from the side, but they don't fully enclose it. Adjustable wrenches (C) and Locking pliers (D) are versatile but don't offer the same enclosed grip as a box-end wrench.

Part 9: Mechanical Comprehension (MC)

1. C) 200 pounds. Explanation: This is a fixed pulley system, where the pulley is only used to change the direction of the force applied but does not provide a mechanical advantage. In a fixed pulley, the amount of force needed to lift the load is equal to the weight of the load. Therefore, to lift the 200-pound weight, the applied force must be:

$$\text{Effort} = \text{Load} = 200 \text{ pounds}$$

2. A) Wrench. Explanation: Although all the objects are at the same temperature, metal is a better conductor of heat than other materials like plastic, wool, or rubber. The wrench will conduct heat away from your hand more quickly, making it feel colder even though its temperature is the same as the other objects.

3. B) magnetism. Explanation: Electric motors work by using the magnetic fields generated by electrical current to create mechanical motion. Options A (heat), C (sound), and D (light) are not related to the working principle of electric motors.

4. B) 3. Explanation: The mechanical advantage of a lever is calculated by dividing the length of the effort arm by the length of the resistance arm. In this case, $\frac{9}{3} = 3$. Therefore, the mechanical advantage is 3.

5. B) The child will fall to the ground. Explanation: Once one child jumps off the seesaw, the side where the remaining child is seated becomes heavier than the other, now empty side. Because the seesaw is no longer balanced, the heavier side (with the remaining child) will fall to the ground. The imbalance of weight causes the seesaw to tip in favor of the heavier side.

6. (B) Counterclockwise. Explanation: In a series of connected gears, each adjacent gear rotates in the opposite direction. If Gear #1 turns counterclockwise, the adjacent gears will alternate in direction. So:

> Gear #2 will turn clockwise.
> Gear #3 will turn counterclockwise.
> Gear #4 will turn clockwise.
> Gear #5 will turn counterclockwise. Therefore, the correct answer should be (B) Counterclockwise.

7. (C) 14 m/s. Explanation: The speed of a falling object can be calculated using the equation: $v = \sqrt{2gh}$, where g is the acceleration due to gravity (approximately 9.8 m/s^2), and h is the height the object falls from. Plugging in the values: $v = \sqrt{2 \times 9.8 \text{ m/s}^2 \times 10 \text{ m}} = \sqrt{196} \approx 14 \text{ m/s}$. The mass of the object does not affect the speed in free fall, which is why choices A is incorrect.

8. (A) 2. Explanation: The number of revolutions is inversely proportional to the number of teeth. The formula is:

$$\text{Revolutions of Gear B} \times \text{Teeth of Gear B} = \text{Teeth of Gear A} \times \text{Revolutions of Gear A}$$

which is equivalent to: $\text{Revolutions of Gear B} = \frac{\text{Teeth of Gear A}}{\text{Teeth of Gear B}} \times \text{Revolutions of Gear A}$

Substituting the values: Revolutions of Gear B $= \frac{10}{50} \times 10 = 2$

Therefore, Gear B will make 2 revolutions when Gear A makes 10 revolutions.

9. (B) 4:1. Explanation: The mechanical advantage of a wheel system is the ratio of the diameters (or radii) of the two wheels. In this case, the larger wheel is 4 times the diameter of the smaller one, so the mechanical advantage is 4:1. This means the larger wheel allows a person to exert one-fourth the force needed to move a load compared to the smaller wheel.

10. (C) First-class lever. Explanation: Scissors are a type of first-class lever. The fulcrum, or pivot point, is located between the input force (where your hands squeeze the handles) and the output force (the blades cutting). This arrangement amplifies the input force, making it easier to cut materials with less effort.

11. C) 20-pound effort. Explanation: The lever's mechanical advantage can be found by dividing the length of the effort arm by the length of the resistance arm: Mechanical Advantage $= \frac{\text{Effort Arm}}{\text{Resistance Arm}} = \frac{6}{2} = 3$

Now, the mechanical advantage tells us how much the effort is reduced. To find the required effort, divide the load (60 pounds) by the mechanical advantage (3): Effort $= \frac{\text{Load}}{\text{Mechanical Advantage}} = \frac{60}{3} = 20$ pounds

So, the boy needs to apply a 20-pound effort to lift the 60-pound rock.

12. (B) 80 N. Explanation: Weight is calculated using $W = m \times g$, where W is weight, m is mass, and g is gravitational acceleration. On Earth, $W = 200$ N, and let's approximate g on earth to be 10, so the mass is $m \approx \frac{200}{10} = 20$ kg. On the fictional planet, the gravitational acceleration is $4 \, m/s^2$, so the weight on is $W = m \times 4 = 20 \times 4 \approx 80$ N.

13. (B) 20 N. Explanation: Work is calculated using $W = F \times d$ where W is work, F is force, and d is distance. Rearranging the formula to solve for force gives $F = \frac{W}{d}$. In this case, $W = 100$ J and $d = 5$ m, so $F = \frac{100}{5} = 20$ N. The net force applied to the object was 20 N.

14. (A) The applied force is less than the force of static friction. Explanation: Since the box doesn't move, the applied force must be less than the static friction force, which prevents the motion. The static friction force must be overcome for the object to start moving. Once it moves, kinetic friction takes over.

15. (B) 3.0 N. Explanation: The weight of the block is $W = mg$ where $m = 0.6$ kg and $g = 9.8 \, m/s^2$. The total weight is $0.6 \, kg \times 9.8 \, m/s^2 = 5.88 \, N$, and since the block is equally supported by two ropes, each rope supports half the weight. So, $5.88/2 = 2.94$ N, or approximately 3.0 N.

Part 10: Assembling Objects (AO)

1. C

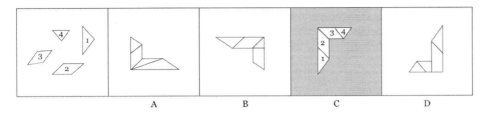

2. D

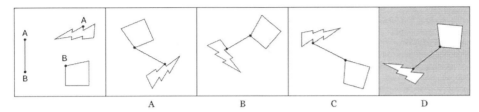

3. B

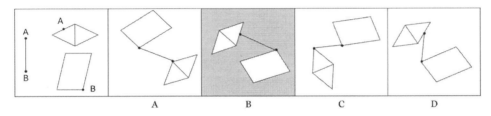

4. B

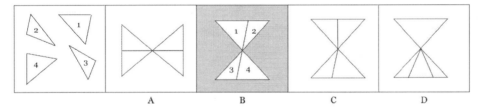

5. A

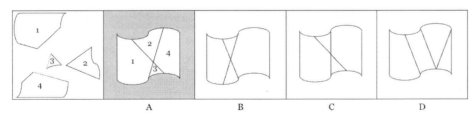

6. C

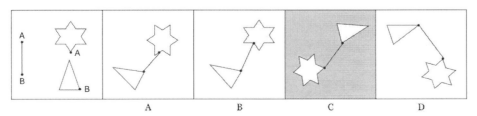

7. A

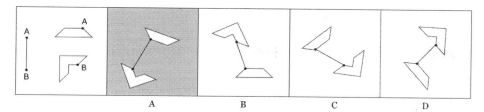

8. A

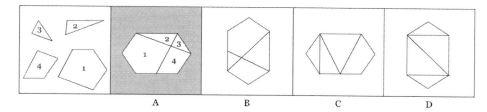

9. D

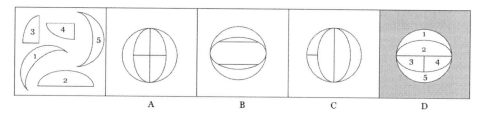

10. A

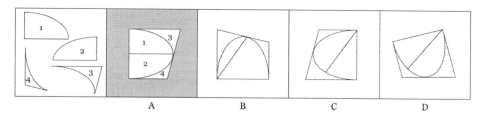

11. C

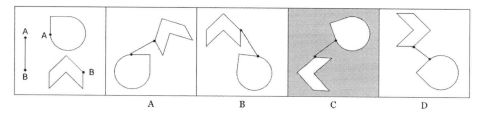

12. A

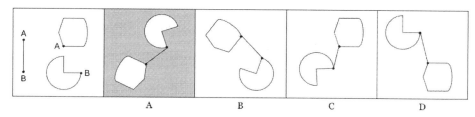

13.

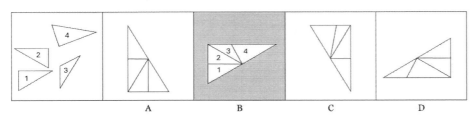

14. D

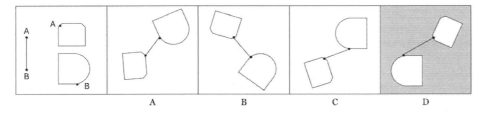

15. C

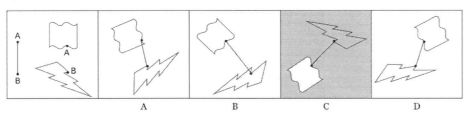

ASVAB Practice Test 2

Part 1: General Science (GS)

Time: 12 minutes for 15 questions

Select the correct answer from the choices given. This practice subtest reflects the number of questions and time limits you'll encounter on the CAT-ASVAB General Science subtest without any tryout questions.

1. What is the layer of the Earth directly below the crust called?

A) Mantle
B) Outer core
C) Inner core
D) Lithosphere

2. What process causes the formation of mountains like the Himalayas?

A) Volcanic activity
B) Divergent boundaries
C) Convergent boundaries
D) Subduction zones

3. In a chemical change, what happens to molecules?

A) Molecules stay the same but their shape changes
B) Bonds between atoms are broken and new ones are formed
C) Molecules increase in size
D) Nothing changes

4. What is a compound?

A) A single type of atom
B) A substance made of two or more different elements chemically bonded
C) A homogeneous mixture
D) A group of identical molecules

5. Which of the following is an example of a homogeneous mixture?

A) Oil and water
B) Saltwater
C) Sand and gravel
D) Salad

6. Which unit is used to measure temperature in the metric system?

A) Celsius
B) Kelvin
C) Fahrenheit
D) Newton

7. What is the smallest unit of the metric prefixes listed below?

A) Centi-
B) Milli-
C) Micro-
D) Nano-

8. What is the primary difference between mass and weight?

A) Mass changes with gravity
B) Weight is constant regardless of location
C) Mass is the amount of matter, weight is the force of gravity on that mass
D) Weight depends on volume

9. If an object has a mass of 10 kg, what is its weight on Earth? (Assume gravity = 9.8 m/s^2)

A) 10 N
B) 9.8 N
C) 98 N
D) 100 N

10. What does velocity measure in physics?

A) Speed
B) Speed with direction
C) Acceleration
D) Distance

11. How does displacement differ from distance?

A) Distance considers direction
B) Displacement measures how far something moved overall
C) Displacement considers the overall change in position
D) Distance always equals displacement

12. Which term refers to organisms that produce their own food?

A) Consumers
B) Producers
C) Decomposers
D) Carnivores

13. What is the function of white blood cells?

A) Transport oxygen
B) Break down food
C) Fight infections
D) Produce hormones

14. Which part of the plant cell is responsible for photosynthesis?

A) Mitochondria
B) Ribosomes
C) Chloroplasts
D) Nucleus

15. Which process describes the copying of DNA before cell division?

A) Translation
B) Transcription
C) Replication
D) Mutation

PART 2: ARITHMETIC REASONING (AR)

Time: 55 minutes for 15 questions

Select the correct answer from the choices given. This practice subtest reflects the number of questions and time limits you'll encounter on the CAT-ASVAB Arithmetic Reasoning subtest without any tryout questions.

1. A bookstore has 30 books in stock. A school purchases one-fifth of the books, a library purchases one-third of the books, and an individual buyer purchases one-sixth of the books. How many books does the bookstore have left?

A) 15
B) 12
C) 9
D) 6

2. A garden sprinkler normally uses 12 liters of water per minute, but due to a leak, it is using 10% more water than usual. How many liters of water does the sprinkler use per minute now?

A) 13.2 liters
B) 14.0 liters
C) 12.5 liters
D) 12.2 liters

3. A culture of bacteria grew by 60,000 cells over a 12-hour period, which was 25% less than the scientists expected. How many cells did the scientists originally expect to grow?

A) 70,000
B) 80,000
C) 75,000
D) 90,000

4. A factory worker used to complete a task in 40 minutes. After improving efficiency, the time to complete the task decreased by 25%. How long does it now take the worker to complete the task?

A) 25 minutes
B) 30 minutes
C) 35 minutes
D) 20 minutes

5. A swimming pool is 50 meters long. If a swimmer wants to swim a total distance of 1 kilometer, how many laps must they complete?

A) 15
B) 18
C) 20
D) 25

6. Your boat uses gasoline at the rate of 15 miles per gallon. If gasoline costs $3.00 per gallon and you travel for 90 miles at a speed of 30 miles per hour, how much will you pay for gasoline for the trip?

A) $15.00
B) $18.00
C) $20.00
D) $22.50

7. A project manager spends $\frac{1}{3}$ of her 50-hour workweek in meetings. How many hours does she spend in meetings?

A) 10 hours
B) 12.5 hours
C) 16.67 hours
D) 20 hours

8. Liam has a coupon for 15% off one pizza. Each pizza costs $12, and he buys two pizzas. How much does he pay?

A) $20.40
B) $22.00
C) $21.60
D) $24.00

9. An engineer needs to cut four pipes, each 1 foot 5 inches long, from a single piece of longer pipe. If the pipe is only sold by the foot, what's the shortest length of pipe the engineer should buy?

A) 5 feet
B) 6 feet
C) 8 feet
D) 7 feet

10. Two cars leave the same point at the same time, one heading east at 65 miles per hour and the other heading west at 75 miles per hour. How far apart will the cars be after 2 hours?

A) 280 miles
B) 250 miles
C) 300 miles
D) 260 miles

11. You are organizing a field trip and need to supply food for 120 students. Each student will receive 3 sandwiches, each weighing 6 ounces. How many pounds of sandwiches will be needed?

A) 128 pounds
B) 135 pounds
C) 138 pounds
D) 146 pounds

12. A rectangular garden has a length of $7\frac{1}{2}$ feet and a width of 4 feet. What is the total perimeter of the garden?

A) 23 feet
B) 22 feet
C) 20 feet
D) 21 feet

13. In a group of 40 students, 10 students wear glasses. What percent of the group wears glasses?

A) 25%
B) 40%
C) 30%
D) 50%

14. A hiker is on a 30-mile journey. She hikes at a speed of 3 miles per hour for the first 15 miles and then at a speed of 2 miles per hour for the remaining 15 miles. How many more hours will it take her to complete the journey than if she hiked the entire trip at 2 miles per hour?

A) 1 hour
B) 2.5 hours
C) 3 hours
D) 4.5 hours

15. In a company, 5 out of 30 employees work in the marketing department. What is the ratio of employees in the marketing department to employees not in the marketing department?

A) $\frac{1}{5}$
B) $\frac{1}{6}$
C) $\frac{1}{4}$
D) $\frac{1}{3}$

PART 3: WORD KNOWLEDGE (WK)

Time: 9 minutes for 15 questions

Each question below includes an underlined word. You may be asked to determine which one of the four answer choices most closely matches the meaning of the underlined word, or which choice has the opposite meaning. If the word is used within a sentence, your task is to select the option that most accurately reflects its meaning in the context of that sentence. This practice subtest reflects the number of questions and time limits you'll encounter on the CAT-ASVAB Word Knowledge subtest without any tryout questions.

1. The word belligerent most nearly means:

   A) peaceful
   B) hostile
   C) calm
   D) timid

2. The word prudent most nearly means:

   A) reckless
   B) careful
   C) hasty
   D) thoughtless

3. The word clandestine most nearly means:

   A) secretive
   B) open
   C) honest
   D) public

4. The camaraderie among the team members helped them win the championship.

   A) rivalry
   B) friendship
   C) isolation
   D) tension

5. He tried to circumvent the system by finding a loophole.

   A) confront
   B) bypass
   C) follow
   D) challenge

6. The young athlete had a voracious appetite after the competition.

   A) moderate
   B) small
   C) insatiable
   D) casual

7. The scientist offered a plausible explanation for the phenomenon.

   A) unlikely
   B) possible
   C) false
   D) imaginary

8. The word most opposite in meaning to arduous is:

   A) easy
   B) difficult
   C) laborious
   D) exhausting

9. The word altruistic most nearly means:

   A) selfish
   B) generous
   C) greedy
   D) stingy

10. The word austere most nearly means:

    A) luxurious
    B) harsh
    C) lavish
    D) generous

11. The beauty of the sunset was ephemeral, lasting only a few moments before the darkness took over.

    A) lasting
    B) brief
    C) permanent
    D) long

12. The CEO's astute business decisions helped the company thrive.

    A) careless
    B) foolish
    C) shrewd
    D) indifferent

13. The athlete's tacit approval was all that was needed for the team to proceed.

    A) expressed
    B) silent
    C) indifferent
    D) verbal

14. His callous remarks about the tragedy shocked everyone.

    A) compassionate
    B) thoughtful
    C) insensitive
    D) caring

15. The journalist's incisive report exposed the corruption within the company.

    A) dull
    B) sharp
    C) vague
    D) irrelevant

PART 4: PARAGRAPH COMPREHENSION (PC)

Time: 27 minutes for 10 questions

This section presents reading paragraphs followed by questions or incomplete statements. Your task is to read the paragraph and choose the option that best completes the statement or answers the question. This practice subtest simulates the number of questions and time constraints you'll face on the CAT-ASVAB Paragraph Comprehension subtest, without any tryout questions.

At the timberline in the Sierra mountains, conifers such as white bark pines grow, but they lack the affinity for water that tamarack pines have. Few birds are present, though chipmunks can be found. One summer, we discovered a sheep's horns lodged in a pine, evidence of a tragic struggle. The tree trunk had grown over them, and the skull was crumbled. The sight left a lasting, disturbing impression, forever tainting my feelings toward Windy Lake.

1. Based on the passage, the author's attitude toward Windy Lake can best be characterized as which of the following?

A) Admiring
B) Indifferent
C) Disdainful
D) Disturbed

The conditions in the camp were unbearable, with overcrowding and a lack of basic sanitation. What the prisoners endured daily was nothing short of inhumane. The treatment by the guards, with their cruelty and disregard for human dignity, was universally regarded as abhorrent. Survivors would later describe their experiences as horrific, detailing acts that no person should ever have to witness or endure.

2. In this passage, *abhorrent* most nearly means:

A) Acceptable
B) Delightful
C) Repulsive
D) Unnoticed

Early in the session of the Congress in December 1839, a bill was discussed abolishing the Military Academy. I saw in this an honorable way to obtain a discharge, and read the debates with much interest, but with impatience at the delay in taking action, for I was selfish enough to favor the bill. It never passed, and I would have been sorry to have seen it succeed. My idea then was to get through the course, secure a detail for a few years as assistant professor of mathematics at the Academy, and afterwards obtain a permanent position as professor in some respectable college; but circumstances always did shape my course different from my plans.

3. Which of the following best summarizes the author's feeling towards the bill regarding abolishing the Military Academy?

A) He was indifferent to the bill and its potential outcomes.
B) He initially supported the bill but later felt relieved it did not pass.
C) He was strongly opposed to the bill from the beginning.
D) He believed the bill would significantly improve the Military Academy.

In the 19th century, Europe's economic system led to the accumulation of vast amounts of capital. While some improvement in living conditions occurred, most of the increased wealth ended up in the hands of the new rich, who preferred investment over spending. Their goal was not immediate enjoyment but accumulating power through investment. This concentration of wealth made it possible for significant capital improvements, which ultimately benefited the entire community, despite the inequality of wealth distribution.

4. How did the author characterize the motivation of the new rich's actions and the results of their actions?

A) The rich sought immediate pleasure and their actions led to widespread consumption.
B) The rich aimed to maximize their power through investment, benefiting the community indirectly.
C) The rich were motivated by philanthropy and directly improved the lives of the poor.
D) The rich preferred to hoard wealth, leading to economic stagnation.

Technological advances have revolutionized the conditions of modern life, yet the public largely lacks an understanding of how these changes occur or how to control them. People experience the effects of technology without fully grasping its workings. Even those who benefit from these advancements cannot systematically understand the system in which they operate. They may exploit certain aspects for personal gain, but they do not comprehend the larger process that drives these advancements.

5. How does the author view the relationship between the public and technological advancement?

A) The public possesses a comprehensive understanding and exerts full control over technological advancements.
B) The public remains largely unaffected by the profound changes brought about by technological advancements.

C) The public is influenced by technological advancements but does not fully understand or manage them.
D) The public benefits equally from technological advancements, regardless of their individual knowledge.

The forest fire had spread rapidly, fueled by the dry underbrush and fierce winds. Trees that had stood tall for centuries were reduced to ash, their leaves turning to embers with frightening speed. Though some plants and animals escaped the blaze, the flames threatened to incinerate everything in their path. The destruction was total, leaving the once-vibrant forest a barren wasteland. It would take years for nature to recover from the intense heat and devastation, but some life, however small, would eventually return.

6. In this passage, *incinerate* most nearly means:

A) Drench
B) Ignite
C) Burn completely
D) Freeze

When a species, owing to highly favorable circumstances, increases inordinately in numbers in a small tract, epidemics—at least, this seems generally to occur with our game animals—often ensue; and here we have a limiting check independent of the struggle for life. But even some of these so-called epidemics appear to be due to parasitic worms, which have from some cause, possibly in part through facility of diffusion among the crowded animals, been disproportionally favored: and here comes in a sort of struggle between the parasite and its prey.

7. What purpose does the epidemics example serve in this passage?

A) To illustrate the natural balance of population control
B) To explain how parasites benefit their hosts
C) To argue against the existence of natural checks
D) To show that game animals are immune to epidemics

When, seven months ago, we rowed a boat under those great black cliffs, and found a disconsolate Emperor penguin chick still in the down, we knew definitely why the Emperor has to nest in midwinter. For if a June egg was still without feathers in the beginning of January, the same egg laid in the summer would leave its produce without practical covering for the following winter. Thus the Emperor penguin is compelled to undertake all kinds of hardships because his children insist on developing so slowly, very much as we are tied in our human relationships for the same reason. It is of interest that such a primitive bird should have so long a childhood.

8. What is the most likely reason the Emperor chick was "disconsolate"?

A) It was separated from its parents.
B) It was not yet fully feathered.
C) It was injured by predators.
D) It was hungry and unable to find food.

Mr. Beecher advised young men to consider going into a small amount of debt to buy land, suggesting that this responsibility, along with marriage, would help them stay focused. However, he strongly cautioned against getting into debt for everyday consumable goods, such as food or clothing. Families that rely on credit for these items often buy things they don't need, leading to deeper financial trouble. Eventually, unpaid debts will catch up, forcing people to break promises and dig themselves into more debt.

9. The primary purpose of the passage is to:
A) Advise young men on the importance of land ownership
B) Warn against the dangers of getting into debt for consumable goods
C) Encourage families to purchase goods on credit
D) Explain the benefits of getting married and owning land

After the shrapnel exploded on the hillside, we realized that settling into siege work was necessary. I moved the troops to a sheltered valley behind the Gatling guns, testing different areas for safety from Spanish sharpshooters hidden in trees. Despite our efforts, a shell hit one of the seemingly safe hollows, injuring a soldier. Eventually, we positioned the troops in secure locations, where they quickly adapted and made themselves as comfortable as possible, under the circumstances.

10. The passage implies which action is most needed in the situation the soldiers were in?
A) Launch a counterattack against the Spanish sharpshooters
B) Find and eliminate the Spanish sharpshooters in the trees
C) Locate and occupy the safest positions for the soldiers
D) Request reinforcements to strengthen their position

PART 5: MATHEMATICS KNOWLEDGE (MK)

Time: 31 minutes for 15 questions

Select the correct answer from the choices given. This practice subtest reflects the number of questions and time limits you'll encounter on the CAT-ASVAB Mathematics Knowledge subtest without any tryout questions.

1. If $\frac{7}{3} + \frac{1}{5} = p$, then the value of p is between which of the following pairs of numbers?

A) 2 and 3
B) 4 and 5
C) 3 and 4
D) 1 and 2

2. Which of the following inequalities is true?

A) $\frac{1}{2} > \frac{3}{5}$
B) $\frac{4}{7} < \frac{3}{6}$
C) $\frac{5}{8} > \frac{4}{5}$
D) $\frac{2}{3} < \frac{4}{5}$

3. Which number in the list below has the greatest value? Given numbers: $\frac{8}{3}$, 2.28, $\frac{10}{12}$, 0.199.

A) $\frac{8}{3}$
B) 2.28
C) $\frac{10}{12}$
D) 0.199

4. 4x - 5y = 11, x = 2

The two lines given by the equations above intersect in the xy-plane. What is the value of the y-coordinate of the point of intersection?

A) -3
B) -0.6
C) 1
D) 0.5

5. Which of the following expressions is equivalent to $(y^3 \cdot y^2)^4$?

A) y^{12}
B) y^{16}
C) y^{20}
D) y^{25}

6. What is the solution to the equation $\frac{1}{2}x + \frac{3}{4}(x + 1) - \frac{1}{4} = 2$?

A) $\frac{3}{2}$
B) $\frac{6}{5}$
C) $\frac{15}{8}$
D) $\frac{17}{8}$

7. The amount of money N, in dollars, Alice earns can be represented by the equation N = 15h + 20, where h is the number of hours Alice works. Which of the following is the best interpretation of the number 20 in the equation?

A) The amount of money, in dollars, Alice earns each hour
B) The total amount of money, in dollars, Alice earns after working for h hours
C) The total amount of money, in dollars, Alice earns after working for one hour
D) The amount of money, in dollars, Alice earns in addition to an hourly wage

8. A company's quarterly sales in the past 2 years are shown in the graph. Which quarter had the greatest increase in sales from Year 1 to Year 2?

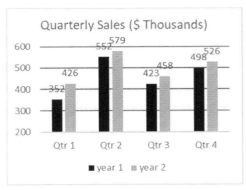

A) Q1
B) Q2
C) Q3
D) Q4

9. Factor $54x^4y^3z + 72x^2y^4$

A) $18x^2y^3(3x^2z + 4y)$
B) $18x^2y^3(3x^2z + 4y^2)$
C) $18x^3y^2(3x^2z + 4y)$
D) $18x^2y^2(3x^2z + 4y)$

10. What are the solutions of the quadratic function $y = 4x^2 - 6x + 1$?

A) $\frac{3\pm\sqrt{5}}{4}$
B) $\frac{6\pm\sqrt{10}}{4}$
C) $\frac{6\pm\sqrt{5}}{8}$
D) $\frac{3\pm\sqrt{10}}{4}$

11. In the figure on the right, the following relationship exists: $\angle\alpha + \angle\beta = 140°$, $\angle A - \angle\beta = 50°$. What is the value of $\angle\alpha$?

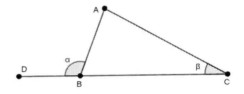

A) 100°
B) 110°
C) 120°
D) 130°

12. A class has 12 students in Grade 8 and 18 students in Grade 9. The Grade 8 students averaged 80 on their final exam, and the Grade 9 students averaged 90. What was the average grade for the entire class?

A) 85
B) 88
C) 84
D) 86

13. Divide the polynomial $6x^3 - 4x^2 + 8x$ by $2x$. What is the result?

A) $3x^2 - 2x + 4$
B) $6x^2 - 2x + 8$
C) $4x^2 + x + 2$
D) $3x^2 + 2x - 4$

14. A circle is inscribed in a square, meaning the circle touches all four sides of the square. If the radius of the circle is 5 units, what is the perimeter of the square?

A) 40 units
B) 20 units
C) 25 units
D) 100 units

15. What's the equation of the line that passes through points $(1, 2)$ and $(3, 6)$?

A) $y = 2x + 1$
B) $y = 2x$
C) $y = x + 1$
D) $y = \frac{1}{2}x + 2$

PART 6: ELECTRONICS INFORMATION (EI)

Time: 10 minutes for 15 questions

Select the correct answer from the choices given. This practice subtest reflects the number of questions and time limits you'll encounter on the CAT-ASVAB Electronics Information subtest without any tryout questions.

1. The process of converting direct current (DC) into alternating current (AC) is known as

A) inversion
B) rectification
C) capacitance
D) conduction

2. How many paths of electrical flow can be found in a parallel circuit

A) one
B) two
C) multiple
D) None

3. What happens if you plug a device designed for DC into an AC power source?

A) The device will operate at half efficiency.
B) The device may overheat and may get damaged.
C) The device will operate normally.
D) The device will reverse its polarity.

4. Which of the following is the most accurate description of voltage?

A) the amount of current flowing in a circuit
B) the measure of electrical potential difference
C) the flow of electrons per unit time
D) the resistance in a circuit

5. What type of device converts electrical energy into mechanical energy?

A) inductor
B) motor
C) resistor
D) transformer

6. Which of the following shows a transistor symbol?

A)

B)

C)

D)

7. A fan operates at 200 watts on a 100-volt power supply. How much current does it draw?

A) 0.5 amperes
B) 2.0 amperes
C) 5.0 amperes
D) 20.0 amperes

8. A number-18 wire, compared to a number-10 wire,

A) is heavier
B) is thicker
C) has a smaller diameter
D) has a larger diameter

9. What is the primary purpose of a circuit breaker?

A) Increase resistance
B) Protect against current surges
C) Store energy
D) Regulate voltage

10. Which type of circuit forces all current to flow through a single path?

A) Open
B) Series
C) Parallel
D) Closed

11. Which component allows current to flow in one direction only?

A) Capacitor
B) Diode
C) Resistor
D) Transformer

12. Four resistors of 3 Ω, 5 Ω, 7 Ω, and 15 Ω are in series. What is their effective resistance?

A) 24 Ω
B) 30 Ω
C) 15 Ω
D) 35 Ω

13. A semiconductor behaves between the properties of a

A) perfect conductor and perfect resistor
B) insulator and conductor
C) battery and resistor
D) inductor and transformer

14. Which component stores energy in a magnetic field and resists changes in current?

A) capacitor
B) resistor
C) inductor
D) diode

15. In the given circuit, a 20V battery is connected across a resistor and a bulb. If the switch connected in series with the bulb is opened, how will the current through the resistor change?

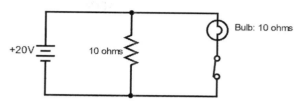

A) The current through the resistor will increase.
B) The current through the resistor will decrease.
C) The current through the resistor will remain the same.
D) The current through the resistor will be zero.

PART 7: AUTO INFORMATION (AI)

Time: 7 minutes for 10 questions

Select the correct answer from the choices given. This practice subtest reflects the number of questions and time limits you'll encounter on the CAT-ASVAB Auto Information subtest without any tryout questions.

1. In a manual transmission, what component is responsible for disengaging the engine from the gearbox to allow for smooth gear changes?

A) Torque Converter
B) Clutch
C) Differential
D) Driveshaft

2. The image below shows the four strokes of an internal combustion engine. Which stroke is responsible for igniting the air-fuel mixture?

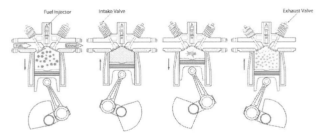

A) Intake
B) Compression
C) Power
D) Exhaust

3. Which emission control system recirculates exhaust gases back into the intake manifold to reduce nitrogen oxide emissions?

A) Positive Crankcase Ventilation (PCV)
B) Evaporative Emission Control (EVAP)
C) Exhaust Gas Recirculation (EGR)
D) Catalytic Converter

4. What component in the cooling system is responsible for circulating coolant throughout the engine to regulate temperature?

A) Radiator
B) Thermostat
C) Oil Pump
D) Water Pump

5. Which of the following steering systems uses a pinion gear to move the wheels in response to the driver's input?

A) Hydraulic Power Steering
B) Electric Power Steering
C) Rack and Pinion Steering
D) Torque Vectoring

6. What is the primary function of shock absorbers in a vehicle's suspension system?

A) To support the vehicle's weight
B) To prevent excessive bouncing by damping suspension movement
C) To reduce friction between the wheels and the road
D) To align the wheels for optimal handling

7. Which of the following is a direct benefit of proper steering alignment?

A) Increased engine horsepower
B) Reduced vibration and improved ride comfort
C) Enhanced brake performance
D) Better fuel injection efficiency

8. Identify the following car part shown in the image:

A) Fuel Pump
B) Oil Filter
C) Air Filter
D) Radiator Cap

9. What is the primary function of the alternator in a vehicle's electrical system?

A) To start the engine by engaging the flywheel
B) To convert electrical energy into mechanical energy for the engine
C) To generate electrical power and recharge the battery once the engine is running
D) To regulate the amount of fuel entering the combustion chamber

10. What is the purpose of a relay in a vehicle's electrical system?

A) To protect circuits from overcurrent by blowing when too much current is drawn
B) To convert mechanical energy into electrical energy
C) To allow a low-current circuit to control a high-current circuit
D) To connect all electrical components in the vehicle

PART 8: SHOP INFORMATION (SI)

Time: 6 minutes for 10 questions

Select the correct answer from the choices given. This practice subtest reflects the number of questions and time limits you'll encounter on the CAT-ASVAB Shop Information subtest without any tryout questions.

1. Which type of saw is best for making intricate, curved cuts in wood or metal?

A) Circular saw
B) Jigsaw
C) Reciprocating saw
D) Chainsaw

2. Four different clamps and vices are shown below. Which of these would be the most appropriate for holding two large boards together while the glue dries over an extended period?

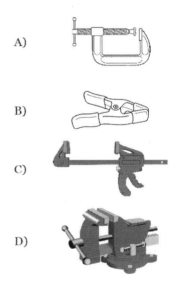

3. What is the main advantage of using a brace and bit in woodworking?

A) Requires less effort for larger holes
B) Provides better control for precise hole drilling
C) Works faster than an electric drill
D) Ideal for creating small, intricate holes

4. Which hammer is best suited for shaping metal and setting rivets?

A) Claw hammer
B) Ball-peen hammer
C) Mallet
D) Sledgehammer

5. What is the primary function of a washer when used with a bolt?

A) To tighten the fastener further
B) To distribute pressure and prevent damage
C) To increase torque on the bolt
D) To prevent bolts from rusting

6. What is a micrometer used for?

A) Measuring large surfaces quickly
B) Measuring very small dimensions with high accuracy
C) Measuring angles in engineering projects
D) Measuring long distances with flexibility

7. Which of the following hammers is best suited for working with a chisel to remove material from wood or metal?

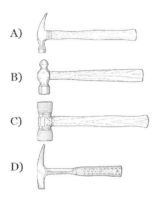

8. What is the primary function of a protractor?

A) Measuring right angles
B) Measuring the internal diameter of an object
C) Measuring angles between 0° and 180° or 0° and 360°
D) Measuring surface lengths in construction projects

9. Which tool is best suited for reaching into tight spaces and handling small objects?

A) Slip-joint Pliers
B) Locking Pliers
C) Needle-nose Pliers
D) Channel-lock Pliers

10 . What is the key feature of a ratchet when used with a socket wrench?

A) It provides better torque for larger fasteners
B) It allows continuous turning without lifting the tool
C) It fits all types of fasteners without changing sockets
D) It is used to measure torque

PART 9: MECHANICAL COMPREHENSION (MC)

Time: 22 minutes for 15 questions

Select the correct answer from the choices given. This practice subtest reflects the number of questions and time limits you'll encounter on the CAT-ASVAB Mechanical Comprehension subtest without any tryout questions.

1. What is the kinetic energy of a 10 kg object moving at 80 m/s?

(A) 16,000 J
(B) 32,000 J
(C) 64,000 J
(D) 80,000 J

2. A person pushes a cart 15 meters with a force of 50 N in 10 seconds. How much power was exerted?

(A) 75 W
(B) 100 W
(C) 150 W
(D) 75 N

3. How much force is needed to apply 60 ft-lb of torque to a bolt using a 3-foot-long wrench?

(A) 20 pounds
(B) 10 pounds
(C) 15 pounds
(D) 30 pounds

4. A box is being pushed with a 50 N force on a surface with a kinetic friction coefficient of 0.2. If the normal force is 200 N, what is the frictional force opposing the box's motion?

(A) 10 N
(B) 20 N
(C) 40 N
(D) 50 N

5. A hiker wears two rectangular snowshoes, each with dimensions 10 inches by 20 inches. The hiker weighs 180 pounds. What pressure does the hiker exert on the snow, assuming both snowshoes bear the weight equally?

(A) 0.35 psi
(B) 0.45 psi
(C) 1.5 psi
(D) 2.0 psi

6. Two blocks are on a frictionless surface. Block A has a mass of 2 kg, and Block B has a mass of 4 kg. If Block A exerts a 10 N force on Block B, how much force does Block B exert on Block A?

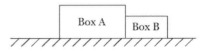

(A) 5 N
(B) 10 N
(C) 15 N
(D) 20 N

7. In the pulley system shown, there are four support segments lifting the load. If the load weighs 400 pounds, what is the effort required to lift it?

A) 100 pounds
B) 200 pounds
C) 400 pounds
D) 50 pounds

8. If the air pressure in a tire is 30 psi, how much force is exerted on a patch of the tire that measures 20 square inches?

A) 600 pounds
B) 150 pounds
C) 300 pounds
D) 50 pounds

9. A machine's chain has a front gear with 60 teeth and a rear gear with 15 teeth. If the front gear turns at 100 revolutions per minute (rpm), how fast will the rear gear rotate?

(A) 400 rpm
(B) 100 rpm
(C) 25 rpm
(D) 15 rpm

10. A 25 kg box is placed on a table and pushed down by an additional 75 N force. What is the normal force acting on the box?

(A) 245 N
(B) 320 N
(C) 250 N
(D) 400 N

11. A block sits on a rough surface and remains stationary when a force is applied. Once enough force is applied to overcome static friction, the block begins to slide, and a smaller force is able to keep it moving at a constant speed. This happens because:

(A) The kinetic friction coefficient decreases with faster motion.
(B) The coefficient of static friction is less than the coefficient of kinetic friction.
(C) The force applied accumulates and increases.
(D) The coefficient of kinetic friction is less than the coefficient of static friction.

12. When a tennis ball hits the ground and bounces back up, the force responsible for the ball's rebound is called:

A) inertia.
B) recoil.
C) elasticity.
D) gravity.

13. A ball rolls down a slope and speeds up as it moves. This happens because:

(A) Its kinetic energy is being converted into potential energy.
(B) Its potential energy is decreasing.
(C) Its potential energy is being converted into kinetic energy.
(D) Its velocity increases.

14. An object that is more difficult to accelerate has:

(A) Greater momentum.
(B) Greater inertia.
(C) More torque.
(D) Higher pressure.

15. A nail is driven into wood using a tool that is designed to transfer force to a small area at its point. Which simple machine does this tool most closely resemble?

(A) Inclined plane
(B) Wedge
(C) Lever
(D) Pulley

Part 10: Assembling Objects (AO)

Time: 18 minutes for 15 questions

Select the correct answer from the choices given. This practice subtest reflects the number of questions and time limits you'll encounter on the CAT-ASVAB Assembling Objects subtest without any tryout questions.

1.

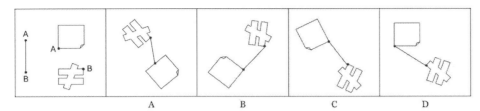

2.

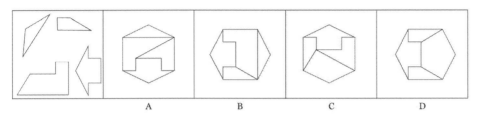

3.

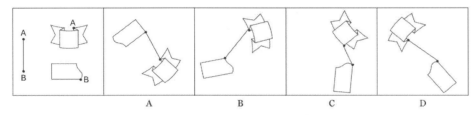

4.

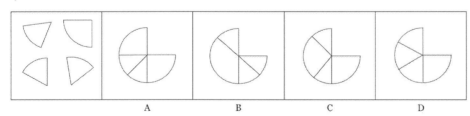

5.

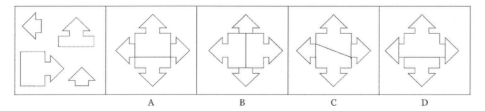

6.

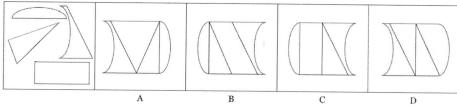

| A | B | C | D |

7.

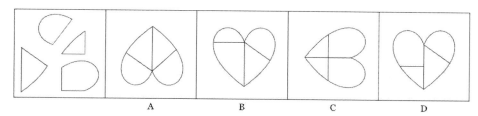

| A | B | C | D |

8.

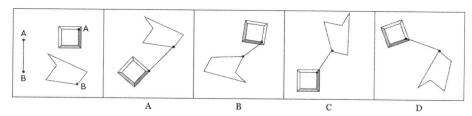

| A | B | C | D |

9.

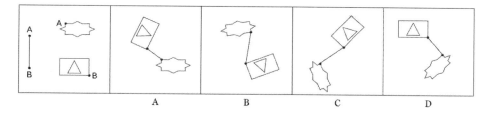

| A | B | C | D |

10.

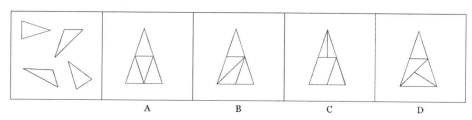

| A | B | C | D |

11.

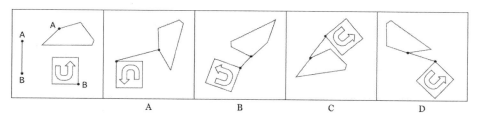

| A | B | C | D |

12.

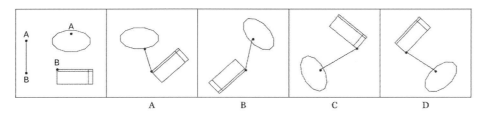

13.

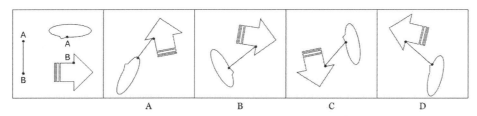

14.

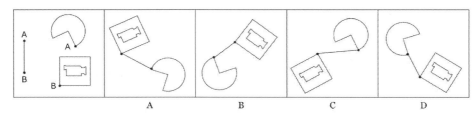

15.

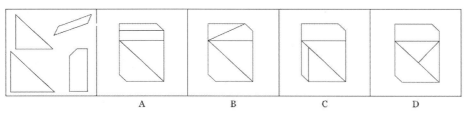

ANSWERS AND EXPLANATIONS—PRACTICE TEST 2

Part 1: General Science (GS)

1. A) Mantle. Explanation: The mantle lies directly beneath the Earth's crust and is made of semi-solid rock that moves slowly, driving plate tectonics.

2. C) Convergent boundaries. Explanation: Mountains form when tectonic plates collide at convergent boundaries, pushing the Earth's crust upward.

3. B) Bonds between atoms are broken and new ones are formed. Explanation: Chemical changes involve breaking and reforming bonds, resulting in the creation of new substances with different properties.

4. B) A substance made of two or more different elements chemically bonded. Explanation: Compounds are substances made from atoms of different elements, such as water (H_2O), where hydrogen and oxygen are chemically bonded.

5. B) Saltwater. Explanation: Salt dissolves uniformly in water, creating a homogeneous mixture where the composition is consistent throughout.

6. B) Kelvin. Explanation: Kelvin is the base unit for temperature in the SI system, used primarily in science. Celsius is more common in everyday usage, but Kelvin is essential for scientific calculations.

7. D) Nano-. Explanation: 'Nano-' means one-billionth (10^{-9}) of a unit, smaller than micro- (10^{-6}), milli- (10^{-3}), and centi- (10^{-2}). It is often used to measure very small quantities, such as in nanotechnology.

8. C) Mass is the amount of matter, weight is the force of gravity on that mass. Explanation: Mass is intrinsic and remains the same regardless of location. Weight varies with gravity, meaning it changes based on the gravitational pull of a planet.

9. C) 98 N. Explanation: Weight is calculated using the formula $F = ma$ where a is gravitational acceleration ($9.8 m/s^2$ on Earth). $F = 10\,\text{kg} \times 9.8\,\text{m/s}^2 = 98\,\text{N}$.

10. B) Speed with direction. Explanation: Velocity is a vector quantity that includes both the speed of an object and its direction of motion, unlike speed, which is a scalar quantity.

11. C) Displacement considers the overall change in position. Explanation: Displacement accounts for both the distance and direction between an object's starting and ending positions, whereas distance only measures the total ground covered.

12. B) Producers. Explanation: Producers, like plants, make their own food through photosynthesis.

13. C) Fight infections. Explanation: White blood cells are part of the immune system and help protect the body from harmful pathogens.

14. C) Chloroplasts. Explanation: Chloroplasts contain chlorophyll, which captures sunlight and initiates the process of photosynthesis.

15. C) Replication. Explanation: DNA replication ensures that each new cell receives an exact copy of the DNA.

Part 2: Arithmetic Reasoning (AR)

1. C) 9. Explanation: First, calculate how many books each buyer purchased: The school buys $\frac{1}{5} \times 30 = 6$ books.

   The library buys $\frac{1}{3} \times 30 = 10$ books. The individual buys $\frac{1}{6} \times 30 = 5$ books. Now, add up the total number of books bought: 6 + 10 + 5 = 21. Thus, the bookstore has 30 - 21 = 9 books left.

2. A) 13.2 liters. Explanation: To find the new water consumption, calculate 10% of 12 liters: $0.10 \times 12 = 1.2$ liters.

   Add this to the normal consumption to find the total: 12 + 1.2 = 13.2 liters.

3. B) 80,000. Explanation: Let the original expectation be x.

   The actual growth was 25% less than expected, so: $x - 0.25x = 60{,}000$. Or, $0.75x = 60{,}000$.

Now, solve for x : $x = \frac{60,000}{0.75} = 80,000$.

4. B) 30 minutes. Explanation: To calculate the percentage decrease, find 25% of 40 minutes: $0.25 \times 40 = 10$.

Now, subtract the decrease from the original time: $40 - 10 = 30$.

5. C) 20. Explanation: Since 1 kilometer is 1000 meters, the total distance is 1000 meters. Now, divide the total distance by the length of one lap: $\frac{1000}{50} = 20$. Thus, the swimmer must complete 20 laps to swim 1 kilometer.

6. B) $18.00. Explanation: First, calculate how many gallons are needed: $\frac{90 \text{ miles}}{15 \text{ miles per gallon}} = 6$ gallons.

Now, multiply the number of gallons by the cost per gallon: $6 \times 3.00 = 18.00$. Thus, the total cost of gasoline for the trip is $18.00. The speed of 30 miles per hour is extraneous information. Don't be tripped up!

7. C) 16.67 hours. Explanation: To find the time spent in meetings, multiply $\frac{1}{3}$ of the workweek: $\frac{1}{3} \times 50 = 16.67$ hours.

8. A) $20.40. Explanation: First, calculate the price of one pizza with the 15% discount:

$12 \times (1 - 0.15) = 12 \times 0.85 = 10.20$. The total price for two pizzas is: $10.20 \times 2 = 20.40$.

9. B) 6 feet. Explanation:

First, calculate the total length required for the four pipes by multiplying 1 foot 5 inches by 4: $1 \text{ foot} \times 4 = 4 \text{ feet}, 5 \text{ inches} \times 4 = 20 \text{ inches}$.

Since 12 inches = 1 foot, convert the extra 20 inches into feet: 20 inches = 1 foot 8 inches. Now, add this to the total: 4 feet + 1 foot 8 inches = 5 feet 8 inches.

Since the pipe is sold by the foot, the engineer will need to purchase at least 6 feet of pipe.

10. A) 280 miles. Explanation: The distance each car travels in 2 hours is: $65 \times 2 = 130$ miles for the first car. $75 \times 2 = 150$ miles for the second car. Add them up: $130 + 150 = 280$ miles. Thus, the cars will be 280 miles apart.

11. B) 135 pounds. Explanation: Step 1: Calculate the total number of sandwiches: $120 \times 3 = 360$ sandwiches

Step 2: Calculate the total weight in ounces: $360 \times 6 = 2,160$ ounces

Step 3: Convert ounces to pounds: Since there are 16 ounces in 1 pound, $\frac{2,160}{16} = 135$ pounds.

12. A) 23 feet. Explanation: The formula for the perimeter of a rectangle is: $P = 2 \times (\text{length} + \text{width})$.

Substitute the values: $P = 2 \times \left(7\frac{1}{2} + 4\right) = 2 \times (7.5 + 4) = 2 \times 11.5 = 23$ feet.

13. A) 25%. Explanation: To find the percentage of students who wear glasses, divide the number of students who wear glasses by the total number of students, and then multiply by 100: $\left(\frac{10}{40}\right) \times 100 = 25\%$.

14. B) 2.5 hours. Explanation: First, calculate the time it would take if she hiked at 2 miles per hour for the entire trip: $\frac{30}{2} = 15$ hours. Now, calculate the time for the actual journey: For the first 15 miles at 3 miles per hour: $\frac{15}{3} = 5$ hours.

For the remaining 15 miles at 2 miles per hour: $\frac{15}{2} = 7.5$ hours. Total time for the actual journey: $5 + 7.5 = 12.5$ hours. The difference between the two times: $15 - 12.5 = 2.5$ hours.

15. A) $\frac{1}{5}$. Explanation: First, calculate the number of employees not in the marketing department: 30 - 5 = 25 So, the ratio of employees in the marketing department to those not in it is: $\frac{5}{25} = \frac{1}{5}$.

Part 3: Word Knowledge (WK)

1. B) hostile. "Belligerent" refers to being aggressive or warlike, the opposite of peaceful.

2. B) careful. "Prudent" describes someone who is cautious and wise in decision-making.

3. A) secretive. "Clandestine" refers to something done in secrecy, usually to avoid detection.

4. B) friendship. "Camaraderie" refers to a sense of friendship and trust among people.

5. B) bypass. "Circumvent" means to find a way around an obstacle or avoid it.

6. C) insatiable. "Voracious" means having a huge appetite or desire for something, especially food.

7. B) possible. "Plausible" means something that seems reasonable or probable.

8. A) easy. "Arduous" means something difficult or requiring great effort, so "easy" is its antonym.

9. B) generous. "Altruistic" describes someone who is selflessly concerned with the welfare of others.

10. B) harsh. "Austere" refers to something severe or strict in manner or appearance, often lacking luxury.

11. B) brief. "Ephemeral" means short-lived or lasting for a very brief time.

12. C) shrewd. "Astute" means having sharp judgment or being shrewd.

13. B) silent. "Tacit" means understood or implied without being openly expressed.

14. C) insensitive. "Callous" means showing or having an insensitive and cruel disregard for others.

15. B) sharp. "Incisive" means clear, sharp, and direct, often cutting to the heart of a matter.

Part 4: Paragraph Comprehension (PC)

1. D) Disturbed

Explanation: The author describes an unsettling discovery of a sheep's horns caught in a tree at Windy Lake and expresses how it tainted their feelings toward the area, indicating a disturbed reaction. Thus, D is the correct choice.

2. C) Repulsive

Explanation: "Abhorrent" refers to something that is repulsive or disgusting. The context, describing cruel and inhumane treatment, makes "repulsive" the most appropriate choice. The other options do not align with the negative tone of the passage.

3. B) He initially supported the bill but later felt relieved it did not pass.

Explanation: The author initially favored the bill as a way to leave the Academy but later realized he would have regretted its passage, showing his change of heart.

4. B) The rich aimed to maximize their power through investment, benefiting the community indirectly.

Explanation: The passage suggests that the new rich were motivated by the power that came from investment, not immediate consumption. Their investments led to capital improvements that, while focused on personal gain, indirectly benefited the community. Thus, B is the correct choice.

5. C) The public is influenced by technological advancements but does not fully understand or manage them.

Explanation: The passage suggests that while technological advances significantly affect people's lives, they lack a full understanding of these changes or the ability to control them. Therefore, the correct answer is C.

6. C) Burn completely

Explanation: "Incinerate" means to completely burn something to ashes. The context of the fire and destruction makes "burn completely" the most appropriate choice. Other options, like "drench" or "freeze," are unrelated to the scenario described.

7. A) To illustrate the natural balance of population control

Explanation: The example of epidemics in the passage demonstrates how natural factors, such as diseases and parasites, serve as limiting checks on the overpopulation of species, thereby maintaining a balance independent of direct competition for resources.

8. B) It was not yet fully feathered.

Explanation: The passage explains that the chick was still in its down and not fully feathered, implying it was likely cold and uncomfortable, making it "disconsolate." This condition highlights the necessity for the Emperor penguin to nest in midwinter.

9. B) Warn against the dangers of getting into debt for consumable goods.

Explanation: The passage primarily warns against accumulating debt for everyday consumables, highlighting the financial pitfalls of relying on credit. While land ownership is discussed, the main focus is on avoiding unnecessary debt. Therefore, B is the correct answer.

10. C) Locate and occupy the safest positions for the soldiers.

Explanation: The passage focuses on the soldiers' efforts to find safe areas from which they could avoid fire from Spanish sharpshooters. The narrator describes testing different locations for safety and settling the troops in protected positions, making C the correct answer.

Part 5: Mathematics Knowledge (MK)

1. A) 2 and 3. Explanation: $\frac{7}{3} + \frac{1}{5} = \frac{35}{15} + \frac{3}{15} = \frac{38}{15} \approx 2.533$.

2. D) $\frac{2}{3} < \frac{4}{5}$. Explanation: $\frac{2}{3} \approx 0.6667, \frac{4}{5} = 0.8, \frac{2}{3} < \frac{4}{5}$.

3. A) $\frac{8}{3}$. Explanation: $\frac{8}{3} \approx 2.6667$, bigger than all the other numbers.

4. B) -0.6. Explanation: Substitute x = 2 into the first equation: $4(2) - 5y = 11$.

$$\text{Thus, } 8 - 5y = 11 \Longrightarrow -5y = 3 \Longrightarrow y = -\frac{3}{5} = -0.6.$$

5. C) y^{20}. Explanation: $(y^3 \cdot y^2)^4 = \left(y^{\{3+2\}}\right)^4 = (y^5)^4 = y^{\{5 \cdot 4\}} = y^{20}$.

6. B) $\frac{6}{5}$. Explanation: $\frac{1}{2}x + \frac{3}{4}(x+1) - \frac{1}{4} = 2 \Longrightarrow \frac{1}{2}x + \frac{3}{4}x + \frac{3}{4} - \frac{1}{4} = 2 \Longrightarrow \frac{1}{2}x + \frac{3}{4}x + \frac{1}{2} = 2$

$$\Longrightarrow \frac{5}{4}x + \frac{1}{2} = 2 \Longrightarrow \frac{5}{4}x = 2 - \frac{1}{2} = \frac{3}{2} \Longrightarrow x = \frac{6}{5}$$

7. D) The amount of money, in dollars, Alice earns in addition to an hourly wage.

Explanation: Given $N = 15h + 20$, Alice makes \$20 even when she works zero hours, or, just by showing up. So, 20 represents a set amount of money earned regardless of hours worked.

8. A) Q1. Explanation: Increase in Q1 sales = $426 - 352 = 74$, which is greater than the increase for any other quarters.

9. A) $18x^2y^3(3x^2z + 4y)$. Explanation: Factor out the greatest common factor $18x^2y^3$, then we have: $54x^4y^3z + 72x^2y^4 = 18x^2y^3(3x^2z + 4y)$.

10. A) $\frac{3 \pm \sqrt{5}}{4}$. Explanation: Use quadratic formula: $x = \frac{-b \pm \sqrt{b^2 - 4ac}}{2a}$.

For $y = 4x^2 - 6x + 1 : a = 4, b = -6, c = 1$.

$$x = \frac{-(-6) \pm \sqrt{(-6)^2 - 4 \cdot 4 \cdot 1}}{2 \cdot 4} = \frac{6 \pm \sqrt{36 - 16}}{8} = \frac{6 \pm \sqrt{20}}{8} = \frac{6 \pm 2\sqrt{5}}{8} = \frac{3 \pm \sqrt{5}}{4}$$

11. B) 110°. Explanation: This is a system of equations problem in a geometry setting, with two equations and three unknowns.

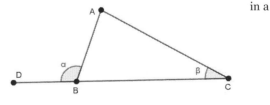

$$\angle\alpha + \angle\beta = 140° \quad (1)$$
$$\angle A - \angle\beta = 50° \quad (2)$$

We'll want to get rid of $\angle A$ first, so we have two unknows with two equations. Because ABC is a triangle, its three internal angles add up to 180°: $\angle A + \angle\beta + (180° - \angle\alpha) = 180°$, where $(180° - \angle\alpha) = \angle ABC$. Hence,

$$\angle A = 180° - (180° - \angle\alpha) - \angle\beta$$
$$\angle A = \angle\alpha - \angle\beta$$

Given that: $\angle A - \angle\beta = 50°$, substitute $\angle A : \angle\alpha - \angle\beta - \angle\beta = 50° \Rightarrow \angle\alpha - 2\angle\beta = 50° \quad (3)$

From the first equation: $\angle\alpha + \angle\beta = 140° \Rightarrow \angle\alpha = 140° - \angle\beta$

Substitute $\angle \alpha$ into equation (3):

$$\left(140° - \angle \beta\right) - 2 \angle \beta = 50°$$
$$140° - 3 \angle \beta = 50°$$
$$3 \angle \beta = 90°$$
$$\angle \beta = 30°$$

Now, substitute $\angle \beta$ back into equation (1) for $\angle \alpha$: $\angle \alpha = 140° - 30° = 110°$.

12. D) 86. Explanation: To find the overall average for the class, we calculate the weighted average based on the number of students in each grade:

$$\text{Average} = \frac{(12 \times 80) + (18 \times 90)}{12 + 18}$$

$$\text{Average} = \frac{960 + 1620}{30} = \frac{2580}{30} = 86$$

13. A) $3x^2 - 2x + 4$. Explanation: To divide the polynomial $6x^3 - 4x^2 + 8x$ by $2x$, divide each term individually:

$$\frac{6x^3}{2x} = 3x^2, \quad \frac{-4x^2}{2x} = -2x, \quad \frac{8x}{2x} = 4$$

Thus, the result is: $3x^2 - 2x + 4$.

14. A) 40 units. Explanation: The radius of the circle is 5 units. Since the circle is inscribed in the square, the diameter of the circle is equal to the side length of the square. The diameter is twice the radius, so:

$$\text{Side length of the square} = 2 \times 5 = 10 \text{ units}$$

The perimeter of a square is given by $4 \times$ side length so: Perimeter of the square $= 4 \times 10 = 40$ units.

15. B) $y = 2x$ Explanation: First, find the slope (m) using the formula:

$$m = \frac{y_2 - y_1}{x_2 - x_1} = \frac{6 - 2}{3 - 1} = \frac{4}{2} = 2$$

Next, use the point-slope form $y - y_1 = m(x - x_1)$ with point $(1,2)$: $y - 2 = 2(x - 1)$

Simplifying: $y - 2 = 2x - 2 \implies y = 2x$

Thus, the equation of the line is $y = 2x$.

Part 6: Electronics Information (EI)

1. A) inversion. Explanation: The process of converting DC to AC is called inversion, and it is done using an inverter.

   B) rectification is the opposite process, converting AC to DC. C) capacitance and D) conduction are unrelated to the AC-DC conversion process.

2. C) multiple. Explanation: Multiple paths are available in a parallel circuit because each component is connected in a way that provides its own separate path for the current to flow.

3. B) The device may overheat and may get damaged. Explanation:

   A) is incorrect because devices designed for DC do not operate on AC, and their efficiency cannot be simply halved; the operation is fundamentally different.

   B) is correct. A DC device plugged into an AC power source is likely to overheat and get damaged because the internal components are not designed to handle the constantly reversing current flow that occurs with AC.

   C) is incorrect because a DC device will not function correctly on AC, as AC current constantly changes direction, which most DC circuits cannot manage.

   D) is incorrect, as polarity reversal is not what typically happens when connecting DC devices to AC power. The issue is more about current type mismatch rather than reversing polarity.

A related question will be: what happens if an AC appliance gets supplied with DC Power? In the scenario, AC appliance generally require the alternating nature of AC for proper operation, and plugging them into DC will either prevent them from functioning or damage the internal circuitry.

4. B) the measure of electrical potential difference. Explanation: Voltage measures the electrical potential difference between two points. A) describes current. C) refers to current flow, not voltage. D) describes resistance.

5. B) motor. Explanation: A motor converts electrical energy into mechanical energy. A) and C) do not perform energy conversion. D) Transformer changes voltage levels but not the form of energy.

6. A). Explanation: A) shows the symbol for a transistor, specifically a bipolar junction transistor (BJT). The three terminals are labeled as B (Base), E (Emitter), and C (Collector), which are the defining features of a transistor symbol. B) shows the symbol for a transformer, which is used to change the voltage level in an AC circuit. It has two sets of coils to indicate the primary and secondary windings, which is not related to a transistor. C) shows the symbol for a diode, which allows current to flow in one direction. It has an arrow and a bar, representing the direction of current flow, but it lacks the three terminals that are characteristic of a transistor. D) shows the symbol for a fuse.

7. B) 2.0 amperes. Explanation: Using Power = Voltage × Current: $200\ W = 100\ V \times I$, therefore, I = 2.0 A. A), C), and D) are incorrect based on this calculation.

8. C) has a smaller diameter. Explanation: Wire gauge numbers indicate diameter, with higher numbers meaning smaller diameters.

9. B) Protect against current surges. Explanation: A circuit breaker interrupts the circuit when there is a current surge to protect devices. A), C), and D) are incorrect as they do not relate to a circuit breaker's function.

10. B) Series. Explanation: In a series circuit, all current flows through a single path. A) Open: No current flows. C) Parallel: Multiple paths are present. D) Closed is a general term and does not specify the circuit type.

11. B) Diode. Explanation: A diode only allows current to flow in one direction. A) stores energy. C) limits but does not direct current. D) steps up or steps down voltage.

12. B) 30 Ω. Explanation: In a series circuit, the total resistance is the sum of all resistances:

$$3 + 5 + 7 + 15 = 30\ \Omega$$

13. B) insulator and conductor. Explanation: A semiconductor has conductivity between that of an insulator and a conductor. A), C), and D) are incorrect, as they do not describe conductivity relationships accurately for semiconductors.

14. C) inductor. Explanation: An inductor stores energy in a magnetic field and resists changes in current. A) stores energy in an electric field. B) and D) do not store energy in magnetic fields.

15. C) The current through the resistor will remain the same.

Explanation: In this circuit, the resistor and bulb are connected in parallel, meaning they each have their own path to the battery. The voltage across both the resistor and the bulb is 20V. When the switch is closed, both elements (the resistor and the bulb) draw current.

If the switch is opened, the bulb is disconnected from the circuit, but the resistor remains directly connected across the 20V source. Therefore, the voltage across the resistor remains unchanged, and according to Ohm's Law (I = V / R), the current through the resistor also remains unchanged.

A) and B) are incorrect because the resistor is unaffected by changes to the switch in the bulb's path.

D) is incorrect because the resistor still has a connection to the power source and will continue to draw current.

Part 7: Auto Information (AI)

1. B) Clutch. Explanation: The clutch disengages the engine from the gearbox when the driver presses the clutch pedal, allowing for smooth gear changes. In automatic transmissions, this function is performed by a torque converter.

2. C) Power. Explanation: During the power stroke, the spark plug ignites the compressed air-fuel mixture, causing combustion. This rapid expansion of gases pushes the piston downward, generating the force needed to power the engine. The other strokes—intake, compression, and exhaust—each have different roles, but the power stroke is where the actual energy for movement is produced.

3. C) Exhaust Gas Recirculation (EGR). Explanation: The EGR system works by recirculating a portion of the exhaust gases back into the engine's intake manifold, lowering the combustion temperature and reducing nitrogen oxide emissions. The PCV system (A) recycles unburned gases, and the EVAP system (B) prevents fuel vapors from escaping into the atmosphere. The catalytic converter (D) reduces toxic emissions but does not recirculate exhaust gases.

4. D) Water Pump. Explanation: The water pump is the component responsible for circulating coolant through the engine and radiator to maintain consistent engine temperatures. The radiator (A) dissipates heat, the thermostat (B) controls the flow of coolant based on temperature, and the oil pump (C) is part of the lubrication system, responsible for circulating engine oil. The water pump ensures continuous coolant flow to prevent overheating.

5. C) Rack and Pinion Steering. Explanation: Rack and pinion steering uses a pinion gear that moves along a metal rack to turn the vehicle's wheels when the driver rotates the steering wheel. Hydraulic (A) and electric (B) power steering systems provide assistance to the driver in turning the wheel but do not involve the rack and pinion mechanism. Torque vectoring (D) is a separate system used to manage power distribution across wheels, not directly related to steering.

6. B) To prevent excessive bouncing by damping suspension movement

Explanation: Shock absorbers dampen the movement of the springs and suspension, preventing excessive bouncing after hitting bumps or uneven surfaces. They convert the kinetic energy from the suspension movement into heat. Option A describes the role of springs and struts, C is related to tires, and D concerns wheel alignment, not the function of shock absorbers.

7. B) Reduced vibration and improved ride comfort. Explanation: Proper steering alignment ensures that the wheels are set to the manufacturer's specifications, reducing vibrations and providing a smoother ride. Misaligned wheels can cause excessive vibrations and uneven tire wear. The other options (A, C, D) are unrelated to steering alignment, focusing on engine and fuel systems instead.

8. B) Oil Filter. Explanation: The oil filter is designed to remove contaminants from the engine oil before it circulates through the engine. This helps maintain proper lubrication and prevents damage from dirt and particles.

9. C) To generate electrical power and recharge the battery once the engine is running

Explanation: The alternator is responsible for generating electrical power by converting mechanical energy from the engine into electrical energy. It supplies power to the vehicle's electrical components and recharges the battery after the engine starts. The starter motor (A) starts the engine, and the alternator does not directly control fuel or combustion (D).

10. C) To allow a low-current circuit to control a high-current circuit

Explanation: A relay is an electrically operated switch that allows a low-current circuit to safely control a high-current circuit, such as the headlights or fuel pump. Fuses (A) protect circuits from overcurrent, while the wiring harness (D) connects electrical components, and the alternator (B) converts mechanical energy into electrical energy. The relay's role is essential for safely controlling powerful devices in the vehicle.

Part 8: Shop Information (SI)

1. B) Jigsaw

Explanation: A jigsaw is designed for making detailed, curved cuts in materials like wood, metal, and plastic. It uses a reciprocating blade, making it ideal for applications requiring precision and complex shapes. A circular saw (A) is better for straight cuts, a reciprocating saw (C) is primarily for demolition, and a chainsaw (D) is used for rough cutting tasks, but none of these are suited for detailed or intricate cutting like a jigsaw.

2. C) Bar Clamp

The best option for holding two large boards together while the glue dries is C) Bar Clamp. Bar clamps provide long, adjustable pressure over a large surface area, making them ideal for tasks like clamping large boards or panels while glue dries.

   A) C-Clamp is versatile but typically used for smaller projects and doesn't span as wide as a bar clamp.

   B) Spring Clamp is useful for quick, temporary holds but lacks the necessary strength and reach for larger gluing tasks.

   D) Bench Vise is stationary and typically used for holding materials while working on them, not for clamping large objects for drying purposes.

3. B) Provides better control for precise hole drilling

Explanation: A brace and bit offer better control when drilling larger holes, particularly in woodworking. The U-shaped handle allows the user to apply steady, controlled pressure, making it ideal for precision tasks. Electric drills (C) are faster, but the brace and bit are used for their accuracy, especially for larger holes, which require more manual control.

4. B) Ball-peen hammer

Explanation: The ball-peen hammer has a rounded end, which makes it ideal for shaping metal and setting rivets without causing damage. It is commonly used in metalworking tasks. The claw hammer (A) is more suited for carpentry, the mallet (C) for softer strikes on wood, and the sledgehammer (D) for heavy demolition, making them less appropriate for metalworking.

5. B) To distribute pressure and prevent damage

Explanation: Washers are placed between a bolt and the surface of a material to distribute the pressure and prevent damage to the surface. They can also improve the stability of the joint. Options A and C are incorrect because washers do not directly affect torque or tightness, and D is unrelated to the washer's purpose.

6. B) Measuring very small dimensions with high accuracy

Explanation: A micrometer is a precision tool used to measure very small objects, often to within thousandths of an inch or hundredths of a millimeter. It provides highly accurate readings, making it ideal for engineering and machining. It is not suitable for measuring large surfaces, angles, or long distances.

7. D) Hammer Chisel

Explanation: A hammer chisel is specifically designed to work with chisels in woodworking or metalworking, providing controlled force for cutting or shaping material. The hammer chisel's flat surface allows precise strikes, ensuring the chisel removes material efficiently.

   A) Claw Hammer is mainly used for driving nails and removing them with the claw.

   B) Ball-Peen Hammer is used for shaping metal and riveting, but not typically with chisels.

   C) A mallet is a soft-headed striking tool used when a softer impact is needed.

8. C) Measuring angles between 0° and 180° or 0° and 360°

Explanation: A protractor is used to measure angles, typically between 0° and 180° or 0° and 360°, depending on the type of protractor. It is an essential tool for ensuring precision in tasks that involve cutting or assembling at specific angles. It is not used for measuring right angles, internal diameters, or lengths.

9. C) Needle-nose Pliers

Explanation: Needle-nose pliers have long, slender jaws that make them ideal for gripping small objects in tight spaces, especially in electrical or mechanical work. Slip-joint pliers (A) and channel-lock pliers (D) are adjustable but not designed for precision work, while locking pliers (B) are meant for gripping with strong force, not delicate tasks.

10 . B) It allows continuous turning without lifting the tool

Explanation: The ratchet mechanism allows the user to move the handle back and forth without removing and repositioning the socket wrench, making it ideal for tightening or loosening fasteners in tight spaces. Options A, C, and D are incorrect: while the ratchet can improve efficiency, it does not inherently increase torque, fit all fasteners, or measure torque like a torque wrench does.

Part 9: Mechanical Comprehension (MC)

1. (B) 32,000 J. Explanation: The formula for kinetic energy is: $KE = \frac{1}{2}mv^2$, where m is the mass (10 kg) and v is the velocity (80 m/s). Substituting the values:

$$KE = \frac{1}{2} \times 10\,\text{kg} \times (80\,\text{m/s})^2 = 5 \times 6400 = 32,000\,\text{J}$$

2. (A) 75 W. Explanation: Power is the rate of work done over time. The formula is: $\text{Power} = \frac{\text{Work}}{\text{Time}} = \frac{F \cdot d}{t}$

Where: $F = 50\,\text{N}, d = 15\,\text{m}$, and $t = 10$ seconds. Hence, calculate the work done: $W = F \cdot d = 50\,\text{N} \times 15\,\text{m} = 750\,\text{J}$

Now, calculate the power: $\text{Power} = \frac{750\,\text{J}}{10\,\text{seconds}} = 75\,\text{W}$.

3. (A) 20 pounds. Explanation: Torque is calculated by multiplying the force applied by the length of the lever arm. Here, the torque is given as 60 ft-lb, and the wrench length is 3 feet. The formula for torque is $T = F \times r$, so solving for force gives $F = \frac{T}{r} = \frac{60}{3} = 20$ pounds. This means applying a 20-pound force at the end of the wrench generates the required torque.

4. (B) 20 N. Explanation: The frictional force is calculated using the formula $f = \mu \times N$ where μ is the coefficient of friction, and N is the normal force. In this case, $\mu = 0.2$ and $N = 200\,\text{N}$ so $f = 0.2 \times 200 = 40\,\text{N}$. The frictional force opposes the motion of the box, slowing it down.

5. (B) 0.45 psi. Explanation: The formula for pressure is: $\text{Pressure} = \frac{\text{Force}}{\text{Area}}$

The force is the hiker's weight, 180 pounds. The total area of both snowshoes is:

$$2 \times (10\,\text{in} \times 20\,\text{in}) = 400\,\text{square inches}$$

Now calculate the pressure: $\text{Pressure} = \frac{180\,\text{lb}}{400\,\text{in}^2} = 0.45\,\text{psi}$.

6. (B) 10 N. Explanation: According to Newton's third law, for every action, there is an equal and opposite reaction. Therefore, Block B will exert the same force of 10 N on Block A but in the opposite direction.

7. A) 100 pounds. Explanation: In this block and tackle pulley system, the mechanical advantage is determined by the number of support segments. Here, there are four support segments, meaning the mechanical advantage is 4. The effort required is the load divided by the mechanical advantage:

$$\text{Effort} = \frac{\text{Load}}{\text{Mechanical Advantage}} = \frac{400\,\text{pounds}}{4} = 100\,\text{pounds}$$

8. A) 600 pounds. Explanation: Force is calculated by multiplying the pressure by the area. In this case, $30\,\text{psi} \times 20\,\text{in}^2 = 600\,\text{pounds}$.

9. (A) 400 rpm. Explanation: The rear gear will rotate faster since it has fewer teeth. Since the front gear has 4 times as many teeth as the rear gear, the rear gear will rotate 4 times as fast as the front gear: $100 \times 4 = 400$ rpm.

10. (B) 320 N. Explanation: The normal force is the sum of the weight of the object and the additional force acting on it. The weight of the box is:

$$W = m \times g = 25\,\text{kg} \times 9.8\,\text{m/s}^2 = 245\,\text{N}$$

Now, adding the extra 75 N force: Normal Force $= 245\,\text{N} + 75\,\text{N} = 320\,\text{N}$.

11. (D) The coefficient of kinetic friction is less than the coefficient of static friction.

Explanation: The coefficient of static friction is usually higher than that of kinetic friction. Static friction must first be overcome to move an object. Once moving, less force is required to keep it moving because the kinetic friction coefficient (which opposes motion) is lower than static friction coefficient.

12. C) elasticity. Explanation: Elasticity is the property of a material (like a tennis ball) to return to its original shape after deformation, which causes the ball to bounce back up after hitting the ground. Options A, B, and D refer to different physical concepts that do not apply in this context.

13. (C) Its potential energy is being converted into kinetic energy.

Explanation: As an object moves down a slope, its height decreases, reducing its potential energy. This lost potential energy is converted into kinetic energy, causing the object to speed up.

14. (B) Greater inertia. Explanation: Inertia is the property of an object that resists changes to its motion. Objects with more mass have more inertia, making them harder to accelerate. Momentum depends on motion, torque relates to rotational force, and pressure isn't relevant to this scenario.

15. (B) Wedge. Explanation: A nail acts as a wedge because it transfers force applied to its head into a splitting force at its point, allowing it to penetrate wood. An inclined plane would not create a splitting force, and a lever is used to lift or pry objects. A pulley is designed for lifting loads and/or redirecting force using ropes.

Part 10: Assembling Objects (AO)

1. B

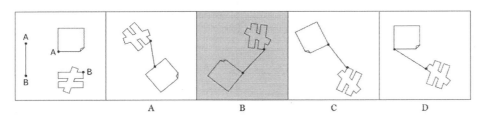

2. B

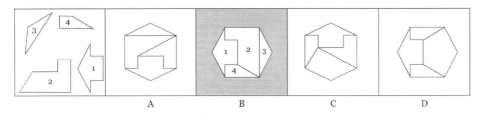

3. D

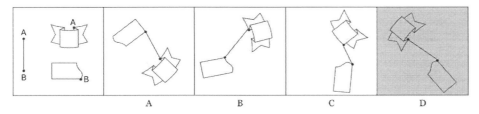

4. D

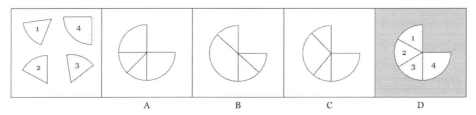

5. A

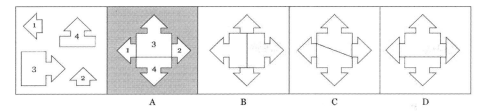

6. C

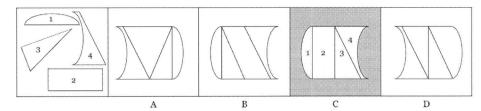

7. D

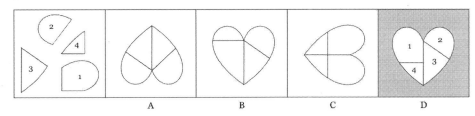

8. C

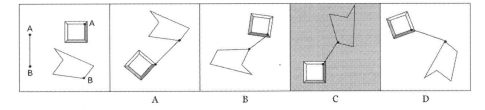

9. B

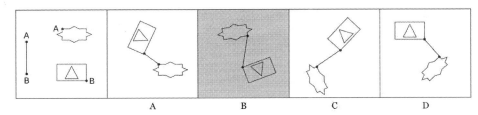

10. B

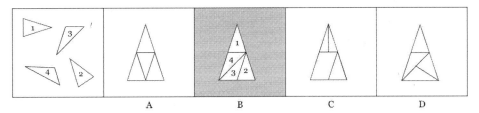

11. A

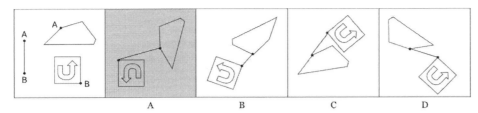

12. B

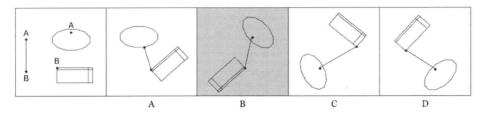

13. C

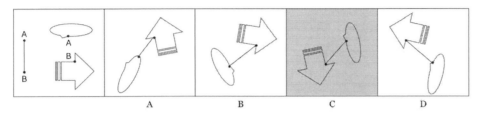

14. B

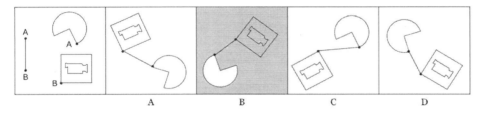

15. C

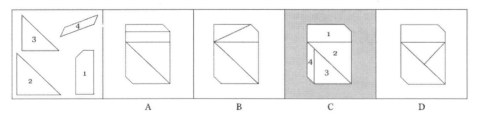

ASVAB PRACTICE TEST 3

PART 1: GENERAL SCIENCE (GS)

Time: 12 minutes for 15 questions

Select the correct answer from the choices given. This practice subtest reflects the number of questions and time limits you'll encounter on the CAT-ASVAB General Science subtest without any tryout questions.

1. What term refers to the maintenance of a stable internal environment in organisms?

A) Homeostasis
B) Photosynthesis
C) Cellular respiration
D) Evolution

2. Which organelle controls cell activities and stores genetic information?

A) Mitochondria
B) Ribosome
C) Nucleus
D) Golgi apparatus

3. Which system is primarily involved in gas exchange in the body?

A) Digestive system
B) Nervous system
C) Respiratory system
D) Skeletal system

4. What is the process of cell division in which two identical cells are produced?

A) Meiosis
B) Mitosis
C) Transcription
D) Replication

5. What is the primary function of stomata in plants?

A) Transporting sugars throughout the plant
B) Absorbing sunlight
C) Gas exchange and regulation of water loss
D) Breaking down nutrients

6. What does the momentum of an object depend on?

A) Its mass and velocity
B) Its velocity and acceleration
C) Its mass and direction
D) Its speed and distance

7. If a 5 kg object moves at a velocity of 10 m/s, what is its momentum?

A) 50 N
B) 50 $kg \cdot m/s$
C) 100 $kg \cdot m/s$
D) 100 N

8. What does Newton's First Law of Motion state?

A) Force is equal to mass times acceleration
B) Every action has an equal and opposite reaction
C) An object at rest stays at rest unless acted upon by an external force
D) Acceleration is proportional to force applied

9. What happens to the total momentum in a closed system during a collision?

A) It increases
B) It decreases
C) It is conserved
D) It depends on the masses

10. Which unit is used to measure power?

A) Joule
B) Watt
C) Newton
D) Kilogram

11. Which of the following is a physical change?

A) Rusting of iron
B) Burning of wood
C) Melting of ice
D) Cooking an egg

12. How are acids defined in chemistry?

A) Substances that release hydrogen ions (H^+) in water
B) Substances that accept electrons
C) Substances that release hydroxide ions (OH^-)
D) Substances that are always neutral

13. What is the atomic mass of an element?

A) Total number of protons
B) Total number of neutrons
C) Average mass of an atom accounting for isotopes
D) Electrons orbiting the nucleus

14. What is the dominant gas in Earth's atmosphere?

A) Oxygen
B) Carbon dioxide
C) Argon
D) Nitrogen

15. How are sedimentary rocks primarily formed?

A) By the cooling of magma
B) Through the compaction of sediments
C) By heat and pressure
D) Through volcanic activity

PART 2: ARITHMETIC REASONING (AR)

Time: 55 minutes for 15 questions

Select the correct answer from the choices given. This practice subtest reflects the number of questions and time limits you'll encounter on the CAT-ASVAB Arithmetic Reasoning subtest without any tryout questions.

1. A company has 25 employees and provides 36 square feet of workspace per employee. If five more employees are hired, how much less workspace will each employee have?

A) 4 square feet
B) 5 square feet
C) 6 square feet
D) 7 square feet

2. Tina rides her bike at a speed of 12 miles per hour. If she needs to travel a distance of 6 miles to get to the park, how long will it take her to get there?

A) 20 minutes
B) 30 minutes
C) 45 minutes
D) 60 minutes

3. Lena is hiking in Canada, where the distances on the trail signs are posted in kilometers. She sees that the next rest stop is 10 kilometers away. Lena knows that 1 kilometer is approximately $\frac{5}{8}$ of a mile. How many miles away is the rest stop? Round to the nearest integer.

A) 5 miles
B) 6 miles
C) 7 miles
D) 8 miles

4. A right triangle has one leg of 6 meters and another leg of 8 meters. What is the length of the hypotenuse?

A) 11 meters
B) 12 meters
C) 9 meters
D) 10 meters

5. A roller-skating rink is 200 meters around. Sarah wants to skate 3 kilometers. How many laps around the rink must she complete to reach her goal?

A) 12
B) 15
C) 18
D) 20

6. A chemical reaction produced 120 grams of a compound, which was 20% more than the theoretical yield. What was the theoretical yield of the compound?

A) 100 grams
B) 105 grams
C) 110 grams
D) 115 grams

7. A juice shop prepared 48 bottles of fresh juice. A gym buys one-fourth of the bottles, a café buys one-third of the bottles, and a customer buys one-sixth of the bottles. How many bottles of juice does the shop have left?

A) 10
B) 8
C) 12
D) 5

8. A family is driving for 2.5 hours at an average speed of 60 miles per hour. How far will they travel during this time?

A) 100 miles
B) 120 miles
C) 150 miles
D) 180 miles

9. A personal trainer earns $15.00 an hour for a 40-hour week. Her overtime pay is 1.5 times her base pay. If she works 45 hours in a week, what is her total weekly pay?

A) $690.00
B) $712.50
C) $697.50
D) $750.00

10. In June, which has 30 days, Jamie worked 3 out of every 5 days at either a library or a café. He worked at the library for 12 days, and at the café for each of the remaining days that he worked. How many days did he work at the café?

A) 4 days
B) 5 days
C) 6 days
D) 8 days

11. On a flight from Paris to Tokyo, a total of 300 passengers each ordered a dinner whose main dish was beef, chicken, or fish. The number of passengers who ordered beef was 105, while 95 ordered fish. How many passengers ordered chicken?

A) 100
B) 95
C) 105
D) 110

12. Sam bikes to the park at a speed of 10 miles per hour and returns home at 20 miles per hour along the same route. What is his average speed for the entire trip?

A) 12 mph
B) 13.3 mph
C) 14.5 mph
D) 15 mph

13. A worker packs 120 books in 30 minutes. At this rate, how long will it take to pack 40 books?

A) 5 minutes
B) 10 minutes
C) 12 minutes
D) 15 minutes

14. Sara has a collection of pens and notebooks. The ratio of pens to notebooks is 3:5, and she has 45 pens. How many notebooks does Sara have?

A) 60
B) 50
C) 75
D) 80

15. A burger and a box of fries costs $5.50. Two burgers and a box of fries cost $8.50. What is the cost of a box of fries?

A) $1.00
B) $1.50
C) $2.00
D) $2.50

PART 3: WORD KNOWLEDGE (WK)

Time: 9 minutes for 15 questions

Each question below includes an underlined word. You may be asked to determine which one of the four answer choices most closely matches the meaning of the underlined word, or which choice has the opposite meaning. If the word is used within a sentence, your task is to select the option that most accurately reflects its meaning in the context of that sentence. This practice subtest reflects the number of questions and time limits you'll encounter on the CAT-ASVAB Word Knowledge subtest without any tryout questions.

1. The word underlined audacious most nearly means:

   A) timid
   B) bold
   C) cautious
   D) hesitant

2. The word eloquent most nearly means:

   A) inarticulate
   B) fluent
   C) awkward
   D) clumsy

3. The word ostentatious most nearly means:

   A) modest
   B) pretentious
   C) oblique
   D) plain

4. The artist was known for his esoteric style, understood only by a few.

   A) common
   B) obscure
   C) simple
   D) popular

5. The word most opposite in meaning to benign is:

   A) gentle
   B) friendly
   C) harmful
   D) kind

6. The word frivolous most nearly means:

   A) important
   B) trivial
   C) serious
   D) necessary

7. The word meticulous most nearly means:

   A) careless
   B) precise
   C) sloppy
   D) reckless

8. The word acumen most nearly means:

   A) foolishness
   B) insight
   C) ignorance
   D) confusion

9. The calamity struck the town, leaving destruction in its wake.
   A) success
   B) disaster
   C) celebration
   D) victory

10. The new evidence may vindicate her from all accusations.

   A) accuse
   B) punish
   C) justify
   D) convict

11. The word empathy most nearly means:

   A) indifference
   B) understanding
   C) hatred
   D) disregard

12. The criminal showed contrition after hearing the sentence.

   A) arrogance
   B) indifference
   C) remorse
   D) joy

13. The town's insular location made it difficult for outsiders to visit.

   A) central
   B) isolated
   C) populous
   D) inclusive

14. He did nothing but exacerbate the situation by bringing up past conflicts.

   A) improve
   B) worsen
   C) resolve
   D) ignore

15. The manager had to delegate some tasks to her team to meet the deadline.

   A) avoid
   B) manage
   C) assign
   D) complete

PART 4: PARAGRAPH COMPREHENSION (PC)

Time: 27 minutes for 10 questions

This section presents reading paragraphs followed by questions or incomplete statements. Your task is to read the paragraph and choose the option that best completes the statement or answers the question. This practice subtest simulates the number of questions and time constraints you'll face on the CAT-ASVAB Paragraph Comprehension subtest, without any tryout questions.

The thieves planned their heist meticulously, waiting for the perfect moment to strike. Under the cover of darkness, they quietly gathered the valuables and made their way toward the exit. However, as soon as the alarm blared, they had no choice but to abandon their careful plan and abscond into the night. They vanished quickly, leaving behind only a few scattered items. Their disappearance left the authorities baffled, and despite the efforts of local law enforcement, they were unable to track down the criminals.

1. In this passage, abscond most nearly means:

A) Escape
B) Surrender
C) Hesitate
D) Confess

In 1962, the Cuyahoga River in Ohio became infamous for catching fire due to extreme pollution levels. The river, heavily contaminated with industrial waste, was a symbol of environmental neglect. The most notable fire occurred in 1969, drawing national attention to the dire state of water pollution in America. Although the Cuyahoga River is the most well-known, rivers in Pennsylvania, such as the Schuylkill River, faced similar pollution issues. Decades of industrial dumping had turned these rivers into hazardous waterways, sparking movements for environmental reform and stricter pollution controls.

2. What was the primary cause of rivers catching fire in Pennsylvania?

A) Overfishing
B) Deforestation
C) Industrial pollution
D) Natural gas leaks

While many plants have green leaves due to chlorophyll, others, such as those with red or purple leaves, also undergo photosynthesis. In these plants, pigments like anthocyanins give the leaves their red or purple color. However, chlorophyll is still present, and it plays a key role in absorbing light for photosynthesis. The other pigments may help absorb additional light wavelengths or protect the plant from harsh sunlight. Despite their color differences, these leaves are still able to capture sunlight and convert it into energy.

3. How do red and purple leaves perform photosynthesis?

A) They lack chlorophyll and use other pigments instead.
B) They use chlorophyll along with other pigments to absorb light.
C) They rely solely on anthocyanins for energy production.
D) They cannot photosynthesize and rely on their roots for energy.

During a recession, the stock market often experiences volatility, with stock prices declining as investors grow concerned about economic conditions. Companies face reduced consumer spending, leading to lower profits and reduced stock values. However, stock market performance doesn't always mirror the overall economy. Sometimes, investors anticipate recovery and begin buying stocks before the recession ends, causing a market rebound. It's essential to note that different sectors may perform differently during a recession, with some industries, like utilities, often showing resilience.

4. What's the main purpose of this paragraph?

A) To explain why all sectors perform poorly during a recession.
B) To highlight the causes of stock market growth during a recession.
C) To describe the typical relationship between recessions and stock market performance.
D) To emphasize the consistent growth of stock prices during economic downturns.

As humans age, the cartilage in joints naturally undergoes changes that can lead to stiffness and reduced mobility. Cartilage, which cushions the ends of bones, becomes thinner and loses its elasticity over time. This thinning reduces its ability to absorb shock, making the joints more susceptible to damage. The decline in collagen and proteoglycan production, key components of cartilage, further weakens its structure. Although cartilage does not regenerate easily, maintaining a healthy lifestyle and staying active can help slow down these degenerative processes, providing relief from joint pain associated with aging.

5. How does aging affect cartilage?

A) It regenerates more easily.
B) It becomes thicker and more flexible.
C) It becomes thinner and loses its elasticity.
D) It becomes immune to damage over time.

It was our third day hiking through the rugged beauty of Cascade National Park. My dog, Luna, trotted ahead, tail wagging with excitement as we followed a narrow trail that wound through towering trees and along the edge of a crystal-clear lake. The crisp mountain air filled my lungs, but the climb was steep, and I could feel the burn in my legs. As we reached a small clearing, I paused to take in the breathtaking view of snow-capped peaks in the distance. Luna barked happily, her energy endless, urging me forward.

6. How does the narrator describe her hiking experience in Cascade National Park?

A) Exhausting but rewarding
B) Boring and uneventful
C) Relaxing and easy-going
D) Disappointing due to bad weather

The group had planned every detail of their trip, from the destinations to the itinerary. However, halfway through the journey, they abandoned their schedule and decided to take a spontaneous detour to an unplanned location. This decision, made on a whim, ended up being the highlight of their travels. They experienced a level of adventure they hadn't anticipated. The joy of these unplanned moments reminded them that sometimes the best experiences come when least expected.

7. In this passage, spontaneous most nearly means:

A) Planned
B) Deliberate
C) Impulsive
D) Hesitant

When the world buzzed with tales of Arctic gold, Carter Weatherbee, a tired and weary clerk, decided to abandon his stable life. Turning half of his savings over to his wife, he invested the rest in outfitting himself for the treacherous journey north. Weatherbee wasn't chasing romance or adventure; he simply wanted to escape the monotony of his job and seek fortune. Foolishly, he ignored the well-traveled routes used by experienced pioneers, rushing to Edmonton. There, he joined a group of men, a decision that would prove fateful for his journey and soul alike.

8. What motivated Carter Weatherbee to leave his job?

A) A love for adventure and romance
B) A desire for wealth and escape from monotony
C) The lure of becoming a pioneer
D) Pressure from his family to find riches

Benjamin Franklin's life was deeply intertwined with his commitment to public service and civic improvement. He played a crucial role in founding the first public library in America and establishing the University of Pennsylvania. Franklin also founded the American Philosophical Society, promoting intellectual advancement and collaboration. Additionally, his contributions to journalism, particularly through his ownership of The Pennsylvania Gazette, significantly impacted the field. Franklin's lasting legacy is a reflection of his relentless pursuit of knowledge and his dedication to the betterment of society.

9. What was one of Benjamin Franklin's key contributions to American society?

A) Writing the Declaration of Independence
B) Establishing the first public library in America
C) Leading a revolutionary army
D) Founding the Smithsonian Institution

Stoicism, a philosophical school founded in ancient Greece by Zeno of Citium, teaches that true happiness comes from accepting things outside our control and focusing on what we can change—our actions and reactions. Stoics believe in cultivating inner virtue, wisdom, and emotional resilience, encouraging individuals to remain calm and composed in the face of adversity. Key figures such as Seneca, Epictetus, and Marcus Aurelius emphasized the importance of aligning with nature and using rational thought to navigate life's challenges. Stoicism's central message is to live in harmony with nature while developing self-discipline.

10. What is the central belief of Stoicism?

A) Acquiring material wealth leads to happiness
B) Accepting things outside of our control leads to inner peace
C) Embracing emotions is the key to a fulfilling life
D) Pursuing pleasure is the ultimate goal of existence

PART 5: MATHEMATICS KNOWLEDGE (MK)

Time: 31 minutes for 15 questions

Select the correct answer from the choices given. This practice subtest reflects the number of questions and time limits you'll encounter on the CAT-ASVAB Mathematics Knowledge subtest without any tryout questions.

1. Emily tracked her steps for a month and found that she walked 22 days out of the last 30 days. What percentage of these days did she walk?

A) 62.5%
B) 73.33%
C) 72.5%
D) 80%

2. Which of the following inequalities is correct?

A) $\frac{6}{7} > \frac{5}{8}$
B) $\frac{7}{10} > \frac{8}{11}$
C) $\frac{9}{10} < \frac{8}{9}$
D) $\frac{5}{6} < \frac{4}{5}$

3. What is 3.4567 rounded to the nearest hundredth?

A) 3.45
B) 3.46
C) 3.457
D) 3.456

4. $\frac{4}{5} \div \frac{2}{3} =$

A) $\frac{4}{3}$
B) $\frac{6}{5}$
C) $\frac{5}{8}$
D) $\frac{5}{2}$

5. If you simplify (3x + 4)(2x - 3) - 4(x - 1), what's the result?

A) $6x^2 + 5x - 4$
B) $6x^2 - 5x - 4$
C) $6x^2 - 5x - 8$
D) $6x^2 + 5x - 8$

6. If $14.8x - 3.4 = 15.3x + 1.6$, then x equals

A) 8
B) -7
C) 0.8
D) -10

7. In a graph, the line intersects the points (1, 2) and (5, 8). What is the equation of this line?

A) $y = \frac{3}{4}x + \frac{5}{4}$
B) $y = \frac{3}{2}x + \frac{1}{2}$
C) $y = 2x - 1$
D) $y = \frac{3}{2}x - \frac{1}{2}$

8. What is the greatest common factor of $18x^3y^2z$ and $24x^2yz^3$?

A) $3xy^2z$
B) $6x^2yz$
C) $6x^2yz^3$
D) $12xy^2z$

9. If a = 2 and b = -4, then $5a^2 + 2ab - 3b^2 =$

A) -52
B) 52
C) -44
D) -92

10. The following table lists data about the 40 employees in a company, dividing the group into departments and then dividing each of these two groups into those who are managers and those who are not. What percentage of the company are managers in the Marketing department?

	Managers	Non-Managers	Total
Marketing	5	15	20
Sales	10	10	20
Total	15	25	40

A) 10%
B) 12.5%
C) 15%
D) 25%

11. If $y = mx + b$ is a linear function with a slope of 5 that intersects the point
(2, -7), what are the values of m and b ?

A) $m = 5, \ b = -10$
B) $m = 5, \ b = -17$
C) $m = -5, \ b = 17$
D) $m = -5, \ b = -7$

12. A right triangle has one leg that is 3 units longer than the other leg. The hypotenuse is 15 units long. What are the lengths of the legs of the triangle?

A) 5 units and 12 units
B) 6 units and 13 units
C) 8 units and 15 units
D) 9 units and 12 units

13. $(3x^2y^3)(4x^5)^2 =$

A) $36x^7y^3$
B) $48x^{10}y^6$
C) $72x^{11}y^3$
D) $72x^{13}y^6$

14. The following graph shows the monthly production at a factory from January to December in 2020. In which month did the factory see the greatest increase in production compared with the previous month?

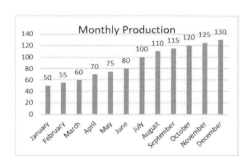

A) February
B) April
C) July
D) October

15. Two triangles are shown to the right. Given DF=AB, which of the following condition can prove the two triangles are congruent.

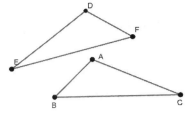

A) $\angle D = \angle A$ and BC=EF
B) $\angle E = \angle C$
C) EF=BC
D) $\angle D = \angle A$ and $\angle F = \angle B$

PART 6: ELECTRONICS INFORMATION (EI)

Time: 10 minutes for 15 questions

Select the correct answer from the choices given. This practice subtest reflects the number of questions and time limits you'll encounter on the CAT-ASVAB Electronics Information subtest without any tryout questions.

1. If a 240-volt power supply is protected by a 15-amp circuit breaker, what is the maximum power an appliance can safely use?

A) 2,400 watts
B) 3,000 watts
C) 3,600 watts
D) 4,000 watts

2. Which instrument is used to measure the voltage in a circuit?

A) ohmmeter
B) voltmeter
C) ammeter
D) wattmeter

3. All of the following statements about capacitors are true EXCEPT

A) Capacitors store electrical energy in an electric field
B) Capacitors block direct current but allow alternating current to pass
C) The unit of capacitance is the farad
D) Capacitors store energy in a magnetic field

4. Which of the following components has a specific direction for current flow?

A) inductor
B) resistor
C) diode
D) transformer

5. A phototransistor changes its current output in response to

A) temperature
B) pressure
C) light intensity
D) voltage

6. In an open electrical circuit,

A) current flows continuously.
B) there is no complete path for current to flow.
C) voltage drops as current flows across components.
D) resistance is zero.

7. In the given circuit, a 24V battery is connected across a 10-ohm bulb with a 2A fuse. If the switch is closed, what will happen in the circuit?

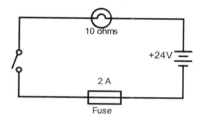

A) The fuse will blow, interrupting the circuit.
B) The bulb will light up, and the fuse will remain intact.
C) The current will be low because the fuse rating is too high.
D) The bulb will not light up as the voltage is too low.

8. Which type of current flows in only one direction continuously?

A) AC
B) DC
C) Alternating
D) Transient

9. What happens when a motor operates below its rated voltage?

A) It runs faster but overheats.
B) It runs slower and with less efficiency.
C) It runs at the same speed without impact.
D) It draws more current than normal.

10. What happens if a magnetic field is moved relative to a conductor?

A) A current is induced in the conductor.
B) The conductor loses resistance.
C) The magnetic field disappears.
D) The voltage drops to zero.

11. What is the main function of an inverter?

A) Convert DC to AC
B) Store energy
C) Reduce resistance
D) Step down voltage

12. A circuit breaker is used to

A) provide constant current.
B) disconnect the circuit during overload.
C) reduce resistance in the circuit.
D) convert DC to AC.

13. The following is a symbol for

A) Resistor
B) Capacitor
C) Inductor
D) Diode

14. The main purpose of an inductor is to

A) resist changes in current.
B) step up AC voltage.
C) store electric charges.
D) convert DC to AC.

15. A transistor typically has three terminals. Which of the following are the correct names for these terminals?

A) Gate, drain, and source
B) Input, output, and ground
C) Base, collector, and emitter
D) Positive, neutral, and negative

PART 7: AUTO INFORMATION (AI)

Time: 7 minutes for 10 questions

Select the correct answer from the choices given. This practice subtest reflects the number of questions and time limits you'll encounter on the CAT-ASVAB Auto Information subtest without any tryout questions.

1. What is one of the main advantages of an All-Wheel Drive (AWD) system?

A) It allows the driver to manually engage four-wheel drive.
B) It provides power only to the rear wheels for better handling.
C) It automatically adjusts power distribution to all four wheels for enhanced traction and stability.
D) It improves weight distribution for high-performance sports cars.

2. Which type of suspension allows each wheel to move independently of the others, improving ride comfort and handling?

A) Solid Axle Suspension
B) Independent Suspension
C) Leaf Spring Suspension
D) Torsion Bar Suspension

3. What component is responsible for engaging the engine's flywheel to initiate the combustion process and start the engine?

A) Alternator
B) Starter Motor
C) Voltage Regulator
D) Ignition Coil

4. What is the primary function of the chassis in a vehicle?

A) To regulate the engine's temperature
B) To provide the structural framework supporting all vehicle components
C) To manage the vehicle's fuel efficiency
D) To control the vehicle's electrical system

5. Identify the car part shown in the image:

A) Fuel Injector
B) Spark Plug
C) Piston
D) Oil Filter

6. How do shock absorbers dissipate the energy generated by the suspension system?

A) By converting motion energy into sound energy
B) By converting motion energy into heat energy
C) By converting motion energy into kinetic energy
D) By converting motion energy into magnetic energy

7. In a modern engine, where are multiple fuel injectors most commonly located?

A) In the exhaust manifold
B) In the intake manifold
C) In the cooling system
D) In the carburetor

8. What is the primary function of piston rings in an engine?

A) To clean the combustion chamber and remove impurities in fuel
B) To seal the combustion chamber and allow the pistons to move freely
C) To protect the cylinder from the destructive force of combustion
D) To provide lubrication to the piston cylinder

9. What can result from driving a vehicle with incorrect tire pressure?

A) Improved fuel efficiency and longer tire life
B) Even tire wear and better handling
C) Uneven tire wear, reduced handling, and increased risk of tire failure
D) Enhanced traction in all road conditions

10. Why is wheel balancing important for vehicle performance?

A) It ensures the wheels are properly aligned with the steering system
B) It prevents uneven tire wear and reduces vibrations at higher speeds
C) It improves fuel efficiency by reducing rolling resistance
D) It allows for better traction in wet conditions

PART 8: SHOP INFORMATION (SI)

Time: 6 minutes for 10 questions

Select the correct answer from the choices given. This practice subtest reflects the number of questions and time limits you'll encounter on the CAT-ASVAB Shop Information subtest without any tryout questions.

1.Which tool is able to lock in place, providing a firm and secure grip?

A) Needle-nose Pliers
B) Slip-joint Pliers
C) Locking Pliers
D) Adjustable Wrench

2. Which of the following saws would be best suited for cutting curved shapes in wood?

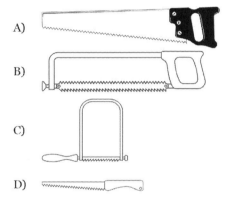

A)

B)

C)

D)

3. Which tool is designed for use when a softer impact is needed to avoid damaging a workpiece?

A) Claw hammer
B) Ball-peen hammer
C) Mallet
D) Sledgehammer

4. What is a square primarily used for in a shop environment?

A) Checking and measuring right angles
B) Measuring small diameters
C) Measuring angles over 90°
D) Measuring internal dimensions

5. Which type of tool is designed to cut holes in materials when attached to a power drill?

A) Auger
B) Brace
C) Drill Bit
D) Hole Saw

6. Which tool provides better leverage for heavy-duty demolition tasks, such as dismantling wooden structures?

A) Pry Bar
B) Nail Puller
C) Crowbar
D) Claw Hammer

7. What are ring fasteners, such as circlips, primarily used for?

A) Joining wood pieces
B) Holding components onto a shaft
C) Driving screws into metal
D) Aligning mechanical parts

8. What is the primary difference between a screw and a bolt?

A) Screws require a hammer, bolts need a screwdriver
B) Screws are driven directly into materials, bolts require a nut
C) Bolts are only used for wood, screws are only used for metal
D) Screws are temporary fasteners, bolts are permanent

9. Which process joins metals by melting them together at high temperatures?

A) Soldering
B) Welding
C) Riveting
D) Bolting

10. Which of the following tasks is best performed with the tools shown in the image?

A) Smoothing rough metal edges
B) Cutting wood into precise shapes
C) Driving screws into wood
D) Stripping electrical wires

PART 9: MECHANICAL COMPREHENSION (MC)

Time: 22 minutes for 15 questions

Select the correct answer from the choices given. This practice subtest reflects the number of questions and time limits you'll encounter on the CAT-ASVAB Mechanical Comprehension subtest without any tryout questions.

1. The force that attracts objects toward each other is explained by which of Newton's laws?

(A) Newton's first law.
(B) Newton's second law.
(C) Newton's law of universal gravitation.
(D) Newton's third law.

2. When a stone is thrown upward, its maximum potential energy occurs:

(A) When it reaches the top of its arc and its velocity is zero.
(B) Just before it leaves the thrower's hand.
(C) Just before it hits the ground.
(D) When its velocity is highest.

3. A beam is supported at two points. The left point is 2 feet from the center, and the right point is 4 feet from the center. Which side holds more of the load?

(A) Left
(B) Right
(C) Both hold the load equally
(D) Not enough information

4. Power is measured in which unit?

(A) Joules
(B) Watts
(C) Newtons
(D) Kilograms

5. Which of the following statements is true about simple machines?

(A) The work put out by a simple machine can sometimes exceed the work put in.
(B) The work put out by a simple machine always exceeds the work put in.
(C) The work put out by a simple machine can never exceed the work put in.
(D) The work put out by a simple machine is always equal to the work put in.

6. The design of a bottle opener is based on which of the following simple machines?

(A) First-class lever
(B) Second-class lever
(C) Third-class lever
(D) Inclined plane

7. To increase the force in a first-class lever, the fulcrum should be

(A) moved toward where the effort is applied.
(B) kept in the same position.
(C) moved toward where the object is moved.
(D) removed altogether.

8. Which of the following shelves can support the most weight?

(A)

(B)

(C)

(D)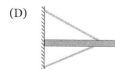

9. A mechanic uses a hydraulic car lift to raise a vehicle. He notices that the car, which weighs 2,000 pounds, can be lifted with only 50 pounds of effort applied to the small piston. What is the primary reason the mechanic can lift such a heavy load with relatively little effort?

(A) The car lift uses a system of pulleys.
(B) The car lift reduces the force required through mechanical advantage.
(C) The hydraulic fluid eliminates friction between the pistons.
(D) The car lift uses electrical power to multiply the force applied.

10. An astronaut on Earth weighs 180 pounds. When the astronaut travels to the Moon, he notices that he feels much lighter. Why is that the case?

(A) The astronaut's mass increases on the Moon.
(B) The force of gravity on the Moon is weaker than on Earth.
(C) The astronaut's muscles are stronger in space.
(D) The astronaut's body is closer to the Sun while on the Moon.

11. One horsepower is equivalent to how many watts?

(A) 746
(B) 855
(C) 1,000
(D) 1,200

12. The design of a door handle is based on which of the following simple machines?

(A) Pulley
(B) Wheel and axle
(C) Wedge
(D) Inclined plane

13. In the pulley system shown, if the load weighs 300 pounds and there are three support segments holding the load, what is the effort required to lift the load?

A) 100 pounds
B) 150 pounds
C) 300 pounds
D) 50 pounds

14. The difference between a screw and a wedge is that:

(A) A screw is designed to rotate, whereas a wedge is designed to stay stationary.
(B) A screw applies force in a rotational motion, whereas a wedge applies force in a linear motion.
(C) A screw decreases friction, while a wedge increases friction.
(D) A screw is used for cutting, whereas a wedge is used for lifting.

15. A hydraulic jack multiplies the force applied by a factor of 5. This increase in force is always accompanied by which of the following changes in distance moved?

(A) An increase
(B) A decrease
(C) No change
(D) A slight increase and decrease at different times

PART 10: ASSEMBLING OBJECTS (AO)

Time: 18 minutes for 15 questions

Select the correct answer from the choices given. This practice subtest reflects the number of questions and time limits you'll encounter on the CAT-ASVAB Assembling Objects subtest without any tryout questions.

1.

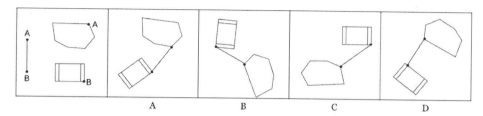

A B C D

2.

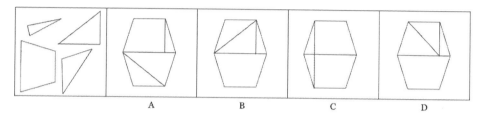

A B C D

3.

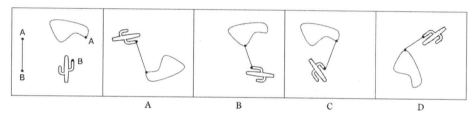

A B C D

4.

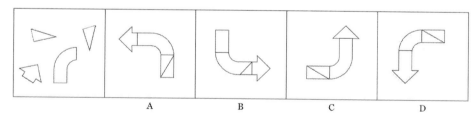

A B C D

5.

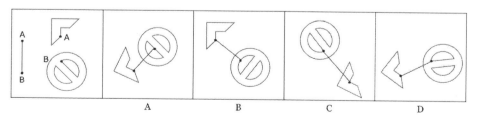

A B C D

6.

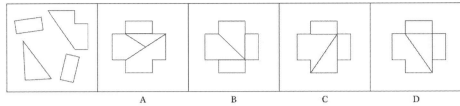

A   B   C   D

7.

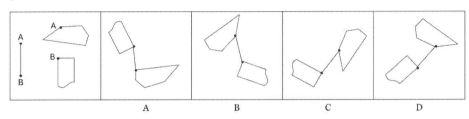

A   B   C   D

8.

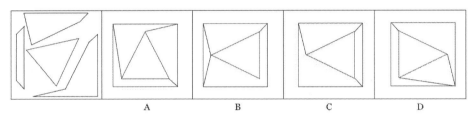

A   B   C   D

9.

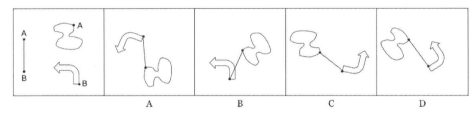

A   B   C   D

10.

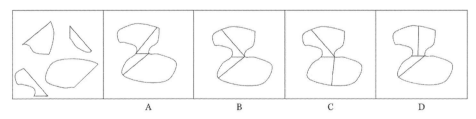

A   B   C   D

11.

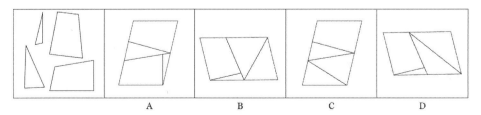

A   B   C   D

12.

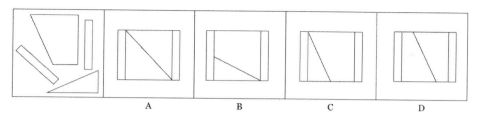

| | A | B | C | D |

13.

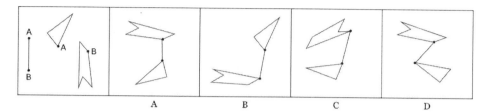

| | A | B | C | D |

14.

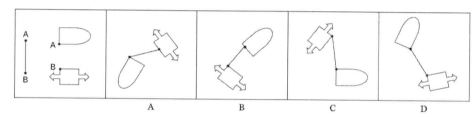

| | A | B | C | D |

15.

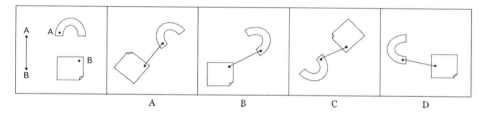

| | A | B | C | D |

ANSWERS AND EXPLANATIONS—PRACTICE TEST 3

Part 1: General Science (GS)

1. A) Homeostasis. Explanation: Homeostasis is the process by which organisms regulate internal conditions to maintain balance despite external changes.

2. C) Nucleus. Explanation: The nucleus is the control center of the cell, housing DNA and directing cell functions.

3. C) Respiratory system. Explanation: The respiratory system is responsible for taking in oxygen and expelling carbon dioxide through the lungs.

4. B) Mitosis. Explanation: Mitosis is the process of cell division that results in two genetically identical daughter cells.

5. C) Gas exchange and regulation of water loss. Explanation: Stomata are tiny openings on leaves that allow plants to exchange gases (oxygen and carbon dioxide) and control water evaporation through transpiration.

6. A) Its mass and velocity. Explanation: Momentum is the product of an object's mass and its velocity, calculated as $p = mv$ and it plays a crucial role in understanding collisions.

7. B) 50 $kg \cdot m/s$. Explanation: Momentum is calculated as $p = mv$ For this object, $p = 5 \, \text{kg} \times 10 \, \text{m/s} = 50 \, \text{kg·m/s}$.

8. C) An object at rest stays at rest unless acted upon by an external force. Explanation: Newton's First Law, or the Law of Inertia, explains that an object will remain in its current state of motion unless an external force causes a change.

9. C) It is conserved. Explanation: In a closed system with no external forces, the total momentum before and after a collision remains constant, according to the principle of conservation of momentum.

10. B) Watt. Explanation: Power is measured in watts (W), where one watt is equal to one joule per second. This unit expresses the rate of energy transfer.

11. C) Melting of ice. Explanation: Melting ice is a physical change because the chemical structure of water remains the same, even though its state changes from solid to liquid. Cooking an egg causes chemical changes inside of the egg.

12. A) Substances that release hydrogen ions (H^+) in water. Explanation: Acids release hydrogen ions (H^+) when dissolved in water, giving them their characteristic sour taste and corrosive properties.

13. C) Average mass of an atom accounting for isotopes. Explanation: The atomic mass represents the average mass of an element's atoms, considering all of its isotopes and their relative abundance.

14. D) Nitrogen. Explanation: Nitrogen makes up approximately 78% of the Earth's atmosphere, followed by oxygen at 21%.

15. B) Through the compaction of sediments. Explanation: Sedimentary rocks form when layers of sediments are compressed and cemented together over time.

Part 2: Arithmetic Reasoning (AR)

1. C) 6 square feet. Explanation: First, calculate the total workspace: $25 \times 36 = 900$ square feet.

   After hiring 5 more employees, the company now has 30 employees. To find the new workspace per employee: $\frac{900}{30} = 30$ square feet per employee.

   Now, find the difference in workspace per employee: $36 - 30 = 6$ square feet.

2. B) 30 minutes. Explanation: To find how long it takes, use the formula time $= \frac{\text{distance}}{\text{speed}}$. The distance is 6 miles, and the speed is 12 miles per hour, so: time $= \frac{6}{12} = 0.5$ hours $= 30$ minutes.

3. B) 6 miles. Explanation: To convert kilometers to miles, multiply the distance in kilometers by $\frac{5}{8}$: $10 \times \frac{5}{8} = 6.25$ miles.

4. D) 10 meters. Explanation: Use the Pythagorean Theorem: $a^2 + b^2 = c^2$, where $a = 6$, $b = 8$, and c is the hypotenuse. Hence, $6^2 + 8^2 = c^2 \Rightarrow 36 + 64 = c^2 \Rightarrow 100 = c^2 \Rightarrow c = \sqrt{100} = 10$ meters.

5. B) 15. Explanation: First, convert the total distance into meters: 3 kilometers is 3000 meters. Then, divide the total distance by the length of one lap: $\frac{3000}{200} = 15$. Thus, Sarah must complete 15 laps to skate 3 kilometers.

6. A) 100 grams. Explanation: Let the theoretical yield be x. The actual yield was 20% more than the theoretical yield, so: $1.2x = 120$. Hence, $x = \frac{120}{1.2} = 100$. Thus, the theoretical yield was 100 grams.

7. C) 12. Explanation: First, add up the fractions of the bottles that were purchased: $\frac{1}{4} + \frac{1}{3} + \frac{1}{6} = \frac{3}{12} + \frac{4}{12} + \frac{2}{12} = \frac{9}{12} = \frac{3}{4}$.

Hence, $1 - \frac{3}{4} = \frac{1}{4}$ was left. Calculate $\frac{1}{4}$ of 48 bottles: $\frac{1}{4} \times 48 = 12$. Therefore, the shop has 12 bottles left.

8. C) 150 miles. Explanation: To find the distance, use the formula distance = speed × time. The speed is 60 miles per hour, and the time is 2.5 hours, so: distance = $60 \times 2.5 = 150$ miles.

9. C) $697.50. Explanation: First, calculate the base pay for 40 hours: $40 \times 15.00 = 600.00$.

Next, calculate the overtime pay. The trainer worked 5 overtime hours, and overtime is paid at 1.5 times the base rate: $5 \times (15.00 \times 1.5) = 5 \times 22.50 = 112.50$.

Now, add the base pay and the overtime pay: $600.00 + 112.50 = 712.50$.

10. C) 6 days. Explanation: $\frac{3}{5} \times 30 = 18$ days worked. $18 - 12 = 6$ days at the café.

11. A) 100. Explanation: $300 - 105 - 95 = 100$.

12. B) 13.3 mph. Explanation: Let the distance to the park be d. The time taken to the park is: $t_1 = \frac{d}{10}$.

The time taken to return is: $t_2 = \frac{d}{20}$. The total time for the trip is: $t_{total} = t_1 + t_2 = \frac{d}{10} + \frac{d}{20} = \frac{3d}{20}$.

The total distance is $2d$, so: Average speed $= \frac{2d}{t_{total}} = \frac{2d}{\frac{3d}{20}} = \frac{2 \times 20}{3} \approx 13.3$ mph.

13. B) 10 minutes. Explanation: The worker packs 120 books in 30 minutes, so they pack: $\frac{120}{30} = 4$ books per minute.

To pack 40 books, the worker will need: $\frac{40}{4} = 10$ minutes.

14. C) 75. Explanation: The ratio of pens to notebooks is 3:5.

Let the number of notebooks be x Set up a proportion: $\frac{3}{5} = \frac{45}{x}$.

Hence: $3x = 45 \times 5 = 225 \Rightarrow x = \frac{225}{3} = 75$. Thus, Sara has 75 notebooks.

15. D) $2.50. Explanation: Let the price of a burger be b and the price of a box of fries be f. We are given:

$$b + f = 5.50 \quad \text{and} \quad 2b + f = 8.50$$

Subtract the first equation from the second: $(2b + f) - (b + f) = 8.50 - 5.50 \Rightarrow b = 3.00$.

Now substitute $b = 3.00$ into $b + f = 5.50$: $3.00 + f = 5.50 \Rightarrow f = 2.50$.

Thus, the cost of fries is $2.50.

Part 3: Word Knowledge (WK)

1. B) bold. "Audacious" means being daring or fearless, the opposite of timid or hesitant.

2. B) fluent. "Eloquent" describes someone who speaks clearly and persuasively.

3. B) pretentious. "Ostentatious" means characterized by vulgar or pretentious display; designed to impress.

4. B) obscure. "Esoteric" means intended to be understood by only a small, specialized group.

5. C) harmful. "Benign" refers to something harmless or gentle, so the opposite is "harmful."

6. B) trivial. "Frivolous" describes something that is not serious or lacks importance.

7. B) precise. "Meticulous" describes someone who is very careful and pays attention to detail.

8. B) insight. "Acumen" refers to sharpness of mind or keen insight.

9. B) disaster. "Calamity" refers to a great disaster or misfortune, so "disaster" is the best synonym.

10. C) justify. "Vindicate" means to clear someone of blame or suspicion, proving them right or justified.

11. B) understanding. "Empathy" refers to the ability to understand and share the feelings of others.

12. C) remorse. "Contrition" means showing sincere remorse or guilt.

13. B) isolated. "Insular" means isolated or separated from others.

14. B) worsen. "Exacerbate" means to make a bad situation even worse.

15. C) assign. "Delegate" means to assign responsibility or authority to another person to carry out specific tasks.

Part 4: Paragraph Comprehension (PC)

1. A) Escape

Explanation: "Abscond" means to leave hurriedly and secretly, typically to avoid capture or legal consequences. In the context of the passage, the thieves escaped when the alarm went off, making "escape" the most appropriate choice.

2. C) Industrial pollution

Explanation: The passage highlights industrial waste as the main contributor to the fires and pollution in Pennsylvania's rivers. This severe pollution, caused by years of dumping, ultimately led to environmental reform. Therefore, "industrial pollution" is the correct answer.

3. B) They use chlorophyll along with other pigments to absorb light.

Explanation: Although red and purple leaves contain pigments like anthocyanins, they still rely on chlorophyll to perform photosynthesis. The additional pigments help absorb different light wavelengths or protect the plant.

4. C) To describe the typical relationship between recessions and stock market performance.

Explanation: The paragraph outlines how the stock market typically behaves during a recession, explaining both the volatility and the potential for recovery, making option C the correct answer.

5. C) It becomes thinner and loses its elasticity.

Explanation: The passage explains that aging causes cartilage to thin and lose its flexibility, making it less effective at cushioning joints and more susceptible to damage. This highlights how aging affects cartilage function and structure.

6. A) Exhausting but rewarding.

Explanation: The narrator describes feeling the burn in her legs from the steep climb but also expresses awe at the beautiful views and Luna's excitement, making the experience physically challenging yet fulfilling. This makes option A the best choice.

7. C) Impulsive

Explanation: "Spontaneous" refers to something done without prior planning or premeditation. In the context of the passage, the group's decision to take an unplanned detour was impulsive, making "impulsive" the most appropriate choice.

8. B) A desire for wealth and escape from monotony.

Explanation: The passage emphasizes that Weatherbee wasn't motivated by romance or adventure but by his exhaustion with his job and desire for wealth. He saw the Arctic gold rush as an opportunity to escape monotony and seek potential fortune, making B the correct answer.

9. B) Establishing the first public library in America.

Explanation: The passage highlights Benjamin Franklin's role in founding the first public library, along with his other contributions to education and intellectual advancement, making option B the correct choice.

10. B) Accepting things outside of our control leads to inner peace.

Explanation: Stoicism emphasizes accepting what we cannot control and focusing on inner virtue and rational responses to challenges. This mindset leads to inner peace and resilience, making B the correct choice.

Part 5: Mathematics Knowledge (MK)

1. B) 73.33%. Explanation: $\frac{22}{30} \times 100 = 73.33\%$.

2. A) $\frac{6}{7} > \frac{5}{8}$. Explanation: Using cross multiplication to compare $\frac{6}{7}$ and $\frac{5}{8}$: Cross multiply:

$$6 \times 8 \quad \text{and} \quad 7 \times 5$$

$$6 \times 8 = 48, 7 \times 5 = 35$$

Since: 48 > 35, Therefore: $\frac{6}{7} > \frac{5}{8}$. Using cross multiplication to compare the other choices, none is true.

3. B) 3.46. Explanation: $3.4567 \approx 3.46$.

4. B) $\frac{6}{5}$. Explanation: $\frac{4}{5} \div \frac{2}{3} = \frac{4}{5} \times \frac{3}{2} = \frac{12}{10} = \frac{6}{5}$.

5. C) $6x^2 - 5x - 8$. Explanation: $(3x+4)(2x-3) - 4(x-1) = 6x^2 - 9x + 8x - 12 - 4x + 4 = 6x^2 - 5x - 8$.

6. D) -10. Explanation:

$$14.8x - 15.3x = 3.4 + 1.6$$
$$-0.5x = 5$$
$$x = -10$$

7. B) $y = \frac{3}{2}x + \frac{1}{2}$. Explanation:

1. Find the slope m using the points $(x_1, y_1) = (1,2)$ and $(x_2, y_2) = (5,8)$:

$$m = \frac{y_2 - y_1}{x_2 - x_1} = \frac{8-2}{5-1} = \frac{6}{4} = \frac{3}{2}$$

2. Use the point-slope form $y - y_1 = m(x - x_1)$ with point (1, 2) and slope $m = \frac{3}{2}$:

$$y - 2 = \frac{3}{2}(x - 1)$$
$$y - 2 = \frac{3}{2}x - \frac{3}{2}$$
$$y = \frac{3}{2}x + \frac{1}{2}$$

8. B) $6x^2yz$. Explanation:

1. Find the common factors for each term:

$$\text{Factors of } 18x^3y^2z = 2 \cdot 3^2 \cdot x^3 \cdot y^2 \cdot z$$

$$\text{Factors of } 24x^2yz^3 = 2^3 \cdot 3 \cdot x^2 \cdot y \cdot z^3$$

2. Identify the common factors: Common factors: $2 \cdot 3 \cdot x^2 \cdot y \cdot z$.

3. Multiply the common factors: $6x^2yz$. Thus, the greatest common factor is 6xyz.

9. C) -44. Explanation:

$$5a^2 + 2ab - 3b^2 = 5(2)^2 + 2(2)(-4) - 3(-4)^2$$
$$= 5(4) + 2(-8) - 3(16)$$
$$= 20 - 16 - 48$$
$$= -44$$

10. B) 12.5%. Explanation: Percentage of managers in Marketing $= \frac{5}{40} \times 100 = 12.5\%$.

11. B) $m = 5, \ b = -17$. Explanation: Step 1. Identify the given values: $m = 5, \quad \text{point}(x_1, y_1) = (2, -7)$. Step 2. Substitute the point and slope into the equation $y = mx + b$ to find b :

$$-7 = 5(2) + b$$
$$-7 = 10 + b$$
$$b = -17$$

Thus, the values are: $B) \ m = 5, \ b = -17$.

12. D) 9 units and 12 units. Explanation: Let x be the length of the shorter leg. Then, the longer leg is $x + 3$. Use the Pythagorean theorem: $x^2 + (x + 3)^2 = 15^2$, solve it:

$$x^2 + x^2 + 6x + 9 = 225$$
$$2x^2 + 6x - 216 = 0$$
$$x^2 + 3x - 108 = 0$$
$$x = \frac{-3 \pm \sqrt{3^2 + 4 \cdot 108}}{2}$$
$$x = \frac{-3 \pm \sqrt{9 + 432}}{2}$$
$$x = \frac{-3 \pm 21}{2}$$

Hence, $x = 9$, and we ignore the negative value. Therefore, the legs of the triangle are:

- Shorter leg = 9 units

- Longer leg 9+3=12 units

13. B) $48x^{10}y^6$. Explanation:

1. Apply the exponent to the term: $(4x^5)^2$: $(4x^5)^2 = 4^2 \cdot (x^5)^2 = 16x^{10}$

2. Multiply the terms: $(3x^2y^3)(16x^{10}) = 3 \cdot 16 \cdot x^{2+10} \cdot y^3 = 48x^{12}y^3$.

14. C) July. Explanation: Analyze the monthly production data and we can see the greatest increase is from June to July with 20. Thus, the month with the greatest increase is July.

15. D) $\angle D = \angle A$ and $\angle F = \angle B$. Explanation: A) This fits the SSA criteria, it cannot prove congruency. B) A single angle and one side are insufficient to prove congruency. C) Two sides are insufficient to prove congruency. D)This fits the ASA criteria; it is sufficient to prove congruency.

Part 6: Electronics Information (EI)

1. C) 3,600 watts. Explanation: Using Electrical Power Formula for power calculation:

$$P = V \times I = 240 \ V \times 15 \ A = 3,600 \ W$$

Hence, the maximum power the appliance can use is 3,600 watts.

2. B) voltmeter. Explanation: A voltmeter measures the voltage in a circuit. A) Ohmmeter measures resistance. C) Ammeter measures current. D) Wattmeter measures power.

3. D) Capacitors store energy in a magnetic field. Explanation: Capacitors store energy in an electric field, not a magnetic field. A), B), and C) are correct statements regarding capacitors.

4. C) diode. Explanation: A diode is polarized, meaning it allows current to flow in only one direction. A) and B) are not polarized components. D) is incorrect; transformers operate in both directions based on electromagnetic induction.

5. C) light intensity. Explanation: A phototransistor changes its current output based on light intensity. A), B), and D) are incorrect, as they do not influence a phototransistor directly.

6. B) there is no complete path for current to flow. Explanation: In an open circuit, there is an incomplete path, so current cannot flow. A) and C) are incorrect as they apply to a closed circuit. D) is incorrect; resistance is not zero in an open circuit.

7. A) The fuse will blow, interrupting the circuit.

Explanation: To determine what will happen when the switch is closed, we need to calculate the current in the circuit using Ohm's Law: $I = \frac{V}{R} = \frac{24V}{10\,\Omega} = 2.4A$. So, the current flowing through the circuit is 2.4A. Since the fuse is rated for 2A, this current exceeds the fuse's limit, causing the fuse to blow and interrupt the circuit to protect the components.

8. B) DC. Explanation: Direct Current (DC) flows in only one direction, unlike AC, which changes direction periodically. A) AC changes direction, making it incorrect. C) Alternating is just another term for AC. D) Transient refers to temporary current changes.

9. B) It runs slower and with less efficiency. Explanation: Running a motor below its rated voltage results in lower speed and decreased efficiency due to inadequate energy. A) and D) are incorrect since lower voltage typically reduces speed and current. C) is incorrect because under-voltage affects performance.

10. A) A current is induced in the conductor. Explanation: When a magnetic field moves relative to a conductor, electromagnetic induction causes a current to be induced. B) is incorrect; resistance does not change based on the movement of the magnetic field. C) and D) are incorrect as they do not occur due to the movement of a magnetic field.

11. A) Convert DC to AC. Explanation: An inverter converts DC to AC, which is essential in systems like solar power setups for household use. B) and C) do not relate to the function of an inverter. D) is incorrect because inverters do not step down voltage; that is a transformer's function.

12. B) disconnect the circuit during overload. Explanation: A circuit breaker disconnects the circuit when it senses an overload or short circuit. A) is incorrect; a circuit breaker does not provide constant current. C) and D) are incorrect because they do not relate to the function of a circuit breaker.

13. C) Inductor. Explanation: The symbol shown mimics a series of loops or coils, which represents an inductor. A resistor is typically represented by a zigzag line or a rectangle, not by the coiled symbol shown.

14. A) resist changes in current. Explanation: An inductor resists changes in current by storing energy in a magnetic field. B) refers to transformers, not inductors. C) applies to capacitors. D) applies to inverters.

15. C) Base, collector, and emitter. Explanation: Base, collector, and emitter are the correct names for the three terminals of a bipolar junction transistor (BJT). The base controls the current flow between the collector and the emitter in a BJT transistor.

Part 7: Auto Information (AI)

1. C) It automatically adjusts power distribution to all four wheels for enhanced traction and stability.

Explanation: AWD systems provide power to all four wheels and automatically adjust power distribution between the front and rear wheels as needed. This enhances traction and stability, especially on rough or slippery surfaces, without requiring manual input from the driver.

2. B) Independent Suspension. Explanation: In independent suspension systems, each wheel moves independently of the others, allowing for better handling and comfort, especially on uneven surfaces. Solid axle suspension (A) connects the wheels via a single axle, causing both wheels to move together. Leaf spring (C) and torsion bar (D) suspensions describe specific types of springs used in various suspension systems but do not specifically refer to independent or solid axle designs.

3. B) Starter Motor. Explanation: The starter motor engages the flywheel, which is connected to the engine's crankshaft, initiating the engine's rotation to start the combustion process. Once the engine starts, the starter motor disengages. The alternator (A) generates power after the engine is running, the voltage regulator (C) controls electrical output, and the ignition coil (D) provides the spark for combustion but does not engage the flywheel.

4. B) To provide the structural framework supporting all vehicle components

Explanation: The chassis is the vehicle's structural framework, supporting and holding all major components, including the suspension, steering system, and drivetrain. It provides strength, stability, and rigidity, ensuring that all parts are securely attached and aligned. Options A, C, and D refer to different systems in the vehicle, but the chassis primarily provides the structural backbone.

5. B) Spark Plug. Explanation: The spark plug is responsible for igniting the air-fuel mixture inside the engine's combustion chamber, generating the combustion that powers the engine.

6. B) By converting motion energy into heat energy. Explanation: Shock absorbers dissipate energy by converting the kinetic energy from suspension movement into heat energy, which is then dispersed. This process controls the vehicle's bouncing and ensures a smooth ride. They do not convert energy into sound, kinetic, or magnetic forms, as suggested by the incorrect options.

7. B) In the intake manifold. Explanation: Multiple fuel injectors are generally located in the intake manifold, where they inject fuel into the air before it enters the combustion chamber for optimal combustion. They are not found in the exhaust manifold, cooling system, or carburetor, which serve entirely different functions in the vehicle.

8. B) To seal the combustion chamber and allow the pistons to move freely

Explanation: Piston rings are designed to seal the combustion chamber, preventing gases from escaping while allowing the piston to move smoothly within the cylinder. They also help control oil consumption by scraping excess oil off the cylinder walls.

9. C) Uneven tire wear, reduced handling, and increased risk of tire failure

Explanation: Driving with incorrect tire pressure, whether over-inflated or under-inflated, can lead to uneven tire wear, reduced handling capability, and a higher risk of tire failure. Proper tire pressure ensures optimal traction, fuel efficiency, and even tire wear, while incorrect pressure compromises the safety and performance of the vehicle. Options A and B describe benefits of proper tire pressure, not the effects of incorrect pressure, and D is unrelated to tire pressure issues.

10. B) It prevents uneven tire wear and reduces vibrations at higher speeds

Explanation: Wheel balancing ensures that the weight is evenly distributed around the wheel and tire assembly, preventing vibrations and promoting even tire wear. Without proper balancing, the vehicle can experience vibrations at higher speeds, which can lead to discomfort and premature tire wear. Wheel balancing does not directly affect fuel efficiency (C), alignment (A), or traction in wet conditions (D), but it is essential for ride quality and tire longevity.

Part 8: Shop Information (SI)

1. C) Locking Pliers

Explanation: Locking pliers, also known as vise-grips, can be locked into position, providing a secure and stable grip on an object for an extended period. Needle-nose pliers (A) are for precision gripping, slip-joint pliers (B) adjust to different sizes but do not lock, and an adjustable wrench (D) is used for turning nuts and bolts but does not lock in place.

2. C) Coping Saw

Explanation: The coping saw is specifically designed for cutting curved or intricate shapes in wood, as its thin, narrow blade can easily maneuver around tight corners and curves.

A) Hand Saw is a general-purpose saw for straight cuts in wood but isn't ideal for intricate curves.

B) Hacksaw is used for cutting metal or plastic, not wood.

D) Drywall Saw is designed for cutting through drywall, making rough cuts for outlets or fixtures, and is not suited for detailed or curved cuts.

3. C) Mallet

Explanation: A mallet, typically made of wood or rubber, delivers a softer impact compared to metal hammers, which makes it ideal for tasks like tapping chisels or joining parts without damaging the surface. Claw hammers (A) and ball-peen hammers (B) are made of metal and are used for harder strikes, while a sledgehammer (D) is too powerful for delicate work.

4. A) Checking and measuring right angles

Explanation: A square is a tool used to check and measure right angles (90°) in construction and fabrication projects. It ensures that edges and corners are accurately aligned, making it essential for tasks like framing or marking perpendicular lines. It is not used for measuring diameters, internal dimensions, or angles over 90°.

5. C) Drill Bit

Explanation: Drill bits are cutting tools that attach to a power drill or hand drill to create holes in various materials, such as wood, metal, or masonry. Each type of drill bit is suited for a specific task, such as twist bits for general drilling or masonry bits for harder surfaces. The auger (A) is for deeper holes, and the brace (B) is used manually, while a hole saw (D) cuts larger diameter holes.

6. C) Crowbar

Explanation: A crowbar, with its longer length and heavy-duty design, provides excellent leverage for large demolition tasks, making it ideal for dismantling wooden structures. A pry bar (A) is smaller and more versatile, typically used for precision work in tight spaces. Nail pullers (B) and claw hammers (D) are more suited for specific tasks like removing nails.

7. B) Holding components onto a shaft

Explanation: Ring fasteners, like circlips, are used to hold components such as gears or bearings onto a shaft, preventing lateral movement. They fit into a groove to provide a secure hold. Options A and C describe functions related to nails and screws, and option D is not relevant to the purpose of ring fasteners.

8. B) Screws are driven directly into materials, bolts require a nut

Explanation: Screws are designed to be driven directly into materials like wood, metal, or plastic, often without the need for a nut. Bolts, on the other hand, are used with a nut to secure parts together, typically requiring a wrench or socket for installation. Options A and D are incorrect, and C oversimplifies the use of screws and bolts across different materials.

9. B) Welding

Explanation: Welding joins metals by melting them at high temperatures and fusing them together, creating a strong, permanent bond. Soldering (A) uses a fusible metal alloy to join components, typically at lower temperatures, and is commonly used in electronics. Riveting (C) and bolting (D) involve mechanical fasteners, not the melting of materials.

10. A) Smoothing rough metal edges

Explanation: The tools shown in the image are files. Files are hand tools used to shape and smooth materials like metal, plastic, or wood by removing small amounts of material. They are ideal for finishing rough edges, especially in metalwork, where precision is important.

   B) Cutting wood is better performed with a saw.

   C) Driving screws requires a screwdriver.

   D) Stripping wires requires a wire stripper, not a file.

Part 9: Mechanical Comprehension (MC)

1. (C) Newton's law of universal gravitation. Explanation: Newton's law of universal gravitation explains how every object in the universe is attracted to every other object with a force that is determined by their masses and the distance between them. Other options refer to motion laws (first, second, and third laws), which describe motion dynamics rather than gravitational attraction.

2. (A) When it reaches the top of its arc and its velocity is zero. Explanation: At the highest point in its arc, the stone's velocity is zero, and its potential energy is at a maximum. The moment it starts falling, potential energy begins converting back to kinetic energy. Other options are wrong because the stone's potential energy increases as it ascends and is highest when velocity is zero.

3. (A) Left. Explanation: The closer a support is to the load, the more force it must bear. Since the left support is closer to the center (2 feet versus 4 feet), it holds more of the load. The load is not distributed equally because the distances are not the same.

Answers and Explanations—Practice Test 3 | 313

4. (B) Watts. Explanation: Power is the rate at which work is done, and it is measured in watts (W). Joules measure work or energy, newtons measure force, and kilograms measure mass, not power. Watts combine energy and time, which makes them the correct unit for power.

5.(C) The work put out by a simple machine can never exceed the work put in.

Explanation: Due to the law of conservation of energy, the work output of a simple machine can never exceed the work input. The machine may change the direction of the force or reduce the effort needed, but energy losses (like friction) ensure that the output is less than or equal to the input.

6. (B) Second-class lever. Explanation: A bottle opener is an example of a second-class lever, where the fulcrum is at one end, the effort is applied at the opposite end, and the load (the bottle cap) is in the middle. This lever type maximizes force at the load for easy bottle opening.

7. (C) Moved toward where the object is moved. Explanation: In a first-class lever, moving the fulcrum closer to the load reduces the distance that the load has to move, which increases the force applied to the load, making it easier to lift.

8. D. Explanation: The shelf in Choice D has both a top support (a rope or wire) and a bottom brace, both extending far to the right. This combination provides the most stability because the forces acting on the shelf are distributed along both the top and bottom supports. The top rope prevents the shelf from tilting downward, while the bottom brace resists sagging under the weight. Since both supports in Choice D extend out at least as much as in other options, this shelf can handle more weight than them.

9. (B) The car lift reduces the force required through mechanical advantage. Explanation: Hydraulic systems rely on Pascal's Law, which states that pressure applied to a confined fluid is transmitted equally in all directions. In a hydraulic lift, the smaller piston requires much less force to lift a heavy load because the larger piston multiplies the force based on the difference in surface areas between the pistons, creating a mechanical advantage. This allows the mechanic to lift the heavy vehicle with minimal effort.

10. (B) The force of gravity on the Moon is weaker than on Earth. Explanation: The astronaut's mass, which is the amount of matter in their body, remains the same no matter where they are in space. However, weight is the force exerted on an object due to gravity. Since the Moon's gravitational pull is weaker than Earth's (approximately one-sixth as strong), the astronaut weighs less on the Moon, even though their mass hasn't changed.

11. (A) 746. Explanation: Horsepower (hp) is a unit of power that measures the rate of doing work. One horsepower is equivalent to approximately 746 watts, which represents the work done per second.

12. (B) Wheel and axle. Explanation: A door handle works like a wheel and axle. Turning the handle (the wheel) transfers force to the axle (the internal mechanism), which then opens the door. A wedge is used for splitting, a pulley redirects force, and an inclined plane raises objects over a distance.

13. A) 100 pounds. Explanation: This is a block and tackle pulley system with three support segments holding the load. The mechanical advantage is equal to the number of support segments. The effort required to lift the load can be calculated by dividing the weight of the load by the number of support segments:

$$\text{Effort} = \frac{\text{Load}}{\text{Mechanical Advantage}} = \frac{300 \text{ pounds}}{3} = 100 \text{ pounds}$$

14. (B) A screw applies force in a rotational motion, whereas a wedge applies force in a linear motion.

Explanation: A screw applies force by rotating around its axis, which pulls or pushes materials together. A wedge, on the other hand, splits or lifts objects by applying linear force. The other answers either confuse the roles of these machines or involve irrelevant details like friction.

15. (B) A decrease. Explanation: The principle of conservation of energy means that when a machine, like a hydraulic jack, increases force, it decreases the distance moved. In this case, the increased force applied through the hydraulic system results in a corresponding decrease in the movement distance of the load.

Part 10: Assembling Objects (AO)

1. B

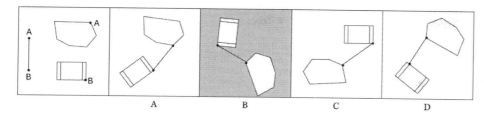

2. B

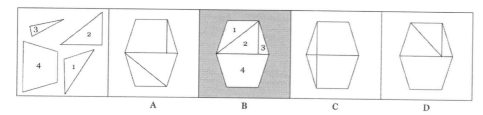

3. A

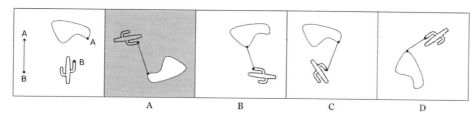

4. A

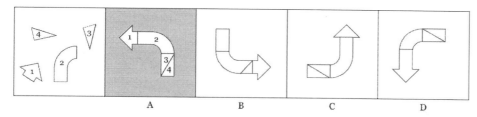

5. D

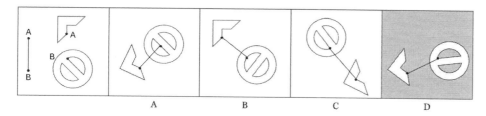

6. D

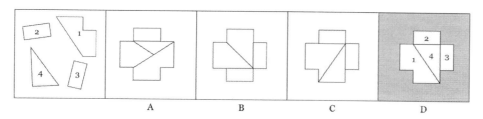

7. C

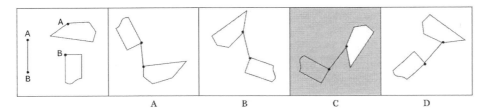

	A	B	C	D

8. C

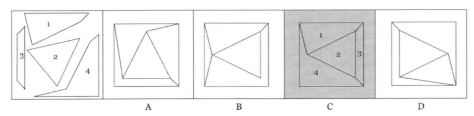

	A	B	C	D

9. A

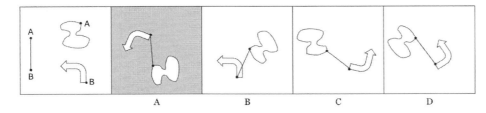

	A	B	C	D

10. B

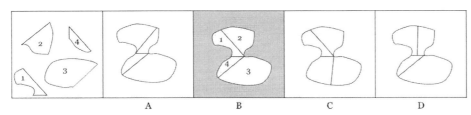

	A	B	C	D

11. A

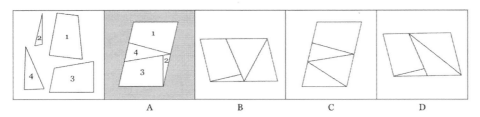

	A	B	C	D

12. C

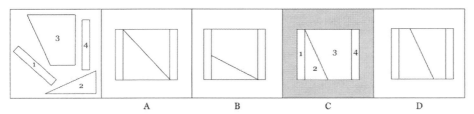

	A	B	C	D

13. A

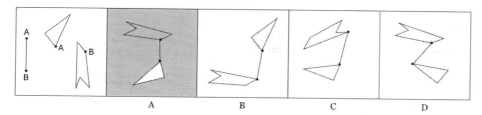

A   B   C   D

14. D

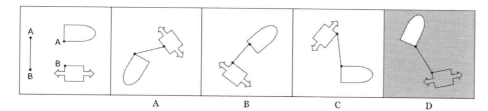

A   B   C   D

15. C

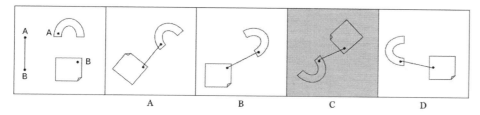

A   B   C   D

FINAL THOUGHTS

Congratulations on reaching the end of this comprehensive ASVAB Study Guide! If you have made it this far, you can feel confident in your preparation. This book has been meticulously designed to cover all aspects of the ASVAB test, providing you with the knowledge and practice needed to excel. You have invested time and effort into your studies, and that dedication is commendable. As you approach your test date, be confident that you are well-prepared.

Also, remember that this is just one step in your academic and career journey. Your performance on this test does not define your worth or potential. Approach the test with a positive mindset and trust in your preparation.

Finally, thank you for choosing Spire Study System's ASVAB Study Guide. Your support and trust in this book mean a lot to us. If you have found this guide helpful and comprehensive, please leave a positive review on Amazon. Your feedback helps other students find the right resources and supports the continued creation of quality study materials.

Best of luck with your ASVAB test, and may your hard work lead you to success in your academic endeavors!

Andrew T. Patton

Andrew T. Patton
Chief Editor
Spire Study System
Email: MyBookFeedback@outlook.com

Made in United States
Orlando, FL
08 November 2024